T0215749

Lecture Notes in Computer Science   9383

Commenced Publication in 1973
Founding and Former Series Editors:
Gerhard Goos, Juris Hartmanis, and Jan van Leeuwen

Editorial Board

More information about this series at http://www.springer.com/series/7407

Henning Wachsmuth

Text Analysis Pipelines

Towards Ad-hoc Large-Scale Text Mining

 Springer

Author

Henning Wachsmuth
Bauhaus-Universität Weimar
Weimar
Germany

This monograph constitutes a revised version of the author's doctoral dissertation, which was submitted to the University of Paderborn, Faculty of Electrical Engineering, Computer Science and Mathematics, Department of Computer Science, Warburger Straße 100, 33098 Paderborn, Germany, under the original title "Pipelines for Ad-hoc Large-Scale Text Mining", and which was accepted in February 2015.

Cover illustration: The image on the front cover was created by Henning Wachsmuth in 2015. It illustrates the stepwise mining of structured information from large amounts of unstructured text with a sequential pipeline of text analysis algorithms.

ISSN 0302-9743   ISSN 1611-3349   (electronic)
Lecture Notes in Computer Science
ISBN 978-3-319-25740-2   ISBN 978-3-319-25741-9   (eBook)
DOI 10.1007/978-3-319-25741-9

Library of Congress Control Number: 2015951772

LNCS Sublibrary: SL1 – Theoretical Computer Science and General Issues

Springer Cham Heidelberg New York Dordrecht London

Printed on acid-free paper

Springer International Publishing AG Switzerland is part of Springer Science+Business Media (www.springer.com)

To Max, my son.

Foreword

The last few years have given rise to a new and lasting technology hype that is receiving much attention, not only in academia and industry but also in the news and politics: *big data*. Hardly anything in the computer science world has been as controversial as the ubiquitous storage and analysis of data. While activists keep on warning that big data will take away our privacy and freedom, industry celebrates it as the holy grail that will enhance everything from decisions over processes to products. The truth lies somewhere in the middle.

Extensive data is collected nowadays about where we are, what we do, and how we think. Being aware of that, dangers like not getting a job or paying higher health insurance fees just because of one's private behavior seem real and need to be tackled. In this respect, big data indeed reduces freedom in that we are forced to refrain from doing things not accepted by public opinion. On the upside, big data has the potential to improve our lives and society in many respects including health care, environment protection, problem solving, decision making, and so forth. It will bring unprecedented insights into diseases and it will greatly increase the energy efficiency of infrastructure. It will provide immediate information access to each of us and it will let influencers better understand what people really need. Striving for such goals definitely makes it worth and honorable working on big data.

Mature technologies exist for storing and analyzing structured data, from databases to distributed computing clusters. However, most data out there (on the web, in business clouds, on personal computers) is in fact unstructured, given in the form of images, videos, music, or—above all—natural language text. Today, the most evolved technologies to deal with such text are search engines. Search engines excel in finding texts with the information we need in real time, but they do not understand what information is actually relevant in a text. Here, *text mining* comes into play.

Text mining creates structured data from information found in unstructured text. For this purpose, analysis algorithms are executed that aim to understand natural language to some extent. Natural language is complex and full of ambiguities. Even the best algorithms therefore create incorrect data from time to time, especially when a processed text differs from expectation. Usually, a whole bunch of algorithms is assembled together in a sequential pipeline. Although text mining targets large-scale data, such pipelines still tend to be too inefficient to cope with the scales encountered today in reasonable time. Moreover, the assembly of algorithms in a pipeline depends on the information to be found, which is often only known ad-hoc.

Henning Wachsmuth addresses these problems of *pipelines for ad-hoc large-scale text mining* in his dissertation, on which the book at hand is based. He systematically follows engineering principles to design pipelines automatically and to execute them optimally. A focus is put on the optimization of the run-time efficiency of pipelines, both in theory and in different practically relevant scenarios. In addition, Henning pays special attention to the fundamental question of how to make the processing of natural language robust to text of any kind.

Owing to its interdisciplinarity, the work of Henning Wachsmuth was supervised cooperatively by my colleague Benno Stein from the Bauhaus-Universität Weimar and me. In particular, Henning leverages artificial intelligence (AI) to solve software engineering tasks. The design and execution of efficient pipelines benefit from classic AI techniques that represent and reason about expert knowledge and environment information. For robustness, Henning uses modern AI techniques, summarized under the term "machine learning." Machine learning solves tasks automatically based on statistical patterns found in data. It is of upmost importance for text mining and the analysis of big data as a whole. According to current trends at leading companies like Google or Yahoo, its combination with classic AI techniques and engineering methods becomes more and more necessary for facing the challenges of search engines and many other software technologies.

In my work as a professor at the University of Paderborn, I experience the growing relevance of big data for our industrial partners. Still, major challenges remain, especially when it comes to the analysis of text. This book is one the first that brings together cutting-edge research from natural language processing with the needs of real-world applications. As such, the results presented here are of great pratical importance. They have been evaluated in close collaboration with companies in technology transfer projects at our s-lab – Software Quality Lab. At the same time, Henning developed novel text analysis approaches of great scientific value. All his main findings have been published in proceedings of renowned international conferences. On one of these conferences, Henning Wachsmuth received the "Best Presentation Award," exemplifying that his work is acknowledged by the community and that he knows how to make it understandable for a large audience.

Overall, Henning shows with his dissertation that his research achieves a high level of excellence. He deeply investigates the problem of performing text mining ad-hoc in the large. Building upon the state of the art, he provides both theoretical solutions and practical approaches for each major facet of this problem. All approaches are implemented as open-source software applications. Some properties of the approaches are proven formally, others are evaluated in extensive experiments. In doing so, Henning Wachsmuth demonstrates his broad knowledge in computer science and his expertise in the area of natural language processing. The book at hand proves that he can advance this and other areas originally.

August 2015   Gregor Engels

Preface

People search on the web to find relevant information on topics they wish to know more about. Accordingly, companies analyze big data to discover new information that is relevant for their business. Today's search engines and big data analytics seek to fulfill such information needs ad-hoc i.e., immediately in response to a search query or similar. Often, the relevant information is hidden in large numbers of natural language texts from web pages and other documents. Instead of returning potentially relevant texts only, leading search and analytics applications have recently started to return relevant information directly. To obtain the information sought for from the texts, they perform *text mining*.

Text mining deals with tasks that target the inference of structured information from collections and streams of unstructured input texts. It covers all techniques needed to identify relevant texts, to extract relevant spans from these texts, and to convert the spans into high-quality information that can be stored in databases and analyzed statistically. Text mining requires task-specific text analysis processes that may consist of several interdependent steps. Usually, these processes are realized with *text analysis pipelines*. A text analysis pipeline employs a sequence of natural language processing algorithms where each algorithm infers specific types of information from the input texts. Although effective algorithms exist for various types, the use of text analysis pipelines is still restricted to a few predefined information needs. We argue that this is due to three problems:

First, text analysis pipelines are mostly constructed manually for the tasks to be addressed, because their design requires expert knowledge about the algorithms to be employed. When information needs have to be fulfilled that are unknown beforehand, text mining hence cannot be performed ad-hoc. Second, text analysis pipelines tend to be inefficient in terms of run-time, because their execution often includes analyzing texts with computationally expensive algorithms. When information needs have to be fulfilled ad-hoc, text mining hence cannot be performed in the large. And third, text analysis pipelines tend not to robustly achieve high effectiveness on all input texts (in terms of the correctness of the inferred information), because they often include algorithms that rely on domain-dependent features of texts. Generally, text mining hence cannot guarantee to infer high-quality information at present.

In this book, we tackle the outlined problems by investigating how to fulfill information needs from text mining ad-hoc in a run-time efficient and domain-robust manner. Text mining is studied within the broad field of computational linguistics, bringing together research from natural language processing, information retrieval, and data mining. On the basis of a concise introduction to the foundations and the state of the art of text mining, we observe that knowledge about a text analysis process as well as information obtained within the process can be exploited in order to improve the design, the execution, and the output of the text analysis pipeline that realizes the process. To do this fully automatically, we apply different techniques from classic and statistical artificial intelligence.

In particular, we first develop knowledge-based artificial intelligence approaches for an ad-hoc pipeline construction and for the optimal execution of a pipeline on its input. Then, we show how to theoretically and practically optimize and adapt the schedule of the algorithms in a pipeline based on information in the analyzed input texts in order to maximize the pipeline's run-time efficiency. Finally, we learn novel patterns in the overall structures of input texts statistically that remain strongly invariant across the domains of the texts and that, thereby, allow for more robust analysis results in a specific set of text analysis tasks.

We analyze all the developed approaches formally and we sketch how to implement them in software applications. On the basis of respective Java open-source applications that we provide online, we empirically evaluate the approaches on established and on newly created collections of texts. In our experiments, we address scientifically and industrially important text analysis tasks, such as the extraction of financial events from news articles or the fine-grained sentiment analysis of reviews.

Our findings presented in this book show that text analysis pipelines can be designed automatically, which process only portions of text that are relevant for the information need to be fulfilled. Through an informed scheduling, we improve the run-time efficiency of pipelines by up to more than one order of magnitude without compromising their effectiveness. Even on heterogeneous input texts, efficiency can be maintained by learning to predict the fastest pipeline for each text individually. Moreover, we provide evidence that the domain robustness of a pipeline's effectiveness substantially benefits from focusing on overall structure in argumentation-related tasks such as sentiment analysis.

We conclude that the developed approaches denote essential building blocks of enabling ad-hoc large-scale text mining in web search and big data analytics applications. In this regard, the book at hand serves as a guide for practitioners and interested readers that desire to know what to pay attention to in the context of text analysis pipelines. At the same time, we are confident that our scientific results prove valuable for other researchers who work on the automatic understanding of natural language and on the future of information search.

Acknowledgments

The findings described in this book should not be attributed to a single person. Although I wrote this book and the dissertation it is based on at the Database and Information Systems Group and the Software Quality Lab of the University of Paderborn myself, many people worked together with me or they helped me in other important respects during my PhD time.

First, I would like to thank both my advisor, Gregor Engels, and my co-advisor, Benno Stein, for supporting me throughout and for giving me the feeling that my research is worth doing. Gregor, I express to you my deep gratitude for showing me what a dissertation really means and showing me the right direction while letting me take my own path. Benno, thank you so much for teaching me what science is all about, how thoroughly I have to work for it, and that the best ideas emerge from collaboration. I would like to thank Bernd Bohnet for the collaboration and for directly saying "yes," when I asked him to be the third reviewer of my dissertation. Similarly, I thank Hans Kleine Büning and Friedhelm Meyer auf der Heide for serving as members of my doctoral committee.

Since the book at hand reuses the content of a number of scientific publications, I would like to thank all my co-authors not named so far. In chronological order, they are Peter Prettenhofer, Kathrin Bujna, Mirko Rose, Tsvetomira Palakarska, and Martin Trenkmann. Thank you for your great work. Without you, parts of this book would not exist. Some parts have also profited from the effort of students who worked at our lab, wrote their thesis under my supervision, or participated in our project group ID|SE. Special thanks go to Joachim Köhring and Steffen Beringer. Moreover, some results presented here are based on work of companies we cooperated with in two research projects. I want to thank Dennis Hannwacker in this regard, but also the other employees of Resolto Informatik and Digital Collections.

The aforementioned projects including my position were funded by the German Federal Ministry of Education and Research (BMBF), for which I am very grateful. For similar reasons, I want to thank the company HRS, the German Federal Ministry for Economic Affairs and Energy (BMWI), as well as my employer, the University of Paderborn, in general.

I had a great time at the university, first and foremost because of my colleagues. Besides those already named, I say thank you to Fabian Christ and Benjamin Nagel for all the fun discussions, for tolerating my habits, and for becoming friends. The same holds for Christian Soltenborn and Christian Gerth, who I particularly thank for making me confident about my research. Further thanks go to Jan Bals, Markus Luckey, and Yavuz Sancar for exciting football matches, to the brave soccer team of the AG Engels, and to the rest of the group. I express my gratitude to Friedhelm Wegener for constant and patient technical help as well as to Stefan Sauer for managing all the official matters, actively supported by Sonja Saage and Beatrix Wiechers.

I am especially grateful to Theo Lettmann for pushing me to apply for the PhD position, for guiding me in the initial phase, and for giving me advice whenever needed without measurable benefit for himself. Thanks to my new group, the web is group in Weimar, for the close collaboration over the years, and to the people at the University of Paderborn who made all my conference attendances possible. Because of you, I could enter the computational linguistics community, which I appreciate so much, and make new friends around the world. I would like to mention Julian Brooke, who I enjoyed discussing research and life with every year at a biannual conference, as well as Alberto Barron, who opened my eyes to my limited understanding of the world with sincerity and a dry sense of humor.

Aside from my professional life, I deeply thank all my dear friends for so many great experiences and fun memories, for unconditionally accepting how I am, and for giving me relief from my everyday life. I would like to name Annika, Carmen, Dirk, Fabian, Kathrin, Lars, Sebastian, Semih, Stephan, and Tim here, but many more current and former Bielefelders and Paderborners influenced me, including but not limited to those from the HG Kurzfilme and the Projektbereich Eine Welt. I thank my parents for always loving and supporting me and for being the best role models I can imagine. Ipke, the countless time you spent for the great corrections and your encouraging feedback helped me more than I can tell. Thanks also to the rest of my family for being such a wonderful family.

Finally, my greatest thanks go to my young small family, Katrin and Max, for letting me experience that there are much more important things in life than work, for giving me the chance to learn about being some sort of father, for giving me a home throughout my PhD, for accepting my long working hours, and for all the love and care I felt. I hope that the effort I put into my dissertation and this book as well as my excitement for research and learning will give you inspiration in your life.

August 2015   Henning Wachsmuth

Symbols

The basic notations used in this thesis are listed here. Specific forms and variations of these notations are introduced where needed and are marked explicitly with the respective indices or similar.

Analysis

A	A text analysis algorithm.
A	A set or a repository of text analysis algorithms.
π	The schedule of the algorithms in a text analysis pipeline.
Π	A text analysis pipeline or a filtering stage within a pipeline.
Π	A set of text analysis pipelines.

Text

d	A portion of text or a unit of a text.
D	A text.
D	A collection or a stream of texts.
S	A scope, i.e., a sequence of portions of a text.
S	A set of scopes.

Information

c	A piece of information, such as a class label, an entity, a relation, etc.
C	An information type or a set of pieces of information.
C	A set of information types or a specification of an information need.
f	A flow, i.e., the sequence of instances of an information type in a text.
F	A set or a cluster of flows.
F	A flow clustering, i.e., a partition of a set of flows.
f*	A flow pattern, i.e., the average of a set of flows.
F^*	A set of flow patterns.
x	A feature used to model an input in machine learning.
x	A feature vector, i.e., an ordered set of features.
X	A set of feature vectors.

Task

γ A query that specifies a combination of information needs.
γ^* A scoped query, i.e., a query that specifies sizes of relevant portions of text.
Γ A dependency graph that respresents the depedencies in a scoped query.
Λ An agenda, i.e., a list of input requirements of text analysis algorithms.
μ A machine that executes text analysis pipelines.
Φ A planning problem that specifies a goal to achieve within an environment.
Ω A universe or an ontology, each of which specifies an environment.

Quality

q A quality value or a quality estimation.
$\mathbf{q}$ A vector of quality estimations.
Q A quality criterion.
$\mathbf{Q}$ A set of quality criteria.
ρ A quality prioritization, defined as an ordered set of quality criteria.

Measures

t A run-time, possibly averaged over a certain unit of text.
a An accuracy value, i.e., an achieved ratio of correct decisions.
p A precision value, i.e., an achieved ratio of information inferred correctly.
r A recall value, i.e., an achieved ratio of correct information that is inferred.
f_1 An F_1-score, i.e., the harmonic mean of a precision and a recall value.
$\mathscr{D}$ The averaged deviation, i.e., a measure of text heterogeneity.
$\mathscr{H}$ A heuristic that predicts the run-time of a text analysis pipeline.
$\mathscr{Q}$ A quality function that maps analysis results to quality values.
$\mathscr{Y}$ A machine learning model that maps features to information.

Contents

Chapter 1
Introduction

In turning from the smaller instruments in frequent use to the larger and more important machines, the economy arising from the increase of velocity becomes more striking.

– Charles Babbage

Abstract The future of information search is not browsing through tons of web pages or documents. In times of big data and the information overload of the internet, experts in the field agree that both everyday and enterprise search will gradually shift from only retrieving large numbers of texts that potentially contain relevant information to directly mining relevant information in these texts (Etzioni 2011; Kelly and Hamm 2013; Ananiadou et al. 2013). In this chapter, we first motivate the benefit of such *large-scale* text mining for today's web search and big data analytics applications (Sect. 1.1). Then, we reveal the task specificity and the process complexity of analyzing natural language text as the main problems that prevent applications from performing text mining *ad-hoc*, i.e., immediately in response to a user query (Sect. 1.2). Section 1.3 points out how we propose to tackle these problems by improving the design, efficiency, and domain robustness of the pipelines of algorithms used for text analysis with artificial intelligence techniques. This leads to the contributions of the book at hand (Sect. 1.4).

1.1 Information Search in Times of Big Data

Information search constitutes an integral part of almost everybody's everyday life. Today's web search engines achieve to rank the most relevant result highest for a large fraction of the information needs implied by search queries. Following Manning et al. (2008), an *information need* can be seen as a topic about which a user desires to know more. A result is *relevant* if it yields information that helps to fulfill the information need at hand.

Instead of directly providing relevant information, however, state-of-the-art web search engines mostly return only links to web pages that may contain relevant information, often thousands or millions of them. This can make search time-consuming

1

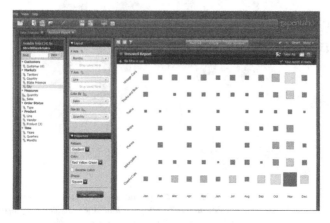

Fig. 1.1 Screenshot of PENTAHO BIG DATA ANALYTICS as an example for an enterprise software. The shown "heat grid" visualizes the vehicle sales of a company.

or even unsuccessful for queries where relevant information has to be derived (e.g. for the query `locations of search companies`), should be aggregated (e.g. `user opinions on bing`), seems like a needle in a haystack (e.g. `"if it isn't on google it doesn't exist" original source`), and so forth.

For enterprise environments, big data analytics applications aim to infer such *high-quality information* in the sense of relations, patterns, and hidden facts from vast amounts of data (Davenport 2012). Figure 1.1 gives an example, showing the enterprise software of PENTAHO.[1] As with this software, big data analytics is still only on the verge of including unstructured texts into analysis, though such texts are assumed to make up 95 % of all enterprise-relevant data (HP Labs 2010). To provide answers to a wide spectrum of information needs, relevant texts must be filtered and relevant information must be identified in these texts. We hence argue that search engines and big data analytics applications need to perform more *text mining*.

1.1.1 Text Mining to the Rescue

Text mining brings together techniques from the research fields of information retrieval, data mining, and natural language processing in order to infer structured high-quality information from usually large numbers of unstructured texts (Ananiadou and McNaught 2005). While *information retrieval* deals, at its heart, with indexing and searching unstructured texts, *data mining* targets at the discovery of patterns in structured data. *Natural language processing*, finally, is concerned with algorithms and engineering issues for the understanding and generation of speech and human-readable text (Tsujii 2011). It bridges the gap between the other fields by

---

[1]Taken from the PENTAHO blog, http://www.pentaho.com/blog/2012/06/07/diary-construction-manger-love-his-bi-tool, accessed on June 15, 2015.

converting unstructured into structured information. Text mining is studied within the broad interdisciplinary field of *computational linguistics*, as it addresses computational approaches from computer science to the processing of data and information while operationalizing findings from linguistics.

According to Sarawagi (2008), the most important text mining techniques for identifying and filtering relevant texts and information within the three fields refer to the areas of *information extraction* and *text classification*. The former aims at extracting entities, relations between entities, and events the entities participate in from mostly unstructured text. The latter denotes the task of assigning a text to one or more predefined categories, such as topics, genres, or sentiment polarities. Information extraction, text classification, and similar tasks are considered in both natural language processing and information retrieval. In this book, we summarize these tasks under the term *text analysis*. All text analyses have in common that they can significantly increase the velocity of information search in many situations.

In our past research project INFEXBA[2], for instance, we developed algorithms for a fast extraction and aggregation of financial forecast events from online news articles, thereby supporting strategic business decision making. The events sought for describe financial developments of organizations and markets over time. They may have an author, a date, and similar. Entities and events of the implied types can be found in texts like *"If Apple does end up launching a television in the next two years as has been rumored, it could help Apple's annual revenue skyrocket to $400 billion by 2015, according to Morgan Stanley analyst Katy Huberty."*[3] In contrast, the goal of our research project ARGUANA[4] was to classify and summarize opinions on products and their features found in large numbers of review texts. To this end, we analyzed the sequence of local sentiment on certain product features found in each of the reviews in order to account for the argumentation of texts.

Of course, major search engines already use text analysis when addressing information needs (Pasca 2011). E.g., a GOOGLE search in late 2014 for `Charles Babbage`, the author of this chapter's introductory quote, led to the results in Fig. 1.2, which convey that Babbage was recognized as a person entity with a number of attributes and related entities.[5] The exact extent to which today's search engines perform text analyses is hard to guess, since they also rely on knowledge bases like FREEBASE.[6] However, the presentation of analysis results as answers is currently restricted to some frequent entity types, such as persons or locations. Correspondingly, the few text-based applications for analyzing big data focus on predefined information needs of wide interest. E.g., APPINIONS continuously mines and aggregates opinions

---

[2]INFEXBA – Information Extraction for Business Applications, funded by the GERMAN FEDERAL MINISTRY OF EDUCATION AND RESEARCH (BMBF), http://infexba.upb.de.

[3]Taken from BUSINESS INSIDER, http://www.businessinsider.com/how-apples-annual-revenue-could-hit-400-billion-by-2015-2012-5, accessed on June 8, 2015.

[4]ARGUANA – Argumentation Analysis in Customer Opinions, also funded by the BMBF, http://www.arguana.com. Details on both research projects are given in Sect. 2.3.

[5]GOOGLE, http://www.google.com/#hl=en&q=Charles+Babbage, December 8, 2014.

[6]FREEBASE, http://www.freebase.com, accessed on June 15, 2015.

Fig. 1.2 GOOGLE result page for the query `Charles Babbage`, showing an example of directly providing relevant information instead of returning only web links.

on specified topics for monitoring purposes.[7] But, in accordance with the quote of Babbage, the benefit of text mining arising from the increase of velocity becomes more striking when turning from predefined text analyses in frequent use to arbitrary and more complex *text analysis processes*.

1.2 A Need for Efficient and Robust Text Analysis Pipelines

Text mining deals with tasks that often entail complex text analysis processes, consisting of several interdependent steps that aim to infer sophisticated *information types* from collections and streams of natural language input texts (cf. Chap. 2 for details). In the mentioned project INFEXBA, different entity types (e.g. organization names) and event types (e.g. forecasts) had to be extracted from input texts and correctly brought into relation, before they could be normalized and aggregated. Such steps require syntactic annotations of texts, e.g. part-of-speech tags and parse tree labels (Sarawagi 2008). These in turn can only be added to a text that is segmented into lexical units, e.g. into tokens and sentences. Similarly, text classification often relies on so called features (Manning et al. 2008) that are derived from lexical and syntactic annotations or even from entities, like in ARGUANA.

To realize the steps of a text analysis process, *text analysis algorithms* are employed that annotate new information types in a text or that classify, relate, normalize, or filter previously annotated information. Such algorithms perform analyses of different computational cost, ranging from the typically cheap evaluation of single rules and regular expressions, over the matching of lexicon terms and the statistical classification of text fragments, to complex syntactic analyses like dependency parsing (Bohnet 2010). Because of the interdependencies between analyses, the standard way to realize a text analysis process is in the form of a *text analysis pipeline*, which sequentially applies each employed text analysis algorithm to its input.

---

[7]APPINIONS, www.appinions.com, accessed on June 15, 2015.

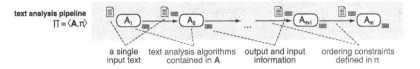

Fig. 1.3 A text analysis pipeline $\Pi = \langle \mathbf{A}, \pi \rangle$ with algorithm set $\mathbf{A} = \{A_1, \ldots, A_m\}$ and schedule π. Each text analysis algorithm $A_i \in \mathbf{A}$ takes a text and information of certain types as input and A_i provides information of certain types as output.

1.2.1 Basic Text Analysis Scenario

Conceptually, a text analysis pipeline can be modeled as a tuple $\Pi = \langle \mathbf{A}, \pi \rangle$ where $\mathbf{A} = \{A_1, \ldots, A_m\}$ is an *algorithm set* consisting of $m \geq 1$ text analysis algorithms, while π is the pipeline's *schedule* that defines the order of algorithm application (Wachsmuth et al. 2011). Each algorithm $A_i \in \mathbf{A}$ takes on one text analysis, producing information of certain information types as output. In order to work properly, A_i requires a text as well as information of a (possibly empty) set of information types as input. This information has to be produced by the algorithms preceding A_i within the schedule π. Hence, π has to ensure that the input requirements of all algorithms in $\mathbf{A}$ are fulfilled. Figure 1.3 illustrates the defined concepts.

Text analysis pipelines process input texts in order to produce output information of a structured set of information types $\mathbf{C}$ that is relevant for an information need at hand. Here, $\mathbf{C}$ may consist of both atomic types that stand on their own (like entity types) and compounds of types (like relation types). Accordingly, the basic *text analysis task* that is addressed with a pipeline Π and that we refine later on can be stated as follows:

> **Text Analysis Task.** Given a collection or a stream of input texts $\mathbf{D}$, process $\mathbf{D}$ in order to infer all output information of a structured set of information types $\mathbf{C}$.

Depending on the task, $\mathbf{D}$ may refer to anything from a small closed-domain collection of texts to a never-ending input stream of open-domain texts from the web. Also, the types in $\mathbf{C}$ may represent different semantic concepts, linguistic annotations, and similar. As a matter of fact, the composition of text analysis algorithms in Π is task-specific; it follows from the concrete types in $\mathbf{C}$ to be inferred and from the language, quality, style, and other properties of the input texts in $\mathbf{D}$. Traditionally, a pipeline Π is therefore predefined when given a text analysis task by selecting and scheduling an appropriate subset of all available text analysis algorithms.

The whole described text analysis scenario is sketched in Fig. 1.4. We will see that many text analysis processes conform with this scenario or with extensions or variations of it, especially those in information extraction and text classification. We detail the underlying concepts in Chap. 2.

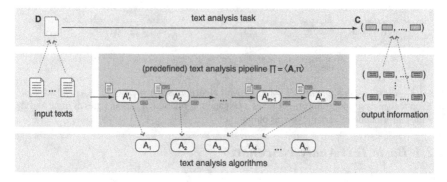

Fig. 1.4 The basic text analysis scenario discussed in this book: A text analysis pipeline $\Pi = \langle \mathbf{A}, \pi \rangle$ composes a subset $\mathbf{A}$ of all available text analysis algorithms $A_1, \ldots, A_n$ in order to infer output information of a structured set of information types $\mathbf{C}$ from a collection or a stream of input texts $\mathbf{D}$.

1.2.2 Shortcomings of Traditional Text Analysis Pipelines

In principle, text analysis pipelines can be applied to tackle arbitrary text analysis tasks, i.e., to infer output information of arbitrary types from arbitrary input texts. This information will not always be correct, as it results from analyzing ambiguous natural language text. Rather, a pipeline achieves a certain *effectiveness* in terms of the quality of the inferred information, e.g. quantified as the relative frequency of output information that is correct in the given task (cf. Chap. 2 for details).

The inference of high-quality information can be seen as the most general goal of text mining. Search engines and big data analytics applications, in particular, aim to infer such information immediately and/or from large numbers of texts. Both of them deal with *ad-hoc information needs*, i.e., information needs that are stated ad-hoc and are, thus, unknown beforehand. We argue that the process complexity and task specificity outlined above prevent such *ad-hoc large-scale text mining* today due to three problems:

First, the *design* of text analysis pipelines in terms of selecting and scheduling algorithms for the information needs at hand and the input texts to be processed is traditionally made manually, because it requires human expert knowledge about the functionalities and interdependencies of the algorithms (Wachsmuth et al. 2013a). If information needs are stated ad-hoc, also the design of pipelines has to be made ad-hoc, which takes time when made manually, even with proper tool support (Kano et al. 2010). Hence, text mining currently cannot be performed immediately.

Second, the run-time *efficiency* of traditionally executing text analysis pipelines is low, because computationally expensive analyses are performed on the whole input texts (Sarawagi 2008). Techniques are missing that identify the portions of input texts, which contain information relevant for the information need at hand, and that restrict expensive analyses to these portions. Different texts vary in the distribution of relevant information, which additionally makes these techniques input-dependent (Wachsmuth and Stein 2012). While a common approach to avoid efficiency problems is to analyze input texts in advance when they are indexed (Cafarella et al. 2005), this is not feasible for ad-hoc information needs. Also, the application of faster algorithms (Pantel et al. 2004) seems critical because it mostly also results in a reduced effectiveness. Hence, ad-hoc text mining currently cannot be performed on large numbers of texts.

Third, text analysis pipelines tend not to infer high-quality information with high *robustness*, because the employed algorithms traditionally rely on features of input texts that are dependent on the domains of the texts (Blitzer et al. 2007). The applications we target at, however, may process texts from arbitrary domains, such that pipelines will often fail to infer information effectively. An approach to still achieve user acceptance under limited effectiveness is to explain how information was inferred (Li et al. 2012b), but this is difficult for pipelines, as they realize a process with several complex and uncertain decisions about natural language (Das Sarma et al. 2011). Hence, text mining cannot generally guarantee high quality.

1.2.3 Problems Approached in This Book

Altogether, we summarize that traditional text analysis pipelines fail to address information needs ad-hoc in an efficient and domain-robust manner. The hypothesis of this book is that three problems must be solved in order to enable ad-hoc large-scale text mining within search engines and big data analytics applications:

1. **Automation of pipeline design.** In order to address ad-hoc information needs, pipelines need to be designed automatically for the given text analysis tasks.
2. **Optimization of pipeline efficiency.** In order to address ad-hoc information needs in the large, pipelines need to analyze relevant portions of input texts only and analyze these portions as efficient as possible.
3. **Improvement of pipeline robustness.** In order to achieve high quality in addressing ad-hoc information needs, pipelines need to infer information from input texts effectively irrespective of the domain of the texts.

Some recent publications tackle parts of these problems, such as an automatic design (Kano 2012) or the optimization of efficiency (Shen et al. 2007). However, neither covers any publication all problems, nor is any of the problems solved in general. Details on related research will be given at the end of Chap. 2. In the next section, we outline how we propose to approach the three problems with the help of techniques from artificial intelligence.

1.3 Towards Intelligent Pipeline Design and Execution

In this book, we consider the task of efficiently and effectively addressing ad-hoc information needs in large-scale text mining. We contribute to this task by showing how to make the design and execution of text analysis pipelines more intelligent. Our approach relies on knowledge and information available for such pipelines.

1.3.1 Central Research Question and Method

As motivated in Sect. 1.2, the design, efficiency, and robustness of text analysis pipelines depend on the realized text analysis processes. With this in mind, the central research question underlying this book can be formulated as follows:

Central Research Question. How can we exploit knowledge about a text analysis process as well as information obtained within the process in order to automatically improve the design, the execution, and the results of the text analysis pipelines that realize the process?

The distinction between knowledge and information is controversial and not always unambiguous (Rowley 2007). For our purposes, it suffices to follow the simple view that knowledge is an interpretation of data, which is assumed to be true irrespective of the context (e.g., APPLE is a company), while information is data, which has been given meaning by a particular context (e.g., in the book at hand the term "Apple" denotes a company). In this regard, knowledge can be understood as specified beforehand, while information is inferred during processing. Now, when speaking of "knowledge about a text analysis process", we basically mean two kinds:

1. **Knowledge about the text analysis task to be addressed**, namely, the information need at hand, expected properties of the input texts to be processed, as well as efficiency and effectiveness criteria to be met.
2. **Knowledge about the text analysis algorithms to be employed**, namely, their input and output information types, restrictions of their applicability, as well as their expected efficiency and effectiveness.

Similarly, we distinguish the following three kinds of "information obtained within the process":

1. **Information about the processed input texts**, namely, their concretely observed properties, especially domain-independent properties.
2. **Information about the produced output**, namely, the occurrence and distribution of the different types of information in the input texts.
3. **Information about the executed text analysis pipelines**, namely, the schedule of the employed text analysis algorithms as well as their achieved efficiency and effectiveness as far as observable.

The exploitation of knowledge and information for automatic problem solving is closely related to the field of *artificial intelligence*. Artificial intelligence describes the ability of software and machines to think and act rationally or human-like. An according system aims to find efficient solutions to problems based on operationalized expert knowledge and a perception of its environment (Russell and Norvig 2009). While text mining itself can be viewed as a subfield of artificial intelligence, we here develop approaches that use classical and statistical artificial intelligence techniques like planning, reasoning, and machine learning to improve traditional text mining approaches using the stated kinds of knowledge and information.

Our goal is to provide widely applicable approaches to the three problems outlined at the end of Sect. 1.2, which is why we also cover aspects of *software engineering*, such as the modeling of domains and the scaling of methods. To investigate our central research question, we evaluate all approaches with respect to the three problems. Some properties are proven formally, whereas in all other cases we have implement the approaches as open-source JAVA applications that can be freely accessed online. Using these applications, we have conducted experiments in terms of empirical analyses, which are based on both existing and new text corpora designed and compiled for that purpose. Most experiment settings are controlled and compare the efficiency and effectiveness of our approaches and traditional approaches. They either refer to text analysis tasks from the mentioned projects INFEXBA and ARGUANA or they address tasks that are well-known in the field. Where appropriate, we also provide software frameworks and stand-alone tools to demonstrate the correctness and practical applicability of our approaches.

1.3.2 An Artificial Intelligence Approach

The proposed overall approach of this book to enable ad-hoc large-scale text mining relies on three core ideas, which we will discuss more detailed below:

1. **Ad-hoc large-scale text analysis pipelines.** We can automatically select the algorithms to be employed in a text analysis pipeline based on the set of

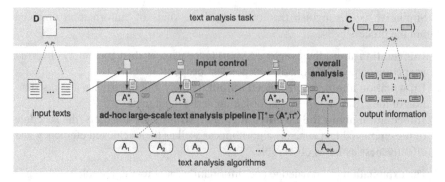

Fig. 1.5 Our overall approach to enable ad-hoc large-scale text mining: Each algorithm A_i^* in the automatically constructed *ad-hoc large-scale text analysis pipeline* $\Pi^* = \langle \mathbf{A}^*, \pi^* \rangle$ gets only portions of text from the *input control* its output is relevant for. The schedule π^* is optimized in terms of efficiency, while the effectiveness of Π^* is improved through an *overall analysis* that produces the final output information.

available algorithms and the information need at hand, and we can optimize their schedule based on information about their achieved efficiency and the produced output.

2. **Input control.** We can automatically infer the portions of input texts that need to be processed by each algorithm in a text analysis pipeline from the information need at hand, the algorithm's output information types, and the output information produced so far.

3. **Overall analysis.** We can automatically improve the domain robustness of specific algorithms in a text analysis pipeline by focusing on information about the overall structure of the processed input texts within their analyses while abstracting from their content.

Figure 1.5 illustrates how these ideas can be operationalized to replace the traditional predefined pipeline in the basic text analysis scenario. By that, Fig. 1.5 serves as an overall view of all proposed approaches of this book. We detail the different approaches in the following.

For ad-hoc information needs, we construct *ad-hoc text analysis pipelines* immediately before analysis. To this end, we formalize the classical process-oriented view of text analysis that is e.g. realized by the leading software frameworks for text analysis, APACHE UIMA[8] and GATE:[9] Each algorithm serves as an action that, if applicable, transforms the state of a text (i.e., its input annotations) into another state (extended by the algorithm's output annotations). So, ad-hoc pipeline construction means to find a viable sequence of actions, i.e., a planning problem (Russell and

---

[8]APACHE UIMA, http://uima.apache.org, accessed on June 15, 2015.

[9]GATE, http://gate.ac.uk, accessed on June 15, 2015.

Norvig 2009). We tackle this problem with partial order planning while considering efficiency and effectiveness criteria (Wachsmuth et al. 2013a). Partial order planning conforms to paradigms of ideal pipeline design and execution that we identified to be always reasonable, e.g. lazy evaluation (Wachsmuth et al. 2011).

Instead of directly handing over the whole input texts from one algorithm in a pipeline to the next, we introduce a novel *input control* that manages the input to be processed by each algorithm, as sketched in Fig. 1.5. Given the output information of all algorithms applied so far, the input control determines and filters only those portions of the current input text that may contain all information required to fulfill the information need at hand.[10] For this information-oriented view, we realize the input control as a truth maintenance system (Russell and Norvig 2009), which models the relevance of each portion of text as a propositional formula. Reasoning about all formulas then enables algorithms to analyze only relevant portions of text. Thereby we avoid unnecessary analyses and we can influence the efficiency-effectiveness tradeoff of a pipeline (Wachsmuth et al. 2013c).

Based on the information-oriented view, we next transform every pipeline into a *large-scale text analysis pipeline*, meaning that we make it as run-time efficient as possible. In particular, we found that a pipeline's schedule strongly affects its efficiency, since the run-time of each employed algorithm depends on the filtered portions of text it processes. The filtered portions in turn result from the distribution of relevant information in the input texts. Given the run-times on the filtered portions, we apply dynamic programming (Cormen et al. 2009) to obtain an optimal schedule (Wachsmuth and Stein 2012). In practice, these run-times can only be estimated for the texts at hand. We thus propose to address scheduling with informed best-first search (Russell and Norvig 2009), either in a greedy manner using estimations of the algorithms' run-times only or, for a more optimized scheduling, using information from a sample of texts (Wachsmuth et al. 2013a).

Now, problems occur in case input texts are heterogeneous in the distribution of relevant information, since such texts do not allow for accurate run-time estimations. We quantify the impact of text heterogeneity on the efficiency of a pipeline in order to estimate the optimization potential of scheduling. A solution is to perform an adaptive scheduling that chooses a schedule depending on the text (Wachsmuth et al. 2013b). For this purpose, the characteristics of texts need to be mapped to the run-times of pipelines. We induce such a mapping with self-supervised online learning, i.e., by incrementally learning from self-generated training data obtained during processing (Witten and Frank 2005; Banko et al. 2007). The scheduling approach has implications for pipeline parallelization that we outline.

Finally, we present a new *overall analysis* that aims to improve domain robustness by analyzing the overall structure of input texts while abstracting from their content. As Fig. 1.5 depicts, the overall analysis is an alternative last algorithm in a pipeline. Its structure-oriented view of text analysis specifically targets at the classification of

---

[10]Throughout this book, we assume that information needs are already given in a processable form (defined later on). Accordingly, we will not tackle problems from the areas of *query analysis* and *user interface design* related to information search (Hearst 2009).

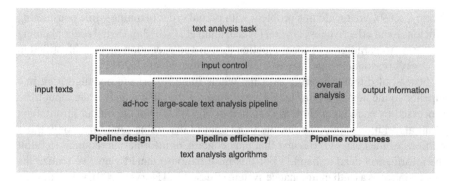

Fig. 1.6 The three high-level contributions of this book: We present approaches (1) to automatically design text analysis pipelines that optimally process input texts ad-hoc, (2) to optimize the run-time efficiency of pipelines on all input texts, and (3) to improve the robustness of pipelines on input texts from different domains.

argumentative texts. It is based on our observation from Wachsmuth et al. (2014b) that the sequential flow of information in a text is often decisive in those text classification tasks where analyzing content does not suffice (Lipka 2013). The overall analysis first performs a supervised variant of clustering (Witten and Frank 2005) to statistically learn common flow patterns of argumentative texts (Wachsmuth et al. 2014a). Then, it uses the learned patterns as features for a more domain-robust classification. The same patterns and their underlying information can be exploited to explain the results of the analysis afterwards.

1.4 Contributions and Outline of This Book

We claim that our approach makes the design and execution of text analysis pipelines more intelligent: Efficient solutions to text analysis tasks (i.e., pipelines) are found and accomplished automatically based on human expert knowledge and informa-tion perceived in the environment (i.e., the processing of texts). More precisely, we contribute to the enablement of ad-hoc large-scale text mining in three respects:

1. **Pipeline design.** Through ad-hoc pipeline construction, we can immedi-ately design text analysis pipelines to perform text mining ad-hoc. Through the input control, we achieve to execute each pipeline in an optimal manner, thereby enabling efficiency optimizations.
2. **Pipeline efficiency.** Through optimized scheduling, we can greatly im-prove the run-time efficiency of traditional text analysis pipelines, which benefits large-scale text mining. Through adaptive scheduling, we main-tain efficiency even on highly heterogeneous texts.

3. **Pipeline robustness.** Through the overall analysis, we can significantly improve the domain robustness of text analysis pipelines for the classification of argumentative texts over traditional approaches.

Figure 1.6 shows how these high-level main contributions relate to the three core ideas within our overall approach. In the following, we summarize the most important findings described in this book for each main contribution.

1.4.1 New Findings in Ad-Hoc Large-Scale Text Mining

We analyze the impact of an optimal design of text analysis pipelines on industrially relevant information extraction tasks from the INFEXBA project. Our results convey that the run-time efficiency of a pipeline can be improved by more than one order of magnitude without harming the effectiveness of the employed algorithms (Wachsmuth et al. 2011). We have realized our approach to ad-hoc pipeline construction as a freely available expert system (Wachsmuth et al. 2013a). Experiments with this system in the INFEXBA context and on the scientifically important biomedical extraction task GENIA (Kim et al. 2011) indicate that efficient and effective pipelines can be designed in near-zero time. Open problems are largely due to automation only, such as a missing weighting of the quality criteria to be met.

The use of our input control comes even without any notable drawback. We have operationalized the input control as an open-source extension of the APACHE UIMA framework (Wachsmuth et al. 2013c), and we provide a proof-of-concept for a number of tasks related to INFEXBA on well-known text corpora of different languages. While the concrete impact of filtering naturally depends on the employed algorithms and the density of relevant information, our findings are convincing: The input control allows us to optimize the run-time of arbitrary text analysis pipelines and it provides an intuitive means to trade efficiency for effectiveness.

Regarding efficiency optimization, we show that the ideal scheduling of a set of text analysis algorithms is a dynamic programming problem (Wachsmuth and Stein 2012). Our experiments reveal, however, that an ideal solution is too expensive, as it depends on the input texts. We formally prove that the irrelevant portions of text decide the optimality of a schedule. Still, the ideal solution serves as a benchmark for practical approaches to optimized scheduling. We implemented different approaches as open-source applications to evaluate them for a number of extraction tasks. Our results indicate that a run-time optimal schedule can often be found very efficiently. Sometimes, even simple greedy scheduling suffices (Wachsmuth et al. 2013a).

Cases where optimal schedules are hard to find tend to emanate from a high heterogeneity of the input texts, as we discover in experimental analyses (Wachsmuth et al. 2013b). On this basis, we develop new measures that quantify the optimization potential of scheduling. Experiments on precisely constructed text corpora suggest that our adaptive scheduling approach still achieves near-optimal efficiency even where the optimal fixed schedule significantly fails. Conversely, the approach encounters problems in low-heterogeneity scenarios, because of limitations in the effectiveness of our self-supervised online learning algorithm.

For classifying argumentative texts, we offer evidence that a focus on their overall structure improves the domain robustness of text analysis. In experiments, we stress the impact of sequential flows of information as well as the domain dependence of traditional approaches. We have realized the analysis of the flows in an open-source software, deployed as a prototypical web application. An evaluation of sentiment analysis in the context of our ARGUANA project emphasizes the benefit of modeling overall structure in this manner in terms of effectiveness and robustness. Also, we sketch how an according model helps users understand the results of text analyses.

1.4.2 Contributions to the Concerned Research Fields

This book presents, at its heart, findings that refer to the field of computer science. In particular, the outlined main contributions largely deal with the development and application of algorithms, especially artificial intelligence algorithms. Most of them benefit the practical applicability of text mining in big data scenarios. Our main field of application is computational linguistics. According to our motivation of improving information search, some of the implications for this field are connected to central concepts from information retrieval, such as information needs or filtering.

Concretely, our approaches to pipeline design and efficiency affect the information extraction area in the first place. In many extraction tasks, huge amounts of text are processed to find the tiny portions of text with relevant information (Sarawagi 2008). Still, existing approaches waste much effort processing irrelevant portions. If at all, they filter only based on heuristics or vague statistical models (cf. Sect. 2.4 for details). In contrast, our input control infers relevance formally and it is well-founded in the theory of truth maintenance systems. We see the input control as a logical extension of software frameworks like APACHE UIMA or GATE.

The efficiency of information extraction has long been disregarded to a wide extent, but it is getting increasing attention in the last years (Chiticariu et al. 2010b). Unlike related approaches, we neither require to lower the effectiveness of extraction, nor do we consider only rule-based extraction algorithms, as we do not change the algorithms themselves at all. Thereby, our approach achieves a very broad applicability in several types of text analysis tasks. It addresses an often overseen means to scale information extraction to large numbers of texts (Agichtein 2005).

In terms of domain robustness, we aim at argumentation-related text classification tasks, like sentiment analysis. Our overall analysis improves effectiveness on texts from domains unknown beforehand by considering the previously disregarded overall structure of texts. While the ultimate goal of guaranteeing high-quality information in ad-hoc large-scale text mining is far from being solved, we are confident that our approach denotes an important step towards more intelligent text analysis.

In this regard, we also provide new insights into the pragmatics of computational linguistics, i.e., the study of the relation between utterances and their context (Jurafsky 2003). Here, the most important findings refer to our work on the argumentation of a text. In particular, we statistically determine common patterns in the way people structure their argumentation in argumentative texts. Additionally, we claim that our model and quantification of the heterogeneity of texts constitutes a substantial building block for a better understanding of the processing complexity of texts.

To allow for a continuation of our research, a verifiability of our claims, and a reproducibility of our experiments, we have made most developed approaches freely available in open-source software (cf. Appendix B). Moreover, we provide three new text corpora for the study of different scientifically and industrially relevant information extraction and text classification problems (cf. Appendix C).

1.4.3 Structure of the Remaining Chapters

In Fig. 1.7, we illustrate the organization of Chaps. 3–5. In each of these chapters, we first develop an abstract solution to the respective problem. Then, we present and evaluate practical approaches. The approaches rely on concrete models of text analysis and/or are motivated by our own experimental analyses. We conclude each main chapter with implications for the area of application.

Before, Chap. 2 provides the required background knowledge. First, we introduce basic concepts and approaches of text mining relevant for our purposes (Sect. 2.1). We point out the importance of text analysis processes and their realization through pipelines in Sect. 2, while case studies that we resort to in examples and experiments follow in Sect. 2.3. Section 2.4 then summarizes the state of the art.

As Fig. 1.7 shows, Chap. 3 deals with the automation of pipeline design. In Sect. 3.1, we present paradigms of an ideal pipeline construction and execution. On this basis, we formalize key concepts from Sect. 2.2 in a process-oriented view of text analysis (Sect. 3.2) and then address ad-hoc pipeline construction (Sect. 3.3). In Sect. 3.4, we develop an information-oriented view of text analysis, which can be operationalized to achieve an optimal pipeline execution (Sect. 3.5). This view provides new ways of trading efficiency for effectiveness (Sect. 3.6).

Next, we optimize pipeline efficiency in Chap. 4, starting with a formal solution to the optimal scheduling of text analysis algorithms (Sect. 4.1). We analyze the impact of the distribution of relevant information in Sect. 4.2, followed by our approach to optimized scheduling (Sect. 4.3) that also requires the filtering view from Sect. 3.4. An analysis of the heterogeneity of texts (Sect. 4.4) then motivates the need for adaptive scheduling, which we approach in Sect. 4.5. Scheduling has implications for pipeline parallelization, as we discuss in Sect. 4.6.

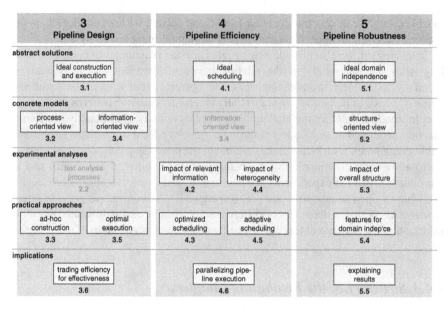

Fig. 1.7 The structure of this book, organized according to the book's three main contributions. The white boxes show short names of all sections of the three main chapters.

In Chap. 5, finally, we present a novel approach for improving pipeline robustness, which refers to an ideal domain independence (Sect. 5.1). We model text analysis from a structure-oriented viewpoint (Sect. 5.2), which emphasizes the impact of the overall structure in the classification of argumentative texts (Sect. 5.3). The model forms the basis for our overall analysis in Sect. 5.4 and it can also be exploited for an explanation of pipeline results (Sect. 5.5).

We conclude the book in Chap. 6 with a summary of our contributions and remaining problems (Sect. 6.1). As a closing step, we sketch implications for the given and other areas of computer science (Sect. 6.2). Information on all text analysis algorithms, software, and corpora referred to in this book is found in Appendices A to C.

1.4.4 Published Research Within This Book

In the book at hand, the complete picture of our approach to enable ad-hoc large-scale text mining is published for the first time. However, most of the main findings described in the book have already been presented in peer-reviewed scientific papers at renowned international conferences from the fields of computational linguistics and information retrieval. An overview is given in Table 1.1. Moreover, some parts of this book integrate content of four master's theses that were written in the context of the doctoral dissertation the book is based on. Most notably, the results of Rose (2012)

Table 1.1 Overview of peer-reviewed publications this book is based on. For each publication, the short name of the venue and the number of pages are given as well as a short sketch of the topic and the main sections of this book, in which content of the publication is reused.

Publication	Venue	Pages	Topic	Sections
Wachsmuth et al. (2010)	COLING	9	Information extraction	2.3, C.1
Wachsmuth et al. (2011)	CIKM	4	Efficient pipeline design	3.1
Wachsmuth and Bujna (2011)	IJCNLP	9	Text classification	3.6; 5.3; C.3
Wachsmuth and Stein (2012)	COLING	10	Optimal pipeline scheduling	3.1; 4.1–4.2
Wachsmuth et al. (2013a)	CICLing	12	Ad-hoc pipeline construction	3.2–3.3; 4.3
Wachsmuth et al. (2013b)	IJCNLP	9	Adaptive pipeline scheduling	4.4–4.5
Wachsmuth et al. (2013c)	CIKM	10	Input control	3.4–3.5
Wachsmuth et al. (2014a)	COLING	12	Robustness of overall structure	5.2; 5.4–5.5
Wachsmuth et al. (2014b)	CICLing	13	Impact of overall structure	5.3, C.2

significantly influenced the approach to ad-hoc pipeline construction presented in Sect. 3.3. Apart from that, short excerpts from Beringer (2012), Melzner (2012), and Mex (2013) are reused in Sects. 3.6, 4.3, and 4.4, respectively.

The exact reuse of content from the papers and theses is outlined in the respective sections. In most cases, this book provides many new details and more comprehensive information on the discussed concepts as well as extended evaluations and tool descriptions. In addition, some parts of this book represent original contributions that have not been published before, as pointed out where given.

Chapter 2
Text Analysis Pipelines

I put my heart and my soul into my work, and have lost my mind in the process.

– Vincent van Gogh

Abstract The understanding of natural language is one of the primary abilities that provide the basis for human intelligence. Since the invention of computers, people have thought about how to operationalize this ability in software applications (Jurafsky and Martin 2009). The rise of the internet in the 1990s then made explicit the practical need for automatically processing natural language in order to access relevant information. Search engines, as a solution, have revolutionized the way we can find such information ad-hoc in large amounts of text (Manning et al. 2008). Until today, however, search engines excel in finding relevant texts rather than in understanding what information is relevant in the texts. Chapter 1 has proposed text mining as a means to achieve progress towards the latter, thereby making information search more intelligent. At the heart of every text mining application lies the analysis of text, mostly realized in the form of text analysis pipelines. In this chapter, we present the basics required to follow the approaches of this book to improve such pipelines for enabling text mining ad-hoc on large amounts of text as well as the state of the art in this respect.

Text mining combines techniques from information retrieval, natural language processing, and data mining. In Sect. 2.1, we first provide a focused overview of those techniques referred to in this book. Then, we define the text analysis processes and pipelines that we consider in our proposed approaches (Sect. 2.2). We evaluate the different approaches based on texts and pipelines from a number of case studies introduced in Sect. 2.3. Finally, Sect. 2.4 surveys and discusses related existing work in the broad context of ad-hoc large-scale text mining.

2.1 Foundations of Text Mining

In this section, we explain all general foundations of text mining the book at hand builds upon. After a brief outline of text mining, we organize the foundations along the three main research fields related to text mining. The goal is not to provide a formal and comprehensive introduction to these fields, but rather to give exactly the information that is necessary to follow our discussion. At the end, we describe how to develop and evaluate approaches to text analysis. Basic concepts of text analysis processes are defined in Sect. 2.2, while specific concepts related to our overall approach are directly defined where needed in Chaps. 3–5.[1]

2.1.1 Text Mining

Text mining deals with the automatic or semi-automatic discovery of new, previously unknown information of high quality from large numbers of unstructured texts (Hearst 1999). Different than sometimes assumed, the types of information to be inferred from the texts are usually specified manually beforehand, i.e., text mining tackles given tasks. As introduced in Sect. 1.1, this commonly requires to perform three steps in sequence, each of which can be associated to one field (Ananiadou and McNaught 2005):

1. **Information retrieval.** Gather input texts that are potentially relevant for the given task.
2. **Natural language processing.** Analyze the input texts in order identify and structure relevant information.[2]
3. **Data mining.** Discover patterns in the structured information that has been inferred from the texts.

Hearst (1999) points out that the main aspects of text mining are actually the same as those studied in empirical computational linguistics. Although focusing on natural language processing, some of the problems computational linguistics is concerned with are also addressed in information retrieval and data mining, such as text classification or machine learning. In this book, we refer to all these aspects with the general term text analysis (cf. Sect. 1.1). In the following, we look at the concepts of the three fields that are important for our discussion of text analysis.

---

[1]Notice that, throughout this book, we assume that the reader has a more or less graduate-level background in computer science or similar.

[2]Ananiadou and McNaught (2005) refer to the second step as information extraction. While we agree that information extraction is often the important part of this step, also other techniques from natural language processing play a role, as discussed later in this section.

2.1.2 Information Retrieval

Following Manning et al. (2008), the primary use case of information retrieval is to search and obtain those texts from a large collection of unstructured texts that can satisfy an information need, usually given in the form of a query. In ad-hoc web search, such a query consists of a few keywords, but, in general, it may also be given by a whole text, a logical expression, etc. An information retrieval application assesses the relevance of all texts with respect to a query based on some similarity measure. Afterwards, it ranks the texts by decreasing relevance or it filters only those texts that are classified as potentially relevant (Manning et al. 2008).

Although the improvement of ad-hoc search denotes one of the main motivations behind this book (cf. Chap. 1), we hardly consider the retrieval step of text mining, since we focus on the inference of information from the potentially relevant texts, as detailed in Sect. 2.2. Still, we borrow some techniques from information retrieval, such as filtering or similarity measures. For this purpose, we require the following concepts, which are associated to information retrieval rather than to text analysis.

Vectors. To determine the relevance of texts, many approaches map all texts and queries into a *vector space model* (Manning et al. 2008). Such a model defines a common vector representation $\mathbf{x} = (x_1, \ldots, x_k)$, $k \geq 1$, for all inputs where each $x_i \in \mathbf{x}$ formalizes an input property. A concrete input like a text D is then represented by one value $x_i^{(D)}$ for each x_i. In web search, the standard way to represent texts and queries is by the frequencies of words they contain from a set of (possibly hundreds of thousands) words. Generally, any measurable property of an input can be formalized, though, which becomes particularly relevant for tasks like text classification.

Similarity. Given a common representation, similarities between texts and queries can be computed. Most word frequencies of a search query will often be 0. In case they are of interest, a reasonable similarity measure is the cosine distance, which puts emphasis on the properties of texts that actually occur (Manning et al. 2008). In Chap. 5, we compute similarities of whole texts, where a zero does not always mean the absence of a property. Such scenarios suggest other measures. In our experiments, we use the *Manhattan distance* between two vectors $\mathbf{x}^{(1)}$ and $\mathbf{x}^{(2)}$ of length k (Cha 2007), which is defined as:

$$\text{Manhattan distance}(\mathbf{x}^{(1)}, \mathbf{x}^{(2)}) = \sum_{i=1}^{k} |\mathbf{x}_i^{(1)} - \mathbf{x}_i^{(2)}|$$

Indexing. While queries are typically stated ad-hoc, the key to efficient ad-hoc search is that all texts in a given collection have been indexed before. A query is then matched against the *search index*, thereby avoiding to process the actual texts during search. Very sophisticated indexing approaches exist and are used in today's web search engines (Manning et al. 2008). In its basic form, a search index contains one entry for every measured property. Each entry points to all texts that are relevant with respect to the property. Some researchers have adapted indexing to information extraction by building specialized search indexes based on concepts like entities, such as Cafarella et al. (2005). We discuss in Sect. 2.4 in how far they reduce the need for ad-hoc large-scale text mining that we tackle in this book.

Filtering. While the ranking of texts by relevance is not needed in this book, we filter relevant portions of texts in Chap. 3. Filtering is addressed in information retrieval on two levels: *Text filtering* classifies complete texts as being relevant or irrelevant (Sebastiani 2002), whereas *passage retrieval* aims to determine the passages of a text that are relevant for answering a given query (Cui et al. 2005). We investigate the difference between our and existing filtering approaches in Sect. 2.4 and their integration at the end of Chap. 3. Filtering is usually seen as a classification task (Manning et al. 2008) and, thus, addressed as a text analysis. We cover text classification as part of natural language processing, which we describe next.

2.1.3 Natural Language Processing

Natural language processing covers algorithms and engineering issues for the understanding and generation of speech and human-readable text (Tsujii 2011). In the book at hand, we concentrate on the analysis of text with the goal of deriving structured information from unstructured texts.

In text analysis, algorithms are employed that, among others, infer lexical information about the words in a text, syntactic information about the structure between words, and semantic information about the meaning of words (Manning and Schütze 1999). Also, they may analyze the discourse and pragmatic level of a text (Jurafsky and Martin 2009). In Chaps. 3–5, we use lexical and syntactic analyses as preprocessing for information extraction and text classification. Information extraction targets at semantic information. Text classification may seek for both semantic and pragmatic information. To infer information of certain types from an input text, text analysis algorithms apply rules or statistics, as we detail below.

Generally, natural language processing faces the problem of *ambiguity*, i.e., many utterances of natural language allow for different interpretations. As a consequence, all text analysis algorithms need to resolve ambiguities (Jurafsky and Martin 2009). Without sufficient context, a correct analysis is hence often hard and can even be impossible. For instance, the sentence *"SHE'S AN APPLE FAN."* alone leaves undecidable whether it refers to a fruit or to a company.

Technically, natural language processing can be seen as the production of *annotations* (Ferrucci and Lally 2004). An annotation marks a text or a span of text that represents an instance of a particular type of information. We discuss the role of annotations more extensively in Sect. 2.2, before we formalize the view of text analysis as an annotation task in Chap. 3.

Lexical and Syntactic Analyses. For our purposes, we distinguish three types of lexical and syntactical analyses: The *segmentation* of a text into single units, the *tagging* of units, and the *parsing* of syntactic structure.

Mostly, the smallest text unit considered in natural language processing is a *token*, denoting a word, a number, a symbol, or anything similar (Manning and Schütze 1999). Besides the *tokenization* of texts, we also refer to *sentence splitting* and *paragraph splitting* as segmentation in this book. In terms of tagging, we look at *part-of-speech*, meaning the categories of tokens like nouns or verbs, although much more specific *part-of-speech tags* are used in practice (Jurafsky and Martin 2009). Also, we perform *lemmatization* in some experiments to get the *lemmas* of tokens, i.e., their dictionary forms, such as "be" in case of "is" Manning and Schütze (1999). Finally, we use shallow parsing, called *chunking* (Jurafsky and Martin 2009), to identify different types of phrases, and *dependency parsing* to infer the dependency tree structure of sentences (Bohnet 2010). Appendix A provides details on all named analyses and on the respective algorithms we rely on. The output of parsing is particularly important for information extraction.

Information Extraction. The basic semantic concept is a named or numeric *entity* from the real world (Jurafsky and Martin 2009). Information extraction analyzes usually unstructured texts in order to recognize references of such entities, *relations* between entities, and *events* the entities participate in Sarawagi (2008). In the classical view of the MESSAGE UNDERSTANDING CONFERENCES, information extraction is seen as a template filling task (Chinchor et al. 1993), where the goal is to fill entity slots of relation or event templates with information from a collection or a stream of texts **D**.

The set of information types **C** to be recognized is often predefined, although some recent approaches address this limitation (cf. Sect. 2.4). Both rule-based approaches, e.g. based on regular expressions or lexicons, and statistical approaches, mostly based on machine learning (see below), are applied in information extraction (Sarawagi 2008). The output is structured information that can be stored in databases or directly displayed to the users (Cunningham 2006). As a matter of fact, information extraction plays an important role in today's database research (Chiticariu et al. 2010a), while it has its origin in computational linguistics (Sarawagi 2008). In principle, the output qualifies for being exploited in text mining applications, e.g. to provide relevant information like GOOGLE in the example from Fig. 1.2 (Sect. 1.1). However, many information types tend to be domain-specific and application-specific (Cunningham 2006), making their extraction cost-intensive. Moreover, while some types can be extracted accurately, at least from hiqh-quality texts of common languages (Ratinov and Roth 2009), others still denote open challenges in current research (Ng 2010).

Information extraction often involves several subtasks, including *coreference resolution*, i.e., the identification of references that refer to the same entity (Cunningham 2006), and the *normalization* of entities and the like. In this book, we focus mainly on the most central subtasks, namely, named and numeric *entity recognition*, binary *relation extraction*, and *event detection* (Jurafsky and Martin 2009). Concrete analyses and algorithms that realize the analyses are found in Appendix A. As an example, Fig. 2.1(a) illustrates instances of different information types in a sample text. Some refer to a relation of the type *Founded(Organization, Time)*.

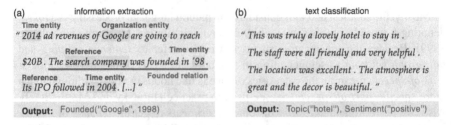

Fig. 2.1 **a** Illustration of an information extraction example: Extraction of a relation of the type *Founded(Organization, Time)* from a sample text. **b** Illustration of a text classification example: Classification of the topic and the sentiment polarity of a sample text.

In Sect. 2.3, we introduce the more sophisticated extraction of financial events from news articles that we consider in many experiments in this book. Without exception, we extract information only *within* but not *across* texts unlike e.g. Li et al. (2011). Also, we restrict our view to unstructured texts and, hence, omit to present approaches that target at structured or semi-structured texts like wrapper induction (Kushmerick 1997).

Text Classification. Text classification (or text categorization) denotes the task of assigning each text from a collection or a stream of texts **D** to one of a set of predefined *classes* $C = \{c_1, \ldots, c_k\}$, $k \geq 2$ (Jurafsky and Martin 2009). We call C the *classification scheme* here. The standard approach to text classification is to statistically learn an assignment based on a set of training texts with known classes (Manning et al. 2008). To this end, every text is converted into a vector representation consisting of a number of (typically lexical or shallow syntactic) features of the text (Sebastiani 2002). We introduce this representation as part of the data mining foundations below.

Several text classification tasks are studied in natural language processing (Manning and Schütze 1999) and information retrieval (Manning et al. 2008). The classic *topic detection* (Lewis et al. 2004) targets at the main topic of a text, whereas in *non-standard text classification tasks*, classes go beyond the subjects of texts (Lipka 2013). Examples are the identification of the *genre* of a text in terms of the form, purpose, and/or intended audience of the text (Stein et al. 2010), or *authorship attribution* where the author of a text is to be determined (Stamatatos 2009). In *automatic essay grading*, the goal is to assign ratings from a usually numeric classification scheme to texts like essays (Dikli 2006), and *stance recognition* seeks for the stance of a person with respect to some topic (Somasundaran and Wiebe 2010). All these and some related tasks are discussed more or less detailed in this book.

Of highest importance in our experiments is *sentiment analysis*, which has become one of the most widely investigated text classification tasks in the last decade. By default, sentiment analysis refers to the classification of the *sentiment polarity* of a text as being positive or negative (Pang et al. 2002). An example is shown in Fig. 2.1(b). Sometimes, also an objective (or neutral) "polarity" is considered, although this class rather refers to *subjectivity* (Pang and Lee 2004). Moreover, sentiment can also be assessed on numeric scales (Pang and Lee 2005), which we call

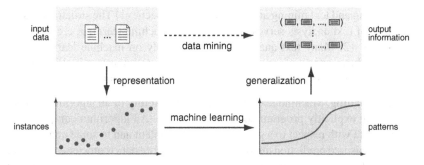

Fig. 2.2 Illustration of a high-level view of data mining. Input data is represented as a set of instances, from which a model is derived using machine learning. The model is then generalized to infer new output information.

sentiment scoring here. We employ a number of sentiment analysis algorithms in Sect. 5. They are listed in Appendix A.

As passage retrieval (see above), text classification does not always deal with complete texts. In Chap. 5, we classify the subjectivity of single discourse units, where objective units can be seen as *facts* and subjective units as *opinions*. In *opinion mining*, such techniques are combined with information extraction techniques to find opinions on certain topics (Popescu and Etzioni 2005), as done in one of our case studies (cf. Sect. 2.3). Sentiment analysis and opinion mining are of high practical relevance, because they can be used in text mining applications that analyze the people's opinions on products and brands in social media, online review sites, and similar (Pang and Lee 2008).[3] For this purpose, data mining needs to be performed on the output of the respective algorithms.

2.1.4 Data Mining

Data mining primarily aims at the inference of new information of specified types from typically huge amounts of input data, already given in structured form (Witten and Frank 2005). To address such a *prediction problem*, the data is first converted into instances of a defined representation and then handed over to a *machine learning* algorithm. The algorithm recognizes statistical patterns in the instances that are relevant for the prediction problem. This process is called *training*. The found patterns are then generalized, such that they can be applied to infer new information from unseen data, generally referred to as *prediction*. In this regard, machine learning can be seen as the technical basis of data mining applications (Witten and Frank 2005). Figure 2.2 shows a high-level view of the outlined process.

---

[3]Unlike us, some researchers do not distinguish between sentiment analysis and opinion mining, but they use these two terms interchangeably (Pang and Lee 2008).

Data mining and text mining are related in two respects: (1) The structured output information of text analysis serves as the input to machine learning, e.g. to train a text classifier. (2) Many text analyses themselves rely on machine learning algorithms to produce output information. Both respects are important in this book. In the following, we summarize the basic concepts relevant for our purposes.[4]

Machine Learning. Machine learning describes the ability of an algorithm to learn without being explicitly programmed (Samuel 1959). An algorithm can be said to learn from data with respect to a given prediction problem and to some quality measure, if the measured prediction quality increases the more data is processed (Mitchell 1997).[5] Machine learning aims at prediction problems where the *target function*, which maps input data to output information, is unknown and which, thus, cannot be (fully) solved by following hand-crafted rules. In the end, all non-trivial text analysis tasks denote such prediction problems, even though many tasks have been successfully tackled with rule-based approaches.[6]

A machine learning algorithm produces a *model* $\mathscr{Y} : \mathbf{x} \to C$, which generalizes patterns found in the input data in order to approximate the target function. $\mathscr{Y}$ defines a mapping from represented data $\mathbf{x}$ to a *target variable* C, where C captures the type of information sought for. In text analysis, the target variable may represent classes of texts (e.g. topics or genres), types of annotations (e.g. part-of-speech tags or entity types), etc. Since machine learning generalizes from examples, the learned prediction of output information cannot be expected to be correct in all cases. Rather, the goal is to find a model $\mathscr{Y}$ that is optimal with respect to a given quality measure (see below). Besides the input data, the quality of $\mathscr{Y}$ depends on how the data is represented and how the found patterns are generalized.

Representation. Similar to information retrieval, most machine learning algorithms rely on a vector space model. In particular, the input data is represented by a set X of *feature vectors* of the form $\mathbf{x}$. $\mathbf{x}$ defines an ordered set of *features*, where each feature $x \in \mathbf{x}$ denotes a measurable property of an input (Hastie et al. 2009). In text mining, common features are e.g. the frequency of a particular word in a given text or the shape of a word (say, capitalized or not). Representing input data means to create a set of instances of $\mathbf{x}$, such that each instance contains one *feature value* for every feature in $\mathbf{x}$.[7] In many cases, hundreds or thousands of features are considered in combination. They belong to different *feature types*, like *bag-of-words* where each feature means the frequency of a word (Manning et al. 2008).

---

[4]Besides the references cited below, parts of the summary are inspired by the COURSERA machine learning course, https://www.coursera.org/course/ml (accessed on June 15, 2015).

[5]A discussion of common quality measures follows at the end of this section.

[6]The question for what text analysis tasks to prefer a rule-based approach over a machine learning approach lies outside the scope of this book.

[7]Throughout this book, we consider only features whose values come from a metric scale. Other features are transformed, e.g. a feature with values "red", "green", and "blue" can be represented by three 0/1-features, one for each value. All values are normalized to the same interval, namely [0,1], which benefits learning (Witten and Frank 2005).

The feature representation of the input data governs what patterns can be found during learning. As a consequence, the development of features, which predict a given target variable C, is one of the most important and often most difficult steps in machine learning.[8] Although common feature types like bag-of-words help in many text analysis tasks, the most discriminative features tend to require expert knowledge about the task and input. Also, some features generalize worse than others, often because they capture domain-specific properties, as we see in Chap. 5.

Generalization. As shown in Fig. 2.2, generalization refers to the inference of output information from unseen data based on patterns captured in a learned model (Witten and Frank 2005). As such, it is strongly connected to the used machine learning algorithm. The training of such an algorithm based on a given set of instances explores a large space of models, because most algorithms have a number of parameters. An important decision in this regard is how much to bias the algorithm with respect to the complexity of the model to be learned (Witten and Frank 2005). Simple models (say, linear functions) induce a high bias, which may not fit the input data well, but regularize noise in the data and, thus, tend to generalize well. Complex models (say, high polynomials) can be fitted well to the data, but tend to generalize less. We come back to this problem of *fitting* in Sect. 5.1.[9]

During training, a machine learning algorithm incrementally chooses a possible model and evaluates the model based on some cost function. The choice relies on an optimization procedure, e.g. *gradient descent* stepwise heads towards a local minimum of the cost function until convergence by adapting the model to all input data (Witten and Frank 2005). In large-scale scenarios, a variant called *stochastic gradient descent* is often more suitable. Stochastic gradient descent repeatedly iterates over all data instances in isolation, thereby being much faster while not guaranteeing to find a local minimum (Zhang 2004). No deep understanding of the generalization process is needed in this book, since we focus only on the question of how to address text analysis tasks with existing machine learning algorithms in order to then select an adequate one. What matters for us is the type of learning that can or should be performed within the task at hand. Mainly, we consider two very prominent types in this book, supervised learning and unsupervised learning.

Supervised Learning. In *supervised learning*, a machine learning algorithm derives a model from known *training data*, i.e., from pairs of a data instance and the associated correct output information (Witten and Frank 2005). The model can then be used to predict output information for unknown data. The notion of being supervised refers to the fact that the learning process is guided by examples of correct predictions. In this book, we use supervised learning for both statistical classification and statistical regression.

---

[8]The concrete features of a feature type can often be chosen automatically based on input data, as we do in our experiments, e.g. by taking only those words whose occurrence is above some threshold. Thereby, useless features that would introduce noise are excluded.

[9]Techniques like feature selection and dimensionality reduction, which aim to reduce the set of considered features to improve generalizability and training efficiency among others (Hastie et al. 2009), are beyond the scope of this book.

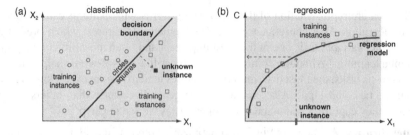

Fig. 2.3 Illustration of supervised learning: **a** In classification, a decision boundary can be derived from training instances with known classes (open circles and squares) based on their feature values, here for x_1 and x_2. The boundary decides the class of unknown instances. **b** In regression, a regression model can be derived from training instances (represented by the feature x_1) with known value for the target variable C. The model decides the values of all other instances.

Classification describes the task to assign a data instance to the most likely of a set of two or more predefined discrete classes (Witten and Frank 2005). In case of binary classification, machine learning algorithms seek for an optimal *decision boundary* that separates the instances of two classes, as illustrated in Fig. 2.3(a). Multi-class classification is handled through approaches like one-versus-all classification (Hastie et al. 2009). The applications of classification in text mining are manifold. E.g., it denotes the standard approach to text classification (Sebastiani 2002) and it is also often used to classify candidate relations between entities (Sarawagi 2008). In all respective experiments below, we perform classification with a *support vector machine* (Witten and Frank 2005). Support vector machines aim to maximize the margin between the decision boundary and the training instances of each class. They have been shown to often perform well (Meyer et al. 2003) while not being prone to adapt to noise (Witten and Frank 2005).[10]

In case of *regression*, the task is to assign a given data instance to the most likely value of a metric and continuous target variable (Witten and Frank 2005). The result of learning is a *regression model* that can predict the target variable for arbitrary instances (cf. Fig. 2.3(b)). We restrict our view to *linear regression* models, which we apply in Chap. 4 to predict the run-times of pipelines. In our experiments, we learn these models with stochastic gradient descent for efficiency purposes.

Unsupervised Learning. In contrast to supervised learning, *unsupervised learning* is only given data instances without output information. As a consequence, it usually does not serve for predicting a target variable from an instance, but merely for identifying the organization and association of input data (Hastie et al. 2009). The most common technique in unsupervised learning is *clustering*, which groups a set of instances into a possibly but not necessarily predefined number of *clusters* (Witten and Frank 2005). Here, we consider only hard clusterings, where each instance belongs to a single cluster that represents some class. Different from

---

[10]Some existing text analysis algorithms that we employ rely on other classification algorithms, though, such as *decision trees* or *artificial neural networks* (Witten and Frank 2005).

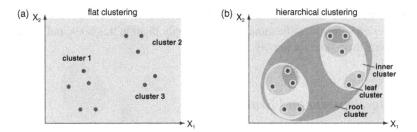

Fig. 2.4 Illustration of unsupervised learning: **a** Flat clustering groups a set of instances into a (possibly predefined) number of clusters. **b** Hierarchical clustering creates a binary hierarchy tree structure over the instances.

classification, the meaning of a class is usually unknown in clustering, though. Clustering learns patterns in the similarities of instances based on similarity measures like those used in information retrieval (see above). The resulting model can assign arbitrary instances to one of the given clusters. In text mining, clustering is e.g. used to detect texts with similar properties.

Conceptually, two basic types of clustering exist, as shown in Fig. 2.4. While *flat clustering* partitions instances without specifying associations between the created clusters, *hierarchical clustering* organizes instances in a hierachical tree (Manning et al. 2008). Each node in the tree represents a cluster of a certain size. The root cluster consists of all instances and each leaf refers to a single instance. A flat clustering can be derived from a hierarchical clustering through cuts in the tree. The tree is incrementally created by measuring distances between instances and clusters. To this end, a cluster is e.g. represented by its *centroid*, i.e., the average of all instances in the cluster (Manning et al. 2008). In general, both clustering types have certain advantages with respect to efficiency and cluster quality. We rely on hierarchical clustering in Chap. 5 for reasons discussed there. In particular, we perform *agglomerative hierarchical clustering* where the hierarchy is created bottom-up, beginning with the single instances (Manning et al. 2008).

Further Learning Types. Some other machine learning types are used more or less frequently in text mining, part of which are variations of supervised learning. Sporadically, we talk about *semi-supervised learning* in this book, which targets at tasks where much input data is available, but little known training data. Intuitively, semi-supervised learning first derives patterns from the training data and then applies knowledge about these patterns to find similar patterns in the other data (Chapelle et al. 2006). Some research in information extraction proposes *self-supervised learning* approaches that aim to fully overcome the need for known data by generating training data on their own (Banko et al. 2007). This can work when some output information is accessible without uncertainty. We present an according approach in Chap. 5. Also, we employ an entity recognition algorithm that relies on *sequence labeling* (cf. Appendix A). Sequence labeling classifies each of a sequence of instances, exploiting information about the other instances.

While there are more learning types, like reinforcement learning, recommender systems or one-class classification, we do not apply them in this book and, so, omit to introduce them here for brevity.

2.1.5 Development and Evaluation

As discussed, text analysis aims to approximate unknown target functions, which map input texts to output information. To this end, both rule-based and statistical text analysis approaches are usually developed based on a collection of input texts with known properties. Still, the output information they produce will, in general, not always be correct. The reasons behind relate to the ambiguity of natural language (see above) and to the incompleteness and inexactness of the input data (Witten and Frank 2005).

As a consequence, an empirical evaluation of the quality of a text analysis approach is of high importance and mostly closely connected to its development. Here, with quality we primarily refer to the effectiveness and efficiency of an approach, as outlined in Sect. 1.2.[11] While the concrete quality measures that are adequate for evaluation partly differ between the mentioned tasks from information retrieval, natural language processing, and data mining, in principle all three fields rely on similar methods (Manning et al. 2008; Jurafsky and Martin 2009; Witten and Frank 2005). In particular, experiments are performed, in which an approach is first developed on a collection of input texts. Then, its quality is measured on previously unseen input texts and compared to alternative approaches. In the following, we detail the outlined concepts for text analysis.

Text Corpora. In this book, we approach text analysis in a *corpus linguistics* manner, i.e., we address all tasks based on the analysis of samples of real-world texts, called text corpora. A *text corpus* is a principled collection of texts that has been compiled to analyze a problem related to language (Biber et al. 1998). Here, we consider corpora that serve for the development of text analyses (e.g. for sentiment analysis). Text corpora often contain annotations, especially annotations of the target variable that represents the output information to be inferred (e.g. the sentiment polarity of a text). In contrast to the annotations produced by text analysis algorithms, corpus annotations have usually been created manually in a cost-intensive *annotation process*. To avoid such a process, they can sometimes be derived from existing metadata (such as the author or star rating of a review). In both cases, they are seen as *ground truth* annotations (Manning et al. 2008).

---

[11]Besides effectiveness and efficiency, we also investigate the *robustness* and *intelligibility* of text analysis in Chap. 5. Further details are given there.

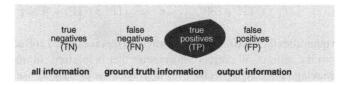

Fig. 2.5 Venn diagram showing the four sets that can be derived from the ground truth information of some type in a collection of input texts and the output information of that type inferred from the input texts by a text analysis approach.

To allow for generalization, the compilation of texts in a text corpus usually aims to be *representative* for some target variable C, i.e., it includes the full range of variability of texts with respect to C (Biber et al. 1998). We discuss representativeness at the beginning of Chap. 5. For evaluation, also the distribution of texts over the values of C should be representative for the real distribution. In machine learning, though, a *balanced* distribution, where all values of C are evenly represented, is favorable according to statistical learning theory (Batista et al. 2004).

Effectiveness. Text analysis approaches are mostly evaluated with respect to their effectiveness, which quantifies the extent to which output information is correct. Given a collection of input texts with ground truth annotations for the target variable C of a text analysis approach, the effectiveness of all approaches relevant in this book can be evaluated in the sense of a two-class classification task, i.e., whether the decision to produce each possible instance of C is correct or not.

We call the output instances of an approach the *positives* and all other instances the *negatives*. On this basis, four different sets can be distinguished (Witten and Frank 2005): *True positives (TP)* are all positives that belong to the ground truth, *true negatives (TN)* are all negatives that do not belong to the ground truth, *false negatives (FN)* are all negatives that belong to the ground truth, and *false positives (FP)* are all positives that do not belong to the ground truth. Figure 2.5 illustrates all sets.

Once the four sets are given, effectiveness can directly be quantified with different measures whose adequateness depends on the task at hand. One measure is the *accuracy a*, which denotes the ratio of correct decisions:

$$a \ = \ (|\text{TP}| + |\text{TN}|) \ / \ (|\text{TP}| + |\text{TN}| + |\text{FP}| + |\text{FN}|)$$

The accuracy is an adequate measure, when all decisions are of equal importance. This holds for many text classification tasks as well as for other text analysis tasks, in which every portion of an input text is annotated and, thus requires a decision, such as in tokenization. In contrast, especially in information extraction tasks like entity recognition, the output information usually covers only a small amount of the processed input texts. As a consequence, high accuracy can be achieved by simply producing no output information at all. Thus, accuracy is inadequate if the true negatives are of low importance. Instead, it seems more suitable to measure effectiveness in terms of the *precision p* and the *recall r* (Manning and Schütze 1999):

$$p \;=\; |TP| \,/\, (|TP| + |FP|) \qquad r \;=\; |TP| \,/\, (|TP| + |FN|)$$

Precision quantifies the ratio of output information that is inferred correctly, while recall refers to the ratio of all correct information that is inferred. In many cases, however, achieving either high precision or high recall is as easy as useless. E.g., perfect recall can be obtained by producing all possible output information. If both high precision and high recall are desired, their harmonic mean can be computed, called the F_1-score (or F_1-measure), which rewards an equal balance between p and r (van Rijsbergen 1979):

$$f_1 \;=\; 2 \cdot p \cdot r \,/\, (p + r)$$

The four defined effectiveness measures are used in a number of experiments in this book. In addition, we compute the mean *regression error* of numeric predictions in Chap. 5, which is defined as the average difference between a predicted and a correct value. Also, we talk about the *labeled attachment score* in Chap. 3, which denotes the proportion of correctly classified tokens in dependency parsing (Bohnet 2010). Other effectiveness measures are left out here for lack of relevance.

Efficiency. Since we aim to perform text analysis on large amounts of input texts, not only effectiveness is important in this book, but also efficiency. In general, efficiency quantifies costs in terms of the consumption of time or memory (Cormen et al. 2009). While we sporadically discuss the effects of high memory consumptions in the subsequent chapters, we always refer to efficiency here as the *run-time* (also called running time) an approach takes to process a given input. We use the terms efficiency and *run-time efficiency* interchangeably from here on.

We quantify the efficiency of each algorithm A_i and pipeline Π in terms of two measures, both specified in seconds or milliseconds: First, the absolute *overall run-times* $t_i(D)$ and $t_\Pi(D)$ on an input text D, and second, the average *run-time per portion of text* (mostly, per sentence), $t(A_i)$ and $t(\Pi)$. All run-times are averaged over a defined number of runs (either 5 or 10) and complemented by their *standard deviation* σ. In some cases, we compute specific run-times (say, the training time), as defined where given.

Experiments. In corpus linguistics, the general method to develop and evaluate both rule-based and statistical text analysis approaches is to perform experiments using a split of a corpus into different *datasets*. One (or the union of some) of these datasets is analyzed manually or automatically for the development, and the others are processed to evaluate a developed approach (Jurafsky and Martin 2009).[12] We realize the process underlying this method in the following two ways in this book, both of which are very common in statistical evaluation (Witten and Frank 2005).

---

[12]The development of statistical approaches benefits from a balanced dataset (see above). This can be achieved through either undersampling minority classes or oversampling majority classes. Where needed, we mostly perform the latter using random duplicates.

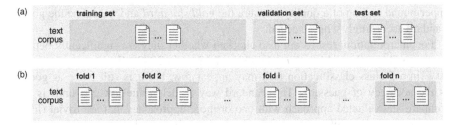

Fig. 2.6 Two ways of splitting a corpus for development and evaluation: **a** A training set is used for development, a validation set for optimizing parameters, and a test set for evaluation. **b** Each fold i out of n folds serves for evaluation in the i-th of n runs. All others are used for development.

In most cases, we split a given text corpus into a training set, a validation set, and a test set, as illustrated in Fig. 2.6(a).[13] After developing an approach on the *training set*, the quality of different configurations of the approach (e.g. with different feature vectors or learning parameters) is iteratively evaluated on the *validation set*. The validation set thereby serves for optimizing the approach, while the approach adapts to the validation set. The best configuration is then evaluated on the *test set* (also referred to as the held-out set). A test set represents the unseen data. It serves for estimating the quality of an approach in practical applications.[14]

The described method appears reasonable when each dataset is of sufficient size and when the given split prevents from bias that may compromise the representativeness of the respective corpus. In other cases, an alternative is to perform (stratified) *n-fold cross-validation* (Witten and Frank 2005). In n-fold cross-validation, a text corpus is split into n (e.g. 10) even folds, assuring that the distribution of the target variable is similar in all folds. The development and evaluation then consist of n runs, over which the measured quality of an approach is averaged. In each run i, the i-th fold is used for evaluation and all others for development. Such a split is shown in Fig. 2.6(b). We conduct according experiments once in Chap. 5.

Comparison. The measured effectiveness and efficiency results of a text analysis approach are usually compared to alternative ways of addressing the given task in order to assess whether the results are good bad. For many tasks, an upper-bound ceiling of effectiveness is assumed to be the effectiveness a human would achieve (Jurafsky and Martin 2009).[15] For simplicity, effectiveness is thus often measured with respect to the human-annotated ground truth. While there is no general upper-bound efficiency ceiling, we see in the subsequent chapters that optimal efficiency can mostly be determined in a given experiment setting. We call every

---

[13]Many text corpora already provide an according corpus split, including most of those that we use in our experiments (cf. Appendix C).

[14]In some of our efficiency experiments, no parameter optimization takes place. We leave out the use of validation set in these cases, as pointed out where relevant.

[15]Some exceptions to the truth of this assumption exist, of course. For instance, authorship attribution (see above) is expected to be often hard for humans.

upper-bound ceiling of a quality measure the *gold standard* and we define the gold standard accordingly where needed.

For interpretation, results are also checked whether they are significantly better than some lower bound *baseline* (Jurafsky and Martin 2009). E.g., an accuracy of 40 % in a 5-class classification task may appear low, but it is still twice as good as the accuracy of guessing. The standard way to determine lower bounds is to compare an evaluated approach with one or more approaches that are trivial (like guessing), standard (like a bag-of-words approach in text classification), state-of-the-art or at least well known from the literature. We compare our approaches to according baselines in all our experiments in Chaps. 3–5. In these experiments, we mostly consider complex text analysis processes realized by pipelines of text analysis algorithms, as presented next.

2.2 Text Analysis Tasks, Processes, and Pipelines

In Sect. 1.2, we have roughly outlined that text mining requires task-specific text analysis processes with several classification, extraction, and similar steps. These processes are realized by text analysis pipelines that infer output information from input texts in order to satisfy a given information need. Since text analysis pipelines are in the focus of all approaches proposed in this book, we now explain the outlined concepts of text analysis more comprehensively and we illustrate them at the end. Thereby, we define the starting point for all discussions in Chaps. 3–5.

2.2.1 Text Analysis Tasks

As specified in Sect. 1.2, we consider tasks in which we are given input texts and an information need to be addressed. The goal is to infer output information from the input texts that is relevant with respect to the information need. Here, we detail basic concepts behind such tasks. An extension of these concepts by quality criteria to be met follows in Chap. 3 after discussing the optimality of text analysis pipelines.

Input Texts. In principle, the input we deal with in this book may be either given in the form of a *collection of texts* or a *stream of texts*. The former denotes a set of natural language texts $\{D_1, \ldots, D_n\}$, $n \geq 1$, usually compiled with a purpose, like a text corpus (see above). With the latter, we refer to continuously incoming natural language text data. We assume here that such data can be split into logical segments $D_1, D_2, \ldots$ (technically, this is always possible). Given that the speed of processing a stream can be chosen freely, we can then deal with collections and streams in the same way except for the constraint that streaming data must be processed in the order in which it arrives. We denote both a collection and a stream as **D**.

We see a single text $D \in \mathbf{D}$ as the atomic input unit in text analysis tasks. While no general assumptions are made about the length, style, language, or other properties of D, we largely restrict our view to fully *unstructured texts*, i.e., plain texts that have no explicit structure aside from line breaks and comparable character-level formattings. Although text mining may receive several types of documents as input, such as HTML files in case of web applications, our restriction is not a limitation but rather a focus: Most text analysis approaches work on plain text. If necessary, some content extraction is, thus, usually performed in the beginning that converts the documents into plain text (Gottron 2008). Besides, some of our approaches in the subsequent chapters allow the input texts to already have annotations of a certain set of zero or more information types $\mathbf{C}_0$, which holds for many text corpora in computational linguistics research (cf. Sect. 2.1).

Output Information. In Sect. 2.1, different information types have been mentioned, e.g. tokens, part-of-speech tags, concrete types of entities and relations, certain text classification schemes, etc. In general, an information type $C = \{c_1, c_2, \ldots\}$ denotes the set of all pieces of information $c \in C$ that represent a particular lexical, syntactic, semantic, or pragmatic concept. We postpone a more exact definition of information types to Chap. 3, where we formalize the expert knowledge for tackling text analysis tasks automatically. A concrete information type is denoted with an upper-case term in this book, such as the *Token* type or a relation type *Founded*. To signal that an information type is part of an event or relation type, we append it to that type in lower case, such as *Token.lemma* or *Founded.time*.

Now, in many tasks from information extraction and text classification, the goal is to infer output information of a specific set of information types $\mathbf{C}$ from texts or portions of texts. Here, we use the set notation as in propositional logic (Kleine et al. 1999), i.e., a set $\mathbf{C} = \{C_1, \ldots, C_k\}$, $k \geq 1$, can be understood as a conjunction $C_1 \wedge \ldots \wedge C_k$. In case of *Founded(Organization, Time)* from Sect. 2.1, for example, a text or a portion of text that contains an instance of this relation type must comprise an organization name and a time information as well as a representation of a foundation relation between them. Hence, the relation type implicitly refers to a conjunction *Founded* $\wedge$ *Founded.organization* $\wedge$ *Founded.time*, i.e., a set *{Founded, Founded.organization, Founded.time}*.

Information Needs. Based on the notion of information types, we can define what information is relevant with respect to an information need in that it helps to fulfill the need. The goal of text mining is to infer new information of specified types from a collection or a stream of input texts $\mathbf{D}$ (cf. Sect. 2.1). From a text analysis perspective, addressing an information need hence means to return *all* instances of a given set of information types $\mathbf{C}$ that are found in $\mathbf{D}$. In this regard, $\mathbf{C}$ itself can be seen as a specification of an information need, a single information need in particular. Accordingly, a combination of $k > 1$ information needs (say, the desire to get information of $k = 2$ relation types at the same time) refers to a disjunction $\mathbf{C}_1 \vee \ldots \vee \mathbf{C}_k$. In practical text mining applications, parts of an information need might be specified beforehand. E.g., *Founded(Organization, "1998")* denotes the request to extract all names of organizations founded in the year 1998.

We assume in this book that information needs are already given in a formalized form. Consequently, we can concentrate on the text analysis processes required to address information needs. Similar to information types, we actually formalize information needs later on in Chap. 3.

2.2.2 Text Analysis Processes

In real-world text analysis tasks, information needs refer to combinations of concrete information types from natural language processing. We have introduced the general analyses that can infer these information types from input texts in Sect. 2.1. However, even the inference of a single information type often requires several analysis steps, each of which refers to one text analysis. The reason is that many text analyses require as input the output of other text analyses, which in turn depend on further text analyses, and so forth. As a consequence, addressing an information need means the realization of a complex text analysis process. Common examples refer to the areas of information extraction and text classification, as sketched below. In general, also other natural language processing tasks entail a number of analysis steps, like *semantic role labeling*, which seeks for the associations between the verb in a sentence and its arguments (Gildea and Jurafsky 2002). Some processes in the intersection of the different areas comprise almost 30 steps (Solovyev et al. 2013).

Information Extraction. As discussed in Sect. 2.1, information extraction often aims at filling complex event templates whose instances can be stored in databases. Therefore, information extraction processes are made up of possibly tens of analysis steps, covering the whole spectrum from lexical and syntactic preprocessing over entity recognition, relation extraction, and event detection to coreference resolution and normalization. While we investigate processes with up to 11 distinguished analysis steps in the experiments of the subsequent chapters, for brevity we here exemplify only that even binary relation extraction may already require several steps.

In particular, assume that instances of the above-mentioned relation type *Founded* shall be extracted from the sentences of an input text using supervised classification (cf. Sect. 2.1). Before features can be computed for classification, both organization and time entities need to be recognized in the sentences. Entity recognition often relies on the output of a chunker, while relation extraction benefits from information about the positions of candidate entities in a dependency parse tree (Sarawagi 2008). These analyses are usually based on part-of-speech tags and lemmas, which mostly makes a preceding tokenization and sentence splitting necessary.

Text Classification. In terms of the number of distinguished analysis steps, text classification processes tend to be shorter than information extraction processes, because the focus is usually on the computation of feature values the class of an input text is inferred from. Still, many features rely on the existence of previously produced instances of information types, especially those resulting from lexical and shallow syntactic analyses (cf. Sect. 2.1). In sentiment analysis, for example, some baseline approaches derive features from the output of tokenization and part-of-speech tagging only (Pang et al. 2002), while others e.g. also perform chunking, and extract relations between recognized domain-specific terms (Yi et al. 2003). Moreover, some text classification approaches rely on fine-grained information from semantic and pragmatic text analyses, such as the sentiment analysis in our case study ARGUANA that we introduce in Sect. 2.3.

Realization. The complexity of common text analysis processes raises the question of how to approach a text analysis task without losing the mind in the process, like van Gogh according to the introductory quote of this chapter. As the examples above indicate, especially the dependencies between analysis steps are not always clear in general (e.g. some entity recognition algorithms require part-of-speech tags, while others do not). In addition, errors may propagate through the analysis steps, because the output of one step serves as input to subsequent steps (Bangalore 2012). This entails the danger of achieving limited overall effectiveness, although each single analysis step works fine. A common approach to avoid error propagation is to perform joint inference, where all or at least some steps are performed concurrently. Some studies indicate that joint approaches can be more effective in tasks like information extraction (cf. Sect. 2.4 for details).[16]

For our purposes, joint approaches entail limitations, though, because we seek to realize task-specific processes ad-hoc for arbitrary information needs from text analysis. Moreover, joint approaches tend to be computationally expensive (Poon and Domingos 2007), since they explore larger search spaces emanating from combinations of information types. This can be problematic for the large-scale scenarios we target at. Following Buschmann et al. (1996), our requirements suggest the resort to a sequence of small analysis steps composed to address a task at hand. In particular, small analysis steps allow for an easy recombination and they simplify the handling of interdepedencies. Still, a joint apprach may be used as a single step in an according sequence. We employ a few joint approaches (e.g. the algorithm ENE described in Appendix A.1) in the experiments of this book. Now, we present the text analysis pipelines that realize sequences of analysis steps.

2.2.3 Text Analysis Pipelines

Pipelines denote the standard approach to realize text analysis processes. Although the application of pipelines is ubiquitous in natural language processing (Hollingshead and Roark 2007), rarely their design and execution are defined formally. As sketched in Sect. 1.2, a text analysis pipeline processes a collection or a stream of

---

[16]A simple example is the interpretation of periods in tokenization and sentence splitting: Knowing sentence boundaries simplifies the determination of tokens with periods like abbreviations, but knowing the abbreviations also helps to determine sentence boundaries.

input texts with a sequence of algorithms in order to stepwise produce a set of output information types.[17] We model a text analysis pipeline in the following way:[18]

> **Text Analysis Pipeline.** A text analysis pipeline Π is a 2-tuple $\langle \mathbf{A}, \pi \rangle$ where
>
> 1. **Algorithm Set.** $\mathbf{A} = \{A_1, \ldots, A_m\}$ is a set of $m \geq 1$ text analysis algorithms, and
> 2. **Schedule.** $\pi \subset \{(A_i < A_j) \mid A_i, A_j \in \mathbf{A}\}$ is a strict total order on $\mathbf{A}$.

For a concise presentation, we sometimes shorten the notation of a text analysis pipeline with m algorithms in this book as $\Pi = (A_1, \ldots, A_m)$ and we often refer to text analysis pipelines as *pipelines* only. Also, we discuss some special pipeline cases, namely, *empty pipelines* with $m = 0$ algorithms, *partial pipelines* that employ a subset of the algorithms in $\mathbf{A}$ only, and *partially ordered pipelines* that have a *partial schedule*, defining a partial order only.

Text Analysis Algorithms. According to our motivation from Chap. 1, we consider pipelines in a *universe* Ω where the set $\mathbf{A}_\Omega$ of all available text analysis algorithms is arbitrary but fixed. Each algorithm from $\mathbf{A}_\Omega$ employed in a pipeline $\Pi = \langle \mathbf{A}, \pi \rangle$ realizes one analysis step of a text analysis process, performing any text analysis like those outlined in Sect. 2.1. By that, such an algorithm can be seen as the atomic processing unit in text analysis.

While an algorithm may perform several analyses, feature computations, and similar, we handle all algorithms in a black-box manner, not considering their internal operations. Instead, we describe each algorithm $A_i \in \mathbf{A}$ by its input and output behavior. In particular, A_i requires a text and instances of a (possibly empty) set of information types $\mathbf{C}_i^{(in)}$ as input and A_i produces instances of a set $\mathbf{C}_i^{(out)}$ as output. A more formal definition is provided in Chap. 3, where we also talk about the effects of language and other input properties on the applicability and quality of an algorithm. Technically, algorithms produce annotations of texts or portions of texts, as discussed in Sect. 2.1. In some parts of this book, we assume that no text analysis is performed by more than algorithm in a pipeline (as mentioned where relevant). In this case, an algorithm adds annotations to a text, but it never deletes or overwrites annotations given already.

---

[17]Some related work speaks about *workflows* rather than pipelines, such as (Shen et al. 2007). The term workflow is more general, also covering cascades where the input can take different paths. Indeed, such cascades are important in text analysis, e.g. when the sequence of algorithms to be executed depends on the language of the input text. From an execution viewpoint, however, we can see each taken path as a single pipeline in such cases.

[18]While named differently, the way we represent pipelines and the algorithms they compose here largely conforms to their realization in standard software frameworks for text analysis, like APACHE UIMA, http://uima.apache.org, accessed on June 15, 2015.

Schedules. The schedule π of a pipeline $\Pi = \langle \mathbf{A}, \pi \rangle$ prescribes the order in which the algorithms in $\mathbf{A}$ are applied to every input text. As such, π rules whether the input requirements of each algorithm $A_i \in \mathbf{A}$ are fulfilled, i.e., whether all information types in $\mathbf{C}_i^{(in)}$ are produced by the algorithms preceding A_i. While some algorithms will fail completely if their requirements are not met (e.g. entity recognition must precede the extraction of respective relations), others will behave unpredictably, usually degrading significantly in effectiveness. Schedules play an important role in the appraches proposed in Chaps. 3 and 4. We formalize desired properties of schedules in Chap. 3. Afterwards, we reveal that *scheduling*, i.e., the definition of a schedule for a given algorithm set, impacts pipeline efficiency.

Pipeline Design. The general design style of text analysis pipelines is fixed. According to their definition above, it largely corresponds to the architectural pattern *pipes and filters*. Pipes and filters divides a process into several sequential processing steps that are connected by the data flow of the process (Buschmann et al. 1996). In particular, the output data of one processing step is the input to the subsequent step. Different from pipes and filters architectures in areas like computer graphics (Angel 2008), however, usual text analysis algorithms do not really transform their input, but they add information in the sense of annotations to their input only. In terms of data management, text analysis pipelines hence rather follow a *blackboard architecture* (Hayes-Roth 1985), i.e., they have a shared knowledge base (with texts and annotations) that all algorithms can access.

In principle, text analysis processes may also be realized with so called tees and joins, i.e., with algorithms that have more than one predecessor or successor (Buschmann et al. 1996). Without parallelization, a respective pipeline needs to be linearized for execution anyway. In the mentioned area of computer graphics, different orderings of processing steps like transformations can lead to different possibly useful results (Angel 2008). In contrast, as long as annotations are only added to a text, either the ordering of two algorithms does not matter (in case they are independent) or there is exactly one correct ordering (otherwise). We discuss limitations of the pipeline architecture in Sect. 2.4 and we clarify both the notion of correct orderings and the effects of parallelization in Chap. 3.

Since the analysis steps to be performed depend on the text analysis task to be tackled, pipelines are task-specific. Traditionally, a pipeline $\Pi = \langle \mathbf{A}, \pi \rangle$ is designed manually by a human expert by when given a task by selecting and scheduling an appropriate subset $\mathbf{A}$ of the set of available text analysis algorithms $\mathbf{A}_\Omega$ (Ferrucci and Lally 2004).

Pipeline Execution. Figure 2.7 illustrates how a pipeline Π is traditionally executed on a collection or a stream of input texts $\mathbf{D}$, for which a set of information types $\mathbf{C}_0$ is already provided in advance (see above). For a clear presentation, the type level is shown for most of the concepts explained on the previous pages. Actually, each text from $\mathbf{D}$ runs sequentially through the m algorithms in Π, and each algorithm A_i in Π produces instances of a set of information types $\mathbf{C}_i^{(out)}$ as output by adding annotations to the text. After the execution of A_i, the union $\bigcup_{j=0}^{i} \mathbf{C}_j$ of information

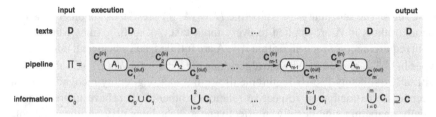

Fig. 2.7 Abstract view of executing a text analysis pipeline $\Pi = (A_1, \ldots, A_m)$ on a collection or a stream of input texts $\mathbf{D}$ in order to produce a set of output information types $\mathbf{C}$. For every text in $\mathbf{D}$, each algorithm A_i, $1 \leq i \leq m$, adds instances of a set of information types $\mathbf{C}_i^{(out)}$ to the instances of all inferred information types $\bigcup_{j=0}^{i} \mathbf{C}_j$. This set is initialized with instances of a possibly empty set of information types $\mathbf{C}_0$.

types inferred so far is given. The union of information types inferred by all algorithms employed in Π is supposed to be a superset of the set of information types $\mathbf{C}$, which represents the information need to be addressed. So, we observe that the pipeline controls the process of creating all information sought for.

At the same time, the processed input texts themselves do not change at all within the realized text analysis process, as emphasized in the upper part of Fig. 2.7. I.e., each algorithm tradionally processes each input text completely. We present an enhancement of such an execution in Chap. 3 after summarizing existing approaches in Sect. 2.4. Before, we introduce the case studies we examine in order to evaluate all of our approaches.

2.3 Case Studies in This Book

In this book, we aim to improve the design, efficiency, and robustness of the text analysis pipelines defined in Sect. 2.2. All developed approaches are evaluated in empirical experiments with text analysis tasks that refer to a selection of scientifically and/or industrially relevant case studies. Some of these case studies are associated to two of our research projects, INFEXBA and ARGUANA, whereas the others are known from related research. We briefly outline all of them in this section.

2.3.1 InfexBA – Information Extraction
for Business Applications

INFEXBA is a research project that was funded by the GERMAN FEDERAL MINISTRY OF EDUCATION AND RESEARCH (BMBF) from 2008 to 2010 under contract number 01IS08007A. The primary goal of INFEXBA was to develop text mining applications

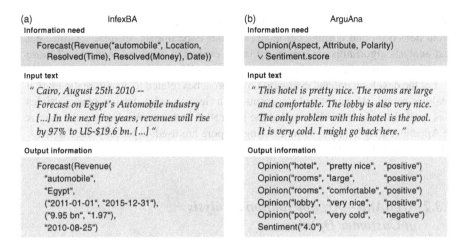

Fig. 2.8 Example for output information inferred from an input text to address the main information needs in **a** the INFEXBA project and **b** the ARGUANA project.

for an automatic market analysis in the sense of a focused web search engine. Given an organization or market name, the search engine retrieves a set of candidate web pages, extracts, normalizes, and aggregates information about financial forecasts for the given subject from the web pages, and visualizes the aggregated information. More details about the project and its results can be found at http://infexba.upb.de.

Within the project, we proposed to perform text mining in a sequence of eight information retrieval, natural language processing, and data mining stages (Wachsmuth et al. 2010), but the focus was on those stages related to information extraction. In particular, information extraction begins after converting all retrieved web pages into plain texts and ends after normalization. We can view the set of these plain texts as a collection of input texts **D**. One of the main tasks tackled in INFEXBA was to extract each revenue forecast for the given organization or market at a certain location (including the date it was published) from **D** and to bring the time and money information associated to the forecast into resolved and normalized form. We can specify the underlying information need as follows:

Forecast(Revenue(Subject, Location, Resolved(Time), Resolved(Money), Date))

Given the market *"automobile"* as the subject, Fig. 2.8(a) exemplifies for one input text what information is meant to satisfy the specified need. Some information is directly found in the text (e.g. *"Egypt"*), some must be computed (e.g. the money amount of *"9.95 bn"* at the end of 2010).

We refer to the INFEXBA project in the majority of those experiments in Chaps. 3 and 4 that deal with pipeline design and optimization. For a focused discussion, we evaluate different simplifications of the presented information need, though. One such need, for instance, targets at all related pairs of time and money information that belong to revenue forecasts. Accordingly, the text analysis pipelines that we evaluate still perform several preprocessing, entity recognition, relation extraction, event detection, and normalization steps in our experiments. In total, 21 different text analysis algorithms are employed in the evaluated pipelines, namely, all those described in Appendix A that are not used for classification or discourse parsing.

For the development and evaluation of approaches related to an automatic market analysis, a manually annotated text corpus with German online business news articles was created within INFEXBA, called the REVENUE CORPUS. We describe the corpus in Appendix C.1. Besides, some existing corpora are used, especially the CoNLL-2003 dataset (cf. Appendix C.4).

2.3.2 ArguAna – Argumentation Analysis in Customer Opinions

As INFEXBA, ARGUANA is a research project that was funded by the GERMAN FEDERAL MINISTRY OF EDUCATION AND RESEARCH (BMBF). It ran from 2012 to 2014 under contract number 01IS11016A. The project aimed at the development of novel text analysis algorithms for fine-grained opinion mining from customer product reviews. In particular, a focus was on the analysis of the sequence of single arguments in a review in order to capture and interpret the review's overall argumentation. From the results of a set of reviews, a text mining application cannot only infer collective opinions about different aspects of a product, but also provide a precise classification of the sentiment of customers with respect to the product. More information about ARGUANA is given at http://www.arguana.com.

In the project, we developed a complex text analysis process to tackle the underlying text classification and information extraction tasks: First, the body of each review text from a collection of input texts **D** is segmented into its single subsentence-level discourse units. Every unit is classified as being either an objective fact, a positive, or a negative opinion. Discourse relations between the units are then extracted as well as products and aspects the units are about, together with their attributes. Finally, a sentiment score in the sense of the review's overall rating is predicted. The output information helps to address the following information need:

Opinion(Aspect, Attribute, Polarity) ∧ *Sentiment.score*

As for this information need, the disjunctions defined in Sect. 2.2 should not be misunderstood in the sense that addressing one of the two connected conjunctions suffices. Rather, it states that instances of either of them is relevant. Figure 2.8(b) shows the output information for a sample hotel review. The sentiment score comes from a scale between 1 (worst) and 5 (best).

We refer to the ARGUANA project mostly in the evaluation of pipeline robustness in Chap. 5. There, we omit the recognition of products, aspects, and attributes, but we focus on text classification approaches based on the extracted facts, opinions, and discourse relations. The remaining text analysis process is realized with the following pipeline: $\Pi_{\text{ARGUANA}} = (\text{SSE}, \text{STO}_2, \text{TPO}_1, \text{PDU}, \text{CSB}, \text{CSP}, \text{PDR}, \text{CSS})$. For details on the algorithms, see Appendix A.

The experiments related to the ARGUANA project are based on two English collections of texts, consisting of reviews from the hotel domain and the film domain, respectively. In particular, we rely on our own ARGUANA TRIPADVISOR CORPUS developed within the project (cf. Appendix C.2) as well as on the widely used SENTIMENT SCALE DATASET (cf. Appendix C.4).

2.3.3 Other Evaluated Text Analysis Tasks

Most of the concrete text analysis tasks in this book are at least loosely connected to the presented projects INFEXBA and ARGUANA. In some cases, though, we provide complementary results obtained in other experiments in order to achieve more generality or to analyze the generalizability of our approaches. All noteworthy results of this kind are associated to the following three text analysis tasks.

Genia Event Extraction. GENIA denotes one of the main evaluation tasks of the BIONLP SHARED TASK (Kim et al. 2011). While the latter deals with the general question of how text mining can help to recognize changes of states of bio-molecules described in the biomedical literature, the former specifically targets at the extraction of nine different event types that relate a number of proteins, other entities, or other events. For instance, a *Phosphorylation* event refers to an entity of the *Protein* type as well as to some information that denotes a binding site of the protein (Kim et al. 2011). In the evaluation of automatic pipeline design in Chap. 3, we consider the formal specifications of several entity recognition and event detection algorithms that infer information types relevant in the GENIA task.

Named Entity Recognition. A *named entity* is an entity that refers to a unique concept from the real world. While numerous types of named entities exist, most of them tend to be rather application-specific (Jurafsky and Martin 2009). Some types, though, occur in diverse types of natural language texts, of which the most common are person names, location names, and organization names. They have been in the focus of the CoNLL-2003 shared task on *named entity recognition* (Tjong et al. 2003). In Chap. 4, we analyze the distribution of the three entity types in several text corpora from Appendix C in the context of influencing factors of pipeline efficiency. There, we rely on a common sequence labeling approach to named entity recognition (cf. Sect. 2.1), using the algorithm ENE (cf. Appendix A) in the pipeline $\Pi_{\text{ENE}} = (\text{SSE}, \text{STO}_2, \text{TPO}_1, \text{PCH}, \text{ENE})$.

Language Function Analysis. Finally, we address the text classification task *language function analysis* in this book. We introduced this task in Wachsmuth and Bujna (2011). As argued there, every text can be seen as being predominantly expressive, appellative, or informative. These *language functions* define an abstract classification scheme, which can be understood as capturing a single aspect of genres (Wachsmuth and Bujna 2011). In Chap. 5, we concretize the scheme for product-related texts in order to then outline how much text classification depends on the domain of the input texts. Moreover, in Chap. 3 we integrate CLF in the information extraction pipelines from INFEXBA (see above). In particular, we employ CLF to filter possibly relevant candidate input texts, which can be seen as one of the most common applications of text classification in text mining.

2.4 State of the Art in Ad-Hoc Large-Scale Text Mining

With the approaches developed in this book, we seek to enable the use of text analysis pipelines for ad-hoc large-scale text mining (cf. Sect. 1.3). Several other approaches have been proposed in the literature that tackle similar problems or that tackle different problems but pursue similar goals. In this section, we survey the state of the art in these respects, focusing on text analysis to a wide extent, and we stress how our approaches extend the state of the art. From an abstract viewpoint, our discussion follows the overall structure of this book. It reuses content from the related work sections of most of our publications listed in Table 1.1 (Sect. 1.4).

2.4.1 Text Analysis Approaches

As defined in Sect. 2.2, we consider the classic realization of a text analysis process in the form of a pipeline, where each algorithm takes as input the output of all proceeding algorithms and produces further output. Pipelines represent the most widely adopted text analysis approach (Bangalore 2012). The leading software frameworks for text analysis, APACHE UIMA and GATE, target at pipelines (cf. Sect. 1.3). Some of our approaches assume that no analysis is performed by more than one algorithm in a pipeline. This is usual, but not always the case (Whitelaw et al. 2008). As a consequence, algorithms can never make up for errors of their predecessors, which may limit the overall effectiveness of pipelines (Bangalore 2012). In addition, the task dependency of effective text analysis algorithms and pipelines (cf. Sects. 2.1 and 2.2) renders their use in the ad-hoc search scenarios we focus on problematic (Etzioni 2011). In the following, we describe the most important approaches to tackle these problems, grouped under the topics *joint inference*, *pipeline enhancement*, and *task independence*.

Joint Inference. We have already outlined joint inference as a way to avoid the problem of error propagation in classic pipelines in Sect. 2.2. Joint approaches infer different types of information at the same time, thereby mimicking the way humans process and analyze texts (McCallum 2009). Among others, tasks like entity recognition and relation extraction have been said to benefit from joint inference (Choi et al. 2006). However, the possible gain of effectiveness comes at the cost of lower efficiency and less reusability (cf. Sect. 2.2), which is why we do not target at joint approaches in this book, but only integrate them when feasible.

Pipeline Enhancement. Other researchers have addressed the error propragation through iterative or probabilistic pipelines. In case of the former, a pipeline is executed repeatedly, such that the output of later algorithms in a pipeline can be used to improve the output of earlier algorithms (Hollingshead and Roark 2007).[19] In case of the latter, a probability model is built based on different possible outputs of each algorithm (Finkel et al. 2006) or on confidence values given for the outputs (Raman et al. 2013). While these approaches provide reasonable enhancements of the classic pipeline architecture, they require modifications of the available algorithms and partly also significantly reduce efficiency. Both does not fit well to our motivation of enabling ad-hoc large-scale text mining (cf. Sect. 1.1).

Task Independence. The mentioned approaches can improve the effectiveness of text analysis. Still, they have to be designed for the concrete task at hand. For the extraction of entities and relations, Banko et al. (2007) introduced *open information extraction* to overcome such task dependency. Unlike traditional approaches for predefined entity and relation types (Cunningham 2006), their system TEXTRUNNER efficiently looks for general syntactic patterns (made up of verbs and certain part-of-speech tags) that indicate relations. Instead of task-specific analyses, it requires only a keyword-based query as input that allows identifying task-relevant relations. While Cunningham (2006) argues that high effectiveness implies high specificity, open information extraction targets at web-scale scenarios. There, precision can be preferred over recall, which suggests the exploitation of redundancy in the output information (Downey et al. 2005) and the resort to highly reliable extraction rules, as in the subsequent system REVERB (Fader et al. 2011).

Open information extraction denotes an important step towards the use of text analysis in web search and big data analytics applications. Until today, however, it is restricted to rather simple binary relation extraction tasks (Mesquita et al. 2013). In contrast, we seek to be able to tackle arbitrary text analysis tasks, for which appropriate algorithms are available. With respect to pipelines, we address the problem of task dependency in Chap. 3 through an automatic design of text analysis pipelines.

2.4.2 Design of Text Analysis Approaches

In Sect. 2.2, we have discussed that text analysis processes are mostly realized manually in regard of the information need to be addressed. Also, the resulting text analysis approaches traditionally process all input texts completely. Not only APACHE UIMA and GATE themselves provide *tool support* for the construction and execution of

---

[19] Iterative pipelines are to a certain extent related to compiler pipelines that include feedback loops (Buschmann et al. 1996). There, results from later compiler stages (say, semantic analysis) are used to resolve ambiguities in earlier stages (say, lexical analysis).

according text analysis pipelines, as outlined below. In order to address information needs ad-hoc on large numbers of texts, a number of approaches have been proposed that, similar to us, aim for an *automatic construction* of text analysis approaches as well as for optimizing their execution by *filtering* relevant texts and portions of text. In Chap. 3, we detail that the key to make the approaches successful is the existence of a pool of reusable and formally specified text analysis algorithms and the like (Wimalasuriya and Dou 2010).

Tool Support. Kano et al. (2010) introduced U- COMPARE, which supports an easy but manual construction of text analysis pipelines. U- COMPARE targets at the automatic evaluation of pipelines on text corpora. Similarly, Yang et al. (2013) describe a framework for the comparison of different pipelines for the same task. Conversely, the tool WEBLICHT, associated to the project CLARIN- D on interoperable and scalable infrastructure for language research, allows setting up pipelines for automatic corpus annotation (Hinrichs et al. 2010). In contrast to these works, we realize pipeline construction fully automatically in order to enable ad-hoc text mining.

Automatic Construction. For automation, we rely on the artificial intelligence technique *planning* (Russell and Norvig 2009). Dezsényi et al. (2005) have proposed planning for composing information extraction algorithms. Unlike us, however, the authors neither realize nor evaluate planning and they disregard the quality of the composition. In related areas, approaches exist that plan knowledge discovery workflows of minimum length given an ontology of data mining algorithms (Žáková et al. 2011) or that sum up the costs of a planned sequence of data stream processing steps (Riabov and Liu 2006). While these approaches generally seem transferrable to text analysis, their quality functions do not apply to the efficiency and effectiveness criteria relevant here (cf. Sect. 2.1). Recently, Kano (2012) presented a first glance of the software platform KACHAKO, which composes and executes a defined set of algorithms largely automatically based on the standard algorithm descriptions of APACHE UIMA. While KACHAKO appears to be similar to our expert system for ad-hoc pipeline design described in Chap. 3, it is still not available yet, rendering an exact comparison hard.

An alternative to the automatic design of text analysis pipelines is implemented in SYSTEMT, which seeks to address the needs of enterprise analytics applications, such as scalability and usability (Chiticariu et al. 2010b). SYSTEMT follows the paradigms of *declarative information extraction* (Krishnamurthy et al. 2009): a user defines analysis steps with logical constraints in the form of a query, while the system manages the workflow (Doan et al. 2009). We do not adopt the declarative approach here, as it is restricted to rule-based text analyses (Reiss et al. 2008). Still, we rely on similar concepts. E.g., SYSTEMT restricts some analyses to scopes of a text based on location conditions in the given query (Shen et al. 2007), which resembles the filtering of the input control that we develop in Chap. 3.

Filtering. Our input control filters only relevant portions of an input text in each analysis step. The idea of filtering relevant texts and portions of texts is well-known in text analysis. Traditionally, filtering is performed based on word statistics or predefined patterns (Cowie and Lehnert 1996). Lewis and Tong (1992) analyze how the filtering of complete texts at different positions in a pipeline impacts the effectiveness in complex extraction tasks. Other researchers observe that also classifying the relevance of sentences can help to improve effectiveness (Patwardhan and Riloff 2007; Jean-Louis et al. 2011). Nedellec et al. (2001) stress the importance of such filtering for all extraction tasks where relevant information is sparse. According to Stevenson (2007), a restriction to sentences may also limit effectiveness in event detection tasks, though. While we use filtering to improve efficiency, we provide evidence that our approach maintains effectiveness. Still, we allow specifying the sizes of filtered portions to trade efficiency for effectiveness.

Filtering approaches for efficiency often target at complete texts, e.g. using fast text classification (Stein et al. 2005) or querying approaches trained on texts with the relations of interest (Agichtein and Gravano 2003). A technique that filters portions of text is passage retrieval (cf. Sect. 2.1). While many text mining applications do not incorporate filtering until today, passage retrieval is common where information needs must be addressed in real-time, e.g. in question answering (Krikon et al. 2012). Cardie et al. (2000) compare the benefit of statistical and linguistic knowledge for filtering candidate passages, and Cui et al. (2005) propose a fuzzy matching of questions and possibly relevant portions of text. Sarawagi (2008) sees the efficient filtering of relevant portions of input texts as a main challenge of information extraction in large-scale scenarios. She complains that existing techniques are still restricted to hand-coded heuristics. Common heuristics aim for high recall in order not to miss relevant information later on, whereas precision can be preferred on large collections of texts under the assumption that relevant information appears redundantly (Agichtein 2005).

Different from all the outlined approaches, our filtering approach does not *predict* relevance, relying on vague models derived from statistics or hand-crafted rules. In contrast, our approach *infers* the relevant portions of an input text formally from the currently available information. Moreover, we discuss in Chap. 3 that the input control can be integrated with common filtering approaches. At the same time, it does not prevent most other approaches to improve the efficiency of text analysis.

2.4.3 Efficiency of Text Analysis Approaches

Efficiency has always been a main aspect of algorithm research (Cormen et al. 2009). For a long time, most rewarded research on text analysis focused on effectiveness as did the leading evaluation tracks, such as the MESSAGE UNDERSTANDING CONFERENCES (Chinchor et al. 1993) or the CoNLL SHARED TASK. In the latter, efficiency has at least sometimes been an optional evaluation criterion (Hajič et al. 2009). In times of big data, however, efficiency is getting increasing attention in both research and industry (Chiticariu et al. 2010b). While the filtering techniques from above denote one way to improve efficiency, the filtered texts or portions of texts still often run through a process with many expensive analysis steps (Sarawagi 2008).

Other techniques address this process, ranging from *efficient algorithms* over an optimization through *scheduling* to *indexing* and *parallelization*.

Efficient Algorithms. Efficient algorithms have been developed for several text analyses. For instance, Al-Rfou' and Skiena (2012) present how to apply simple heuristics and caching mechanisms in order to increase the velocity of segmentation and tagging (cf. Sect. 2.1). Complex syntactic analyses like dependency parsing can be approached in linear time by processing input texts from left to right only (Nivre 2003). Bohnet and Kuhn (2012) show how to integrate the knowledge of deeper analyses in such transition-based parsing while still achieving only quadratic complexity in the worst case. van Noord (2009) trades parsing efficiency for effectiveness by learning a heuristic filtering of useful parses. For entity recognition, Ratinov and Roth (2009) demonstrate that a greedy search (Russell and Norvig 2009) can compete with a more exact sequence labeling (cf. Sect. 2.1). Others offers evidence that simple patterns based on words and part-of-speech tags suffice for relation extraction, when given enough data (Pantel et al. 2004). In text classification tasks like genre identification, efficiently computable features are best practice (Stein et al. 2010). Also, the feature computation itself can be sped up through unicode conversion and string hash computations (Forman and Kirshenbaum 2008).

All these approaches aim to improve the efficiency of *single* text analyses, mostly at the cost of some effectiveness. We do not compete with these approaches but rather complement them, since we investigate how to improve pipelines that realize *complete* processes consisting of different text analyses. In particular, we optimize the efficiency of pipelines without compromising effectiveness through scheduling.

Scheduling. Some approaches related to text mining optimally schedule different algorithms for the same analysis. For instance, Stoyanov and Eisner (2012) effectively resolve coreferences by beginning with the easy cases, and Hagen et al. (2011) efficiently detect sessions of search queries with the same information need by beginning with the fastest detection steps. The ordering in which information is sought for can also have a big influence on the run-time of text analysis (Sarawagi 2008). In Chap. 4, we seize on this idea where we optimize the schedules of pipelines that filter only relevant portions of texts. However, the optimal schedule is input-dependent, as has been analyzed by Wang et al. (2011) for rule-based information extraction. Similar to the authors, we process samples of input texts in order to estimate the efficiency of different schedules.

In this regard, our research is in line with approaches in the context of the above-mentioned SYSTEMT. Concretely, Shen et al. (2007) and Doan et al. (2009) exploit dependencies and distances between relevant text regions to optimize the schedules of declarative information extraction approaches, yielding efficiency gains of about one order of magnitude. Others obtain comparable results through optimization strategies such as the integration of analysis steps (Reiss et al. 2008).

In these works, the authors provide only heuristic hints on the reasons behind their empirical results. While some algebraic foundations of SYSTEMT are established in Chiticariu et al. (2010a), these foundations again reveal the limitation of declarative information extraction, i.e., its restriction to rule-based text analysis. In contrast, we approach scheduling for arbitrary sets of text analysis algorithms. While we achieve similar gains as SYSTEMT through an optimized scheduling, our adaptive scheduling approach is, to our knowledge, the first that maintains efficiency on heterogeneous input texts. In addition, we show that the theoretically optimal schedule can be found with dynamic programming (Cormen et al. 2009) based on the run-times and filtered portions of text of the employed algorithms.

In the database community, dynamic programming is used since many years to optimize the efficiency of *join* operations (Selinger et al. 1979). However, the problem of filtering relevant portions of text for an information need corresponds to processing *and*-conditioned queries (cf. Sect. 2.2). Such queries select those tuples of a database table whose values fulfill some attribute conjunction, as e.g. in SELECT * FROM forecasts WHERE (time>2011 AND time<2015 AND organization=IBM). Different from text analysis, the optimal schedule for an and-conditioned query is obtained by ordering the involved attribute tests (e.g. time>2011) according to the numbers of expected matches (Ioannidis 1997), i.e., without having to consider algorithm run-times.

Indexing. An alternative to optimizing the efficiency of text analysis is to largely avoid the need for efficient analyses by indexing relevant information for each input text beforehand (cf. Sect. 2.1). For instance, Cafarella et al. (2005) have presented the KNOWITNOW system, which builds specialized index structures using the output of information extraction algorithms. Their approach has then been adopted in the open information extraction systems discussed above. Also, the GOOGLE KNOWLEDGE GRAPH is operationalized in an index-like manner as far as known.[20]

In the best case, indexing renders text analysis unnecessary when addressing information needs (Agichtein 2005). In the database analogy from above, the run-times of the tests (that correspond to the text analysis algorithms) drop out then. By that, indexing is particularly helpful in scenarios like ad-hoc search. However, it naturally applies only to anticipated information needs and to input texts that can be preprocessed beforehand. Both cannot be assumed in the tasks that we consider in this book (cf. Sect. 1.2).

Parallelization. With the goal of efficiency finally arises the topic of parallelization. As discussed, we concentrate on typical text analysis algorithms and pipelines, which operate over each input text independently, making many parallelization techniques easily applicable (Agichtein 2005). This might be the reason for the limited literature on parallel text analysis, despite the importance of parallelization for practical text mining applications. Here, we focus on process-related approaches as opposed to distributed memory management (Dunlavy et al. 2010) or algorithm schemes like MAPREDUCE for text analysis (Lués and de Matos 2009).[21]

---

[20]GOOGLE KNOWLEDGE GRAPH, http://googleblog.blogspot.co.uk/2012/05/introducing-knowledge-graph-things-not.html, accessed on June 15, 2015.

[21]Accordingly, we omit to talk about infrastructural technologies for distributed computing, such as APACHE HADOOP, http://hadoop.apache.org, accessed on June 15, 2015.

Text analysis can be parallelized on various levels: Different algorithms may run distributed, both to increase the load of pipelines (Ramamoorthy and Li 1977) and to parallelize independent analyses. Pokkunuri et al. (2011) run different pipelines at the same time, and Dill et al. (2003) report on the parallelization of different algorithms. The two latter do not allow interactions between the parallelized steps, while others also consider synchronization (Egner et al. 2007). A deep analysis of parallel scheduling strategies was performed by Zhang (2010). Apart from these, different texts can be processed in parallel (Gruhl et al. 2004), and the execution of analysis steps like parsing is commonly parallelized for different portions of text (Bohnet 2010). Kalyanpur et al. (2011) even run different pipelines on the same text in parallel in order to provide results as fast as possible in ad-hoc question answering.

At the end of Chap. 4, we see that input-based parallelization is always applicable to the pipelines that we employ. The same holds for the majority of other approaches, as discussed there. Because of filtering, synchronization entails new challenges with respect to our approaches, though.

2.4.4 Robustness of Text Analysis Approaches

In Chap. 5, we seek to improve the domain robustness of text analysis in order to produce high-quality information in applications where the domain of input texts cannot be anticipated, like ad-hoc web search. Most text analysis approaches at least partly rely on features of texts that are specific to a domain of application (Blitzer et al. 2007) and, hence, significantly drop in effectiveness when being applied in a new domain. Early work in this context often aimed to reduce the cost of adapting to new domains by exploiting machine learning techniques for obtaining training data automatically, surveyed by Turmo et al. (2006). However, the predominant approach today is to tackle domain dependence through *domain adaptation* (Daumé and Marcu 2006), as explained below. Some approaches also strive for *domain independence* based on generally valid features. From these approaches, we adopt the idea of focusing on structure, especially on the *argumentation structure* of texts, which in turn relates to *information structure* and *discourse structure*. Since robustness does not mean perfect effectiveness, we end with existing work on how to increase the *user acceptance* of erroneous results.

Domain Adaptation. The scenario usually addressed in domain adaptation is that many training texts are given from some source domain, but only few from a target domain (Blitzer et al. 2008). The goal is to learn a model on the source texts that works well on unknown target texts. In information extraction, most domain adaptation approaches share that they choose a representation of the source texts that makes them close the distribution of the target texts (Gupta and Sarawagi 2009). Similarly, domain adaptation is often tackled in text classification by separating the domain-specific from the domain-independent features and then exploiting knowledge about the latter (Daumé and Marcu 2006). Also, structural correspondences can be learned between domains (Blitzer et al. 2007; Prettenhofer and Stein 2011). In particular, domain-specific features are aligned based on a few domain-independent features, e.g. *"Stay away!"* in the hotel domain might have a similar meaning as *"Read the book!"* in the film domain.

Domain adaptation, however, does not really apply to ad-hoc search and similar applications, where it is not possible to access texts from all target domains in advance. This also excludes the approach of Gupta and Sarawagi (2009) who derive domain-independent features from a comparison of the set of all unknown target texts to the set of known source texts.

Domain Independence. Since domains are often characterized by content words and the like (cf. Chap. 5 for details), most approaches that explicitly aim for domain independence try to abstract from content. Glorot et al. (2011), for instance, argue that higher-level intermediate concepts obtained through the non-linear input transformations of deep learning help in cross-domain sentiment analysis of reviews. While we evaluate domain robustness for the same task, we do not presume a certain type of machine learning algorithms. Rather, we work on the features to be learned. Lipka (2013) observes that style features like character trigrams serve the robustness of text quality assessment. Similar results are reported for authorship attribution in Sapkota et al. (2014). The authors reveal the benefit of mixed-domain training sets for developing robust text analysis algorithms.

Some experiments that we perform in Chap. 5 suggest that style features are still limited in their generalizability. We therefore propose features that model the structure of texts. This resembles the idea of open information extraction, which avoids the resort to any domain-dependent features, but captures only generally valid syntactic patterns in sentences (see above). However, we seek for domain independence in tasks, where complete texts have to be classified. For authorship attribution, Choi (2011) provide evidence that structure-based features like function word n-grams achieve high effectiveness across domains. We go one step further by investigating the argumentation structure of texts.

Argumentation Structure. Argumentation is studied in various disciplines, such as logic, philosophy, and artificial intelligence. We consider it from the linguistics perspective, where it is pragmatically viewed as a regulated sequence of speech or text (Walton and Godden 2006). The purpose of argumentation is to provide persuasive arguments for or against a decision or claim, where each argument itself can be seen as a claim with some evidence. Following the pioneer model of Toulmin (1958), the structure of an argumentation relates a claim to facts and warrants that are justified by backings or countered by rebuttals. Most work in the emerging research area of *argumentation mining* relies on this or similar models of argumentation (Habernal et al. 2014). Concretely, argumentation mining analyzes natural language texts in order to detect different types of arguments as well as their interactions (Mochales and Moens 2011).

Within our approach to robustness, we focus on texts that comprise a monological and positional argumentation, like reviews, essays, or scientific articles. In such a text, a single author collates and structures a choice of facts, pros, and cons in order to persuade the intended recipients about his or her conclusion (Besnard and Hunter 2008). Unlike *argumentative zoning* (Teufel et al. 2009), which classifies segments of scientific articles according to their argumentative functions, we aim to find argumentation patterns in these texts that help to solve text classification tasks. For this purpose, we develop a shallow model of argumentation structure in Chap. 5.

Information Structure. Our model captures sequences of task-specific information in the units of a text as well as relations between them. By that, it is connected to information structure, which refers to the way information is packaged in a text (Lambrecht 1994). Different from approaches like (Bohnet et al. 2013), however, we do not analyze the abstract information structure within sentences. Rather, we look for patterns of how information is composed in whole texts (Gylling 2013). In sentiment-related tasks, for instance, we claim that the sequence of subjectivities and polarities in the facts and opinions of a text represents the argumentation of the text. While Mao and Lebanon (2007) have already investigated such sequences, they have analyzed the positions in the sequences only separately (cf. Chap. 5 for details). In contrast, we develop an approach that learns patterns in the complete sequences found in texts, thereby capturing the overall structure of the texts. To the best of our knowledge, no text analysis approach to capture overall structure has been published before.

Discourse Structure. The information structure that we consider is based on the discourse structure of a text (Gylling 2013). Discourse structure refers to organizational and functional relations between the different parts of a text (Mann and Thompson 1988), as presented in Chap. 5. There, we reveal that patterns also exist in the sequences of discourse relations that e.g. cooccur with certain sentiment. Gurevych (2014b) highlight the close connection between discourse structure and argumentation, while Ó Séaghdha and Teufel (2014) point out the topic independence of discourse structure. The benefit of discourse structure for sentiment analysis, especially in combination with opinion polarities, has been indicated in recent publications (Villalba and Saint-Dizier 2012; Chenlo et al. 2014). We use according features as baselines in our domain robustness experiments.

User Acceptance. Even a robust text mining application will output erroneous results occasionally. If users do not understand the reasons behind, their acceptance of such an application may be limited (Lim and Dey 2009). While in some technologies related to text mining much attention is paid to the transparency of results, like recommender systems (Sinha and Swearingen 2002), according research for text analysis is limited. We consider the explanation of text classification, which traditionally outputs only a class label, possibly extended by some probability estimate (Manning et al. 2008). Alvarez and Martin (2009) present an explanation approach to general supervised classification that puts the decision boundary in the focus (cf. Sect. 2.1). Kulesza et al. (2011) visualize the internal logic of a text classifier, and Gabrilovich and Markovitch (2007) stress the understandability of features that correspond to real-world concepts. At the end of Chap. 5, we sketch explanation approaches that follow the intuitions of the two latter using knowledge about the employed pipelines and information about the developed features. We believe that the user acceptance of erroneous results is decisive for the success of ad-hoc large-scale text mining applications.

Chapter 3
Pipeline Design

Once you eliminate the impossible, whatever remains, no matter how improbable, must be the truth.

– Arthur Conan Doyle

Abstract The realization of a text analysis process as a sequential execution of the algorithms in a pipeline does not mimic the way humans approach text analysis tasks. Humans simultaneously investigate lexical, syntactic, semantic, and pragmatic clues in and about a text (McCallum 2009) while skimming over the text to fastly focus on the portions of text relevant for a task (Duggan and Payne 2009). From a machine viewpoint, however, the decomposition of a text analysis process into single executable steps is a prerequisite for identifying relevant information types and their interdependencies. Until today, this decomposition and the subsequent construction of a text analysis pipeline are mostly made manually, which prevents the use of pipelines for tasks in ad-hoc text mining. Moreover, such pipelines do not focus on the task-relevant portions of input texts, making their execution slower than necessary (cf. Sect. 2.2). In this chapter, we show that both parts of pipeline design (i.e., construction and task-specific execution) can be fully automated, once given adequate formalizations of text analysis.

In Sect. 3.1, we discuss the optimality of text analysis pipelines and we introduce paradigms of an ideal pipeline construction and execution. For automatic construction, we model the expert knowledge underlying text analysis processes formally (Sect. 3.2). On this basis, we operationalize the cognitive skills of constructing pipelines through partial order planning (Sect. 3.3). In our evaluation, the construction always takes near zero-time, thus enabling ad-hoc text mining. In Sect. 3.4, we then reinterpret text analysis as the task to filter the portions of a text that contain relevant information, i.e., to consistently imitate skimming. We realize this information-oriented view by equipping a pipeline with an input control. Based on the dependencies between relevant information types, the input control determines for each employed algorithm in advance what portions of text its output is relevant for (Sect. 3.5). Such an automatic truth maintenance of the relevant portions results in an optimal pipeline execution, since all unnecessary analyses of input texts are avoided. This does not only improve pipeline efficiency significantly in all our experiments, but it also creates the efficiency potential of pipeline scheduling that

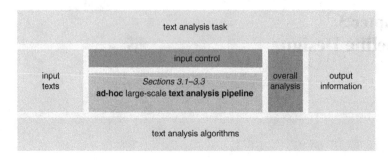

Fig. 3.1 Abstract view of the overall approach of this book (cf. Fig. 1.5). Sections 3.1–3.3 discuss the automatic design of *ad-hoc text analysis pipelines*.

we target at in Chap. 4. In addition, it implies different ways of trading efficiency for effectiveness, which we examine before (Sect. 3.6).

3.1 Ideal Construction and Execution for Ad-Hoc Text Mining

In this section, we formally develop the notion of optimal text analysis pipelines. Then, we introduce generic paradigms of constructing and executing such pipelines in ad-hoc text analysis tasks. The descriptions of the paradigms and a subsequent case study of its impact are based on and partly reuse content from Wachsmuth et al. (2011). Figure 3.1 highlights the contribution of this section as well as of the two subsequent sections to the overall approach of this book. Concretely, this section contains a great deal of the theory behind ad-hoc large-scale text analysis pipelines, which will be completed by the optimal solution to pipeline scheduling in Sect. 4.1.

3.1.1 The Optimality of Text Analysis Pipelines

The term "optimal" always relates to some measure of quality. Informally, a text analysis pipeline can be called optimal if it achieves a higher quality in what it does than any other text analysis pipeline. Accordingly, the optimality is associated to the tackled text analysis task, i.e., to a particular information need C and a collection or a stream of input texts D.

When we speak of the quality of a pipeline in this book, we refer to the effectiveness of the pipeline's results with respect to C and to the (run-time) efficiency of its execution on D. Both can be quantified in terms of the quality criteria introduced in

Sect. 2.1, which provide the basis for defining optimality. As soon as more than one criterion is considered, finding an optimal pipeline becomes a multi-criteria optimization problem (Marler and Arora 2004): Usually, more effective pipelines are less efficient and vice versa, because, in principle, higher effectiveness implies deeper and, thus, more expensive analyses (cf. Sect. 2.4). Sometimes, the optimal pipeline is the most efficient one under all most effective ones. Sometimes, the opposite holds, and sometimes, there may also be a reasonable weighting of quality criteria. In general, some *quality function* $\mathcal{Q}$ is required that specifies how to compute the quality of a pipeline from the pipeline's measured effectiveness and efficiency in the given text analysis task. Without loss of generality, we assume here that a higher value for $\mathcal{Q}$ means a higher quality. The notion of $\mathcal{Q}$ implies how to define *pipeline optimality*:

Pipeline Optimality. Let **D** be a collection or a stream of texts and let **C** be an information need. Further, let $\boldsymbol{\Pi} = \{\Pi_1, \ldots, \Pi_{|\boldsymbol{\Pi}|}\}$ be the set of all text analysis pipelines for **C** on **D**. Then, $\Pi^* \in \boldsymbol{\Pi}$ is optimal for **C** on **D** with respect to a quality function $\mathcal{Q}$ if and only if the following holds:

$$\forall \Pi' \in \boldsymbol{\Pi} : \quad \mathcal{Q}(\Pi^*|\mathbf{C}, \mathbf{D}) \geq \mathcal{Q}(\Pi'|\mathbf{C}, \mathbf{D}) \tag{3.1}$$

Now, the question is how to design an optimal pipeline Π^* for a given information need **C** and a collection or a stream of input texts **D**. Our focus is realizing complete text analysis processes rather than single text analyses. Therefore, we consider the question for a universe Ω where the set $\mathbf{A}_\Omega$ of all available algorithms is predefined (cf. Sect. 2.2). Under this premise, the quality of a pipeline follows only from its construction and its execution.

As presented in Sect. 2.2, the design style of a pipeline $\Pi = \langle \mathbf{A}, \pi \rangle$ is fixed, consisting in a sequence of algorithms where the output of one algorithm is the input of the next. Consequently, *pipeline construction* means the selection of an algorithm set **A** from $\mathbf{A}_\Omega$ that can address **C** on **D** as well as the definition of a schedule π of the algorithms in **A**. Similarly, we use the term *pipeline execution* to refer to the application of a pipeline's algorithms to the texts in **D** and to its production of output information of the types in **C**. While the process of producing output from an input is defined within an algorithm, the execution can be influenced by controlling what part of the input is processed by each algorithm. As a matter of fact, pipeline optimality follows from an optimal selection and scheduling of algorithms as well as from an optimal control of the input of each selected algorithm.

The dependency of optimality on a specified quality function $\mathcal{Q}$ suggests that, in general, there is not a single pipeline that is always optimal for a given text analysis task. However, one prerequisite of optimality is to ensure that the respective pipeline behaves correct. Since it is not generally possible to design pipelines that achieve maximum effectiveness (cf. Sect. 2.1), we speak of the *validity* of a pipeline if it tackles the task it is meant to solve:

Validity. Let **D** be a collection or a stream of texts and let $\mathbf{C}_0$ be the set of information types known in advance for each text in **D**. Further, let **C** be an information need. Then, a text analysis pipeline $\Pi = \langle \mathbf{A}, \pi \rangle = (A_1, \ldots, A_m)$ is valid for **C** on **D** if and only if Π is both *complete* and *admissible*:

1. **Completeness.** The algorithm set $\mathbf{A} = \{A_1, \ldots, A_m\}$ produces all information types needed to address **C** on **D**, i.e.,

$$\mathbf{C} \subseteq \mathbf{C}_0 \cup \bigcup_{i=1}^{m} \mathbf{C}_i^{(out)} \tag{3.2}$$

2. **Admissibility.** The schedule π fulfills the input constraints of all algorithms in **A**, i.e.,

$$\forall A_i \in (A_1, \ldots, A_m): \quad \mathbf{C}_i^{(in)} \subseteq \mathbf{C}_0 \cup \bigcup_{j=1}^{i-1} \mathbf{C}_j^{(out)} \tag{3.3}$$

A complete algorithm set does not guarantee that an admissible schedule exists, since it may yield circular or unfulfillable dependencies. So, both properties are necessary for validity. Only valid pipelines allow the employed algorithms to produce output information in the way they are supposed to do, which is why we restrict our view to such pipelines throughout this book. Admissibility has an important implication, which can be exploited during pipeline construction and execution: Given that no information type is output by more than one algorithm of an algorithm set **A**, all admissible pipelines based on **A** achieve the same effectiveness, irrespective of the tackled text analysis task.[1]

We come back to this implication when we prove the correctness of our solution to optimal scheduling in Sect. 4.1. The intuition is that, under admissibility, the schedule of any two algorithms is only variable if neither depends on the other. In this case, applying the algorithms in sequence is a commutative operation, which leads to the same result irrespective of the schedule. In our project INFEXBA (cf. Sect. 2.3), for instance, we extracted relations between time and money entities from sentences. No matter which entity type is recognized first, relation extraction must take place only on those sentences that contain both a time entity and a money entity.

---

[1]The limitation to pipelines with only one algorithm for each information type could be dropped by extending the definition of admissibility, which we leave out here for simplicity. Admissibility would then require that an algorithm $A_i \in \mathbf{A}$ with required input information types $\mathbf{C}_i^{(in)}$ is not scheduled before any algorithm A_j for which $\mathbf{C}_j^{(out)} \cap \mathbf{C}_i^{(in)} \neq \emptyset$ holds.

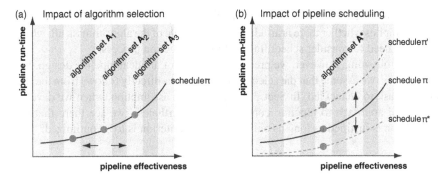

Fig. 3.2 The impact of the selection and the schedule of the algorithms in a text analysis pipeline: **a** Selecting a more effective algorithm set improves a pipeline's effectiveness, but it also takes more run-time. **b** Scheduling can improve the pipeline's run-time without impairing its effectiveness.

What we get from admissibility is that we can subdivide the problem of finding an optimal pipeline $\Pi^* = \langle \mathbf{A}^*, \pi^* \rangle$ into two subproblems. The first subproblem is to select an algorithm set $\mathbf{A}^*$ that best matches the efficiency-effectiveness tradeoff to be made, which has to be inferred from the quality function $\mathcal{Q}$ at hand. This situation is illustrated in Fig. 3.2(a). Once $\mathbf{A}^*$ is given, the second subproblem breaks down to a single-criterion optimization problem that is independent from $\mathcal{Q}$, namely, to schedule and execute the selected algorithms in the most efficient manner, because all pipelines based on $\mathbf{A}^*$ are of equal effectiveness. Accordingly, the best pipeline for $\mathbf{A}^*$ in Fig. 3.2(b) refers to the one with lowest run-time. We conclude that only the selection of algorithms actually depends on $\mathcal{Q}$. Altogether, the developed *pipeline optimization problem* can be summarized as follows:[2]

Pipeline Optimization Problem. Let $\mathbf{D}$ be a collection or a stream of texts and let $\mathbf{C}$ be an information need. Then, the optimal text analysis pipeline $\Pi^* = \langle \mathbf{A}^*, \pi^* \rangle$ for $\mathbf{C}$ on $\mathbf{D}$ with respect to a quality function $\mathcal{Q}$ is found by solving the following subproblems:

1. **Algorithm Selection.** Determine an algorithm set $\mathbf{A}^*$ that is complete with respect to $\mathbf{C}$ and that is optimal for $\mathbf{C}$ on $\mathbf{D}$ with respect to $\mathcal{Q}$.
2. **Pipeline Scheduling.** Given an algorithm set $\mathbf{A}^*$ that is complete with respect to $\mathbf{C}$, determine a schedule π^* such that $\langle \mathbf{A}^*, \pi^* \rangle$ is run-time optimal on $\mathbf{D}$ under all admissible pipelines for $\mathbf{A}^*$.

Unfortunately, the two subproblems are not fully separable in practice if $\mathcal{Q}$ is based on both effectiveness and efficiency criteria, since the efficiency of a pipeline

---

[2]The second subproblem of the pipeline optimization problem has originally been presented in the context of the theory on optimal scheduling in Wachsmuth and Stein (2012).

is decided by both the selection and the scheduling. In general, the algorithm selection already implies whether there is an admissible schedule of the algorithms at all, which raises the need to consider scheduling within the selection process.

In the following, however, we present paradigms of an ideal pipeline design. For this purpose, we assume that the selection of algorithms directly follows from the text analysis task to be tackled. In Sect. 3.3, we drop this assumption, when we develop a practical approach to pipeline construction. Nevertheless, we see there that the assumption is justified as long as only one quality criterion is to be optimized.

3.1.2 Paradigms of Designing Optimal Text Analysis Pipelines

We consider the pipeline optimization problem for an arbitrary but fixed text analysis task, i.e., for a collection or a stream of input texts $\mathbf{D}$ and an information need $\mathbf{C}$. In Sect. 2.2, we have discussed that such a task requires a text analysis process that infers instances of $\mathbf{C}$ from the texts in $\mathbf{D}$. To realize this process, we can choose from a set of available text analysis algorithms $\mathbf{A}_\Omega$. On this basis, we argue that an optimal text analysis pipeline Π^* for $\mathbf{C}$ on $\mathbf{D}$ results from following four paradigms:[3]

a. **Maximum Decomposition.** Split the task of addressing $\mathbf{C}$ on $\mathbf{D}$ into a sequential process of single text analyses. Realize the process with a pipeline with one algorithm from $\mathbf{A}_\Omega$ for each text analysis.
b. **Early Filtering.** After each algorithm that produces information types from $\mathbf{C}$, insert a *filtering step* that maintains only those portions of text from $\mathbf{D}$, which contain instances of these types.
c. **Lazy Evaluation.** Postpone each algorithm within the pipeline before the first algorithm that depends on it. Interdependent algorithms together with their filtering steps are called *filtering stages*.
d. **Optimal Scheduling.** Rearrange the schedule of these filtering stages such that the resulting pipeline is run-time optimal under all admissible pipelines of the filtering stages.

Figure 3.3 illustrates the paradigms. Below, we explain each of them in detail.

---

[3]The given steps revise the pipeline construction method from Wachsmuth et al. (2011). There, we named the last step *"optimized* scheduling". We call it *"optimal* scheduling" here, since we discuss the theory behind pipeline design rather than a practical approach. The difference between optimal and optimized scheduling is detailed in Chap. 4.

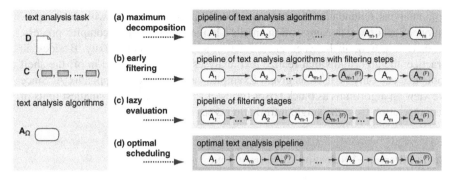

Fig. 3.3 Sample illustration of the four steps of designing an optimal text analysis pipeline for a collection or a stream of input texts **D** and an information need **C** using a selection $A_1, \ldots, A_m$ of the set of all text analysis algorithms $\mathbf{A}_\Omega$.

Maximum Decomposition of a Text Analysis Task

Given a text analysis task, *maximum decomposition* splits the process of addressing **C** on **D** into single text analyses, such that the output of each text analysis can be inferred with one algorithm A in $\mathbf{A}_\Omega$. As stated above, in this section we assume temporarily that the decomposition directly implies the algorithm set $\mathbf{A} \subseteq \mathbf{A}_\Omega$ to be employed, while the text analysis process suggests an initial schedule $\pi^{(a)}$ of a pipeline $\Pi^{(a)} = \langle \mathbf{A}, \pi^{(a)} \rangle$. This is reflected in the top part of Fig. 3.3. The assumption reduces the pipeline optimization problem to the pipeline scheduling problem (i.e., to find an optimal schedule π^*). In general, the more a text analysis task is decomposed into single text analyses, the better the schedule of the algorithms that realize the analyses can be optimized.

As motivated in Sect. 1.1, we consider mainly tasks from information extraction and text classification. In information extraction, the intuitive unit of decomposition is given by a text analysis that produces a certain information type, e.g. author name annotations or the part-of-speech tags of tokens. In principle, it would be useful to even decompose single text analyses. Different analyses often share similar elements and, so, a finer decomposition avoids redundant analyses. This fact gets more obvious, when we look at text classification. Consider a pipeline that first classifies the subjectivity of each text and then the sentiment polarity of each subjective text, as used in our case study ARGUANA (cf. Sect. 2.3). Both classifiers rely on certain preprocessing and feature computation steps. While it is common to separate the preprocessors, it would also be reasonable to decompose feature computation, since every shared feature of the two classifiers is computed twice otherwise. Mex (2013) points out the importance of such a decomposition in efficient approaches to tasks like text quality assessment.

The example also reveals that a non-maximum decomposition can induce redundancy. For the mentioned pipeline, the separation of subjectivity and polarity classification implies the unit of decomposition. If each classifier encapsulates its feature computations, redundancy cannot be avoided. While this is different without encapsulation, an according decomposition entails a longer and thus more complex process, so there is a tradeoff between encapsulation and process complexity. Besides, in practice, the algorithms that realize text analyses are often packed in off-the-shelf tools that can only be used as given. Examples can be found in Appendix A. Since we view all algorithms as black boxes (cf. Sect. 2.2), we derive the smallest units of decomposition from the single information types to be inferred.

Early Filtering of Relevant Portions of Text

The goal of the valid but not yet optimized pipeline $\Pi^{(a)} = \langle \mathbf{A}, \pi^{(a)} \rangle$ is to address the information need $\mathbf{C}$ only. Thus, we propose to perform *early filtering* on the input texts in $\mathbf{D}$, i.e., to maintain only those portions of text at each point of a text analysis process, which are relevant in that they may still contain all information types in $\mathbf{C}$. To this end, we insert filtering steps $A_1^{(F)}, \ldots, A_k^{(F)}$ into $\Pi^{(a)}$ after each of the $k \geq 1$ algorithms in $\mathbf{A}$ that does not annotate all portions of text (i.e., it is not a preprocessor). By that, we obtain a modified algorithm set $\mathbf{A}^* = \{A_1, \ldots, A_m, A_1^{(F)}, \ldots, A_k^{(F)}\}$ and hence a modified schedule $\pi^{(b)}$ in the resulting pipeline $\Pi^{(b)} = \langle \mathbf{A}^*, \pi^{(b)} \rangle$. Such a pipeline is visualized in step (b) of Fig. 3.3.

Especially information extraction tasks like INFEXBA (cf. Sect. 2.3) profit from filtering. To extract all revenue forecasts, for instance, only those portions of text need to be filtered, which contain both a time entity and a money entity and where these entities can be normalized if needed. For many applications on top of INFEX-BA, relevant portions of text will be those only where an arbitrary or even a specific organization or market name is recognized. Also, the classification of forecasts can be restricted to portions that have been identified to refer to revenue.

In the end, the filtering steps give rise to the optimization potential of pipeline scheduling: Without filtering, every admissible pipeline for an algorithm set would have the same run-time on each input text, because each algorithm would then process all portions of all texts. Conversely, filtering the relevant portions of text enables a pipeline to avoid all analyses that are unnecessary for the inference of $\mathbf{C}$ from $\mathbf{D}$ (Wachsmuth et al. 2013c). Thereby, the run-time of pipeline can be optimized without changing its effectiveness. In Sect. 3.5, we discuss filtering in detail, where we see that a consistent filtering is indeed possible automatically and that it also allows a trading of efficiency for effectiveness. There, we substitute the filtering steps by an input control that works independent from the given pipeline.

Lazy Evaluation of Text Analysis Algorithms

Based on the filtering steps, an always reasonable step to further improve the run-time of the pipeline $\Pi^{(b)}$ is *lazy evaluation*, i.e., to delay each algorithm in $\pi^{(b)}$ until its output is needed. More precisely, each $A_i \in \mathbf{A}^*$ is moved directly before the first algorithm $A_j \in \mathbf{A}^*$ in $\pi^{(b)}$, for which $\mathbf{C}_i^{(out)} \cap \mathbf{C}_j^{(in)} \neq \emptyset$ holds (or to the end of $\pi^{(b)}$ if no such A_j exists). Thereby, $\mathbf{A}^*$ is implicitly partitioned into an ordered set of *filtering stages*. We define a filtering stage as a partial pipeline Π_j, consisting of a filtering step $A_j^{(F)}$ and all algorithms $A_i \in \mathbf{A}$ with $\mathbf{C}_i^{(out)} \cap \mathbf{C}_j^{(in)} \neq \emptyset$ that precede $A_j^{(F)}$. We sketch a couple of filtering stages in Fig. 3.3, e.g., the one with A_2, A_{m-1}, and $A_{m-1}^{(F)}$. Of course, no algorithm in $\mathbf{A}^*$ is executed more than once in the resulting pipeline of filtering stages $\Pi^{(c)} = \langle \mathbf{A}^*, \pi^{(c)} \rangle$.[4]

The rationale behind lazy evaluation is that, the more filtering takes place before an algorithm is executed, the less portions of text the algorithm will process. Therefore, an algorithm is, in general, faster if it is scheduled later in a pipeline. The potential of lazy evaluation is rooted in the decomposition of text analysis tasks. E.g., in INFEXBA, tokens were required for time recognition and named entity recognition, but part-of-speech tags only for the latter. So, the decomposition of tokenization and tagging allowed us to tag only tokens of portions with time entities.

Optimal Scheduling of Filtering Stages

Finally, an *optimal scheduling* of the filtering stages in $\Pi^{(c)}$ determines a schedule π^* that minimizes the run-time of all text analysis pipelines based on $\mathbf{A}^*$. Unlike early filtering and lazy evaluation, optimal scheduling cannot be performed irrespective of the collection or stream of input texts $\mathbf{D}$ at hand. To underpin this, in the following we combine parts of the argumentations from Wachsmuth et al. (2011) and our subsequent work on optimal scheduling Wachsmuth and Stein (2012). While the argumentations refer to algorithms, they apply to filtering stages as well.

For an algorithm set $\mathbf{A} = \{A_1, \ldots, A_m\}$, two admissible pipelines can vary in their run-time if they apply the algorithms in $\mathbf{A}$ to different portions of text from $\mathbf{D}$. In particular, the run-time $t_\Pi(D)$ of a pipeline $\Pi = \langle \mathbf{A}, \pi \rangle$ on a text $D \in \mathbf{D}$ sums up the run-time t_i of each algorithm $A_i \in \mathbf{A}$ on the portions of text d_{i-1} filtered by its preceding algorithm A_{i-1} within π. Without loss of generality, assume that π schedules $\mathbf{A}$ as $(A_1, \ldots, A_m)$. Then, A_1 processes D, A_2 processes $d_1(D)$, A_3 processes $d_1(D) \cap d_2(D)$, and so on. So, we have:

$$t_\Pi(D) = t_1(D) + \sum_{i=2}^{m} t_i \left(\bigcap_{j=1}^{i-1} d_j(D) \right) \tag{3.4}$$

---

[4]The given definition of filtering stages revises the definition of (Wachsmuth et al. 2011) where we used the term to denote the partial pipelines resulting from early filtering.

Consequently, optimal scheduling defines an optimization problem, namely, to find an admissible pipeline $\Pi^* = \langle \mathbf{A}^*, \pi^* \rangle$ that minimizes Eq. 3.4.[5] While it thereby resembles the whole pipeline scheduling problem, step (b) and (c) of our method usually significantly reduce the search space to be explored. Chapter 4 presents both the theoretical solution and practical approaches to optimal scheduling. In contrast, in the case study below we approximate solutions by only pairwise computing the optimal schedule of two algorithms A_1, $A_2 \in \mathbf{A}$ based on estimations of their average run-times as well as of their *selectivity* q_1 and q_2, i.e., the ratios of filtered portions of text when first applicable to a text (in the sense of admissibility). Concretely, we let A_1 precede A_2 in π^* if and only if

$$t(A_1) + q_1 \cdot t(A_2) \quad < \quad t(A_2) + q_2 \cdot t(A_1). \tag{3.5}$$

3.1.3 Case Study of Ideal Construction and Execution

In the following, we present an extended version of the application of the four paradigms in the INFEXBA context from Wachsmuth et al. (2011). The goals are (1) to demonstrate how the paradigms can be followed in general and (2) to offer first evidence that, especially in information extraction, filtering and scheduling significantly impacts efficiency without compromising effectiveness. The results provide the basis for all practical approaches and evaluations presented in Chaps. 3 and 4. The JAVA source code of the performed experiments is detailed in Appendix B.4.

Information Need. We study the application of the paradigms for the extraction of all related time and money entities from sentences that denote revenue forecasts. This information need can be modeled as follows:

$\mathbf{C} = \{Relation(Time, Money), Forecast, Revenue\}$

An instance of $\mathbf{C}$ is e.g. found in the sentence *"In 2009, market analysts expected touch screen revenues to reach \$9B by 2015"*.

Input Texts. In the case study, we process the provided split of our REVENUE COR-PUS, for which details are presented in Appendix C.1. We use the training set of the corpus to estimate all run-times and initially filtered portions of text of the employed text analysis algorithms.

Maximum Decomposition. To address $\mathbf{C}$, we need a recognition of time entities and money entities, an extraction of their relations, and a detection of revenue and forecast events. For these text analyses, an input text must be segmented into sentences and tokens before. Depending on the employed algorithms, the tokens may additionally have to be extended by part-of-speech tags, lemmas, and dependency

---

[5]Equation 3.4 assumes that the run-time of each filtering step $A^{(F)} \in \mathbf{A}^*$ is zero. In Sect. 3.5, we offer evidence that the time required for filtering is in fact almost neglible.

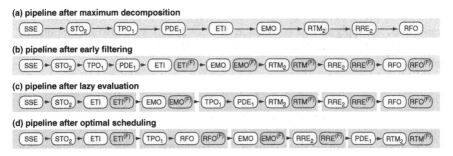

(a) pipeline after maximum decomposition

(b) pipeline after early filtering

(c) pipeline after lazy evaluation

(d) pipeline after optimal scheduling

Fig. 3.4 Application of the paradigms from Fig. 3.3 of designing an optimal pipeline $\Pi_2^* = \langle \mathbf{A}_2^*, \pi^* \rangle$ for addressing the information need *Forecast(Time, Money)* on the REVENUE CORPUS. The application is based on the algorithm set $\mathbf{A}_2$.

parse information. Based on these circumstances, we consider three algorithm sets for **C**, each of them representing a different level of effectiveness:

$$\mathbf{A}_1 = \{\text{SSE}, \text{STO}_2, \text{TPO}_1, \text{ETI}, \text{EMO}, \text{RTM}_1, \text{RRE}_1, \text{RFO}\}$$
$$\mathbf{A}_2 = \{\text{SSE}, \text{STO}_2, \text{TPO}_1, \text{PDE}_1, \text{ETI}, \text{EMO}, \text{RTM}_2, \text{RRE}_2, \text{RFO}\}$$
$$\mathbf{A}_3 = \{\text{SSE}, \text{STO}_2, \text{TPO}_2, \text{TLE}, \text{PDE}_2, \text{ETI}, \text{EMO}, \text{RTM}_2, \text{RRE}_2, \text{RFO}\}$$

For information on the algorithms (input and output, quality estimations, etc.), see Appendix A. Differences between $\mathbf{A}_1$, $\mathbf{A}_2$, and $\mathbf{A}_3$ are that (1) only $\mathbf{A}_3$ contains separated algorithms TPO$_2$ and TLE for part-of-speech tagging and lemmatization, (2) because of the simple rule-based relation extractor RTM$_1$, $\mathbf{A}_1$ requires no dependency parser, and (3) the revenue event detector RRE$_1$ of $\mathbf{A}_1$ is faster but less effective than RRE$_2$. Exemplarily, Fig. 3.4 illustrates the design of an optimal text analysis pipeline for $\mathbf{A}_2$, showing the result of maximum decomposition at the top, i.e., an initial valid pipeline $\Pi_2^{(a)} = \langle \mathbf{A}_2, \pi_2^{(a)} \rangle$. For each algorithm set, the initial pipeline schedules the algorithms in the ordering shown above.

Early Filtering. Next, each of the three algorithm sets is modified by adding filtering steps after every non-preprocessing algorithm. This results in three modified pipelines, such as the pipeline $\Pi_2^{(b)} = \langle \mathbf{A}_2^*, \pi_2 \rangle$ in Fig. 3.4(b). The pipelines $\Pi_1^{(b)}$ to $\Pi_3^{(b)}$ perform filtering on the sentence-level in order to match the information needed to address **C**.

Lazy Evaluation. According to the input and output constraints of the employed algorithms (cf. Appendix A.1), the outputs of the algorithms TPO$_1$ and PDE$_1$ in $\Pi_2^{(b)} = \langle \mathbf{A}_2^*, \pi_2^{(b)} \rangle$ are first needed by RTM2. In $\Pi_2^{(c)} = \langle \mathbf{A}_2^*, \pi_2^{(c)} \rangle$, we hence delay them after ETI and EMO, as shown in Fig. 3.4(c), and we perform similar operations on $\Pi_1^{(b)}$ and $\Pi_3^{(b)}$.

Optimal Scheduling. Finally, we compute an optimal scheduling of the filtering stages in $\Pi_1^{(c)}, \ldots, \Pi_3^{(c)}$ in order to obtain optimal pipelines $\Pi_1^*, \ldots, \Pi_3^*$. Here, we sketch scheduling for $\Pi_2^* = \langle \mathbf{A}_2^*, \pi_2^* \rangle$ only. We know that admissible pipelines based on $\mathbf{A}_2^*$ execute ETI and EMO before RTM$_2$ and ETI also before RFO. Given these constraints, we apply the approximation of Eq. 3.5, i.e., we pairwise compute the optimal schedule of two filtering stages. E.g., for $\Pi_{\mathrm{EMO}} = (\mathrm{SSE}, \mathrm{STO}_2, \mathrm{EMO}, \mathrm{EMO}^{(F)})$ and $\Pi_{\mathrm{RFO}} = (\mathrm{SSE}, \mathrm{STO}_2, \mathrm{TPO}_1, \mathrm{RFO}, \mathrm{RFO}^{(F)})$, we have:

$$t(\mathrm{RFO}) + q_{\mathrm{RFO}} \cdot t(\mathrm{EMO}) = 1.67\,\mathrm{ms} + 0.20\,\mathrm{ms}$$
$$< t(\mathrm{EMO}) + q_{\mathrm{EMO}} \cdot t(\mathrm{RFO}) = 1.77\,\mathrm{ms} + 0.17\,\mathrm{ms}$$

Therefore, we move the algorithms in Π_{RFO} before EMO, which also means that we separate TPO$_1$ from PDE$_1$ to insert TPO$_1$ before RFO. For corresponding reasons, we postpone RTM$_2^{(F)}$ to the end of the schedule. Thereby, we obtain the final pipeline Π_2^* that is illustrated in Fig. 3.4(d). Correspondingly, we obtain the following pipelines for $\mathbf{A}_1^*$, $\mathbf{A}_3^*$, and $\mathbf{A}_4^*$:

$$\Pi_1^* = (\mathrm{SSE}, \mathrm{STO}_2, \mathrm{RRE}_1, \mathrm{RRE}^{(F)}, \mathrm{ETI}, \mathrm{ETI}^{(F)}, \mathrm{EMO}, \mathrm{EMO}^{(F)}, \mathrm{TPO}_1, \mathrm{RFO}, \mathrm{RFO}^{(F)},$$
$$\mathrm{RTM}_1, \mathrm{RTM}^{(F)})$$
$$\Pi_3^* = (\mathrm{SSE}, \mathrm{STO}_2, \mathrm{ETI}, \mathrm{ETI}^{(F)}, \mathrm{EMO}, \mathrm{EMO}^{(F)}, \mathrm{RRE}_1, \mathrm{RRE}^{(F)}, \mathrm{TPO}_2, \mathrm{TLE}, \mathrm{RFO},$$
$$\mathrm{RFO}^{(F)}, \mathrm{PDE}_2, \mathrm{RTM}_2, \mathrm{RTM}^{(F)})$$

Baselines. To show the effects of each paradigm, we consider all constructed intermediate pipelines. E.g., for $\mathbf{A}_2$, this means $\Pi_2^{(a)}$, $\Pi_2^{(b)}$, $\Pi_2^{(c)}$, and Π_2^*. In addition, we compare the schedules of the different optimized pipelines. I.e., for $1 \leq i, j \leq 3$, we compare each $\Pi_i^* = \langle \mathbf{A}_i^*, \pi^* \rangle$ to all pipelines $\langle \mathbf{A}_i^*, \pi_j^* \rangle$ with $i \neq j$ except for π_1^*. π_1^* applies RRE$_1$ before time and money recognition, which would not be admissible for RRE$_2$. For $\langle \mathbf{A}_i^*, \pi_j^* \rangle$, we assume that π_j^* refers to the algorithms of $\mathbf{A}^*$.

Experiments. We compute the run-time per sentence $t(\Pi)$ and its standard deviation σ for each pipeline Π on the test set of the REVENUE CORPUS using a 2 GHz Intel Core 2 Duo MacBook with 4 GB RAM. All run-times are averaged over five runs. Effectiveness is captured in terms of precision p, recall r, and F$_1$-score f_1 (cf. Sect. 2.1).

Table 3.1 The precision p and the recall r as well as the average run-time in milliseconds per sentence $t(\Pi_i^j)$ and its standard deviation σ for each considered pipeline $\Pi_i^j = \langle \mathbf{A}_i, \pi_j \rangle$ based on $\mathbf{A}_1$, $\mathbf{A}_2$, and $\mathbf{A}_3$ on the REVENUE CORPUS.

	$\mathbf{A}_1$			$\mathbf{A}_2$			$\mathbf{A}_3$		
π_j	p	r	$t \pm \sigma$	p	r	$t \pm \sigma$	p	r	$t \pm \sigma$
$\pi_i^{(a)}$	0.65	0.56	$3.23 \pm .07$	0.72	0.58	$51.05 \pm .40$	0.75	0.61	$168.40 \pm .57$
$\pi_i^{(b)}$	0.65	0.56	$2.86 \pm .09$	0.72	0.58	$49.66 \pm .28$	0.75	0.61	$167.85 \pm .70$
$\pi_i^{(c)}$	0.65	0.56	$2.54 \pm .08$	0.72	0.58	$15.54 \pm .23$	0.75	0.61	$45.16 \pm .53$
π_1^*	0.65	0.56	$\mathbf{2.44 \pm .03}$	0.72	0.58	$-$	0.75	0.61	$-$
π_2^*	0.65	0.56	$2.47 \pm .15$	0.72	0.58	$\mathbf{4.77 \pm .06}$	0.75	0.61	$16.25 \pm .15$
π_3^*	0.65	0.56	$2.62 \pm .05$	0.72	0.58	$4.95 \pm .09$	0.75	0.61	$\mathbf{10.19 \pm .05}$

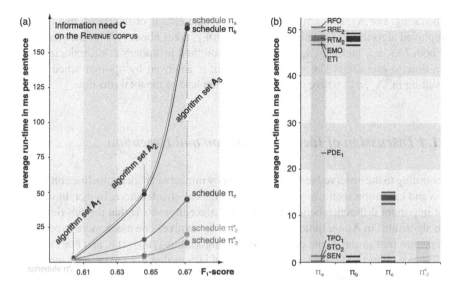

Fig. 3.5 **a** The run-time per sentence of each pipeline $\langle A_i, \pi_j \rangle$ on the test set of the REVENUE CORPUS at the levels of effectiveness represented by A_1, A_2, and A_3. **b** The run-time per sentence of each algorithm $A \in A_2$ on the test set depending on the schedule π_j of the pipeline $\langle A_2, \pi_j \rangle$.

Results. Table 3.1 lists the precision, recall and run-time of each pipeline based on A_1, A_2, or A_3. In all cases, the application of the paradigms does not change the effectiveness of the employed algorithm set.[6] Both precision and recall significantly increase from A_1 to A_2 and from A_2 to A_3, leading to F_1-scores of 0.60, 0.65, and 0.67, respectively. These values match the hypothesis that deeper analyses supports higher effectiveness.

Paradigms (b) to (c) reduce the average run-time of A_1 from 3.23 ms per sentence of $\Pi_1^{(a)}$ to $t(\Pi_1^*) = 2.44$ ms. Π_1^* is indeed the fastest pipeline, but only at a low confidence level according to the standard deviations. The efficiency gain under A_1 is largely due to early filtering and lazy evaluation. In contrast, the benefit of optimal scheduling becomes obvious for A_2 and A_3. Most significantly, Π_3^* clearly outperforms all other pipelines with $t(\Pi_3^*) = 10.19$ ms. It requires less than one fourth of the run-time of the pipeline resulting after step (c), lazy evaluation, and even less than one sixteenth of the run-time of $\Pi_3^{(a)}$.

In Fig. 3.5(a), we plot the run-times of all considered pipelines as a function of their effectiveness in order to stress the efficiency impact of the four paradigms. The shown interpolated curves have the shape sketched in Fig. 3.2. While they grow more rapidly under increasing F_1-score, only a moderate slope is observed after optimal

---

[6]In Wachsmuth et al. (2011), we report on a small precision loss for A_2, which we there assume to emanate from noise of algorithms that operate on token level. Meanwhile, we have found out that the actual reason was an implementation error, which is now fixed.

scheduling. For A_2, Fig. 3.5(b) illustrates the main effects of the paradigms on the employed algorithms: Dependency parsing (PDE$_1$) takes about 90 % of the run-time of both $\langle A_2, \pi_a \rangle$ and $\langle A_2, \pi_b \rangle$. Lazy evaluation then postpones PDE$_1$, reducing the run-time to one third. The same relative gain is achieved by optimal scheduling, resulting in $\langle A_2, \pi_2^* \rangle$ where PDE$_1$ takes less than half of the total run-time.

3.1.4 Discussion of Ideal Construction and Execution

According to the observed results, the efficiency impact of an ideal pipeline construction and execution seems to grow with the achieved effectiveness. In fact, however, the important difference between the studied algorithm sets is that the run-times of the algorithms in A_1 are quite uniform, while A_2 involves one much more expensive algorithm (PDE$_1$) and A_3 involves three such algorithms (TPO$_2$, TLE, and PDE$_2$). This difference gives rise to much of the potential of lazy evaluation and optimal scheduling. Moreover, the room for improvement depends on the density and distribution of relevant information in input texts. With respect to C, only 2 % of the sentences in the test set of the REVENUE CORPUS are relevant. In contrast, the more dense relevant information occurs, the less filtering impacts efficiency, and, the more spread it is across the text, the larger the size of the filtered portions of text must be in order to achieve high recall, as we see later on.

Still, the introduced paradigms are generic in that they work irrespective of the employed algorithms and the tackled text analysis task. To give a first intuition of the optimization potential of the underlying filtering and scheduling steps, we have considered a scenario where the algorithm set is already given. Also, the discussed task is restricted to a single information need with defined sizes of relevant portions of texts. In general, approaches are needed that can (1) choose a complete algorithm set on their own and (2) perform filtering for arbitrary text analysis tasks. We address these issues in the remainder of Chap. 3. On this basis, Chap. 4 then turns our view to the raised optimization problem of pipeline scheduling.

3.2 A Process-Oriented View of Text Analysis

The paradigms introduced in Sect. 3.1 assume that the set of text analysis algorithms to be employed is given. In practice, the algorithms' properties need to be specified in a machine-readable form in order to be able to automatically select and schedule an algorithm set that is complete according to Eq. 3.2 (see above). For this purpose, we now formalize the concepts underlying text analysis processes in a metamodel. Then, we exemplify how to instantiate the metamodel within an application and we discuss its limitations. This section presents an extended version of the model from Wachsmuth et al. (2013a), which in turn consolidates content from the work of Rose (2012) that has also influenced the following descriptions.

3.2.1 Text Analysis as an Annotation Task

Our goal is to automatically design optimal text analysis pipelines for arbitrary text analysis tasks (cf. Eq. 3.1). As motivated in Chap. 1, the design of a pipeline requires human expert knowledge related to the text analysis algorithms to be employed. For automation, we therefore develop a model that formalizes this expert knowledge. To this end, we resort to the use of an *ontology*. Following Gruber (1993), an ontology specifies a conceptualization by defining associations between names in a universe. We rely on OWL-DL, a complete and decidable variant of the *web ontology language*.[7] OWL-DL represents knowledge using *description logic*, i.e., a subset of first-order logic made up of concepts, roles, individuals, and relations (Baader et al. (2003). As Rose (2012) argues, the major advantages of OWL-DL are its wide successful use and its readability for both humans and machines. It is the recommended standard of the W3C (Horrocks 2008), which is why OWL-DL ontologies are normally visualized as *resource description framework (RDF)* graphs.

Now, to formalize the expert knowledge, we slightly refine our basic scenario from Sect. 1.2 by viewing text analysis as an *annotation task*:

Annotation Task. Given a collection or a stream of input texts **D**, process **D** in order to annotate all information of a structured set of information types **C**.

The rationale behind this process-oriented view is that all text analyses can largely be operationalized as an annotation of texts (cf. Sect. 2.2). While both the input texts to be processed and the information need to be addressed depend on the given task, we can hence model general expert knowledge about text analysis processes irrespective of the task. Such an *annotation task metamodel* serves as an upper ontology that is extended by concrete knowledge in a task at hand. In particular, we model three aspects of the universe of annotation tasks:

1. **The information** to be annotated,
2. **the analysis** to be performed for annotation, and
3. **the quality** to be achieved by the annotation.

Each aspect subsumes different abstract concepts, each of which is instantiated by the concrete concepts of the text analysis task at hand. Since OWL-DL integrates types and instances within one model, such an instantiation can be understood as an extension of the metamodel. Figure 3.6 illustrates the complete annotation task metamodel as an RDF graph. In the following, we discuss the representation of all shown concepts in detail. For a concise presentation of limited complexity and for lack of other requirements, we define only some concepts formally.

---

[7]OWL, http://www.w3.org/TR/owl2-overview/, accessed on June 15, 2015.

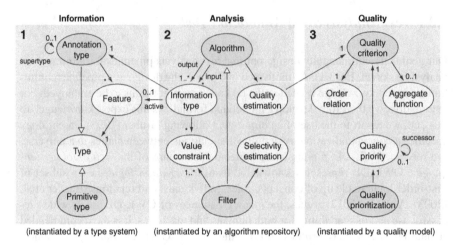

Fig. 3.6 The proposed metamodel of the expert knowledge that is needed for addressing annotation tasks, given in the form of an RDF graph. Black arrowheads denote "has" relations and white arrowheads "subclass" relations. The six non-white abstract concepts are instantiated by concrete concepts in an application.

3.2.2 Modeling the Information to Be Annotated

The information needs addressed in annotation tasks refer to possibly complex real-world concepts, such as semantic roles or relations between entities (cf. Sect. 2.2). Usually, the types of information that are relevant for an according application are implicitly or explicitly predefined in a *type system*. In our case study INFEXBA, for instance, we considered entity types like *Organization, Time,* or *Money* as well as relation and event types based on these types, whereas the type system in ARGUANA specified opinions, facts, product names, and the like (cf. Sect. 2.3).

As for our case studies, most types are specific to the language, domain, or application of interest: Classical natural language processing types emanate from lexical or syntactic units like tokens or sentences. While the set of types is quite stable, their values partly vary significantly across languages. An example is given by part-of-speech tags, for which a universal tagset can only catch the most general concepts (Petrov et al. 2012). In information extraction, some entity types are very common like person names, but there does not even exist an approved definition of the term "entity" (Jurafsky and Martin 2009). Relations and events tend to be both domain-specific and application-specific, like the association of time and money entities to revenue forecasts in INFEXBA. And in text classification, the class attribute and its values differ from application to application, though there are some common classification schemes like the REUTERS topics (Lewis et al. 2004) or the sentiment polarities (Pang et al. 2002).

Since concrete type systems vary across annotation tasks, it does not make sense to generally model a certain set of concrete types. In contrast, we observe that, in principle, all type systems instantiate a subset of the same abstract structures. These structures are defined in our metamodel, as shown on the left of Fig. 3.6.[8]

In particular, we distinguish two abstract *types*: (1) *Primitive types*, such as integers, real numbers, booleans, or strings. In the given context, primitive types play a role where values are assigned to annotations of a text (examples follow below). (1) An *annotation type*, which denotes the set of all annotations of all texts that represent a specific (usually syntactic or semantic) real-world concept. A concrete annotation type might e.g. be *Author*, subsuming all annotations of author names. An instance of the annotation type (i.e., an annotation) assigns the represented concept to a span of text, e.g. it marks a token or an author name. Formally, we abstract from the textual annotations in the definition of an abstract annotation type, which specifies the associated concept only through its identifier:

Annotation Type. An annotation type $C^{(A)}$ represents a specific real-world concept and associates it to a 2-tuple $\langle \mathbf{C}^{(A)}, C'^{(A)} \rangle$ such that

1. **Features.** $\mathbf{C}^{(A)}$ is the set of $|\mathbf{C}^{(A)}| \geq 0$ features of $C^{(A)}$, where each feature is a concept that has a certain abstract type of information.
2. **Supertype.** $C'^{(A)}$ is either undefined or it is the supertype of $C^{(A)}$.

According to the definition, concrete annotation types can be organized hierarchically through *supertypes*. E.g., the supertype of *Author* may be *Person*, whose supertype may in turn be *Named entity*, and so forth. An annotation type has an arbitrary but fixed number of *features*.[9] Each feature has a type itself. The value of a feature is either a primitive or an annotation. Primitive features e.g. represent class values or normalized forms of annotations (say, the part-of-speech tag or the lemma of a token) or they simply specify an annotation's boundary indices or reference address. Through features, annotations can also model relations or events. In our case study ARGUANA from Sect. 2.3, we modeled the type *Discourse relation* on the statement level as an annotation type with two features of the annotation type *Statement* as well as a third primitive string feature that defines the type of relation.

3.2.3 Modeling the Quality to Be Achieved by the Annotation

When addressing information needs, text analysis pipelines target at the optimization of a quality function $\mathcal{Q}$ (cf. Sect. 3.1). Depending on the task, several concrete quality criteria exist, mostly referring to effectiveness and efficiency (cf. Sect. 2.1). The abstract concepts that we consider for quality criteria are shown on the right of Fig. 3.6. In principle, a *quality criterion* simply defines a set of comparable values:

---

[8]The notion of type systems and the modeled structures are in line with the software framework APACHE UIMA, http://uima.apache.org, accessed on June 15, 2015.

[9]We refer to features of annotations in this chapter only. They should not be confused with the machine learning features (cf. Chap. 2.1), which play a role in Chaps. 4 and 5.

Quality Criterion. A quality criterion Q denotes a set of values that has the following properties:

1. **Order Relation.** The values in Q have a defined total order.
2. **Aggregate Function.** Q may have an aggregate function that maps two arbitrary values $q_1, q_2 \in Q$ to an aggregate value $q \in Q$.

Annotation tasks aim at optimizing a set of quality criteria **Q**. While aggregate functions provide a possibility to infer the quality of a solution from the quality of solutions to subtasks, far from all criteria entail such functions. E.g., aggregating the absolute run-times of two text analysis algorithms executed in sequence means computing their sum, whereas there is no general way of inferring an overall precision from the precision of two algorithms. Similarly, quality functions that aggregate values of different quality criteria (as in the case of precision and recall) only rarely exist. Thus, in contrast to several other multi-criteria optimization problems, weighting different *Pareto-optimal* solutions (where any improvement in one criterion worsens others) does not seem reasonable in annotation tasks. Instead, we propose to rely on a *quality prioritization* that defines an order of importance:

Quality Prioritization. A quality prioritization $\rho = (Q_1', \ldots, Q_k')$ is a permutation of a set of quality criteria $\mathbf{Q} = \{Q_1, \ldots, Q_k\}, k \geq 1$.

E.g., the quality prioritization *(run-time, F_1-score, recall)* targets at finding the best solution in terms of recall under all best solutions in terms of F_1-score under all best solutions in terms of run-time. As the example shows, quality prioritizations can at least integrate the weighting of different quality criteria by including an "aggregate quality criterion" like the F_1-score.

In the annotation task metamodel in Fig. 3.6, we define a quality prioritization as a sequence of one more quality priorities, where each *quality priority* points to a quality criterion and has zero or one successor. Within a universe Ω, we call the combination of a set of concrete quality criteria $\mathbf{Q}_\Omega$ and a set of concrete quality prioritizations the *quality model* of Ω. Such a quality model instantiates the concepts of the quality aspect of the annotation task metamodel for a concrete application.

3.2.4 Modeling the Analysis to Be Performed for Annotation

Finally, to address a given information need under some quality prioritization, a text analysis process needs to be realized that performs the annotation of input texts. Each text analysis refers to the inference of certain annotation types or features. It is conducted by a set of text analysis algorithms from a given *algorithm repository* $\mathbf{A}_\Omega$. Within a respective process, not all features of an annotation are always set. Similarly, an algorithm may require or produce only some features of an annotation type. We call a feature an *active feature* if it has a value assigned.

In accordance with Sect. 2.2, an information need can be seen as defining a set of annotation types and active features. In addition, it may specify *value constraints*, i.e., constraints a text span must meet in order to be considered for annotation. In one of our prototypes from INFEXBA, for instance, a user can specify the organization to find forecasts for, say *"Google"* (cf. Sect. 2.3). Only organization annotations that refer to GOOGLE then meet the implied value constraint. Besides such instance-specific constraints, implicitly all text spans must meet the basic constraint that they refer to the real-world concept represented by the respective annotation type. Based on the notion of active features and value constraints, we formally define the abstract information type to be found in annotation tasks as follows:

Information Type. A set of instances of an annotation type denotes an information type C if it contains all instances that meet two conditions:

1. **Active Feature.** The instances in C either have no active feature or they have the same single active feature.
2. **Constraints.** The instances in C fulfill the same value constraints.

By defining an information type C to have at most one active feature, we obtain a normalized unit of information in annotation tasks. I.e., every information need can be stated as a set of information types $\mathbf{C} = \{C_1, \ldots, C_k\}$, meaning a conjunction $C_1 \wedge \ldots \wedge C_k$ with $k \geq 1$, as defined in Sect. 2.2. In this regard, we can denote the above-sketched example information need from INFEXBA as *{Forecast, Forecast.organization = "Google"}*, where *Forecast* is a concrete annotation type with a feature *organization*.

Regarding information types, the internal operations of a text analysis algorithm that infers this type from a text do not matter, but only the algorithm's behavior in terms of the *input types* it requires and the *output types* it produces. The actual quality of an algorithm (say, its efficiency and/or effectiveness) in processing a collection or a stream of texts is, in general, unknown beforehand. For many algorithms, *quality estimations* are known from evaluations, though. Formally, our abstract concept of an *algorithm* in the center of Fig. 3.6 hence has the following properties:

Algorithm. Let $\mathbf{C}$ be a set of information types and $\mathbf{Q}$ a set of quality criteria. Then an algorithm A is a 3-tuple $\langle \mathbf{C}^{(in)}, \mathbf{C}^{(out)}, \mathbf{q} \rangle$ with $\mathbf{C}^{(in)} \neq \mathbf{C}^{(out)}$ and

1. **Input Types.** $\mathbf{C}^{(in)} \subseteq \mathbf{C}$ is a set of input information types,
2. **Output Types.** $\mathbf{C}^{(out)} \subseteq \mathbf{C}$ is a set of output information types, and
3. **Quality Estimations.** $\mathbf{q} \in (Q_1 \cup \{\bot\}) \times \ldots \times (Q_{|\mathbf{Q}|} \cup \{\bot\})$ contains one value q_i for each $Q_i \in \mathbf{Q}$. q_i defines a quality estimation or it is unknown, denoted as $\bot$.

Different from frameworks like APACHE UIMA, the definition does not allow equal input and output types, which is important for ad-hoc pipeline construction. We come back to this disparity in Sect. 3.3.

Now, assume that an algorithm has produced instances of an output type C (say, *Organization*) for an information need $\mathbf{C}$. As discussed in Sect. 3.1, a means to improve efficiency is early filtering, i.e., to further analyze only portions of text that contain instances of C and that, hence, may be relevant for $\mathbf{C}$. Also, portions can be excluded from consideration, if they span only instances that do not fulfill some value constraint in $\mathbf{C}$ (say, *organization* = "Google"). For such purposes, we introduce *filters*, which discard portions of an input text that do not meet some checked value constraint while filtering the others. We formalize filters as follows:

Filter. Let $\mathbf{C}$ be a set of information types. Then a filter is an algorithm $A^{(F)}$ that additionally defines a 2-tuple $\langle \mathbf{C}^{(F)}, q^{(F)} \rangle$ such that

1. **Value Constraints.** $\mathbf{C}^{(F)} \subseteq \mathbf{C}$ is the set of value constraints of $A^{(F)}$,
2. **Selectivity Estimations.** $q^{(F)} \in [0, 1]^*$ is a vector of selectivity estimations of $A^{(F)}$, where each estimation refers to a set of input types.

In line with our case study in Sect. 3.1, the definition states that a filter entails certain selectivities, which depend on the given input types. Selectivities, however, strongly depend on the processed input texts, as we observed in Wachsmuth and Stein (2012). Therefore, reasonable *selectivity estimations* can only be obtained during analysis and then assigned to a given filter.

Filters can be created on-the-fly for information types. A respective filter then has a single input type in $\mathbf{C}^{(in)}$ that equals its output type in $\mathbf{C}^{(out)}$ except that $\mathbf{C}^{(out)}$ additionally meets the filter's value constraints. We use filters in Sect. 3.3 in order to improve the efficiency of text analysis pipelines. In Sects. 3.4 and 3.5, we outsource filtering into an input control, which makes an explicit distinction of filters obsolete.

3.2.5 Defining an Annotation Task Ontology

The metamodel in Fig. 3.6 is instiantiated within a concrete application. We define the knowledge induced thereby as an *annotation task ontology*, which can be understood as a universe for annotation tasks:

Annotation Task Ontology. An annotation task ontology Ω consists in a 3-tuple $\langle \mathbf{C}_\Omega, \mathbf{Q}_\Omega, \mathbf{A}_\Omega \rangle$ such that

1. **Type System.** $\mathbf{C}_\Omega$ is a set of concrete annotation types,
2. **Quality Model.** $\mathbf{Q}_\Omega$ is a set of concrete quality criteria, and
3. **Algorithm Repository.** $\mathbf{A}_\Omega$ is a set of concrete algorithms.

This definition differs from the one in Wachsmuth et al. (2013a), where we define an annotation task ontology to contain the set of all possible information types and quality prioritizations instead of the annotation types and quality criteria. However, the definition in Wachsmuth et al. (2013a) was chosen merely to shorten the discussion. In the end, the set of possible information types implies the given set of annotation types and vice versa. The same holds for quality criteria and prioritizations, given that all possible prioritizations of a set of quality criteria are viable.

To demonstrate the development of concrete concepts based on our annotation task metamodel within an application, we sketch a sample annotation task ontology for our case study ARGUANA (cf. Sect. 2.3). Here, we follow the notation of Rose (2012). Although ARGUANA does not yield insightful instances of *all* abstract concepts, it suffices to outline how to use our annotation task metamodel in practice. In the

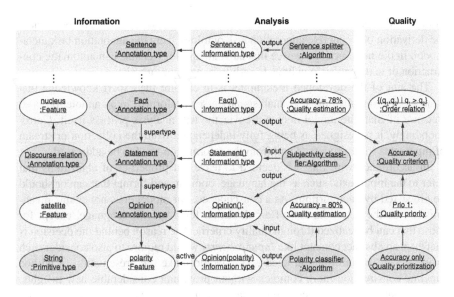

Fig. 3.7   Excerpt from the annotation task ontology associated to the project ARGUANA. The shown concepts instantiate the abstract concepts of the annotation task metamodel from Fig. 3.6.

APACHE UIMA sense, the instantiation process corresponds to the creation of a type system and all analysis engine descriptors. That being said, we observe that quality is not modeled in APACHE UIMA, which gets important in Sect. 3.3.

Figure 3.7 illustrates an excerpt from the sample annotation task ontology. It shows five annotation types, such as *Statement* and *Opinion* where the former is the super-type of the latter. The opinion feature *polarity* is a primitive, whereas *nucleus* and *satellite* of *Discourse relation* define a relation between two statements. Annotation types are referenced by the information types of concrete algorithm concepts. E.g., *Subjectivity classifier* has an output type *Opinion()* without active features, which also serves as the input type of *Polarity classifier*. A polarity classifier sets the value of the polarity feature, represented by the output type *Opinion(polarity)*. In that, it achieves an estimated accuracy of *80%*. *Accuracy* denotes the only quality crite-rion in the quality model of the sample ontology. Its order relation defines that an accuracy value q_1 is better than an accuracy value q_2 if it is greater than q_2. The quality criteria directly imply possible quality prioritizations. Here, the only quality prioritization assigns *Prio 1* to accuracy. A more sophisticated quality model follows in the evaluation in Sect. 3.3.

3.2.6 Discussion of the Process-Oriented View

To conclude, this section has introduced a metamodel that represents a process-oriented view of text analysis in order to formalize knowledge about concepts of information, analysis, and quality related to according tasks. We have demonstrated the derivation of a concrete annotation task ontology from the annotation task metamodel. In the next section, we see that such an ontology enables an automatic construction of text analysis pipelines for arbitrary annotation tasks.

The aim of the developed metamodel is to capture the expert knowledge that is necessary to realize the text analysis processes performed in an annotation task. Because of that, the model does not cover the text analysis process itself. Correspondingly, it is designed as being fully independent from the collection or stream of input texts to be processed and from the information need to be addressed.

In accordance with this, we decided to leave out properties of algorithms that refer to the input texts, such as the language, domain, and format that can or should be processed by an algorithm. As a consequence, our model does not enable mechanisms like the determination of an algorithm for a specific language, except for those that can be realized through quality criteria. The reason behind the decision is that even an abstract concept like *Input property* would require to also consider such properties in the information needs. This would make the presentation of ad-hoc pipeline construction more complex without providing considerable new insights. Besides, our model is perfectly appropriate as long as the given algorithm repository is dedicated to the application at hand. Still, an extension in terms of input properties should be possible without notable problems.

In terms of quality, the chosen prioritization concept entails limitations. When following a quality prioritization, algorithms that target at a middle ground between efficiency and effectiveness will tend not to be considered, as they are neither preferred over very efficient nor over very effective algorithms. Moreover, it is not possible to e.g. prioritize efficiency in one stage of a text analysis process (say, preprocessing) and effectiveness in another (say, entity recognition). Possible solutions to these problems would require more user interaction in an according application, thereby reflecting the inherent tradeoff between automation and manual tuning.

3.3 Ad-Hoc Construction via Partial Order Planning

Based on the proposed process-oriented view of text analysis, this section shows how to construct text analysis pipelines ad-hoc for arbitrary information needs and quality prioritizations. First, we show how to perform partial order planning Russell and Norvig (2009) to select an algorithm set that is complete in terms of the definition in Sect. 3.1 while allowing for an admissible schedule. Then, we present a basic approach to linearize the resulting partial order of the selected algorithms. More efficient linearization approaches follow in Chap. 4 in the context of pipeline scheduling. We realize the pipeline construction process in an expert system that we finally use to evaluate the automation of pipeline construction. As above, this section reuses content of Wachsmuth et al. (2013a) and Rose (2012).

Figure 3.8 exemplarily illustrates the pipeline construction for a sample information need C from our case study INFEXBA (cf. Sect. 2.3), which requests all forecasts

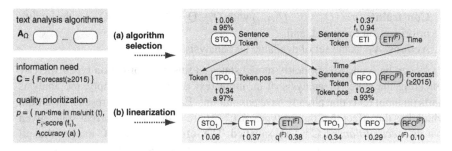

Fig. 3.8 Sample illustration of our approach to ad-hoc pipeline construction: **a** A complete algorithm set $\mathbf{A} \subseteq \mathbf{A}_\Omega$ is selected that addresses a given information need $\mathbf{C}$ while following a given quality prioritization ρ. **b** The partial order of the algorithms in $\mathbf{A}$ is linearized to obtain a text analysis pipeline $\Pi = \langle \mathbf{A}, \pi \rangle$.

for the year 2015 or later. Depending on the given quality prioritization ρ, a set of algorithms that can address $\mathbf{C}$ is selected from an algorithm repository $\mathbf{A}_\Omega$, relying on quality estimations of the algorithms. In addition, filters are automatically created and inserted. The linearization then derives an efficient schedule using measures or estimations of the run-times and selectivities of the algorithms and filters.

3.3.1 Modeling Algorithm Selection as a Planning Problem

The selection and scheduling of an algorithm set, which is optimal for an information need $\mathbf{C}$ on a collection or a stream of input texts $\mathbf{D}$ with respect to a quality function $\mathscr{Q}$ is traditionally made manually by human experts (cf. Sect. 2.2). Based on the presented formalization of expert knowledge in an annotation task ontology Ω, we now introduce an artificial intelligence approach to automatically construct text analysis pipelines, hence enabling ad-hoc text mining (cf. Chap. 1). As discussed at the end of the Sect. 3.2, we leave out the properties of input texts in our approach and we assume $\mathscr{Q}$ to be based on a given quality prioritization ρ.

We consider ad-hoc pipeline construction as a planning problem. In artificial intelligence, the term *planning* denotes the process of generating a viable sequence of actions that transforms an initial state of the world into a specified goal state (Russell and Norvig 2009). A planning problem is defined by the goal (and optional constraints) to be satisfied as well as by the states and actions of the world. Here, we describe the *pipeline planning problem* based on the definition of annotation task ontologies as follows.

Pipeline Planning Problem. Let $\Omega = \langle \mathbf{C}_\Omega, \mathbf{Q}_\Omega, \mathbf{A}_\Omega \rangle$ be an annotation task ontology. Then a pipeline planning problem $\Phi^{(\Omega)}$ is a 4-tuple $\langle \mathbf{C}_0, \mathbf{C}, \rho, \mathbf{A}_\Omega \rangle$ such that

1. **Initial State.** $\mathbf{C}_0 \subseteq \mathbf{C}_\Omega$ is the initially given set of information types,
2. **Goal.** $\mathbf{C} \subseteq \mathbf{C}_\Omega$ is the set of information types to be inferred,

3. **Constraints.** $\rho = (Q_1, \ldots, Q_{|\mathbf{Q}_\Omega|})$ with $Q_i \in \mathbf{Q}_\Omega$ for $1 \leq i \leq |\mathbf{Q}_\Omega|$ is the quality prioritization to be met, and
4. **Actions.** $\mathbf{A}_\Omega$ is the set of available text analysis algorithms.[10]

As can be seen, we implicitly model states as sets of information types, thereby reflecting the states of analysis of an input text. If $\mathbf{C}_0$ is not empty, the analysis starts on input texts that already have annotations. Each $A \in \mathbf{A}_\Omega$ represents an action, which has the effect that output types $A.\mathbf{C}^{(out)}$ are added to the current state, given that its *preconditions* $A.\mathbf{C}^{(in)}$ are satisfied. The information need $\mathbf{C}$ implies that all states $\mathbf{C}_\Phi$ with $\mathbf{C} \subseteq \mathbf{C}_\Phi$ are goal states. To solve a planning problem $\Phi^{(\Omega)}$, we hence need an admissible pipeline $\langle \mathbf{A}, \pi \rangle$ that produces $\mathbf{C} \backslash \mathbf{C}_0$ while complying with ρ.

3.3.2 Selecting the Algorithms of a Partially Ordered Pipeline

For the selection of an algorithm set $\mathbf{A}$, we propose to use *partial order planning*. This backward approach recursively generates and combines subplans (i.e., sequences of actions) for all preconditions of those actions that satisfy a planning goal (Russell and Norvig 2009). In general, actions may conflict, namely, if an effect of one action violates a precondition of another one. In annotation tasks, however, algorithms only produce information. While filters reduce the input to be processed, they do not remove information types from the current state, thus never preventing subsequent algorithms from being applicable (Dezsényi et al. 2005). Consequently, the preconditions of an algorithm will always be satisfied as soon as they are satisfied once. Partial order planning follows a least commitment strategy, which leaves the ordering of the actions as open as possible. Therefore, it is in many cases a very efficient planning variant (Minton et al. 1995).

Pseudocode 3.1 shows our partial order planning approach to algorithm selection. Given a planning problem, the approach creates a complete algorithm set $\mathbf{A}$ together with a partial schedule $\tilde{\pi}$. Only to initialize planning, a helper finish algorithm A_0 is first added to $\mathbf{A}$. Also, the *planning agenda* Λ is derived from the information need $\mathbf{C}$ and the initial state $\mathbf{C}_0$ (pseudocode lines 1–3). Λ stores each open *input requirement*, i.e., a single precondition to be satistified together with the algorithm it refers to. As long as open input requirements exist, lines 4–15 iteratively update the planning agenda while inserting algorithms into $\mathbf{A}$ and respective ordering constraints into $\tilde{\pi}$. In particular, line 5 retrieves an input requirement $\langle C, A \rangle$ from Λ using the method *poll()*. If $\mathbf{C}$ contains C, a filter $A^{(F)}$ is created and integrated on-the-fly (lines 6–9). According to Sect. 3.2, $A^{(F)}$ discards all portions of text that do not comprise instances of C. After replacing $\langle C, A \rangle$ with the input requirement of $A^{(F)}$, line 11 selects an algorithm $A^* \in \mathbf{A}_\Omega$ that produces C and that is best in terms of the quality prioritization ρ. If any C cannot be satisfied, planning fails (line 12) and does not reach line 16 to return a partially ordered pipeline $\langle \mathbf{A}, \tilde{\pi} \rangle$.

---

[10]Because of the changed definition of annotation task ontologies in Sect. 3.1, the definition of planning problems also slightly differs from the one in Wachsmuth et al. (2013a).

PIPELINEPARTIALORDERPLANNING($\mathbf{C}_0$, $\mathbf{C}$, ρ, $\mathbf{A}_\Omega$)

1: Algorithm set $\mathbf{A}$ $\leftarrow \{A_0\}$
2: Partial schedule $\tilde{\pi}$ $\leftarrow \emptyset$
3: Input requirements $\Lambda \leftarrow \{\langle C, A_0\rangle \mid C \in \mathbf{C}\backslash \mathbf{C}_0\}$
4: **while** $\Lambda \neq \emptyset$ **do**
5:     Input requirement $\langle C, A\rangle \leftarrow \Lambda.\text{poll}()$
6:     **if** $C \in \mathbf{C}$ **then**
7:        Filter $A^{(F)}$ $\leftarrow$ CREATEFILTER(C)
8:        $\mathbf{A} \leftarrow \mathbf{A} \cup \{A^{(F)}\}$
9:        $\tilde{\pi} \leftarrow \tilde{\pi} \cup \{(A^{(F)} < A)\}$
10:       $\langle C, A\rangle$ $\leftarrow \langle A^{(F)}.C^{(in)}.\text{poll}(), A^{(F)}\rangle$
11:     Algorithm $A^* \leftarrow$ SELECTBESTALGORITHM(C, $\mathbf{C}$, ρ, $\mathbf{A}_\Omega$)
12:     **if** $A = \bot$ **then return** $\bot$
13:     $\mathbf{A} \leftarrow \mathbf{A} \cup \{A^*\}$
14:     $\tilde{\pi} \leftarrow \tilde{\pi} \cup \{(A^* < A)\}$
15:     $\Lambda \leftarrow \Lambda \cup \{\langle C, A^*\rangle \mid C \in A^*.C^{(in)} \backslash \mathbf{C}_0\}$
16: **return** $\langle \mathbf{A}, \tilde{\pi}\rangle$

Pseudocode 3.1: Partial order planning for selecting an algorithm set $\mathbf{A}$ (with a partial schedule $\tilde{\pi}$) that addresses a planning problem $\Phi^{(\Omega)} = \langle \mathbf{C}_0, \mathbf{C}, \rho, \mathbf{A}_\Omega\rangle$.

Different from Wachsmuth et al. (2013a), we also present the method SELECT-BESTALGORITHM in detail here, shown in Pseudocode 3.2. The underlying process has been defined by Rose (2012) originally. Lines 1 and 2 check if algorithms exist that produce the given precondition C. The set $\mathbf{A}_C$ of these algorithms is then compared subsequently for each quality criterion Q_i in ρ (lines 3–13) in order to determine the set $\mathbf{A}_C^*$ of all algorithms with the best quality estimation q^* (initialized with the worst possible value of Q_i in lines 4 and 5). To build $\mathbf{A}_C^*$, lines 6–11 iteratively compare the quality estimation q of each algorithm A in $\mathbf{A}_C$ with respect to Q_i. Only possibly best algorithms are kept (line 12). In case only one algorithm remains for any Q_i, it constitutes the single best algorithm (line 13). Otherwise, any best algorithm is eventually returned in line 14.

Finally, Pseudocode 3.3 estimates the quality q of an algorithm A from the repository $\mathbf{A}_\Omega$. q is naturally based on the quality estimation $A.q_i$ of A. For lack of better alternatives, we assume q to be the worst possible value of Q_i whenever $A.q_i$ is not specified. If values of Q_i cannot be aggregated (cf. Sect. 3.2), q simply equals $A.q_i$ (lines 1–3). Elsewise, lines 4–9 recursively aggregate the quality estimations $q_{C^{(in)}}^*$ of all best algorithms (in terms of Q_i) that satisfy a precondition $C^{(in)}$ of A. In the worst case, this may require to create a full partial order plan for each precondition. As guaranteed in line 4, however, we consider only algorithms that produce some information type $C^{(in)} \notin \mathbf{C}$. The reason is that other algorithms will be succeeded by a filter in the partial schedule $\tilde{\pi}$ (cf. Pseudocode 3.1). Since filters change the input to be processed, it seems questionable to aggregate quality estimations of algorithms before and after filtering.

SELECTBESTALGORITHM(C, **C**, ρ, **A**$_\Omega$)

1: Algorithm set $\mathbf{A}_C \leftarrow \{A \in \mathbf{A}_\Omega \mid C \in A.\mathbf{C}^{(out)}\}$
2: **if** $|\mathbf{A}_C| = 0$ **then return** $\perp$

3: **for each** Quality criterion $Q_i \in \rho$ **with** i **from** 1 **to** $|\rho|$ **do**
4:     Algorithm set $\mathbf{A}_C^* \leftarrow \emptyset$
5:     Quality estimation $q^* \leftarrow Q_i.\text{worst}()$
6:     **for each** Algorithm $A \in \mathbf{A}_C$ **do**
7:         Quality estimation $q \leftarrow$ ESTIMATEQUALITY(A, Q_i, **C**, **A**$_\Omega$)
8:         **if** $Q_i.\text{isEqual}(q, q^*)$ **then** $\mathbf{A}_C^* \leftarrow \mathbf{A}_C^* \cup \{A\}$
9:         **if** $Q_i.\text{isBetter}(q, q^*)$ **then**
10:           $\mathbf{A}_C^* \leftarrow \{A\}$
11:           $q^* \leftarrow q$
12:     $\mathbf{A}_C \leftarrow \mathbf{A}_C^*$
13:     **if** $|\mathbf{A}_C| = 1$ **then return** $\mathbf{A}_C.\text{poll}()$
14: **return** $\mathbf{A}_C.\text{poll}()$

Pseudocode 3.2: Selection of an algorithm from **A**$_\Omega$ that produces the information type C and that is best in terms of the quality prioritization ρ.

ESTIMATEQUALITY(A, Q_i, **C**, **A**$_\Omega$)

1: Quality estimation $q \leftarrow A.q_i$
2: **if** $q = \perp$ **then** $q \leftarrow Q_i.\text{worst}()$
3: **if** Q_i has no aggregate function **then return** q
4: **for each** Information type $C^{(in)} \in A.\mathbf{C}^{(in)} \setminus \mathbf{C}$ **do**
5:     Quality estimation $q_{C^{(in)}}^* \leftarrow Q_i.\text{worst}()$
6:     **for each** Algorithm $A_{C^{(in)}} \in \mathbf{A}_\Omega$ **with** $C^{(in)} \in A_{C^{(in)}}.\mathbf{C}^{(out)}$ **do**
7:         Quality estimation $q_{C^{(in)}} \leftarrow$ ESTIMATEQUALITY($A_{C^{(in)}}$, Q_i, **C**, **A**$_\Omega$)
8:         **if** $Q_i.\text{isBetter}(q_{C^{(in)}}, q_{C^{(in)}}^*)$ **then** $q_{C^{(in)}}^* \leftarrow q_{C^{(in)}}$
9:     $q \leftarrow Q_i.\text{aggregate}(q, q_{C^{(in)}}^*)$
10: **return** q

Pseudocode 3.3: Computation of a quality estimation q for the algorithm A in terms of the quality criterion Q_i. Given that Q_i has an aggregate function, q recursively aggregates the best quality estimations of all required predecessors of A.

3.3.3 Linearizing the Partially Ordered Pipeline

Before the selected algorithm set **A** can be executed, an admissible schedule π must be derived from the partial schedule $\tilde{\pi}$, as illustrated at the bottom of Fig. 3.8 above. Such a *linearization* of a partial order plan addresses the pipeline scheduling problem from Sect. 3.1.

An algorithm set $\mathbf{A}$ implies a search space with up to $|\mathbf{A}|!$ admissible schedules. As follows from Eq. 3.4, the optimal schedule π^* of $\mathbf{A}$ depends on the run-times and on the filtered portions of text of the employed algorithms. In an annotation task ontology, we model these two properties through estimations. Different from the algorithms' run-time estimations, however, selectivity estimations are never given for the filters created by our partial order planner. This design decision is made, since reliable selectivity estimations cannot be obtained before processing (cf. Sect. 3.2). In the end, an optimal schedule π^* depends on the collection or stream of input texts $\mathbf{D}$, as we analyze in depth in Chap. 4. Among others, there we efficiently explore the mentioned search space on a sample of input texts in order to construct a pipeline for *large-scale* text mining purposes.

In contrast, we predominantly target at *ad-hoc* text mining here. Consequently, processing texts only for pipeline construction may impose much computational overhead, especially because an analysis of these texts could already suffice to directly respond to an information need. We thus propose an approach instead that works irrespective of $\mathbf{D}$ using estimated algorithm run-times only. The approach can be seen as an informed *greedy search*, i.e., it always greedily chooses the best decision given the current knowledge (Cormen et al. 2009).[11] This seems reasonable, knowing that the first algorithms in a pipeline need to process the whole input. At the same time, scheduling can be performed without a sample of texts in a hill-climbing manner, as no text is actually taken into account.

Pseudocode 3.4 shows our greedy approach for finding a pipeline $\langle \mathbf{A}, \pi \rangle$. Lines 3–12 follow the first three paradigms from Sect. 3.1 by determining filtering stages in the given partially ordered pipeline $\langle \mathbf{A}, \tilde{\pi} \rangle$ in order to subsequently schedule the filtering stage $\langle \mathbf{A}_j, \pi_j \rangle$ with the lowest aggregate run-time estimation $q(\langle \mathbf{A}_j, \pi_j \rangle)$ first. To this end, the set $\mathit{\Pi}$ is built with one filtering stage for each not yet scheduled filter $A^{(F)}$ in $\mathbf{A}_\Phi \setminus \mathbf{A}$ (lines 4–9). Using GETPREDECESSORS, line 6 identifies all remaining algorithms in $\mathbf{A} \setminus \mathbf{A}_\Phi$ that must precede $A^{(F)}$ according to $\tilde{\pi}$. A total ordering of the algorithms and a run-time estimation of the resulting filtering stage $\langle \mathbf{A}^{(F)}, \pi^{(F)} \rangle$ are obtained in lines 7 and 8. Then, line 10 determines $\langle \mathbf{A}_j, \pi_j \rangle$. Before $\mathbf{A}$ and $\mathbf{A}_j$ are merged in line 12, π is extended by π_j as well as by ordering constraints for scheduling the algorithms in $\mathbf{A}_j$ after those in $\mathbf{A}$ (line 11).

We do not show pseudocode for the two called methods here, as both refer to classical techniques from the literature: GETPREDECESSORS can be based on a transitive closure of a graph representation of $\langle \mathbf{A}, \tilde{\pi} \rangle$ whose edges (implied by $\tilde{\pi}$) are inverted in order to access predecessors. Rose (2012) suggests to use the FLOYD- WARSHALL ALGORITHM (Cormen et al. 2009) to compute the transitive closure, which has to be done only once per call of GREEDYPIPELINELINEARIZATION. Even simpler, GETANYCORRECTTOTALORDERING can be realized with some standard topological sort approach (Cormen et al. 2009).

---

[11] We assume that run-time estimations of all algorithms in $\mathbf{A}$ are given. In doubt, for each algorithm without a run-time estimation, at least some default value can be used.

GREEDYPIPELINELINEARIZATION($\mathbf{A}, \tilde{\pi}$)

1: Algorithm set $\mathbf{A}_\Phi \leftarrow \emptyset$
2: Schedule $\pi \leftarrow \emptyset$
3: **while** $\mathbf{A}_\Phi \neq \mathbf{A}$ **do**
4:     Filtering stages $\Pi \leftarrow \emptyset$
5:     **for each** Filter $A^{(F)} \in \{A \in \mathbf{A} \setminus \mathbf{A}_\Phi \mid A \text{ is a filter}\}$ **do**
6:         Algorithm set $\mathbf{A}^{(F)} \leftarrow \{A^{(F)}\} \cup \text{GETPREDECESSORS}(\mathbf{A} \setminus \mathbf{A}_\Phi, \tilde{\pi}, A^{(F)})$
7:         Schedule $\pi^{(F)} \leftarrow \text{GETANYCORRECTTOTALORDERING}(\mathbf{A}^{(F)}, \tilde{\pi})$
8:         Estimated run-time $q(\langle \mathbf{A}^{(F)}, \pi^{(F)} \rangle) \leftarrow \sum_{A \in \mathbf{A}^{(F)}} t(A)$
9:         $\Pi \leftarrow \Pi \cup \{\langle \mathbf{A}^{(F)}, \pi^{(F)} \rangle\}$
10:    Filtering stage $\langle \mathbf{A}_j, \pi_j \rangle \leftarrow \underset{\langle \mathbf{A}^{(F)}, \pi^{(F)} \rangle \in \Pi}{\arg\min} \ q(\langle \mathbf{A}^{(F)}, \pi^{(F)} \rangle)$
11:    $\pi \leftarrow \pi \cup \pi_j \cup \{(A < A_j) \mid A \in \mathbf{A}_\Phi \wedge A_j \in \mathbf{A}_j\}$
12:    $\mathbf{A}_\Phi \leftarrow \mathbf{A}_\Phi \cup \mathbf{A}_j$
13: **return** $\langle \mathbf{A}, \pi \rangle$

Pseudocode 3.4: Greedy linearization of a partially ordered pipeline $\langle \mathbf{A}, \tilde{\pi} \rangle$. The pipeline's filtering stages are ordered by increasing estimated run-time.

3.3.4 Properties of the Proposed Approach

We now turn to the properties of our approach in terms of its benefits and limitations as well as its correctness and complexity. Especially the analysis of the correctness and complexity is a new contribution of this book.

Planning operationalizes the first paradigm from Sect. 3.1, maximum decomposition. The actual benefit of partial order planning relates to the second and third paradigm. It originates in the least commitment strategy of partial order planning: As planning proceeds backwards, the constraints in the partial schedule $\tilde{\pi}$ (cf. Pseudocode 3.1) prescribe only to execute an algorithm right before its output is needed, which implies lazy evaluation. Also, $\tilde{\pi}$ allows a direct execution of a filter after the text analysis algorithm it refers to, thereby enabling early filtering.

In the described form, PIPELINEPARTIALORDERPLANNING is restricted to the construction of a pipeline for one information need $\mathbf{C}$. In general, also text analysis tasks exist that target at $k > 1$ information needs at the same time. Because our case studies INFEXBA and ARGUANA do not serve as proper examples in this regard, in the evaluation below we also look at the biomedical event extraction task GENIA (cf. Sect. 2.3). GENIA addresses nine different event types, such as *Positive regulation* or *Binding*. The principle generalization for k planning problems $\Phi_1, \ldots, \Phi_k$ is straightforward: We apply our approach to each Φ_i in isolation, resulting in k partially ordered pipelines $\langle \mathbf{A}_1, \tilde{\pi}_1 \rangle, \ldots, \langle \mathbf{A}_k, \tilde{\pi}_k \rangle$. Then, we unify all algorithm sets and partial schedules, respectively, to create one partially ordered pipeline $\langle \mathbf{A}, \tilde{\pi} \rangle = \langle \bigcup_{i=1}^k \mathbf{A}_i, \bigcup_{i=1}^k \pi_i \rangle$. As a consequence, attention must be paid to filters. For instance, a portion of text without positive regulations still may comprise a binding event. To handle $\Phi_1, \ldots, \Phi_k$ concurrently, a set of relevant portions must be maintained independently for each Φ_i, which is achieved by the input control that follows in Sect. 3.5.

Correctness. Our planner may fail if the given algorithm repository $\mathbf{A}_\Omega$ is not *consistent*, i.e., if there is any algorithm in $\mathbf{A}_\Omega$ whose input types cannot be satisfied by any other algorithm in $\mathbf{A}_\Omega$. We ignore this case, because such an algorithm will never prove helpful and, hence, should be removed from $\mathbf{A}_\Omega$. Similarly, we do not pay attention to algorithms with a *circular dependency*. As an example, assume that we have (1) a tokenizer STO, which requires $\mathbf{C}_{\text{STO}}^{(in)} = \{Sentence\}$ as input and produces $\mathbf{C}_{\text{STO}}^{(out)} = \{Token\}$ as output, and (2) a sentence splitter SSE with $\mathbf{C}_{\text{SSE}}^{(in)} = \{Token\}$ and $\mathbf{C}_{\text{SSE}}^{(out)} = \{Sentence\}$. Given each of them is the best to satisfy the other's precondition, these algorithms would be repeatedly added to the set of selected algorithms $\mathbf{A}$ in an alternating manner. A solution to avoid circular dependencies is to ignore algorithms whose input types are output types of algorithms already added to $\mathbf{A}$. However, this might cause situations where planning fails, even though a valid pipeline would have been possible. Here, we leave more sophisticated solutions to future work. In the end, the described problem might be realistic, but it is in our experience far from common.

Theorem 3.1. *Let $\Phi^{(\Omega)} = \langle \mathbf{C}_0, \mathbf{C}, \rho, \mathbf{A}_\Omega \rangle$ be a planning problem with a consistent algorithm repository $\mathbf{A}_\Omega$ that does not contain circular dependencies. Then* PIPELINEPARTIALORDERPLANNING($\mathbf{C}_0, \mathbf{C}, \rho, \mathbf{A}_\Omega$) *returns a complete algorithm set $\mathbf{A}$ for $\mathbf{C} \backslash \mathbf{C}_0$ iff. such an algorithm set exists in $\mathbf{A}_\Omega$.*

Proof. We provide only an informal proof here, since the general correctness of partial order planning is known from the literature (Minton et al. 1995). The only case where planning fails is when SELECTBESTALGORITHMS finds no algorithm in $\mathbf{A}_\Omega$ that satisfies C. Since $\mathbf{A}_\Omega$ is consistent, this can happen only if $C \in \mathbf{C}$ holds. Then, $\mathbf{C} \backslash \mathbf{C}_0$ must indeed be unsatisfiable using $\mathbf{A}_\Omega$.

If $\mathbf{C} \backslash \mathbf{C}_0$ is satisfiable using $\mathbf{A}_\Omega$, SELECTBESTALGORITHMS always returns an algorithm that satisfies C by definition of $\mathbf{A}_C$. It remains to be shown that Pseudocode 3.1 returns a complete algorithm set $\mathbf{A}$ for $\mathbf{C} \backslash \mathbf{C}_0$ then. Without circular dependencies in $\mathbf{A}_\Omega$, the while-loop in lines 4–15 always terminates, because (1) the number of input requirements added to Λ is finite and (2) an input requirement is removed from Λ in each iteration. As all added input requirements are satisfied, each algorithm in $\mathbf{A}$ works properly, while the initialization of Λ in line 3 ensures that all information types in $\mathbf{C} \backslash \mathbf{C}_0$ are produced. Hence, $\mathbf{A}$ is complete and, so, Theorem 3.1 is correct. $\square$

Theorem 3.2. *Let $\langle \mathbf{A}, \tilde{\pi} \rangle$ be a partially ordered pipeline returned by* PIPELINEPARTIALORDERPLANNING *for a planning problem $\langle \mathbf{C}_0, \mathbf{C}, \rho, \mathbf{A}_\Omega \rangle$. Then* GREEDYPIPELINELINEARIZATION($\mathbf{A}, \tilde{\pi}$) *returns an admissible pipeline $\langle \mathbf{A}, \tilde{\pi} \rangle$ for $\mathbf{C} \backslash \mathbf{C}_0$.*

Proof. To prove Theorem 3.2, we first show the termination of GREEDYPIPELINELINEARIZATION. The guaranteed total order in $\tilde{\pi}$ then follows from induction over the length of $\tilde{\pi}$. According to the pseudocode of our partial order planning (Pseudocode 3.1), each text analysis algorithm in $\mathbf{A}$ is a predecessor of at least one filter in **A**. Since all predecessors of the filter in the filtering stage $\langle \mathbf{A}_j, \pi_j \rangle$, chosen in line 10 of GREEDYPIPELINELINEARIZATION, belong to $\mathbf{A}_j$, $\mathbf{A}_\Phi$ is extended in every iteration of the while-loop (lines 3–12). Thus, $\mathbf{A}_\Phi$ eventually equals **A**, so the method always terminates.

The schedule $\tilde{\pi}$ is initialized with the empty set, which denotes a trivial correct total order. Now, for the inductive step, assume a correct total order in π within some loop iteration. The schedule π_j added to $\tilde{\pi}$ guarantees a correct total order by definition of GETANYCORRECTTOTALORDERING. For each A_j referred to in π_j, line 11 adds ordering constraints to π that prescribe the execution of A_j after all algorithms referred to in π before. Hence, $\tilde{\pi}$ remains a correct total order and, so, Theorem 3.2 must hold.   □

Theorems 3.1 and 3.2 state the correctness and completeness of our approach. In contrast, the quality of the selected algorithms with respect to the given quality function $\mathcal{Q}$ (implied by the quality prioritization ρ) as well as the optimality of the derived schedule remain unclear. Our planner relies on externally defined quality estimations of the algorithms, which e.g. come from related experiments. It works well as long as the algorithms, which are considered best for single text analyses, also achieve high quality when assembled together. Similarly, the greedy linearization can yield a near-optimal schedule only if comparably slow filtering stages do not filter much less portions of the processed texts than faster filtering stages. Other construction approaches like Kano et al. (2010) and Yang et al. (2013) directly compare alternative pipelines on sample texts. However, our primary goal here is to enable ad-hoc text mining, which will often not allow the preprocessing of a significant sample. That is why we decided to remain with an approach that can construct pipelines in almost zero time.

Complexity. To estimate the run-time of PIPELINEPARTIALORDERPLANNING, we determine its asymptotic upper bound using the $\mathcal{O}$-notation (Cormen et al. 2009). The while-loop in Pseudocode 3.1 is repeated once for each precondition to be satisfied. Assuming that an annotation type implies a constant number of related information types, this is at most $\mathcal{O}(|\mathbf{C}_\Omega|)$ times due to the finite number of available annotation types in $\mathbf{C}_\Omega$. Within the loop, SELECTBESTALGORITHM is called. It iterates $\mathcal{O}(|\mathbf{A}_C|)$ times following from the inner for-loop, since the number of iterations of the outer for-loop (i.e., the number of quality criteria in ρ) is constant. In the worst case, each algorithm in the algorithm repository $\mathbf{A}_\Omega$ produces one information type only. Hence, we infer that $\mathcal{O}(|\mathbf{C}_\Omega| \cdot |\mathbf{A}_C|) = \mathcal{O}(|\mathbf{C}_\Omega|)$ holds, so there are actually only $\mathcal{O}(|\mathbf{C}_\Omega|)$ external calls of ESTIMATEQUALITY. For each algorithm A, satisfying all preconditions requires at most all $|\mathbf{A}_\Omega|$ algorithms. This means that the two for-loops in ESTIMATEQUALITY result in $\mathcal{O}(|\mathbf{A}_\Omega|)$ internal calls of ESTIMATEQUALITY that recursively require to satisfy preconditions. This process is reflected in Fig. 3.9. Analog to our argumentation for the preconditions, the maximum recursion depth is $|\mathbf{C}_\Omega|$, which implies a total number of $\mathcal{O}(|\mathbf{A}_\Omega|^{|\mathbf{C}_\Omega|})$ executions of ESTIMATEQUAL-ITY. Therefore, we obtain the asymptotic worst-case overall run-time

$$t_{\text{PIPELINEPARTIALORDERPLANNING}}(\mathbf{C}_\Omega, \mathbf{A}_\Omega) \;\; = \;\; \mathcal{O}\big(|\mathbf{C}_\Omega| \cdot |\mathbf{A}_\Omega|^{|\mathbf{C}_\Omega|}\big). \qquad (3.6)$$

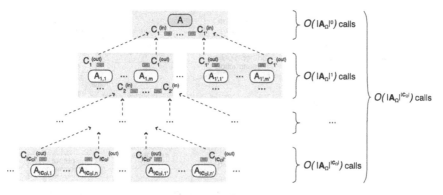

Fig. 3.9 Sketch of the worst-case number $\mathcal{O}(|\mathbf{A}_\Omega|^{|\mathbf{C}_\Omega|})$ of calls of the method ESTIMATEQUALITY for a given algorithm A, visualized by the algorithms that produce a required information type and, thus, lead to a recursive call of the method.

This estimation seems problematic for large type systems $\mathbf{C}_\Omega$ and algorithm repositories $\mathbf{A}_\Omega$. In practice, however, both the while-loop iterations and the recursion depth are governed rather by the number of information types in the information need $\mathbf{C}$. Moreover, the recursion (which causes the main factor in the worst-case run-time) assumes the existence of aggregate functions, which will normally hold for efficiency criteria only. With respect to algorithms, the actual influencing factor is the number of algorithms that serve as preprocessors, called the *branching factor* in artificial intelligence (Russell and Norvig 2009). The average branching factor is limited by $\mathbf{C}$ again. Additionally, it is further reduced through the disregard of algorithms that allow for filtering (cf. line 6 in Pseudocode 3.3).

Given the output $\langle \mathbf{A}, \tilde{\pi} \rangle$ of planning, the run-time of GREEDYPIPELINELINEARI-ZATION depends on the number of algorithms in $\mathbf{A}$. Since the while-loop in Pseudocode 3.4 adds algorithms to the helper algorithm set $\mathbf{A}_\Phi$, it iterates $\mathcal{O}(|\mathbf{A}|)$ times (cf. the proof of Theorem 3.2). So, the driver of the asymptotic run-time is not the number of loop iterations, but the computation of a transitive closure for GET-PREDECESSOR, which typically takes $\mathcal{O}(|\mathbf{A}|^3)$ operations (Cormen et al. 2009). As mentioned above, the computation needs to be performed only once. Thus, we obtain a worst-case run-time of

$$t_{\text{GREEDYPIPELINELINEARIZATION}}(\mathbf{A}) \quad = \quad \mathcal{O}(|\mathbf{A}|^3). \qquad (3.7)$$

$\mathcal{O}(|\mathbf{A}|^3)$ can be said to be easily tractable, considering that the number of algorithms in $\mathbf{A}$ is usually at most in the lower tens (cf. Sect. 2.2). Altogether, we hence claim that the run-time of our approach to ad-hoc pipeline construction will often be negligible in practice. In our evaluation of ad-hoc pipeline construction below, we will offer evidence for this claim.

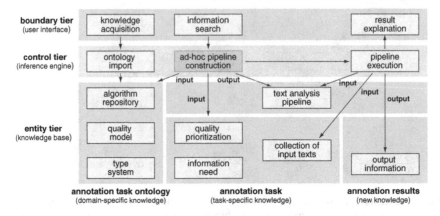

Fig. 3.10 An UML-like class diagram that shows the three-tier architecture of our expert system PIPELINE XPS for ad-hoc pipeline construction and execution.

3.3.5 An Expert System for Ad-Hoc Construction

Rose (2012) has implemented the described ad-hoc construction of pipelines and their subsequent execution as a JAVA software tool on top of the software framework APACHE UIMA already mentioned above. Technical details on the software tool and its usage are found in Appendix B.1. Here, we present an extended version of the high-level view of the main concepts underlying the software tool presented in Wachsmuth et al. (2013a).

The software tool can be regarded as a classical *expert system*. In general, expert systems simulate the reasoning of human experts within a specific domain (Jackson 1990). The purpose of expert systems is either to replace or to assist experts in solving problems that require to reason based on domain- and task-specific expert knowledge. Reasoning is performed by an inference engine, whereas the expert knowledge is represented in a respective knowledge base. To serve their purpose, expert systems must achieve a high efficiency and effectiveness while being capable of explaining their problem solutions. One of the tasks expert systems have most often been used for since the early times of artificial intelligence is the planning of sequences of actions (Fox and Smith 1984). As discussed above, the construction of a text analysis pipeline is an example for such kind of tasks.

To build an expert system, the required expert knowledge must be formalized. Here, our model of text analysis as an annotation task from Sect. 3.2 comes into play. Since the model conforms with basic and already well-defined concepts of APACHE UIMA to a wide extent, we rely on APACHE UIMA in the realization of the expert system. In particular, APACHE UIMA defines text analysis pipelines through so called aggregate analysis engines, which consist of a set of primitive analysis engines (text analysis algorithms) with a specified flow (the schedule). Each analysis engine is represented by a descriptor file with metadata, such as the analysis

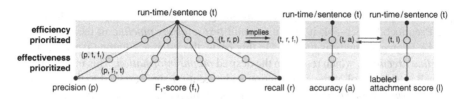

Fig. 3.11 Visualization of the built-in quality model of our expert system. Each of the partially labeled circles denotes one possible quality prioritization. Exemplarily, the shown *implies* relations illustrate that some prioritizations imply others.

engine's input and output annotation types and features. Similarly, the available set of annotation types is specified in a type system descriptor file. In contrast, quality criteria and estimations are not specified by default. For this reason, we allow algorithm developers to integrate quality estimations in the description field of the analysis engine descriptor files via a fixed notation, e.g. "@*Recall 0.7*". The resulting descriptor files comprise all knowledge required by our expert system for ad-hoc pipeline construction, called PIPELINE XPS.

Figure 3.10 sketches the three-tier architecture of PIPELINE XPS in a UML-like class diagram notation (OMG 2011). As usual for expert systems, the architecture separates the *user interface* from the *inference engine*, and both of them from the *knowledge base*. In accordance with Sect. 3.2, the latter stores all domain-specific expert knowledge in an annotation task ontology realized with OWL-DL. Via a *knowledge acquisition* component, users (typically experts) can trigger an automatic *ontology import* that creates an *algorithm repository* and a *type system* from a set of descriptor files. Conversely, we decided to rely on a predefined *quality model* for lack of specified quality criteria in APACHE UIMA (cf. Sect. 3.2) and for convenience reasons: Since the set of quality criteria is rather stable in text analysis, we thereby achieve that users only rarely deal with ontology specifications if at all.

The quality model that we provide is visualized in Fig. 3.11. It contains six criteria from Sect. 2.2, one for efficiency (i.e., *run-time per sentence*) and five for effectiveness (e.g. *accuracy*). Possible quality prioritizations are represented by small circles. Some of these are labeled for illustration, such as (p, t, f_1). In addition, the quality model defines relations between those quality prioritizations where one implies the other, as in the illustrated case of (t, r, f_1) and (t, a). In this way, users can restrict their view to the three effectiveness criteria in the left part of Fig. 3.11, since the expert system can e.g. compare algorithms whose effectiveness is measured as accuracy (say, tokenizers), when e.g. F_1-score is to be optimized. Also, some quality prioritizations are naturally equivalent. For instance, (p, f_1, t) is equivalent to (p, r, t), because, given the best possible precision, the best possible F_1-score follows from the best possible recall. In contrast, (f_1, p, t) is different from (r, p, t), since it prioritizes a high F_1-score over a high recall.

Through the *information search* interface in Fig. 3.10, a user can choose a *quality prioritization*, the *information need* to be addressed, and the *collection of input texts* to be processed. The *ad-hoc pipeline construction* component takes these parts of an annotation task together with the given ontology as input. Implementing Pseudocodes 3.1–3.4, it outputs a valid *text analysis pipeline* in the form of a UIMA aggregate analysis engine. On this basis, the inference engine performs the *pipeline execution*, which results in the desired *output information*. This information as well as a protocol of the construction and execution are presented to the user via a *result explanation* component. A screenshot of the prototypical user interfacace of the implemented expert system from Rose (2012) is found in Appendix B.1.

3.3.6 Evaluation of Ad-Hoc Construction

We evaluate our approach to ad-hoc pipeline construction in controlled experiments for two information extraction tasks introduced in Sect. 2.3 (see Appendix B.4 for information on the used source code): our industrially relevant case study INFEXBA and the scientifically important task GENIA. The presented results greatly increase the comprehensiveness of those reported in Wachsmuth et al. (2013a).

Annotation Task Ontologies. We consider two ontologies, $\Omega_1 = \langle \mathbf{C}_\Omega, \mathbf{Q}_\Omega, \mathbf{A}_{\Omega_1} \rangle$ and $\Omega_2 = \langle \mathbf{C}_\Omega, \mathbf{Q}_\Omega, \mathbf{A}_{\Omega_2} \rangle$, with the same annotation types $\mathbf{C}_\Omega$ and quality criteria $\mathbf{Q}_\Omega$ but different algorithm repositories. $\mathbf{C}_\Omega$ consists of 40 concrete annotation types, and $\mathbf{Q}_\Omega$ complies with the quality model described above. $\mathbf{A}_{\Omega_1}$ comprises 76 algorithms for preprocessing, entity recognition, relation extraction, event detection, and normalization, whereas $\mathbf{A}_{\Omega_2}$ contains exactly half of them. Up to three algorithms exist for an analysis in both cases, but $\mathbf{A}_{\Omega_1}$ provides more alternatives for some analyses. For instance, STO$_1$ and STO$_2$ belong to $\mathbf{A}_{\Omega_1}$, while the only tokenizer in $\mathbf{A}_{\Omega_2}$ is STO$_1$. Information on the algorithms is given in Appendix A.

Text Corpora. Based on Ω_1 and Ω_2, we evaluate pipeline construction and execution. As described, our construction approach is independent from the processed input. In case of execution, we restrict our view to an information need from INFEXBA and, so, rely on the REVENUE CORPUS again, which is outlined in Appendix C.1.

Experiments. All experiments are conducted on an 2 GHz Intel Core 2 Duo MacBook with 4 GB memory by manually triggering the evaluated functionalities of our expert system. In particular, we measure the absolute run-time of ad-hoc pipeline construction in a first experiment. Certainly due to I/O operations (for the creation of APACHE UIMA descriptor files and similar), the standard deviation of this run-time is quite high, which is why we average it over the last 25 of 30 consecutive runs. In a second experiment, we compare the efficiency and effectiveness of different pipelines for the same information need with respect to their average run-time per sentence t as well as with respect to the precision p and recall r they achieve.

Efficiency of Pipeline Construction. To demonstrate the efficiency of our approach, we construct pipelines for seven information needs of increasing complexity for each of the two considered tasks. Table 3.2 gives an overview of the information needs: For both *Revenue* and *PositiveRegulation* events, we first stepwise add required entity

Table 3.2 Each information need C from INFEXBA and GENIA, for which we evaluate the run-time of ad-hoc pipeline construction, and the number of algorithms |A| in the resulting pipeline.

Task	Information need C	|A|
INFEXBA	*Revenue()*	3
	Revenue(Subject)	6
	Revenue(Subject, Location)	9
	Revenue(Subject, Location, Time)	15
	Revenue(Subject, Location, Time, Money)	16
	Revenue(Subject, Location, Time, Money, Date)	18
	Revenue("Apple", "USA", "2012", Money, Date)	21
GENIA	*PositiveRegulation()*	6
	PositiveRegulation(Theme)	12
	PositiveRegulation(Theme, Cause)	14
	PositiveRegulation(Theme, Cause, Site)	17
	PositiveRegulation(Theme, Cause, Site, CSite)	19
	PositiveRegulation("expression", Cause, Site, CSite)	20
	PositiveRegulation("expression", "Eo-VP16", Site, CSite)	21

types to the respective information need (e.g. *Subject* in case of the former). Then, we also require specific values for some of these types (e.g. "Apple" in case of *Subject*). In terms of quality, we prioritize precision over recall and both over the run-time per sentence in all cases. While we construct pipelines once based on Ω_1 and once based on Ω_2, the information needs lead to the same selected algorithm sets for both ontologies. By that, we achieve that we can directly compare the run-time of our expert system under Ω_1 and Ω_2. The cardinalities of the algorithm sets are listed in the right column of Table 3.2.

Figure 3.12 plots interpolated curves of the run-time of our expert system as a function of the number of algorithms in the resulting pipeline. For simplicity, we omit to show the standard deviations, which range between 3.6 ms and 9.8 ms for pipeline construction in total and proportionally lower values for algorithm selection and scheduling. Even on the given far from up-to-date standard computer, both the algorithm selection via partial order planning and the scheduling via greedy linearization take only a few milliseconds for all information needs. The remaining run-time of pipeline construction refers to operations, such as the creation of APACHE UIMA descriptor files. Different from the asymptotic worst-case run-times computed above, the measured run-times seem to grow only linear in the number of employed text analysis algorithms in practice, although there is some noise in the depicted curves because of the high deviations.

As expected from theory, the size of the algorithm repositories has only a small effect on the run-time, since the decisive factor is the number of algorithms available for each required text analysis. Accordingly, scheduling is not dependent on the size at all. Altogether, our expert system takes at most 26 ms for pipeline construction

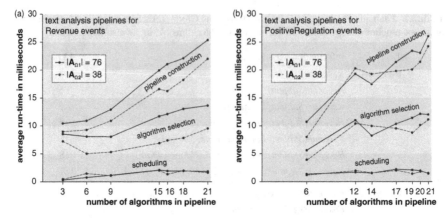

Fig. 3.12 The run-time of our expert system on a standard computer for ad-hoc pipeline construction in total as well as for algorithm selection and scheduling alone, each as a function of the number of algorithms in the constructed pipeline. The algorithms are selected from a repository of 76 (solid curves) or 38 algorithms (dashed) and target at event types from **a** INFEXBA or **b** GENIA.

in all cases, and this efficiency could certainly be significantly improved through an optimized implementation. In contrast, manual pipeline construction would take at least minutes, even with appropriate tool support as given for APACHE UIMA.

Correctness of Pipeline Construction. To offer practical evidence for the correctness of our approach, we evaluate the execution of different pipelines for a single information need, *Revenue(Time, Money)*. We analyze the impact of all six possible quality prioritizations of precision, recall, and the average run-time per sentence. Our expert system constructs three different pipelines for these prioritizations, which we execute on the test set of the REVENUE CORPUS:

$$\Pi_t = (\text{STO}_1, \text{RRE}_1, \text{RRE}^{(F)}, \text{ETI}, \text{ETI}^{(F)}, \text{EMO}, \text{EMO}^{(F)}, \text{TPO}_1, \text{PDE}_1, \text{RTM}_2, \text{RTM}^{(F)})$$
$$\Pi_r = (\text{SSE}, \text{STO}_2, \text{EMO}, \text{EMO}^{(F)}, \text{ETI}, \text{ETI}^{(F)}, \text{RRE}_1, \text{RRE}^{(F)}, \text{TLE}, \text{TPO}_2, \text{PDE}_2,$$
$$\text{RTM}_1, \text{RTM}^{(F)})$$
$$\Pi_p = (\text{SSE}, \text{STO}_2, \text{ETI}, \text{ETI}^{(F)}, \text{EMO}, \text{EMO}^{(F)}, \text{RRE}_2, \text{RRE}^{(F)}, \text{TLE}, \text{TPO}_2, \text{PDE}_2,$$
$$\text{RTM}_2, \text{RTM}^{(F)})$$

Table 3.3 The run-time per sentence t on the test set of the REVENUE CORPUS averaged over ten runs with standard deviation σ as well as the precision p and recall r of each text analysis pipeline resulting from the evaluated quality prioritizations for the information need *Revenue(Time, Money)*.

Pipeline	Quality prioritizations	t	$\pm\sigma$	p	r
Π_t	$(t, p, r), (t, r, p)$	**0.58 ms**	± 0.01 ms	0.6	0.48
Π_r	(r, t, p)	3.53 ms	± 0.03 ms	0.67	0.58
Π_p	$(p, r, t), (p, t, r), (r, p, t)$	20.77 ms	± 0.16 ms	**0.76**	**0.66**

Π_t fully relies on rule-based extraction algorithms and fast preprocessors. Π_r and Π_p include more exact preprocessors, and Π_p additionally performs event detection and relation extraction statistically. For details of the employed algorithms, see Appendix A. The mapping from quality prioritizations to pipelines is given in Table 3.3, which shows the obtained efficiency and effectiveness. In accordance with the quality prioritizations, the pipeline for (t, p, r) and (t, r, p) is one to two orders of magnitude faster than the other ones while achieving the lowest precision (0.6) and recall (0.48). Similarly, Π_p has both the highest precision and the highest run-time. In contrast, the comparably fair recall of Π_r (0.58) appears counterintuitive at first sight. However, it indicates the restricted validity of the quality estimations: favoring algorithms of high quality supports but does not ensure high overall quality, because the output of an employed algorithm is influenced by the quality of its input, which in turn depends on the interaction with other algorithms. In the end, quality can never be predicted perfectly in annotation tasks, as it depends on the domain of application and the processed input texts.

3.3.7 Discussion of Ad-Hoc Construction

In this section, we have presented an artificial intelligence approach for ad-hoc pipeline construction. We have shown its correctness and we have evaluated its run-time efficiency due to its purpose of enabling ad-hoc text mining. In our experience, the evaluated annotation task ontologies are of realistic scale, at least for applications that focus on specific domains. An example of similar scale is the standard configuration of U-COMPARE (Kano et al. 2010), which comes with about 40 text analysis algorithms.[12] For such a scale, the observed run-time of our expert system seems almost neglible even for highly complex information needs. Hence, we argue that our approach is, in general, suitable for ad-hoc text mining. A scenario that would require further investigation is the ad-hoc use of text analysis pipelines within general purpose search engines, which we leave open here.

General limitations of our approach have already been discussed above as part of its properties. Partly, they already emanate from the underlying model (cf. Sect. 3.2). In addition, the realization as an expert system has revealed that text analysis algorithms, which jointly annotate more than one information type, can compromise a given quality prioritization. E.g., a constructed pipeline that targets at effectiveness might schedule TPO$_2$ before TPO$_1$, employing the former for part-of-speech tagging and the latter for lemmatization (cf. Appendix A.1). Since TPO$_1$ also tags part-of-speech, it overwrites the output of TPO$_2$. This problem is not tackled by our expert system. It emanates from a non-maximum decomposition intrinsic to the respective algorithm repository. On the contrary, the expert system handles cases where one algorithm "dominates" another one. Given that efficiency is of upmost priority, for instance, TPO$_2$ would be removed from a pipeline if preceded by TPO$_1$.

---

[12]U-COMPARE version 2.0, http://nactem.ac.uk/ucompare, accessed on June 8, 2015.

A solved challenge relates to the hierarchical structure of annotation types, which implies that interdependencies of information types can result from supertypes. In the information need *PositiveRegulation(Theme)*, for instance, the feature *Theme* might be inherited from a general type *Event*. For this reason, the expert system normalizes the information need into *PositiveRegulation* $\wedge$ *Event(Theme)* while ensuring that only positive regulation events are kept. However, the example also entails a more complex problem: In GENIA, different event types can be themes of positive regulations. But, for scheduling, it suffices to detect one single event type before the extraction of themes. In its current form, our approach then does not select further algorithms, which is not the desired behavior. A solution would be to require all subtypes for types like *Event*, but this is left to future work.

Finally, by now our approach does not completely exploit the potential of filtering outlined in Sect. 3.1. In particular, it integrates filters only for output types, i.e., those types that belong to the information need at hand, but not information types the output types depend on. E.g., the information need from ARGUANA studied in Sect. 3.1 allows for a filtering of opinions, but this would not be recognized by our approach. Moreover, as mentioned above, filtering gets complex when more than one information need shall be addressed at the same time. What is missing is an input control that consistently filters the relevant portions of text depending on the analysis to be performed. The following sections deal with this issue.

3.4 An Information-Oriented View of Text Analysis

While the process-oriented view of text analysis described above is suitable for pipeline construction, we now reinterpret text analysis as the task to filter exactly those portions of input texts that are relevant for the information need at hand. This information-oriented view has originally been developed in Wachsmuth et al. (2013c). Here, we reorganize and detail content of that publication for an improved presentation. The information-oriented view enables us to automatically execute text analysis pipelines in an optimal manner, as we see in the subsequent section, i.e., without performing any unnecessary analyses. Together, Sects. 3.4–3.6 discuss our concept of an input control (cf. Fig. 3.13) as well as its implications.

3.4.1 Text Analysis as a Filtering Task

Traditional text analysis approaches control the process of creating all output information sought for (cf. Sect. 2.2). However, they often do not comprise an efficient control of the processed input texts, thus executing text analysis pipelines in a suboptimal manner. Concretely, much effort is spent for annotating portions of the texts that are not relevant, as they lack certain required information. For instance, consider the text analysis task to annotate all mentions of financial developments of orga-

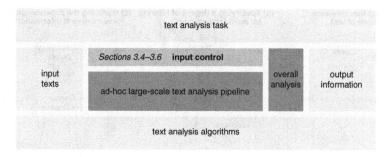

Fig. 3.13   Abstract view of the overall approach of this book (cf. Fig. 1.5). Sections 3.4–3.6 address the extension of a text analysis pipeline by an *input control*.

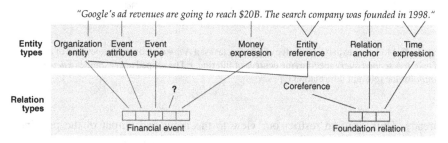

Fig. 3.14   A sample text with instances of information types associated to a financial event and a foundation relation. One information (the time) of the financial event is missing, which can be exploited to filter and analyze only parts of the text.

nizations over time in the sample text at the top of Fig. 3.14, modeled by an event type *Financial(Organization, Sector, Criterion, Time, Money)*. While the text spans instances of most required information types, an appropriate time entity is missing. Hence, the effort of annotating the other information of the financial event is wasted, except for the organization entity, which also indirectly belongs to a binary relation of the type *Founded(Organization, Time)*.

Therefore, instead of simply processing the complete text, we propose to filter only those portions of the text before spending annotation effort that may be relevant for the task. To this end, we reinterpret the basic scenario from Sect. 1.2 and its refined version from Sect. 3.2 as a *filtering task*:

Filtering Task. Given a collection or a stream of input texts **D**, process **D** in order to filter all portions of text that contain information of a structured set of information types **C**.

To address text analysis in this way, we formalize the required expert knowledge again (cf. Sect. 3.2). We assume the employed text analysis pipeline to be given

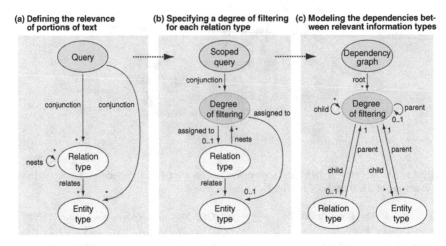

Fig. 3.15 Modeling expert knowledge of filtering tasks: **a** A *query* defines the relevance of a portion of text. **b** A *scoped query* specifies the degrees of filtering. **c** The scoped query implies a *dependency graph* for the relevant information types.

already. Thus, we can restrict our view to the input and output of the pipeline. However, the input and output vary for different text analysis tasks, so we need to model the expert knowledge ad-hoc when a new task is given. For this purpose, we propose the three following steps:

a. **Defining the relevance** of portions of text,
b. **specifying a degree of filtering** for each relation type, and
c. **modeling dependencies** of the relevant information types.

Before we explain the steps in detail, we sketch the information-oriented view of text analysis for the mentioned financial events. Here, a portion of text is relevant if it contains related instances of all types associated to *Financial*, such as *Time*. Now, assume that time entities have already been annotated in the sample text in Fig. 3.14. If the specified degree prescribes to filter sentences, then only the second sentence remains relevant and, thus, needs to be analyzed. According to the schedule of the employed text analysis algorithms, that sentence sooner or later also turns out to be irrelevant for lack of financial events. Filtering the relevant sentences (and disregarding the others) hence prevents a pipeline from wasting time.

By viewing text analysis in this sense, we gain (1) that each algorithm in a text analysis pipeline annotates only relevant portions of input texts, thus optimizing the pipeline's run-time efficiency, and (2) that we can easily trade the run-time efficiency of the pipeline for its effectiveness. We offer evidence for these benefits later on in Sect. 3.5. In accordance with the given examples, the primary focus of the information-oriented view is information extraction and not text analysis as a whole. Still, the view also applies to text classification in principle, if we model the information need to be addressed accordingly. We give a short example below, although we largely restrict our discussion to tasks from information extraction.

Below, Fig. 3.15 models the main concepts that we refer to, separately for each proposed step. To contrast the differences between the three models, the roles of all associations are named. The chosen ontology form merely serves as an analogy to the process-oriented view of text analysis from Sect. 3.2, showing the structural relationships between the concepts. It is not used in the sense of a knowledge base.

3.4.2 Defining the Relevance of Portions of Text

Given a collection or a stream of input texts $\mathbf{D}$, we consider each text $D \in \mathbf{D}$ as an ordered set $(d_1, \ldots, d_n)$ of $n \geq 1$ portions of text. Each portion of text d defines a span of text, such as a sentence, a paragraph, a section, or similar. We come back to the size of a portion of text later on. In order to perform filtering correctly, we must be able to infer the relevance of a portion of text at each point of a text analysis process. To this end, a clear specification of the information sought for in a text analysis task is needed.

As summarized in Sect. 3.2, the concrete types of information sought for can be manifold. There, we have represented all of them by an abstract annotation type with features in order to allow for uniform descriptions of the algorithms in a text analysis pipeline. In this section, however, we are interested in the actual execution of a pipeline, which takes a certain input and produces the information sought for as output. From an output viewpoint, we argue that it rather makes sense to unify the concrete types of information into two other abstract types: An atomic *entity type* C_E, whose instances are represented by annotated spans of text, and a *relation type* C_R, whose instances are expressed in a text, indicating relations between two or more entities. This unification has already been illustrated for the sample information types in Fig. 3.14 above.

Based on the notion of entity and relation types, we can define the relevance of a portion of text for an information need at hand.[13] By now, we have considered an information need as a single set of information types, implicitly meaning a conjunction of the respective types. As stated, tasks like GENIA target at different sets concurrently. Here, we therefore define the relevance in a more general manner with respect to a so called *query*:

Query. A query γ specifies the relevant sets of information types in a text analysis task. Its abstract syntax is defined by the following grammar:
1. **Disjunction.** $\gamma ::= \gamma \vee \gamma \mid \mathbf{C}$
2. **Conjunction.** $\mathbf{C} ::= C_R(\, \mathbf{C} \{, \mathbf{C}\}^* \,) \mid C_E$

---

[13]Especially the term "entity" may be counterintuitive for types that are not core information extraction types, e.g. for *Sentence* or *Opinion*. In the end, however, the output of all pipelines is structured information that can be used in databases. Hence, it serves to fill the (entity) slots of a (relation) template in the language of the classical MUC tasks (Chinchor et al. 1993). Such templates represent the table schemes of databases.

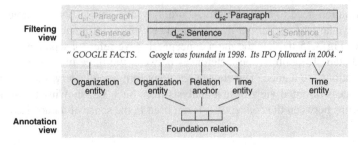

Fig. 3.16 The annotations (bottom) and the relevant portions (top) of a sample text. For the query $\gamma_1 = Founded(Organization, Time)$, the only relevant portion of text is d_{p2} on the paragraph level and d_{s2} on the sentence level, respectively.

According to the definition, every query γ denotes a disjunction of (outer) conjunctions. Each such conjunction **C** binds a number of information types through a relation type C_R that can both relate entity types C_E and nest further (inner) conjunctions, for which the same holds. The structure of the concepts of a query is shown in Fig. 3.15(a), implicitly modeling a disjunction as a set of conjunctions.

Now, addressing information needs can be regarded as fulfilling a given query, i.e., finding all portions of text that contain the information sought for. Similar to the truth of a logical formula, the fulfillment of a query γ follows from the fulfillment of any of the outer conjunctions in γ, which in turn depends on the fulfillment of all its inner conjunctions. Consequently, we define the *relevance of a portion of text* with respect to a conjunction **C** of the query γ to be addressed. In particular, a portion of text can be said to be relevant for **C** at some point of a text analysis process if it still may contain all information needed to fulfill **C**.

As a simple example, consider the following query γ_1 that contains only one conjunction, namely, the binary relation type *Founded* with two associated entity types, which has been introduced in Fig. 3.14:

$$\gamma_1 = Founded(Organization, Time)$$

Before the extraction of *Founded* relations in a text analysis process, all portions of text are relevant that contain at least one instance of both entity types, i.e., an organization and a time entity. Consequently, if time entities are annotated first, then only those portions remain relevant for organization recognition that contain time entities, and vice versa. The portions remaining after relation extraction fulfill γ_1. Figure 3.16 visualizes respective portions for a sample text, both on the paragraph level and on the sentence level. Also, it shows the respective annotations. By that, it opposes the information-oriented view to the process-oriented view of text analysis.

3.4.3 Specifying a Degree of Filtering for Each Relation Type

At each point of a text analysis process, the relevance of a given portion of text can be automatically inferred from the addressed query. However, a query alone does not suffice to perform filtering, because it does not specify the size of the portions to be filtered. Since these portions serve for the fulfillment of single conjunctions, different portions can be relevant for different conjunctions of a query. The following queries exemplify this:

$\gamma_2 = Forecast(Anchor, Time)$
$\gamma_3 = Financial(Money, \gamma_2)$ $= Financial(Money, Forecast(Anchor, Time))$

γ_2 targets at the extraction of forecasts (i.e., statements about the future) with time information that have an explicit anchor, while γ_3 refers to financial events, which relate forecasts to money entities. With respect to the inner conjunction of γ_3 (i.e., the query γ_2), a portion of text without time entities is irrelevant, but since such a portion may still contain a money entity, it remains relevant for the outer conjunction of γ_3 (i.e., the query γ_3 as a whole).

In case of disjunctive queries like γ_4, the relevance of all portions of text is largely decided independently for each of them:

$\gamma_4 = \gamma_1 \lor \gamma_3$ $= Founded(Organization, Time) \lor Financial(Money, \gamma_2)$

Here, a portion of text that does not fulfill the conjunctive query γ_1 can, of course, still fulfill γ_3, except for the constraint that both γ_1 and γ_3 require an instance of the entity type *Time*. In general, every conjunction in a query may entail a different set of relevant portions of text at each step of the analysis of an input text. Therefore, we propose to assign a *degree of filtering* to each conjunction in a query.

Degree of Filtering. A degree of filtering C_S is a type of lexical or syntactic text unit that defines the size of a portion of text, all information of an instance of a conjunction $C_R(\mathbf{C}_1, \ldots, \mathbf{C}_k)$, $k \geq 1$, from a query to be addressed must lie within, denoted as $C_S[C_R(\mathbf{C}_1, \ldots, \mathbf{C}_k)]$.

Degrees of filtering associate instances of conjunctions to units of text.[14] The specification of degrees of filtering accounts for the fact that most text analysis algorithms operate on some text unit level. E.g., sequential classifiers for part-of-speech tagging or entity recognition normally process one sentence at a time. Similarly, most binary relation extractors take as input only candidate entity pairs within that sentence. In contrast, coreference resolution rather analyzes paragraphs or even the entire text. We call a query with assigned degrees of filtering a *scoped query*:

Scoped Query. A scoped query γ^* is a query γ where a degree of filtering is assigned to each contained conjunction $C_R(\mathbf{C}_1, \ldots, \mathbf{C}_k)$, $k \geq 1$, from γ.

---

[14]In Wachsmuth et al. (2013c), we associate the relevance of portions of texts and, hence, also the assignment of degrees of filtering to relation types instead of conjunctions. The resort to conjunctions can be seen as a generalization, because it allows us to determine the relevance of a portion of text also with respect to an atomic entity type only.

Figure 3.15(b) shows how degrees of filtering are integrated in a query to form a scoped query. Every degree of filtering either belongs to a relation type or to an entity type, never to none or both (this cannot be modeled in the chosen ontology notation). Moreover, entity types have an assigned degree of filtering only if they denote an outer conjunction on their own. All other entity types are bound to a relation type and are, thus, covered by the degree of filtering of that relation type. As an example, a scoped version of γ_4 may prescribe to look for the event type *Financial* in paragraphs and for the binary relation types in sentences. I.e.:

$$\gamma_4^* = Sentence[Founded(Organization, Time)]$$
$$\vee\ Paragraph[Financial(Money, Sentence[Forecast(Anchor, Time)])]$$

The definition of a scoped query denotes a design decision and should, in this regard, be performed manually. In particular, degrees of filtering provide a means to influence the tradeoff between the efficiency of a text analysis pipeline and its effectiveness: small degrees allow for the filtering of small portions of text, which positively affects run-time efficiency. Larger degrees provide less room for filtering, but they allow for higher recall if relations exceed the boundaries of small portions. When the degrees match the text unit levels of the employed text analysis algorithms, efficiency will be optimized without losing recall, since an algorithm can never find relevant information that exceeds the respective text units.[15] Hence, knowing the text unit levels of the employed algorithms would in principle also enable an automatic specification of degrees of filtering.

The notion behind the term "scoped query" is that, at each point of a text analysis process, every degree of filtering in a scoped query implies a set of relevant portions of text, which we call a *scope* of the analyzed input text:

Scope. A scope $S = (d_1, \ldots, d_n)$ is an ordered set of $n \geq 0$ portions of text where instances of a conjunction $C_R(\mathbf{C}_1, \ldots, \mathbf{C}_k), k \geq 1$, from a scoped query γ^* may occur.

3.4.4 Modeling Dependencies of the Relevant Information Types

When addressing a scoped query γ^* on a given input text, only the scopes of the text need to be analyzed. However, the scopes change within the text analysis process according to the found instances of the information types that are relevant with respect to γ^*. To maintain the scopes, the dependencies between the entity and relation types in γ^* and their associated degrees of filtering must be known, because the change of one scope may affect another one. For illustration, consider the above-mentioned scoped query γ_4^*. In terms of γ_4^*, paragraphs without time entities will never span

---

[15]There is no clear connection between the specified degrees of filtering and the *precision* of a text analysis. In many applications, however, a higher precision will often be easier to achieve if text analysis is performed only on small portions of text.

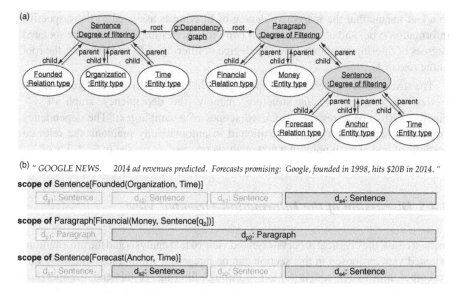

Fig. 3.17 **a** The dependency graph of the scoped query $\gamma_4^* = \gamma_1^* \vee \gamma_3^*$. **b** The scopes of a sample text associated to the degrees of filtering in γ_4^*. They store the portions of text that are relevant for γ_4^* after all text analyses have been performed.

sentences with forecasts and, thus, will not yield financial relations. Similarly, if a paragraph contains no money entities, then there is no need for extracting forecasts from the sentences in the paragraph. So, filtering one of the scopes of *Forecast* and *Financial* affects the other one.[16]

In general, an instance of a conjunction $C_R(\mathbf{C}_1, \ldots, \mathbf{C}_k)$ in γ^* requires the existence of information of the relation type C_R and of all related sets of information types $\mathbf{C}_1, \ldots, \mathbf{C}_k$ within the same portion of text. All these types hence depend on the same degree of filtering. In case of an inner conjunction in an outer conjunction $C_R(\mathbf{C}_1, \ldots, \mathbf{C}_k)$, the relevance of a portion of text with respect to the inner conjunction can depend on the relevance with respect to the outer conjunction and vice versa. So, degrees of filtering depend on the degrees of filtering they subsume and they are subsumed by. We explicitly represent these hierarchical dependencies between the relevant types of information as a *dependency graph*:

Dependency Graph. The dependency graph Γ of a scoped query $\gamma^* = \mathbf{C}_1 \vee \ldots \vee \mathbf{C}_k$, $k \geq 1$, is a set of directed trees with one tree for each conjunction $\mathbf{C}_i \in \{\mathbf{C}_1, \ldots, \mathbf{C}_k\}$. An inner node of any $\mathbf{C}_i$ corresponds to a degree of filtering C_S and a leaf to an entity type C_E or a relation type C_R. An edge from an inner node

---

[16]For complex relation types like *coreference*, the degree of filtering of an inner conjunction may exceed the degree of an outer conjunction. For instance, in the example from Fig. 3.14, foundation relations (outer) might be filtered sentence-wise, while coreferences (inner) could be resolved based on complete paragraphs. In such a case, filtering with respect to the outer conjunction affects the entities to be resolved, but not the entities to be used for resolution.

to a leaf means that the respective degree of filtering is assigned to the respective information type, and an edge between two inner nodes implies that the associated degrees of filtering are dependent. The degree of filtering of C_i itself defines the root of the tree of C_i.

The structure of a dependency graph is given in Fig. 3.15(c) above. Figure 3.17(a) models an instance of this structure, namely, the dependency graph of γ_4^*. Figure 3.17(b) visualizes the associated scopes of a sample text. The dependency graph of a scoped query can be exploited to automatically maintain the relevant portions of text at each point of a text analysis process, as we see in Sect. 3.5.

3.4.5 Discussion of the Information-Oriented View

In most cases, the classical process-oriented view of text analysis and the information-oriented view proposed in this section can be integrated without loss, meaning that no output information sought for is lost through filtering. To this end, the specified degrees of filtering need to match the actual analyses of the employed algorithms, as described above. We offer evidence for this effectiveness preservation in the evaluation of Sect. 3.5.

An exception that is not explicitly covered by the view emanates from algorithms that do not operate on some text unit level, but that e.g. look at a sliding window of an input text without paying attention to text unit boundaries. For instance, an entity recognition algorithm might classify a candidate term based on clues from the three preceding and the three subsequent tokens. Such algorithms will change their behavior when only portions of the text are analyzed. In our experience, though, most important information for according classification decisions is typically found within sentence boundaries, which is why the algorithms will often still work appropriately when considering a text as a set of portions of text (as we do).

As mentioned, the information-oriented view does not help much in usual text classification tasks where complete texts shall be categorized, since these tasks often do not allow for filtering at all. Still, as soon as an analysis can be restricted to some scope of the text, an appropriate modeling of the task may enable filtering. As an example, consider the prediction of sentiment scores from the bodies of review texts in our case study ARGUANA (cf. Sect. 2.3). This task directly implies a degree of filtering *Body*. Additionally, there may be features used for prediction that are e.g. computed based only on statements that denote opinions (as opposed to facts). Therefore, a scoped query may restrict preceding analyses like the recognition of product names or aspects to the according portions of texts:

$$\gamma_{score}^* = Body[SentimentScore(Opinion[Product], \ Opinion[Aspect])]$$

Scoped queries and the derived dependency graphs normally ought to model only the information types explicitly sought for in a text analysis task. In the following section, we use the dependency graphs in order to automatically maintain the relevant portions of an input text based on the output of the employed text analysis algorithms. However, some algorithms produce information types that do not appear in a dependency graph at all, but that only serve as input for other algorithms. Typical examples are basic lexical and syntactic types like *Token* or *Part-of-speech*. Also, annotations of a specific type (say, *Author*) may require annotations of a more general type (say, *Person*) to be given already. We decided not to model any of these *predecessor types* here, because they depend on the employed pipeline. Consequently, it seems more reasonable to determine their dependencies when the pipeline is given. In particular, the dependencies can be automatically determined from the input and output types of the algorithms in the pipeline, just as we have done for the ad-hoc pipeline construction in Sect. 3.3.

3.5 Optimal Execution via Truth Maintenance

The information-oriented view of text analysis can be exploited to analyze only relevant portions of an input text in each step of a text analysis process, thereby operationalizing the way humans skim over texts in a consistent way. To this end, we now adopt the concept of *truth maintenance* (Russell and Norvig 2009) for keeping track of the relevance of each portion of text. Then, we realize such kind of input control as part of a software framework. Using this framework, we conduct several experiments to show the benefit of our approach. As in Sect. 3.4, we reuse content from Wachsmuth et al. (2013c) here, but we also provide many new insights.

3.5.1 Modeling Input Control as a Truth Maintenance Problem

Text analysis processes can be regarded as non-monotonic in that knowledge about the input texts to be processed changes in each step. By knowledge, we mean annotations of entity and relation types here that help to address the information needs at hand (represented by a scoped query).[17] In many cases, no knowledge is given beforehand, meaning that the text analysis process starts on a plain input text. Consequently, each portion d of the text must be assumed relevant in the beginning. During text analysis, new knowledge is inferred through annotation. If, in some step of the process, d lacks any knowledge that is required for the given scoped query, it becomes irrelevant and can be excluded from further analysis.

In artificial intelligence, such non-monotonicity is well-studied. To handle the non-monotonic knowledge used by inference engines, one common approach is to rely on an *assumption-based truth maintenance system* (ATMS), which justifies and retracts assumptions about a problem at hand in order to constantly update what can

---

[17]We omit to distinguish between knowledge and information in this section to emphasize the connection between text analysis and non-monotonicity in artificial intelligence.

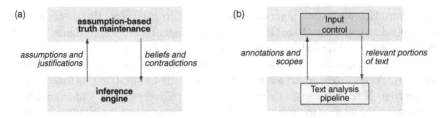

Fig. 3.18 Comparison of **a** the classical high-level concept of an assumption-based truth maintenance system and **b** the proposed input control.

be believed as true, i.e., what inferences can be made based on the currently given knowledge (Russell and Norvig 2009). To this end, the inference engine passes current assumptions and justifications expressed as propositional symbols and formulas to the ATMS. The ATMS then returns the inferrable beliefs and contradictions.

To address text analysis as a filtering task, we adapt the ATMS concept for maintaining the portions of an input text that are relevant with respect to a given scoped query γ^*. In particular, we propose to equip a text analysis pipeline with an input control that takes the annotations and current scopes of a text as input in order to determine in advance of executing a text analysis algorithm what portions of text need to be processed by that algorithm. Figure 3.18 compares the high-level concept of a classical ATMS to the proposed input control.

The input control models the relevance of each portion of text using an independent set of propositional formulas. In a formula, every propositional symbol represents an *assumption* about the portion of text, i.e., the assumed existence of an information type or the assumed fulfillment of the scoped query γ^* or of a conjunction in γ^*. The formulas themselves denote justifications. A *justification* is an implication in definite Horn form whose consequent corresponds to the fulfillment of a query or conjunction, while the antecedent consists of the assumptions under which the fulfillment holds.

Concretely, the following formulas are defined initially. For each portion of text d that is associated to an outer conjunction $C_S[C_R(\mathbf{C}_1, \ldots, \mathbf{C}_k)]$ in γ^*, we denote the relevance of d with respect to the scoped query γ^* as $\gamma^{*(d)}$ and we let the input control model its justification as $\phi^{(d)}$:

$$\phi^{(d)}: \quad C_R^{(d)} \wedge \mathbf{C}_1^{(d)} \wedge \ldots \wedge \mathbf{C}_k^{(d)} \ \rightarrow \ \gamma^{*(d)} \tag{3.8}$$

Additionally, the input control defines a justification of the relevance $\mathbf{C}_i^{(d)}$ of the portion of text d with respect to each inner conjunction of the outer conjunction $C_S[C_R(\mathbf{C}_1, \ldots, \mathbf{C}_k)]$ that has the form $\mathbf{C}_i = C_S'[C_R'(\mathbf{C}_{i1}, \ldots, \mathbf{C}_{il})]$. Based on the portions of text associated to the degree of filtering of $\mathbf{C}_i$, we introduce a formula $\psi_i^{(d')}$ for each such portion of text d':

$$\psi_i^{(d')}: \quad C_R'^{(d')} \wedge \mathbf{C}_{i1}^{(d')} \wedge \ldots \wedge \mathbf{C}_{il}^{(d')} \ \rightarrow \ \mathbf{C}_i^{(d)} \tag{3.9}$$

This step is repeated recursively until each child node $C_{ij}^{(d')}$ in a formula $\psi_i^{(d')}$ represents either an entity type C_E or a relation type C_R. As a result, the set of all formulas $\phi^{(d)}$ and $\psi_i^{(d')}$ of all portions of text defines what can initially believed for the respective input text.

To give an example, we look at the sample text from Fig. 3.17(b). The scoped query γ_4^* to be addressed has two outer conjunctions, γ_1^* and γ_3^*, with the degrees of filtering *Sentence* and *Paragraph*, respectively. For the four sentences and two paragraphs of the text, we have six formulas:

$$\phi^{(d_{s1})} : \quad Founded^{(d_{s1})} \wedge Organization^{(d_{s1})} \wedge Time^{(d_{s1})} \rightarrow \gamma_4^{*(d_{s1})}$$

$$\phi^{(d_{s2})} : \quad Founded^{(d_{s2})} \wedge Organization^{(d_{s2})} \wedge Time^{(d_{s2})} \rightarrow \gamma_4^{*(d_{s2})}$$

$$\phi^{(d_{s3})} : \quad Founded^{(d_{s3})} \wedge Organization^{(d_{s3})} \wedge Time^{(d_{s3})} \rightarrow \gamma_4^{*(d_{s3})}$$

$$\phi^{(d_{s4})} : \quad Founded^{(d_{s4})} \wedge Organization^{(d_{s4})} \wedge Time^{(d_{s4})} \rightarrow \gamma_4^{*(d_{s4})}$$

$$\phi^{(d_{p1})} : \quad Financial^{(d_{p1})} \wedge Money^{(d_{p1})} \wedge \gamma_2^{*(d_{p1})} \rightarrow \gamma_4^{*(d_{p1})}$$

$$\phi^{(d_{p2})} : \quad Financial^{(d_{p2})} \wedge Money^{(d_{p2})} \wedge \gamma_2^{*(d_{p2})} \rightarrow \gamma_4^{*(d_{p2})}$$

In case of the two latter formulas, the relevance depends on the inner conjunction γ_2^* of γ_4^*, for which we define four additional formulas:

$$\psi^{(d_{s1})} : \quad Forecast^{(d_{s1})} \wedge Anchor^{(d_{s1})} \wedge Time^{(d_{s1})} \rightarrow \gamma_2^{*(d_{p1})}$$

$$\psi^{(d_{s2})} : \quad Forecast^{(d_{s2})} \wedge Anchor^{(d_{s2})} \wedge Time^{(d_{s2})} \rightarrow \gamma_2^{*(d_{p2})}$$

$$\psi^{(d_{s3})} : \quad Forecast^{(d_{s3})} \wedge Anchor^{(d_{s3})} \wedge Time^{(d_{s3})} \rightarrow \gamma_2^{*(d_{p2})}$$

$$\psi^{(d_{s4})} : \quad Forecast^{(d_{s4})} \wedge Anchor^{(d_{s4})} \wedge Time^{(d_{s4})} \rightarrow \gamma_2^{*(d_{p2})}$$

The antecedents of these formulas consist of entity and relation types only, so no further formula needs to be added. Altogether, the relevance of the six distinguished portions of the sample text is hence initially justified by the ten defined formulas.

After each text analysis, the formulas of a processed input text must be updated, because their truth depends on the set of currently believed assumptions, which follows from the output of all text analysis algorithms applied so far. Moreover, the set of current formulas implies, whether a portion of text must be processed by a specific text analysis algorithm or not. In particular, an algorithm can cause a change of only those formulas that include an output type of the algorithm. At the end of the text analysis process then, what formula ever remains, must be the truth, just in the sense of this chapter's introductory quote by Arthur Conan Doyle.

Here, by truth, we mean that the respective portions of text are relevant with respect to the scoped query γ^* to be addressed. To maintain the relevant portions of an input text, we have already introduced the concept of scopes that are associated to the degrees of filtering in the dependency graph Γ of γ^*. Initially, these scopes span the whole input text. Updating the formulas then means to filter the scopes according to the output of a text analysis algorithm. Similarly, we can restrict the analysis of that algorithm to those portions of text its output types are relevant for. In the following, we discuss how to perform these operations.

3.5.2 Filtering the Relevant Portions of Text

Given the output of a text analysis algorithm, we update all justifications $\phi^{(d)}$ and $\psi^{(d)}$ of the relevance of an analyzed portion of text d that contain an output type $C^{(out)} \in \mathbf{C}^{(out)}$ of the algorithm. In particular, the assumptions about these types become either true or false. Once an assumption turns out to be false, it will always be false. Instead of maintaining the respective justifications, we can hence delete those that are contradicted, thereby filtering the analyzed scopes of the input text.

For instance, if time entities are found only in the sentences d_{s2} and d_{s4} in Fig. 3.17(b), then all formulas with $Time^{(d_{s1})}$ or $Time^{(d_{s3})}$ are falsified. In the other ones, the respective assumptions $Time^{(d_{s2})}$ and $Time^{(d_{s4})}$ are justified by replacing them with "true" and, consequently, deleting them from the antecedents of the formulas. In addition, updating a formula $\psi^{(d)}$ requires a recursive update of all formulas that contain the consequent of $\psi^{(d)}$. In the given case, the consequent $\gamma_2^{*(d_{p1})}$ of $\psi^{(d_{s1})}$ becomes false, which is why $\phi^{(d_{p1})}$ also cannot hold anymore. This in turn could render the fulfillment of further nested conjunctions useless. However, such conjunctions do not exist in $\phi^{(d_{p1})}$. Therefore, the following formulas remain:

$$\phi^{(d_{s2})} :\ Founded^{(d_{s2})} \wedge Organization^{(d_{s2})}\ \rightarrow\ \gamma_4^{*(d_{s2})}$$

$$\phi^{(d_{s4})} :\ Founded^{(d_{s4})} \wedge Organization^{(d_{s4})}\ \rightarrow\ \gamma_4^{*(d_{s4})}$$

$$\phi^{(d_{p2})} :\ Financial^{(d_{p2})} \wedge Money^{(d_{p2})} \wedge \gamma_2^{*(d_{p2})}\ \rightarrow\ \gamma_4^{*(d_{p2})}$$

$$\psi^{(d_{s2})} :\ Forecast^{(d_{s2})} \wedge Anchor^{(d_{s2})}\ \rightarrow\ \gamma_2^{*(d_{p2})}$$

$$\psi^{(d_{s4})} :\ Forecast^{(d_{s4})} \wedge Anchor^{(d_{s4})}\ \rightarrow\ \gamma_2^{*(d_{p2})}$$

We summarize that the output of a text analysis algorithm is used to filter not only the scopes analyzed by the algorithm, but also the dependent scopes of these scopes. The set of dependent scopes of a scope S consists of the scope S_0 associated to the root of the degree of filtering C_S of S in the dependency graph of γ^* as well as of each scope S' of a descendant degree of filtering of the root. This, of course, includes the scopes of all ancestor degrees of filtering of C_S besides the root.

Pseudocode 3.5 shows how to update the scopes of an input text based on the output types $\mathbf{C}^{(out)}$ of a text analysis algorithm. To enable filtering, all scopes must initially be generated by segmentation algorithms (e.g. by a sentence splitter), i.e., algorithms with an output type $C^{(out)}$ that denotes a degree of filtering in the dependency graph Γ. This is done in lines 1–3 of the pseudocode, given that the employed pipeline schedules the according algorithms first. Independent of the algorithm, the

---

UPDATESCOPES($\mathbf{C}^{(out)}$)

1: **for each** Information type $C^{(out)}$ in $\mathbf{C}^{(out)}$ **do**
2:    **if** $C^{(out)}$ is a degree of filtering in the dependency graph Γ **then**
3:       GENERATESCOPE($C^{(out)}$)

4: Scopes $\mathbf{S} \leftarrow$ GETRELEVANTSCOPES($\mathbf{C}^{(out)}$)
5: **for each** Scope S in $\mathbf{S}$ **do**
6:    Information types $\mathbf{C} \leftarrow$ all $C \in \mathbf{C}^{(out)}$ to which S is assigned
7:    **for each** Portion of text d in S **do**
8:       **if not** d contains an instance of any $C \in \mathbf{C}$ **then** S.remove(d)

9:    Scope $S_0 \leftarrow \Gamma$.getRootScope(S)
10:   **if** $S_0 \neq S$ **then**
11:      **for each** Portion of text d in S_0 **do**
12:         **if not** d intersects with S **then** S_0.remove(d)

13:   Scopes $\mathbf{S}' \leftarrow \Gamma$.getAllDescendantScopes($S_0$)
14:   **for each** Scope $S' \neq S$ in $\mathbf{S}'$ **do**
15:      **for each** Portion of text d in S' **do**
16:         **if not** d intersects with S_0 **then** S'.remove(d)

Pseudocode 3.5: Update of scopes based on the set of output types $\mathbf{C}^{(out)}$ of a text analysis algorithm and the produced instances of these types. An update may lead both to the generation and to the filtering of the affected scopes.

GETRELEVANTSCOPES($\mathbf{C}^{(out)}$)

1: Scopes $\mathbf{S}$
2: **for each** Degree of filtering C_S in the dependency graph Γ **do**
3:    **if** Γ.getChildren(C_S) $\cap$ $\mathbf{C}^{(out)} \neq \emptyset$ **then**
4:       $\mathbf{S}$.add(Γ.getScope(C_S))
5:    **else if** GETPREDECESSORTYPES(Γ.getChildren(C_S)) $\cap$ $\mathbf{C}^{(out)} \neq \emptyset$ **then**
6:       $\mathbf{S}$.add(Γ.getScope(C_S))
7: **return S**

Pseudocode 3.6: Determination of the set **S** of all scopes that are relevant with respect to the output types $\mathbf{C}^{(out)}$ of a text analysis algorithm.

method GETRELEVANTSCOPES next determines the set **S** of scopes that are relevant with respect to the output of the applied algorithm (line 4).[18] For each scope $S \in \mathbf{S}$, a portion of text d is maintained only if it contains an instance of one of the types $\mathbf{C} \subseteq \mathbf{C}^{(out)}$ relevant for S (lines 5–8). Afterwards, lines 9–12 remove all portions of text from the root scope S_0 of S that do not intersect with any portion of text in S. Accordingly, only those portions of text in the set of descendant scopes $\mathbf{S}'$ of S_0 are retained that intersect with a portion in S_0 (lines 13–16).

---

[18]Unlike here, for space reasons we do not determine the relevant scopes within UPDATESCOPES in Wachsmuth et al. (2013c), which requires to store the scopes externally instead.

DETERMINEUNIFIEDSCOPE($\mathbf{C}^{(out)}$)

1: **for each** Information type $C^{(out)}$ in $\mathbf{C}^{(out)}$ **do**
2:   **if** $C^{(out)}$ is a degree of filtering in the dependency graph Γ **then**
3:     **return** the whole input text
4: Scopes $\mathbf{S}$ ← GETRELEVANTSCOPES($\mathbf{C}^{(out)}$)
5: Scope $S_\cup$ ← $\emptyset$
6: **for each** Scope S in $\mathbf{S}$ **do**
7:   **for each** Portion of text d in S **do**
8:     **if not** d intersects with $S_\cup$ **then** $S_\cup$.add(d)
9:     **else** $S_\cup$.merge(d)
10: **return** $S_\cup$

Pseudocode 3.7: Determination of the unified scope $S_\cup$ to be analyzed by a text analysis algorithm based on the given output types $\mathbf{C}^{(out)}$ of the algorithm.

GETRELEVANTSCOPES is given in Pseudocode 3.6: A scope is relevant with respect to $\mathbf{C}^{(out)}$ if at least one of two conditions holds for the associated degrees of filtering: First, a type from $\mathbf{C}^{(out)}$ is a child of the degree in the dependency graph Γ (lines 3 and 4). Second, an information type from $\mathbf{C}^{(out)}$ serves as the required input of another algorithm in the employed pipeline (lines 5–7), i.e., it denotes a predecessor type in the sense discussed at the end of Sect. 3.4. E.g., part-of-speech tags are not specified in γ_4^*, but they might be necessary for the type *Organization*.

3.5.3 Determining the Relevant Portions of Text

Above, we discussed how to filter the relevant portions of text based on the output of a text analysis algorithm. Still, the question is what subset of the current scopes of an input text actually need to be processed by an algorithm. As an example, consider the five mentioned formulas that remain after time recognition when addressing the scoped query $\gamma_4^* = \gamma_1^* \vee \gamma_3^*$. Although the whole paragraph d_{p2} is assumed relevant for γ_4^*, an algorithm that produces *Organization* annotations will only lead to a change of the formulas $\phi^{(d_{s2})}$ and $\phi^{(d_{s4})}$. So, the analysis of the algorithm can be restricted to the scope associated γ_1^*, thus leaving out the sentence d_{s3} of d_{p2}.

In general, an employed text analysis algorithm must be applied to each portion of text d, for which an assumption $\phi^{(d)}$ or $\psi^{(d)}$ exists that depends on one of the output types $\mathbf{C}^{(out)}$ of the algorithm. That is, the algorithm must be applied to the union $S_\cup$ of the set $\mathbf{S}$ of all scopes that are relevant for the algorithm according to the method GETRELEVANTSCOPES.

Pseudocode 3.7 sketches how to determine the unified scope $S_\cup$ that contains all portions of an input text relevant for the output types $\mathbf{C}^{(out)}$ of an employed algorithm. Lines 1–3 check if a type in $\mathbf{C}^{(out)}$ is a degree of filtering. In this case, the employed algorithm is a segmentation algorithm and, so, the whole input text is returned. Elsewise, the set **S** of relevant scopes is identified using GETRELEVANT-SCOPES from Pseudocode 3.6 again. These scopes are then unified in lines 5–9 by collecting all non-overlapping portions of text while merging the overlapping ones.

3.5.4 Properties of the Proposed Approach

We have already discussed the limitations of the information-oriented view at the end of Sect. 3.4, namely, there are two noteworthy prerequisites that must be fulfilled in order to allow for filtering: (1) The algorithms in the employed pipeline must operate on some text unit level. (2) Not all parts of all input texts (and, hence, not all possible annotations) are relevant to fulfill the information needs at hand. In the following, we restrict our view to pipelines where both prerequisites hold. As for the pipeline construction in Sect. 3.3, we look at the correctness and run-time of the developed approaches. In Wachsmuth et al. (2013c), we have sketched these properties roughly, whereas we analyze them more formally here.

Correctness. Concretely, we investigate the question whether the execution of a pipeline that is equipped with an input control, which determines and updates the scopes of an input text before each step of a text analysis process (as presented), is optimal in that it analyzes only relevant portions of text.[19] As throughout this book, we consider only pipelines, where no output type is produced by more than one algorithm (cf. Sect. 3.1). Also, for consistent filtering, we require all pipelines to schedule the algorithms whose output is needed for generating the scopes of an input text before any possible filtering takes place. Given these circumstances, we now show the correctness of our algorithms for determining and updating scopes:

Lemma 3.1. *Let a text analysis pipeline $\Pi = \langle \mathbf{A}, \pi \rangle$ address a scoped query γ^* on an input text D. Let* UPDATESCOPES($\mathbf{C}^{(out)}$) *be called after each execution of an algorithm $A \in \mathbf{A}$ on D with the output types $\mathbf{C}^{(out)}$ of A. Then every scope S of D associated to γ^* always contains exactly those portions of text that are currently relevant with respect to γ^*.*

Proof. We prove the lemma by induction over the number m of text analysis algorithms executed so far. By assumption, no scope is generated before the first algorithm has been executed. So, for $m = 0$, the lemma holds. Therefore, we hypothesize that each generated scope S contains exactly those portions of text that can be relevant with respect to γ^* after the execution of an arbitrary but fixed number m of text analysis algorithms.

---

[19]Here, we analyze the *optimality of pipeline execution* for the case that both the algorithms employed in a pipeline and the schedule of these algorithms have been defined. In contrast, the examples at the beginning of Sect. 3.4 have suggested that the amount of text to be analyzed (and, hence, the *run-time optimal pipeline*) may depend on the schedule. The problem of finding the optimal schedule under the given filtering view is discussed in Chap. 4.

Now, by definition, line 4 of UPDATESCOPES determines all scopes $\mathbf{S}$ whose portions of text need to span an instance of one of the output types $\mathbf{C}^{(out)}$ of the $m+1$-th algorithm in order to be relevant for γ^*.[20] Every such portion d in a scope $S \in \mathbf{S}$ is retained in lines 7 and 8. Because of the induction hypothesis, d can still fulfill the conjunction $\mathbf{C}$ of γ^* its associated degree of filtering is assigned to. Consequently, also the outer conjunction of $\mathbf{C}$ can still be fulfilled by the portions of text that intersect with S in lines 11 and 12 (e.g., the paragraph d_{p2} in Fig. 3.17(b) remains relevant after time recognition, as it intersects with the scope of $Sentence[Forecast(Anchor, Time)]$). If an outer conjunction becomes false (as for d_{p1} after money recognition), the same holds for all inner conjunctions, which is why the respective portions of text (d_{s1} only) are removed in lines 14–16. Altogether, exactly those portions that are relevant with respect to any conjunction in γ^* remain after executing the $m+1$-th algorithm. So, Lemma 3.1 holds.   □

Lemma 3.2. *Let a text analysis pipeline $\Pi = \langle \mathbf{A}, \pi \rangle$ address a scoped query γ^* on an input text D. Further, let each degree of filtering in γ^* have an associated scope S of D. Given that S contains exactly those portions of text that can be relevant with respect to γ^*, the scope $S_{\cup}$ returned by DETERMINEUNIFIEDSCOPE($\mathbf{C}^{(out)}$) contains a portion of text $d \in D$ iff. it is relevant for the information types $\mathbf{C}^{(out)}$.*

Proof. By assumption, every segmentation algorithm must always process the whole input text, which is assured in lines 1–3 of Pseudocode 3.7. For each other algorithm $A \in \mathbf{A}$, exactly those scopes belong to $\mathbf{S}$ where the output of A may help to fulfill a conjunction (line 4). All portions of text of the scopes in $\mathbf{S}$ are unified incrementally (line 5–9) while preventing that overlapping parts of the scopes are considered more than once. Thus, no relevant portion of text is missed and no irrelevant one is analyzed.   □

The two lemmas lead to the optimality of using an input control:

Theorem 3.3. *Let a text analysis pipeline $\Pi = \langle \mathbf{A}, \pi \rangle$ address a scoped query γ^* on an input text D. Let UPDATESCOPES($\mathbf{C}^{(out)}$) be called after each execution of an algorithm $A \in \mathbf{A}$ on D with the output types $\mathbf{C}^{(out)}$ of A, and let each A process only the portions of D returned by DETERMINEUNIFIEDSCOPE($\mathbf{C}^{(out)}$). Then Π analyzes only portions of D that are currently relevant with respect to γ^*.*

Proof. As Lemma 3.1 holds, all scopes contain exactly those portions of D that are relevant with respect to γ^* according to the current knowledge. As Lemma 3.2 holds, each algorithm employed in Π gets only those portions of D its output is relevant for. From that, Theorem 3.3 follows directly.   □

Theorem 3.3 implies that an input-controlled text analysis pipeline does not perform any unnecessary analysis. The intended benefit is to make a text analysis process

---

[20]For the proof, it does not matter whether the instances of an information type in $\mathbf{C}^{(out)}$ are used to generate scopes, since no filtering has taken place yet in this case and, hence, the whole text D can be relevant after lines 1–3 of UPDATESCOPES.

faster. Of course, the maintenance of relevant portions of text naturally produces some overhead in terms of computational cost. In the evaluation below, however, we give experimental evidence that these additional costs only marginally affect the efficiency of an application in comparison to the efficiency gains achieved through filtering. Before, we now analyze the asymptotic time complexity of the proposed methods.

Complexity. The number of output types $|\mathbf{C}^{(out)}|$ of an algorithm is constant. Hence, lines 1–3 of UPDATESCOPES take time linear in the length of the input text D, i.e., $\mathcal{O}(|D|)$. Getting the relevant scopes for $\mathbf{C}^{(out)}$ then requires an iteration over all degrees of filtering $\mathbf{C}_S$ in the scoped query γ^*. Also, the for-loop from line 5 to 16 is executed at most once for each scope S and, thus, again depends on $|\mathbf{C}_S|$. Within one loop iteration, the filtering of S in lines 6–8 needs $\mathcal{O}(|D|)$ operations. Afterwards, S is intersected with at most $|\mathbf{C}_S|$ other scopes. Each intersection can be realized in $\mathcal{O}(|D|)$ time by stepwise comparing the portions of text in all scopes according to their ordering in D. Altogether, the run-time of the for-loop dominates the worst-case run-time of UPDATESCOPES, which can be estimated as

$$t_{\text{UPDATESCOPES}}(D, \mathbf{C}_S) \;=\; \mathcal{O}(|\mathbf{C}_S| \cdot (|\mathbf{C}_S|+1) \cdot |D|) \;=\; \mathcal{O}(|\mathbf{C}_S|^2 \cdot |D|). \quad (3.10)$$

In most cases, the number of degrees of filtering $|\mathbf{C}_S|$ will be a negligibly small constant. In the end, we therefore simply assume a call of UPDATESCOPES to be linear in the length of the analyzed text D.

Analogous to the update of the scopes, the determination of a unified scope in Pseudocode 3.7 begins with $\mathcal{O}(|\mathbf{C}_S|)$ steps in lines 1–3 and $\mathcal{O}(|D|)$ steps in line 4. For a concise presentation, lines 6–9 contain nested loops. As for the intersection of scopes, the unification of scopes can in fact be realized in time linear in the number of portions of text of all scopes through a stepwise comparison and, thus, $\mathcal{O}(|D|)$ operations (we realized an according procedure in the software framework described below). Consequently, the asymptotic run-time of DETERMINEUNIFIEDSCOPE is

$$t_{\text{DETERMINEUNIFIEDSCOPE}}(D, \mathbf{C}_S) \;=\; \mathcal{O}(|\mathbf{C}_S|) + \mathcal{O}(|D|). \quad (3.11)$$

Practically, this again results in time linear to the length of D. We conclude that the filtering view of text analysis can be efficiently realized in the form of an input control that governs the portions of text processed by each algorithm in a text analysis pipeline. In the following, we describe the main concepts of our realization.

3.5.5 A Software Framework for Optimal Execution

To demonstrate how to equip a text analysis pipeline with an input control in practice, we now sketch our realization of the developed approach as a JAVA software framework on top of APACHE UIMA (see above). This FILTERING FRAMEWORK

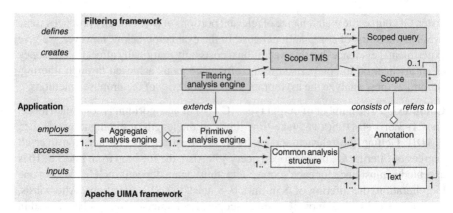

Fig. 3.19 A UML-like class diagram that shows the high-level architecture of realizing an input control as a filtering framework, which extends the APACHE UIMA framework.

was originally presented in Wachsmuth et al. (2013c). A few technical details about the framework and its extension by an application are given in Appendix B.2.

Some concepts of APACHE UIMA have been introduced in Sect. 3.3. Here, we provide a simplified view of its architecture that is illustrated at the bottom of Fig. 3.19 in a UML-like class diagram notation (OMG 2011). An application based on APACHE UIMA inputs at least one but typically much more *texts* and analyzes these texts with *aggregate analysis engines* (text analysis pipelines). An aggregate analysis engine executes a composition of *primitive analysis engines* (say, text analysis algorithms), which make use of *common analysis structures* in order to process and to produce output *annotations* of the input text at hand. Concrete annotation types do not denote entity types only, but also relation types, because they may have features that store values or references to other annotations.

We extend APACHE UIMA with our FILTERING FRAMEWORK. Figure 3.19 shows the four main concepts of this extension at the top:

1. The *filtering analysis engines* that analyze only relevant portions of text,
2. the *scoped query* to be addressed by the analysis engines,
3. the *scopes* that contain the relevant portions of the input text, and
4. the *scope TMS*, which updates and determines all scopes.

Filtering analysis engines inherit from primitive analysis engines and, hence, can be composed in an aggregate analysis engine. Prior to analysis, a filtering analysis engine automatically requests the unified scope its output annotation types and features $C^{(out)}$ are relevant for from the scope TMS. After analysis, it triggers the update of scopes based on $C^{(out)}$ and its produced output annotations.[21]

To enable filtering, an application must define the scoped query γ^* to be addressed by an aggregate analysis engine. In our implementation, γ^* is entered in the form of

---

[21] The set $C^{(out)}$ can be inferred from the so called *result specification* of an analysis engine, which APACHE UIMA automatically derives from the analysis engine's descriptor file.

a string. Then, γ^* is parsed by the FILTERING FRAMEWORK to derive its dependency graph Γ and to prepare the scopes associated to its degrees of filtering. In accordance with Γ, each scope can have at most one root scope and an arbitrary number of descendant scopes. We realize a scope as a set of generic annotations that may have a text unit type assigned (say, *Sentence*). The text unit type can be exploited to improve the efficiency of operations like the unification of scopes.

Since the access points of the APACHE UIMA framework are fixed, analysis engines cannot simply access objects outside the framework. To avoid modifications of the framework's source code, we decided to maintain all scopes using a blackboard architecture. Such an architecture is common in artificial intelligence, defining a shared knowledge base that can be accessed by a group of specialists (cf. Sect. 2.2). Here, the specialists are filtering analysis engines, which determine and update scopes via a globally accessible truth maintenance system. This *scope TMS* maintains the dependency graph Γ of each scoped query γ^*, a mapping from the degrees of filtering in γ^* to the associated scopes, and a mapping from all output types of the filtering analysis engines (including the predecessor types mentioned in Sect. 3.4) to the scopes they are relevant for. Dependencies between the output types are derived from the analysis engines' descriptor files.

For the determination of a unified scope, the scope TMS implements Pseudocode 3.7 that is executed based on the output types $\mathbf{C}^{(out)}$ of the calling filtering analysis engine. Once the filtering analysis engine has processed the scope, the scope TMS updates all respective scopes according to Pseudocode 3.5. Concretely, if an output type $C^{(out)} \in \mathbf{C}^{(out)}$ denotes a degree of filtering, the scope TMS adds all produced instances of $C^{(out)}$ to the associated scope S. Otherwise, it filters all concerned scopes, thus keeping track of the relevant portions of an input text while excluding the others from further analyses.

3.5.6 Evaluation of Optimal Execution

Based on the realized filtering framework, we now evaluate the effects of using an input control on the efficiency and effectiveness of pipeline execution. The impact of the underlying filtering view depends on the amount of information in the given input texts that is relevant for the given text analysis task. This makes a comprehensive evaluation of filtering in text analysis infeasible. Instead, our experiments serve as a reasonable proof-of-concept that (1) analyzes the main parameters intrinsic to filtering and (2) offers evidence for the efficiency of our proposed approach. Appendix B.4 yields information on the JAVA source code of this evaluation.

Input Texts. Our experiments are conducted all on texts from two text corpora of different languages. First, the widely used English dataset of the CoNLL-2003 SHARED TASK that has originally served for the development of approaches to language-independent named entity recognition (cf. Appendix C.4). The dataset consists of 1393 mixed classic newspaper stories. And second, our complete REVENUE

CORPUS with 1128 German online business news articles that we already processed in Sects. 3.1 and 3.3 and that is described in Appendix C.1.

Scoped Queries. From a task perspective, the impact of our approach is primarily influenced by the complexity and the filtering potential of the scoped query to be addressed. To evaluate these parameters, we consider the example queries γ_1 to γ_4 from Sect. 3.4 under three degrees of filtering: *Sentence*, *Paragraph*, and *Text*, where the latter is equivalent to performing no filtering at all. The resulting scoped queries are specified below.

Text Analysis Pipelines. We address the scoped queries with different pipelines, some of which use an input control, while the others do not. In all cases, we employ a subset of eleven text analysis algorithms that have been adjusted to serve as filtering analysis engines. Each of these algorithms can be parameterized to work both on English and on German texts. Concretely, we make use of the segmentation algorithms STO$_2$, SSE, and TPO$_1$ as well as of the chunker PCH for preprocessing. The entity types that appear in the queries (i.e., *Time*, *Money*, and *Organization*) are recognized with ETI, EMO, and ENE, respectively. Accordingly, we extract relations with the algorithms RFO (*Forecast*), RFU (*Founded*), and RFI (*Financial*). While RFO operates only on the sentence level, the other two qualify for arbitrary degrees of filtering. Further information on the algorithms can be found in Appendix A.

All employed algorithms have a roughly comparable run-time that scales linear with the length of the processed input text. While computationally expensive algorithms (such as the dependency parsers in Sect. 3.1) strongly increase the efficiency potential of filtering (the later such an algorithm is scheduled the better), employing them would render it hard to distinguish the effects of filtering from those of the order of algorithm application (cf. Chap. 4).

Experiments. We quantify the filtering potential of our approach by comparing the *filter ratio* (*Filter %*) of each evaluated pipeline Π, i.e., the quotient between the number of characters processed by Π and the number of characters processed by a respective non-filtering pipeline. Similarly, we compute the *time ratio* (*Time %*) of each Π as the quotient between the run-time of Π and the run-time of a non-filtering pipeline.[22] All run-times are measured on a 2 GHz Intel Core 2 Duo MacBook with 4 GB memory and averaged over ten runs (with standard deviation σ). In terms of effectiveness, below we partly count the *positives (P)* only, i.e., the number of extracted relations of the types sought for, in order to roughly compare the recall of pipelines (cf. Sect. 2.1). For the foundation relations, we also distinguish between *false positives (FP)* and *true positives (TP)* to compute the *precision* of extraction. To this end, we have decided for each positive manually whether it is true or false. In particular, an extracted foundation relation is considered a true positive if and only

---

[22]We provide no comparison to existing filtering approaches, as these approaches do not compete with our approach, but rather can be integrated with it (cf. Sect. 3.6).

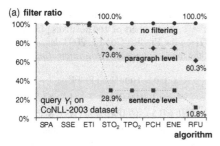
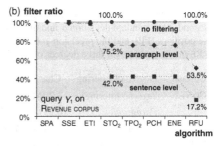

Fig. 3.20   Interpolated curves of the filter ratios of the algorithms in pipeline Π_1 under three degrees of filtering for the query $\gamma_1 = Founded(Organization, Time)$ on **a** the English CoNLL-2003 dataset and **b** the German REVENUE CORPUS.

if its anchor is brought into relation with the correct time entity while spanning the correct organization entity.[23]

Tradeoff between Efficiency and Effectiveness. We analyze different degrees of filtering for the query $\gamma_1 = Founded(Organization, Time)$. In particular, we execute the pipeline $\Pi_1 = (SPA, SSE, ETI, STO_2, TPO_2, PCH, ENE, RFU)$ on both given corpora to address each of three scoped versions of γ_1:

$$\gamma_1^* = Sentence[\gamma_1] \qquad \gamma_{1'}^* = Paragraph[\gamma_1] \qquad \gamma_{1''}^* = Text[\gamma_1]$$

To examine the effects of an input control, we first look at the impact of the degree of filtering. Figure 3.20 illustrates the filter ratios of all single algorithms in Π_1 on each of the two corpora with one interpolated curve for every evaluated degree of filtering. As the beginnings of the curves convey, even the segmentation of paragraphs (given for the paragraph level only) and sentences already enables the input control to disregard small parts of a text, namely those between the segmented text portions. The first algorithm in Π_1, then, that really reduces the number of relevant portions of text is TIM. On the sentence level, it filters 28.9 % of its input characters from the texts in the CoNLL-2003 dataset and 42.0 % from the REVENUE CORPUS. These values are further decreased by ENE, such that RFU has to analyze only 10.8 % and 17.2 % of all characters, respectively. The values for the degree of filtering *Paragraph* behave similar, while naturally being higher.

The resulting overall efficiency and effectiveness values are listed in Table 3.4. On the paragraph level, Π_1 processes 81.5 % of the 12.70 million characters of the CoNLL-2003 dataset that it processes on the text level, resulting in a time ratio of 69.0 %. For both these degrees of filtering, the same eight relations are extracted with a precision of 87.5 %. So, no relation is found that exceeds paragraph boundaries. Filtering on the sentence level lowers the filter ratio to 40.6 % and the time ratio to

---

[23] An exact evaluation of precision and recall is hardly feasible on the input texts, since the relation types sought for are not annotated. Moreover, the given evaluation of precision is only fairly representative: In practice, many extractors do not look for cross-sentence and cross-paragraph relations at all. In such cases, precision remains unaffected by filtering.

Table 3.4 The number of processed characters in millions with filter ratio *Filter %*, the run-time *t* in seconds with standard deviation σ and time ratio *Time %*, the numbers of true positives (TP) and false positives (FP), and the precision *p* of pipeline Π_1 on the English CoNLL-2003 dataset and the REVENUE CORPUS for three degrees of filtering of the query *Founded(Organization, Time)*.

Corpus	Degree of filtering	Char's	Filter %	$t \pm \sigma$	Time %	TP	FP	p
CoNLL	*Text* (no filtering)	12.70 M	100.0 %	75.4 ± 0.3	100.0 %	7	1	87.5 %
	Paragraph	10.35 M	81.5 %	52.1 ± 0.5	69.0 %	7	1	87.5 %
	Sentence	**5.16 M**	**40.6 %**	**24.8 ± 0.2**	**32.9 %**	5	**0**	**100.0 %**
REVENUE	*Text* (no filtering)	30.63 M	100.0 %	157.8 ± 0.3	100.0 %	37	15	71.2 %
	Paragraph	24.95 M	81.4 %	126.5 ± 0.5	80.2 %	27	11	71.1 %
	Sentence	**14.67 M**	**47.9 %**	**74.9 ± 0.2**	**47.5 %**	14	5	**73.7 %**

32.9 %. While this reduces the number of true positives to 5, it also prevents any false positive. Such behavior may be coincidence, but it may also indicate a tendency to achieve better precision, when the filtered portions of texts are small.

On the REVENUE CORPUS, the filter and time ratios are higher due to a larger amount of time entities (which are produced first by Π_1). Still, the use of an input control saves more than half of the run-time *t*, when performing filtering on the sentence level. Even for simple binary relation types like *Founded* and even without employing any computationally expensive algorithm, the efficiency potential of filtering hence becomes obvious. At the same time, the numbers of found true positives in Table 3.4 (37 in total, 27 within paragraphs, 14 within sentences) suggest that the use of an input control provides an intuitive means to trade the efficiency of a pipeline for its recall, whereas precision remains quite stable.

Optimization of Run-Time Efficiency. In Sect. 3.4, we claim that it is possible to optimize the efficiency of a pipeline through an input control without losing effectiveness by specifying degrees of filtering that match the text unit levels of the employed algorithms. For demonstration, we assign the same degrees of filtering as above to the query γ_2 = *Forecast(Anchor, Time)*. Each of the three resulting scoped queries is then addressed using the pipeline Π_2 = (SPA, SSE, ETI, STO2, TPO2, RFO) on the REVENUE CORPUS. As stated, RFO operates on the sentence level only.

Table 3.5 offers evidence for the truth of our claim: Under all three degrees of filtering, Π_1 extracts the same 3622 forecast relations from the 33,364 sentences in the REVENUE CORPUS. Although more than every tenth sentence is hence classified as being relevant with respect to γ_2, the filter ratio is reduced down to 64.8 %.[24]

---

[24] In Table 3.5, the number of characters for *Paragraph* is higher than for *Text* (20.02 M as opposed to 19.14 M), which seems counterintuitive. The reason behind is that the degree of filtering *Paragraph* requires an additional application of the algorithm SPA. A respective non-filtering pipeline for the paragraph level actually processes 22.97 million characters.

Table 3.5 The number of processed characters in millions with filter ratio *Filter* %, the run-time t in seconds with standard deviation σ and time ratio *Time* %, and the number of positives (in terms of extracted relations) of pipeline Π_2 for the query $\gamma_2 = Forecast(Anchor, Time)$ under three degrees of filtering on the REVENUE CORPUS.

Degree of filtering	Char's	Filter %	$t \pm \sigma$	Time %	Positives
Text (no filtering)	19.14 M	100.0 %	58.7 ± 0.4	100.0 %	3622
Paragraph	20.02 M	87.2 %	48.8 ± 1.1	83.1 %	3622
Sentence	**12.40 M**	**64.8 %**	**31.6 ± 0.3**	**53.9 %**	3622

Performing filtering in such a way forms the basis of our approaches to pipeline scheduling that we develop in Chap. 4. Also, related approaches like Shen et al. (2007) rely on similar concepts. Here, the input control improves the run-time of Π_2 by almost factor 2, thus emphasizing its great efficiency optimization potential.

Impact of the Complexity of the Query. Finally, we analyze the benefit and computational effort of filtering on the REVENUE CORPUS under increasing complexity of the addressed query. For this purpose, we consider γ_1^* from the first experiment as well as the following scoped queries:

$$\gamma_3^* = Paragraph[Financial(Money, Sentence[\gamma_2])] \qquad \gamma_4^* = \gamma_1^* \vee \gamma_3^*$$

For γ_1^*, we employ Π_1 again, whereas we use the following pipelines Π_3 and Π_4 to address γ_3^* and γ_4^*, respectively:

$\Pi_3 = (\text{SPA, SSE, EMO, ETI, STO}_2, \text{TPO}_2, \text{RFO, RFI})$
$\Pi_4 = (\text{SPA, SSE, EMO, ETI, STO}_2, \text{TPO}_2, \text{RFO, RFI, PCH, ENE, RFU})$

In Table 3.6, we list the efficiency results and the numbers of positives for the three queries. While the time ratios get slightly higher under increasing query complexity (i.e., from γ_1^* to γ_4^*), the input control saves over 50 % of the run-time of a standard pipeline in all cases. At the same time, up to 1760 relations are extracted from the REVENUE CORPUS (2103 relations without filtering). While the longest pipeline (Π_4) processes the largest number of characters (24.40 millions), the filter ratio of Π_4 (57.9 %) rather appears to be the "weighted average" of the filter ratios of Π_1 and Π_3.

For a more exact interpretation of the results of γ_4^*, Fig. 3.21 visualizes the filter ratios of all algorithms in Π_4. As shown, the interpolated curve does not decline monotonously along the pipeline. Rather, the filter ratios depend on what portions of text are relevant for which conjunctions in γ_4^*, which follows from the dependency graph of γ_4^* (cf. Fig. 3.17(a)). For instance, the algorithm RFO precedes the algorithm PCH, but entails a lower filter ratio (28.9 % vs. 42 %). RFO needs to analyze the portions of text in the scope of γ_3^* only. According to the schedule of Π_5, this means all sentences with a time entity in paragraphs that contain a money entity.

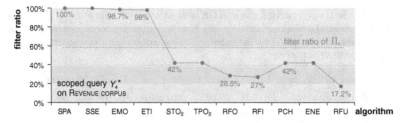

Fig. 3.21 Interpolated curve of the filter ratios of the eleven algorithms in the pipeline Π_4 for the scoped query $\gamma_4^* = \gamma_1^* \vee \gamma_3^*$ on the REVENUE CORPUS.

Table 3.6 The number of processed characters with filter ratio *Filter %* as well as the run-time t in seconds with standard deviation σ and time ratio *Time %* of $\Pi_1, \ldots, \Pi_3$ on the REVENUE CORPUS under increasingly complex queries γ^*. Each run-time is broken down into the times spent for text analysis and for input control. In the right-most column, the positives are listed, i.e., the number of extracted relations.

γ^*	Π	Char's	Filter %	$t \pm \sigma$	Time %	Analysis time	Control time	Positives
γ_1^*	Π_1	14.67 M	47.9 %	74.9±0.2	47.5 %	74.2 (99.0 %)	0.7 (1.0 %)	19
γ_3^*	Π_3	17.86 M	58.3 %	34.9±0.1	48.6 %	34.5 (98.9 %)	0.4 (1.1 %)	1741
γ_4^*	Π_4	24.40 M	57.9 %	91.2±0.5	48.8 %	90.2 (98.8 %)	1.1 (1.2 %)	1760

In contrast, CHU processes *all* sentences with time entities, as it produces a predecessor type required by ENE, which is relevant for the scope of γ_1^*.

Besides the efficiency impact of input control, Table 3.6 also provides insights into the efficiency of our implementation. In particular, it opposes the analysis time of each pipeline (i.e., the overall run-time of the employed text analysis algorithms) to the control time (i.e., the overall run-time of the input control). In case of γ_1^*, the input control takes 1.0 % of the total run-time (0.7 of 74.9 s). This fraction grows only marginally under increasing query complexity, as the control times of γ_3^* and γ_4^* suggest. While our implementation certainly leaves room for optimizations, we thus conclude that the input control can be operationalized efficiently.

3.5.7 Discussion of Optimal Execution

As summarized in Sect. 2.4, the idea of performing filtering to improve the efficiency of text analysis is not new. However, unlike existing approaches such as the prediction of sentences that contain relevant information (Nedellec et al. 2001) or the fuzzy matching of queries and possibly relevant portions of text (Cui et al. 2005), our proposed input control does not rely on vague statistical models. Instead, we formally infer the relevance of a portion of text from the current knowledge.

In general, the goal of equipping a text analysis pipeline with an input control is an optimal pipeline execution. Following Sect. 3.1, this means to fulfill an information need on a collection or a stream of input texts in the most run-time efficient manner. In this section, we have proven that a pipeline $\Pi = \langle \mathbf{A}, \pi \rangle$ based on our input control approach analyzes only possibly relevant portions of text in each step. Given that $\mathbf{A}$ and π are fixed, such an execution is optimal, because no performed analysis can be omitted without possibly missing some information sought for.

Our evaluation has offered evidence that we can optimize the efficiency of a pipeline using an input control while not influencing the pipeline's effecticeness. At the same time, the overhead induced by maintaining the relevant portions of text is low. Even in text analysis tasks that are hardly viable for filtering like most text classification tasks, an input control hence will usually have few negative effects. We therefore argue that, in principle, every text analysis pipeline can be equipped with an input control without notable drawbacks. What we have hardly discussed here, though, is that our current implementation based on APACHE UIMA still requires small modifications of each text analysis algorithm (cf. Appendix B.2 for details). To overcome this issue, future versions of APACHE UIMA could directly integrate the maintenance of scopes in the common analysis structure.

While the exact efficiency potential of filtering naturally depends on the amount of relevant information in the given input texts, our experimental results suggest that filtering can significantly speed up text analysis pipelines. Moreover, the specification of degrees of filtering provides a means to easily trade the efficiency of a pipeline for its effectiveness. This tradeoff is highly important in today's and tomorrow's text mining scenarios, as we sketch in the concluding section of this chapter.

3.6 Trading Efficiency for Effectiveness in Ad-Hoc Text Mining

As we have seen in the previous section, approaching text analysis as a filtering task provides a means to trade efficiency for effectiveness within ad-hoc text mining. We now extend the analysis of this tradeoff by discussing the integration of different filtering approaches. Then, we conclude with the important observation that filtering governs how an optimal solution to the pipeline scheduling problem raised in Sect. 3.1 looks like.

3.6.1 Integration with Passage Retrieval

As surveyed in Sect. 2.4, our input control is not the first approach that filters possibly relevant portions of text. The question is in how far existing approaches integrate with ours. Especially in time-critical ad-hoc text mining applications like question answering, returning a precise result is usually of higher importance than achieving high recall (and, thus, high overall effectiveness), which enables great improvements of run-time efficiency. To this end, only promising candidate passages (i.e., paragraphs or the like) are retrieved in the first place, from which relevant information to answer the question at hand is then extracted (Cui et al. 2005).

A study of Stevenson (2007) suggests that most extraction algorithms operate on the sentence level only, while related information is often spread across passages. Under the above-motivated assumption that extraction is easier on smaller portions of text, precision is hence preferred over recall again. In terms of the filtering view from Sect. 3.4, this makes *Sentence* the most important degree of filtering and it directly shows that passage retrieval techniques should often be integrable with our input control: As long as the size of candidate passages exceeds the specified degrees of filtering, relevance can be maintained for each portion of an input passage just as described above. Therefore, we decided not to evaluate passage retrieval against our approach. Also, we leave the integration for future work.

3.6.2 Integration with Text Filtering

Besides the filtering of *portions of text*, the efficiency and effectiveness of pipelines can also be influenced by filtering *complete texts or documents* that meet certain constraints, while discarding others. In Sect. 2.4, we have already pointed out that such kind of text filtering has been applied since the early times in order to determine candidate texts for information extraction. As such, text filtering can be seen as a regular text classification task.

Usually, the classification of candidate texts and the extraction of relevant information from these texts are addressed in separate stages of a text mining application (Cowie and Lehnert 1996; Sarawagi 2008). However, they often share common text analyses, especially in terms of preprocessing, such as tokenization or part-of-speech tagging. Sometimes, features for text classification are also based on information types like entities, as holds e.g. for the main approach in our project ARGUANA (cf. Sect. 2.3) as well as for related works like Moschitti and Basili (2004). Given that the two stages are separated, all common text analyses are performed twice, which increases run-time and produces redundant or inconsistent output.

To address these issues, Beringer (2012) has analyzed the integration of text classification and information extraction pipelines experimentally in his master's thesis written in the context of the book at hand. In particular, the master's thesis investigates the hypothesis that the later filtering is performed within an integrated pipeline, the higher its effectiveness but the lower its efficiency will be (and vice versa).

While existing works implicitly support this hypothesis, they largely focus on effectiveness, such as Lewis and Tong (1992) who compare text filtering at three positions in a pipeline. In contrast, Beringer (2012) explicitly evaluates the

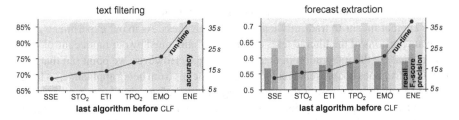

Fig. 3.22 Illustration of the effectiveness of **a** filtering candidate input texts and **b** extracting forecasts from these texts in comparison to the run-time in seconds of the integrated text analysis pipeline $\Pi^*_{2,\text{lfa}}$ depending on the position of the text filtering algorithm CLF in $\Pi^*_{2,\text{lfa}}$. The figure is based on results from Beringer (2012).

efficiency-effectiveness tradeoff, focusing on the INFEXBA process (cf. Sect. 2.3) that has original been proposed in Stein et al. (2005): Informational texts like reports and news articles are first filtered from a collection of input texts. Then, forecasts are extracted from the informational texts. To realize this process, the algorithm CLF from Wachsmuth and Bujna (2011) for language function analysis (cf. Sect. 2.3) is integrated in different positions of the optimized pipeline Π^*_2 that we use in Sect. 3.1. The later CLF is scheduled in the integrated pipeline $\Pi^{(b)}_{2,\text{lfa}}$, the more information is accessed for text classification, but the later the filtering of text portions starts, too. The input control operates on the sentence level, which matches the analyses of all employed algorithms. Therefore, observed effectiveness differences must be caused by the text filtering stage. For this scenario, Beringer (2012) performs several experiments with variations of $\Pi^*_{2,\text{lfa}}$.

Here, we exemplarily look at the main results of one experiment. The experiment has been conducted on the union of the test sets from the REVENUE CORPUS and from the music part of the LFA-11 CORPUS, both of which are described in Appendix C. This combination is not perfect for evaluation, both because the domain difference between the corpora makes text classification fairly easy and because the music texts contain no false positives with respect to the forecast extraction task at all. Still, it suffices to outline the basic effects of the pipeline integration.

Figure 3.22 plots the efficiency and effectiveness of $\Pi^{(b)}_{2,\text{lfa}}$ for different positions of CLF in the pipeline. Run-times were measured on a 3.3 GHz Intel Core i5 Windows 7 system with 8 GB memory. According to Fig. 3.22(a), spending more time improves the accuracy of text filtering in the given case, at least until the application of CLF after TPO_2.[25] This in turn benefits the recall and, thus, the F_1-score of extracting forecasts, which are raised up to 0.59 and 0.64 in Fig. 3.22(b), respectively.[26]

---

[25] As shown in Fig. 3.22(a), the accuracy is already close to its maximum when CLF is integrated after STO_2, i.e., when token-based features are available, such as bag-of-words, bigrams, etc. So, more complex features are not really needed in the end, which indicates that the classification of language functions is comparably easy on the given input texts.

[26] While the extraction precision remains unaffected from the position of integration in the experiment, this is primarily due to the lack of false positives in the LFA-11 CORPUS only.

The observed results indicate that integrating text filtering and text analysis provides another means to trade efficiency for effectiveness. As in our experiments, the relevant portions of the filtered texts can then be maintained by our input control. We do not analyze the integration in detail in this book. However, we point out that the input control does not prevent text filtering approaches from being applicable, as long as it does not start to restrict the input of algorithms before text filtering is finished. Otherwise, less and diffently distributed information is given for text filtering, which can cause unpredictable changes in effectiveness, cf. Beringer (2012).

Aside from the outlined tradeoff, the integration of the two stages generally improves the efficiency of text mining. In particular, the more text analyses are shared by the stages, the more redundant effort can be avoided. For instance, the $\Pi_{2,\mathrm{lfa}}^{(b)}$ requires 19.1 s in total when CLF is scheduled after TPO$_2$, as shown in Fig. 3.22. Separating text filtering and text analysis would require to execute the first four algorithms $\Pi_{2,\mathrm{lfa}}^{(b)}$ double on all filtered texts, hence taking a proportional amount of additional time (except for the time taken by CLF itself). The numeric efficiency impact of avoiding redundant operations has not been evaluated in Beringer (2012). In the end, however, the impact depends on the schedule of the employed algorithms as well as on the fraction of relevant texts and relevant information in these texts, which leads to the concluding remark of this chapter.

3.6.3 Implications for Pipeline Efficiency

In Sect. 3.1, we have defined the pipeline optimization problem as two-tiered, consisting of (1) the selection of a set of algorithms that is optimal with respect to some quality function and (2) determining a run-time optimal schedule of the algorithms. While it should be clear by itself that different algorithm sets vary in terms of efficiency and effectiveness, we have only implicitly answered yet why different schedules vary in their run-time. The reason behind can be inferred directly from the theory of ideal pipeline design in Sect. 3.1, namely, the optimization potential of scheduling emanates solely from the insertion of filtering steps.

By now, we have investigated the efficiency impact of consistently filtering the relevant portions of input texts under the prerequisite that the employed text analysis pipeline $\Pi = \langle \mathbf{A}, \pi \rangle$ is fixed. In accordance with the lazy evaluation step from Sect. 3.1, the later an algorithm from $\mathbf{A}$ is scheduled in π, the less filtered portions of text it will process, in general. Since the algorithms in $\mathbf{A}$ have different run-times and different selectivities (i.e., they filter different portions of text), the schedule π hence affects the overall efficiency of Π. This gives rise to the last step in Sect. 3.1, i.e., to find an optimal scheduling that minimizes Eq. 3.4.

However, both the run-times and the selectivities of the algorithms are not predefined, but they depend on the processed input. Under certain circumstances, it might be reasonable to assume that the run-times behave proportionally (we come back to this in Sect. 4.3). In contrast, the selectivities strongly diverge on different collections

or streams of input texts (cf. Fig. 3.20 in Sect. 3.5). Therefore, an optimal scheduling cannot be found ad-hoc in the sense implied so far in this chapter, i.e., without
processing input texts but based on the text analysis task to be addressed only. As a
consequence, we need to integrate the use of an input control with a mechanism that
determines a run-time optimal schedule for the input texts at hand. This is the main
problem tackled in the following chapter.

Chapter 4
Pipeline Efficiency

*A man who dares to waste one hour of time has not discovered
the value of life.*

– Charles Darwin

Abstract The importance of run-time efficiency is still often disregarded in
approaches to text analysis tasks, limiting their use for industrial size text mining applications (Chiticariu et al. 2010b). Search engines avoid efficiency problems
by analyzing input texts at indexing time (Cafarella et al. 2005). However, this is
impossible in case of ad-hoc text analysis tasks. In order both to manage and to
benefit from the ever increasing amounts of text in the world, we need not only
scale existing approaches to the large (Agichtein 2005), but we also need to develop
novel approaches at large scale (Glorot et al. 2011). Standard text analysis pipelines
execute computationally expensive algorithms on most parts of the input texts, as
we have seen in Sect. 3.1. While one way to enable scalability is to rely on cheap
but less effective algorithms only (Pantel et al. 2004; Al-Rfou' and Skiena 2012), in
this chapter we present ways to significantly speed up arbitrary pipelines by up to
over one order of magnitude. As a consequence, more effective algorithms can be
employed in large-scale text mining.

In particular, we observe that the schedule of a pipeline's algorithms affects the
pipeline's efficiency, when the pipeline analyzes only relevant portions of text (as
achieved by our input control from Sect. 3.5). In Sect. 4.1, we show that the optimal
schedule can theoretically be found with dynamic programming. It depends on the
run-times of the algorithms and the distribution of relevant information in the input
texts. Especially the latter varies strongly between different collections and streams
of texts, often making an optimal scheduling too expensive (Sect. 4.2). In practice, we
thus perform scheduling with informed search on a sample of texts (Sect. 4.3). In cases
where input texts are homogeneous in the distribution of relevant information, the
approach reliably finds a near-optimal schedule according to our evaluation. In other
cases, there is not one single optimal schedule (Sect. 4.4). To optimize efficiency,
a pipeline then needs to adapt to the input text at hand. Under high heterogeneity,
such an adaptive scheduling works well by learning in a self-supervised manner what
schedule is fastest for which text (Sect. 4.5). For large-scale text mining, a pipeline

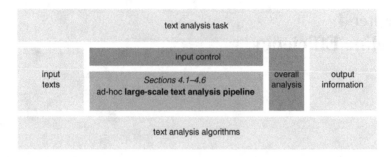

Fig. 4.1 Abstract view of the overall approach of this book (cf. Fig. 1.5). All sections of Chap. 4 contribute to the design of *large-scale text analysis pipelines*.

can finally be parallelized, as we outline in Sect. 4.6. The contribution of Chap. 4 to our overall approach is shown in Fig. 4.1.

4.1 Ideal Scheduling for Large-Scale Text Mining

As defined in Sect. 3.1, the last step of an ideal pipeline design is to optimally schedule the employed text analysis algorithms. In this section, we present an extended version of content from Wachsmuth and Stein (2012), where we compute the solution to an *optimal scheduling* using dynamic programming (Cormen et al. 2009). Given an input control as introduced in Sect. 3.5, the most efficient pipeline follows from the run-times and processed portions of text of the scheduled algorithms. These values must be measured before, which will often make the solution too expensive in practice. Still, it reveals the properties of pipeline scheduling and it can be used to compute benchmarks for large-scale text mining.

4.1.1 The Efficiency Potential of Pipeline Scheduling

As already indicated in Sect. 3.6, a consequence of equipping a text analysis pipeline with an input control is that the pipeline's schedule affects the pipeline's efficiency. In particular, the run-time of two pipelines $\Pi_1 = \langle \mathbf{A}, \pi_1 \rangle$ and $\Pi_2 = \langle \mathbf{A}, \pi_2 \rangle$ can vary on an input text if they apply the algorithms in $\mathbf{A}$ to different portions of the text. At the same time, Π_1 and Π_2 achieve the same effectiveness in the tackled text analysis task, as long as both of them are admissible (cf. Sect. 3.1).

As an example, consider the task to extract all sentences that denote forecasts with a money and an organization entity from a single news article, which is related to our project INFEXBA (cf. Sect. 2.3). Let the article consist of ten sentences, six of which contain money entities. Let two of the six sentences denote forecasts and let four of

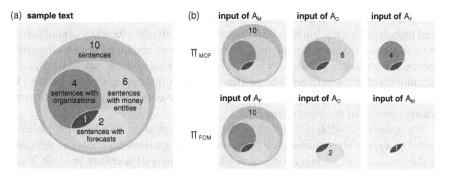

Fig. 4.2 a Venn diagram representation of a sample text with ten sentences, among which one is a forecast that contains a money and an organization entity. **b** The sentences that need to be processed by each text analysis algorithm in the pipelines Π_{MOF} (top) and Π_{FOM} (bottom), respectively.

them contain organization enties. Only one of these also spans an organization entity and, so, contains all information sought for. Figure 4.2(a) represents such an article as a Venn diagram. To tackle the task, assume that three algorithms A_M, A_O, and A_F for the recognition of money entities, organization entities, and forecast events are given that have no interdependencies, meaning that all possible schedules are admissible. For simplicity, let A_M always take $t(A_M) = 4$ ms to process a single sentence, while A_O and A_F need $t(A_O) = t(A_F) = 5$ ms. Without an input control, each algorithm must process all ten sentences, resulting in the following run-time $t(\Pi_{\text{no filtering}})$ of a respective pipeline:

$$t(\Pi_{\text{no filtering}}) \;=\; 10 \cdot t(A_M) + 10 \cdot t(A_O) + 10 \cdot t(A_F) \;=\; 140 \,\text{ms}$$

Now, given an input control that performs filtering on the sentence level, it may appear reasonable to apply the fastest algorithm A_M first, e.g. in a pipeline $\Pi_{\text{MOF}} = (A_M, A_O, A_F)$. This is exactly what our method GREEDYPIPELINELIN-EARIZATION from Sect. 3.3 does. As a result, A_M is applied to all ten sentences, A_O to the six sentences with money entities (assuming all entities are found), and A_F to the four with money and organization entities (accordingly), as illustrated at the top of Fig. 4.2(b). Hence, we have:

$$t(\Pi_{\text{MOF}}) \;=\; 10 \cdot t(A_M) + 6 \cdot t(A_O) + 4 \cdot t(A_F) \;=\; 90 \,\text{ms}$$

Thus, the input control achieves an efficiency gain of 50 ms when using Π_{MOF}. However, in an according manner, we compute the run-time of an alternative pipeline $\Pi_{\text{FOM}} = (A_F, A_O, A_M)$, based on the respective number of processed sentences as (cf. bottom of Fig. 4.2(b)):

$$t(\Pi_{\text{FOM}}) \;=\; 10 \cdot t(A_F) + 2 \cdot t(A_O) + 1 \cdot t(A_M) \;=\; 64 \,\text{ms}$$

As can be seen, Π_{MOF} takes over 40 % more time than Π_{FOM} to process the article, even though its first algorithm is 25 % faster. Apparently, the efficiency gain of using an input control does not depend only on the algorithms employed in a pipeline, but also on the pipeline's schedule, which influences the algorithms' selectivities, i.e., the numbers of portions of text filtered after each algorithm application (cf. Sect. 3.1). The efficiency potential of pipeline scheduling hence corresponds to the maximum possible impact of the input control.

So, optimal scheduling consists in the determination of an admissible schedule π^* of a given algorithm set $\mathbf{A}$ that minimizes Eq. 3.4 from Sect. 3.1, i.e., the sum of the run-times of all algorithms in $\mathbf{A}$ on the portions of text they process. This minimization problem is governed by two paradigms: (1) Algorithms with a small run-time should be scheduled early. (2) Algorithms with a small selectivity should be scheduled early. Due to the exemplified recurrent structure of the run-times and selectivities, however, these paradigms cannot be followed independently, but they require a global analysis. In the following, we perform such an analysis with *dynamic programming*. Dynamic programming refers to a class of algorithms that aim to efficiently find solutions to problems by dividing the problems into smaller subproblems and by solving recurring subproblems only once (Cormen et al. 2009).

4.1.2 Computing Optimal Schedules with Dynamic Programming

According to Eq. 3.4 and to the argumentation above, all admissible pipelines based on an algorithm set $\mathbf{A}$ entail the same relevant portions of an input text D while possibly requiring different run-times for processing D. To model these run-times, we consider a pipeline $\Pi^{(j)} = (A_1, \ldots, A_j)$ with j algorithms. For $j = 1$, $\Pi^{(j)} = (A_1)$ must always process the whole input text, which takes $t_1(D)$ time. For $j > 1$, the run-time $t(\Pi^{(j)})$ of $\Pi^{(j)}$ is given by the sum of (1) the run-time $t(\Pi^{(j-1)})$ of $\Pi^{(j-1)}$ on D and (2) the run-time $t_j(S(\Pi^{(j-1)}))$ of A_j on the scope $S(\Pi^{(j-1)})$ associated to $\Pi^{(j-1)}$. Here, we reuse the concept of scopes from Sect. 3.4 to refer to the portions of texts relevant after applying $\Pi^{(j-1)}$. We can define $t(\Pi^{(j)})$ recursively as:

$$t(\Pi^{(j)}) = \begin{cases} t_1(D) & \text{if } j = 1 \\ t(\Pi^{(j-1)}) + t_j(S(\Pi^{(j-1)})) & \text{otherwise} \end{cases} \qquad (4.1)$$

This recursive definition resembles the one used by the VITERBI ALGORITHM, which operates on *hidden Markov models* (Manning and Schütze 1999). A hidden Markov model describes a statistical process as a sequence of states. A transition from one state to another is associated to some state probability. While the states are not visible, each state produces an observation with an according probability. Hidden Markov models have the *Markov property*, i.e., the probability of a future state depends on the current state only. On this basis, the VITERBI ALGORITHM computes the *Viterbi path*, which denotes the most likely sequence of states for a given sequence of observations.

We adapt the VITERBI ALGORITHM for scheduling an algorithm set $\mathbf{A}$, such that the Viterbi path corresponds to the run-time optimal admissible pipeline $\Pi^* = \langle \mathbf{A}, \pi^* \rangle$ on an input text D. As throughout this book, we restrict our view to pipelines where no algorithm processes D multiple times. Also, under admissibility, only algorithms with fulfilled input constraints can be executed (cf. Sect. 3.1). Putting both together, we call an algorithm A_i *applicable* at some position j in a pipeline's schedule, if A_i has not been applied at positions 1 to $j-1$ and if all input types $A_i.\mathbf{C}^{(in)}$ of A_i are produced by the algorithms at positions 1 to $j-1$ or are already given for D.

To compute the Viterbi path, the original VITERBI ALGORITHM determines the most likely sequence of states for each observation and possible state at that position in an iterative (dynamic programming) manner. For our purposes, we let states of the scheduling process correspond to the algorithms in $\mathbf{A}$, while each observation denotes the position in a schedule.[1] According to the VITERBI ALGORITHM, we then propose to store a pipeline $\Pi_i^{(j)}$ from 1 to j for each combination of a position $j \in \{1, \ldots, m\}$ and an algorithm $A_i \in \mathbf{A}$ that is applicable at position j. To this end, we determine the set $\mathbf{\Pi}^{(j-1)}$ with all those previously computed pipelines of length $j-1$, after which A_i is applicable. The recursive function to compute the run-time of $\Pi_i^{(j)}$ can be directly derived from Eq. 4.1:

$$t(\Pi_i^{(j)}) = \begin{cases} t_i(D) & \text{if } j = 1 \\ \min_{\Pi_l \in \mathbf{\Pi}^{(j-1)}} \left(t(\Pi_l) + t_i(S(\Pi_l)) \right) & \text{otherwise} \end{cases} \qquad (4.2)$$

The scheduling process does *not* have Markov property, as the run-time $t(\Pi_i^{(j)})$ of an algorithm $A_i \in \mathbf{A}$ at some position j depends on the scope it is executed on. Thus, we need to keep track of the values $t(\Pi_i^{(j)})$ and $S(\Pi_i^{(j)})$ for each pipeline $\Pi_i^{(j)}$ during the computation process. After computing all pipelines based on the full algorithm set $\mathbf{A} = \{A_1, \ldots, A_m\}$, the optimal schedule π^* of $\mathbf{A}$ on the input text D is the one of the pipeline $\Pi_i^{(m)}$ with the lowest run-time $t(\Pi_i^{(m)})$.

Pseudocode 4.1 shows our VITERBI ALGORITHM adaptation. A pipeline $\Pi_i^{(1)}$ is stored in lines 1–5 for every algorithm $A_i \in \mathbf{A}$ that is already applicable given D only. The run-time $t(\Pi_i^{(1)})$ and the scope $S(\Pi_i^{(1)})$ of $\Pi_i^{(1)}$ are set to the respective values

---

[1] Different from Wachsmuth and Stein (2012), we omit to explicitly define the underlying model here for a more focused presentation. The adaptation works even without the model.

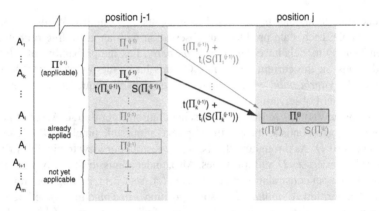

Fig. 4.3 Trellis diagram visualization of OPTIMALPIPELINESCHEDULING, showing the determination of the run-time optimal pipeline $\Pi_i^{(j)}$ from position 1 to j. For illustration purposes, the algorithms $A_1, \ldots, A_m$ are ordered according to their applicability after the pipelines of length $j-1$.

OPTIMALPIPELINESCHEDULING($\{A_1, \ldots, A_m\}, D$)

1: **for each** $i \in \{1, \ldots, m\}$ **do**
2:    **if** A_i is applicable in position 1 **then**
3:       Pipeline $\Pi_i^{(1)} \leftarrow (A_i)$
4:       Run-time
         $t(\Pi_i^{(1)}) \leftarrow t_i(D)$
5:       Scope $S(\Pi_i^{(1)}) \leftarrow S_i(D)$

6: **for each** $j \in \{2, \ldots, m\}$ **do**
7:    **for each** $i \in \{1, \ldots, m\}$ **do**
8:       Pipelines $\boldsymbol{\Pi}^{(j-1)} \leftarrow \{\Pi_l^{(j-1)} \mid A_i \text{ is applicable after } \Pi_l^{(j-1)}\}$
9:       **if** $\boldsymbol{\Pi}^{(j-1)} \neq \emptyset$ **then**
10:         Pipeline $\Pi_k^{(j-1)} \leftarrow \underset{\Pi_l \in \boldsymbol{\Pi}^{(j-1)}}{\arg\min} \left(t(\Pi_l) + t_i(S(\Pi_l)) \right)$
11:         Pipeline $\Pi_i^{(j)} \leftarrow \Pi_k^{(j-1)} \parallel (A_i)$
12:         Run-time $t(\Pi_i^{(j)}) \leftarrow t(\Pi_k^{(j-1)}) + t_i(S(\Pi_k^{(j-1)}))$
13:         Scope $S(\Pi_i^{(j)}) \leftarrow S_i(S(\Pi_k^{(j-1)}))$
14: **return** $\underset{\Pi_i^{(m)}, i \in \{1, \ldots, m\}}{\arg\min} t(\Pi_i^{(m)})$

Pseudocode 4.1: The optimal solution to the computation of a pipeline based on an algorithm set $\{A_1, \ldots, A_m\}$ with a run-time optimal schedule on an input text D.

of A_i. Next, for each algorithm A_i that is applicable at all in position j lines 6–13 incrementally compute a pipeline $\Pi_i^{(j)}$ of length j. Here, the set $\boldsymbol{\Pi}^{(j-1)}$ is computed in line 8. If $\boldsymbol{\Pi}^{(j-1)}$ is not empty (which implies the applicability of A_i), lines 9–11 then create $\Pi_i^{(j)}$ by appending A_i to the pipeline $\Pi_k^{(j-1)}$ that is best in terms of Eq. 4.2.[2] In lines 12 and 13, the run-time and the scope are computed accordingly for $\Pi_i^{(j)}$. After the final iteration, the fastest pipeline $\Pi_i^{(m)}$ of length m is returned as an optimal solution (line 13). A trellis diagram that schematically illustrates the described operations for A_i at position j is shown in Fig. 4.3.

4.1.3 Properties of the Proposed Solution

In Wachsmuth and Stein (2012), we have sketched the basic idea of how to prove that the presented scheduling approach computes an optimal solution. Now, we provide a formal proof of the correctness of the approach. Then, we continue with its complexity and with practical implications.

Correctness. In the proof, we consider only algorithm sets that are consistent and that have no circular dependencies, as defined in Sect. 3.3. These properties ensure that an admissible schedule exists for a given algorithm set $\mathbf{A} = \{A_1, \ldots, A_m\}$. As usual in dynamic programming, the optimality of the pipeline $\Pi_i^{(m)}$ returned by OPTIMALPIPELINESCHEDULING for $\mathbf{A}$ and for an input text D then follows from the optimal solution to all subproblems. Here, this means the optimality of all computed pipelines $\Pi_i^{(j)}$, because $\Pi_i^{(m)}$ is then optimal for the full algorithm set $\mathbf{A}$. The following lemma states that each $\Pi_i^{(j)}$ is run-time optimal under all admissible pipelines that are based on the same algorithm set and that end with the same algorithm:

Lemma 4.1. *Let $\mathbf{A} = \{A_1, \ldots, A_m\}$ be a consistent algorithm set without circular dependencies and let D be a text. Let $\Pi_i^{(j)} = \langle \mathbf{A}_i^{(j)}, \pi^* \rangle = (A_1, \ldots, A_{j-1}, A_i)$, $\mathbf{A}_i^{(j)} \subseteq \mathbf{A}$, be any pipeline that OPTIMALPIPELINESCHEDULING$(\mathbf{A}, D)$ computes. Then for all admissible pipelines $\Pi_i'^{(j)} = \langle \mathbf{A}_i^{(j)}, \pi' \rangle = (A_1', \ldots, A_{j-1}', A_i)$, we have:*

$$t(\Pi_i^{(j)}) \leq t(\Pi_i'^{(j)})$$

Proof. We show the lemma by induction over the length j. For $j = 1$, each pipeline $\Pi_i^{(1)}$ created in line 3 of OPTIMALPIPELINESCHEDULING consists only of the algorithm A_i. As there is only one pipeline of length 1 that ends with A_i, for all $i \in \{1, \ldots, m\}$, $\Pi_i^{(1)} = \Pi_i'^{(1)}$ holds and, so, $\Pi_i^{(1)}$ is optimal. Therefore, we hypothesize that the lemma is true for an arbitrary but fixed length $j-1$. We prove by contradiction that, in this case, it also holds for j. For this purpose, we assume the opposite:

$$\exists \Pi_i'^{(j)} = \langle \mathbf{A}_i^{(j)}, \pi' \rangle = (A_1', \ldots, A_{j-1}', A_i) : \quad t(\Pi_i^{(j)}) > t(\Pi_i'^{(j)})$$

---

[2]Different from the pseudocode in Wachsmuth and Stein (2012), we explicitly check here if $\Pi^{(j-1)}$ is not empty. Apart from that, the pseudocodes differ only in terms of namings.

According to Eq. 4.1, this inequality can be rewritten as follows:

$$t(\Pi^{(j-1)}) + t_i(S(\Pi^{(j-1)})) \quad > \quad t(\Pi'^{(j-1)}) + t_i(S(\Pi'^{(j-1)}))$$

By definition, $\Pi^{(j-1)}$ and $\Pi'^{(j-1)}$ employ the same algorithm set $\mathbf{A}_i^{(j)} \setminus \{A_i\}$. Since both pipelines are admissible, they entail the same relevant portions of text, i.e., $S(\Pi^{(j-1)}) = S(\Pi'^{(j-1)})$. Therefore, the run-time of algorithm A_i must be equal on $S(\Pi^{(j-1)})$ and $S(\Pi'^{(j-1)})$, so we remain with the following inequality:

$$t(\Pi^{(j-1)}) \quad > \quad t(\Pi'^{(j-1)})$$

$\Pi'^{(j-1)}$ must end with a different algorithm A'_{j-1} than A_{j-1} in $\Pi^{(j-1)}$, since $\Pi_i^{(j)}$ would otherwise in lines 10 and 11 of OPTIMALPIPELINESCHEDULING not be created from $\Pi^{(j-1)}$. For the same reason, $\Pi'^{(j-1)}$ cannot belong to the set $\mathbf{\Pi}^{(j-1)}$ computed in line 8. Each pipeline in $\mathbf{\Pi}^{(j-1)}$ is run-time optimal according to the induction hypothesis, including the pipeline—if such a pipeline exists—that ends with the algorithm A'_{j-1}. But, then, $\Pi^{(j-1)}$ cannot be optimal. This means that the assumed opposite must be wrong.   □

Based on the truth of Lemma 4.1, we show the correctness of OPTIMALPIPELINE-SCHEDULING, as represented by Theorem 4.1:

Theorem 4.1. *Let* $\mathbf{A} = \{A_1, \ldots, A_m\}$ *be a consistent algorithm set without circular dependencies and let* D *be a text. Then, the pipeline* $\langle \mathbf{A}, \pi \rangle$ *returned by a call of* OPTIMALPIPELINESCHEDULING($\mathbf{A}$, D) *is run-time optimal on* D *under all admissible pipelines* $\langle \mathbf{A}, \pi_1 \rangle, \ldots, \langle \mathbf{A}, \pi_n \rangle, n \geq 1$.

Proof. We first point out the admissibility of each text analysis pipeline $\Pi_i^{(m)}$ returned by Pseudocode 4.1. Both in line 3 and in line 11, only applicable algorithms are added to the end of the created pipelines $\Pi_i^{(m)}$. By definition of applicability (see above), all input requirements of an applicable algorithm are fulfilled. Therefore, all pipelines $\Pi_i^{(m)}$ must be admissible.

As a consequence, Lemma 4.1 implies that the pipeline computed in the last iteration of lines 6–13 of OPTIMALPIPELINESCHEDULING is run-time optimal under all admissible pipelines of length m that end with A_i. Since no algorithm is added twice under applicability, each $\Pi_i^{(m)}$ contains the complete algorithm set $\mathbf{A}$. The fastest of these pipelines is taken in line 13.   □

Complexity. Knowing that the approach is correct, we now come to its computational complexity. As in Chap. 3, we rely on the $\mathcal{O}$-notation (Cormen et al. 2009) to capture the worst-case run-time of the approach. Given an arbitrary algorithm set $\mathbf{A}$ and some input text D, Pseudocode 4.1 iterates exactly $|\mathbf{A}|$ times over the $|\mathbf{A}|$ algorithms, once for each position in the schedule to be computed. In each of these $|\mathbf{A}|^2$ loop iterations, a pipeline $\Pi_i^{(j)}$ is determined based on at most $|\mathbf{A}|-1$ other pipelines

$\Pi_l^{(j-1)}$, resulting in $\mathcal{O}(|\mathbf{A}|^3)$ operations. For each $\Pi_i^{(j)}$, the run-time $t(\Pi_i^{(j)})$ and the scope $S(\Pi_i^{(j)})$ are stored. In practice, these values are not known beforehand, but they need to be measured when executing $\Pi_i^{(j)}$ on its input. In the worst case, all algorithms in $\mathbf{A}$ have an equal run-time $t_{\mathbf{A}}(D)$ on D and they find relevant information in all portions of text, i.e., $S_i(D) = D$ for each algorithm $A_i \in \mathbf{A}$. Then, all algorithms must indeed process the whole text D, which leads to an overall upper bound of

$$t_{\text{OPTIMALPIPELINESCHEDULING}}(\mathbf{A}, D) \;=\; \mathcal{O}(|\mathbf{A}|^3 \cdot t_{\mathbf{A}}(D)). \tag{4.3}$$

Moreover, while we have talked about a single text D up to now, a more reasonable input will normally be a whole collection of texts in practice.[3] This underlines that our theoretical approach is not made for practical applications in the first place: Since each algorithm employed in a text analysis pipeline $\Pi = \langle \mathbf{A}, \pi \rangle$ processes its input at most once, even without an input control the run-time of Π is bound by $\mathcal{O}(|\mathbf{A}| \cdot t_{\mathbf{A}}(D))$ only.

Besides the unrealistic nature of the described worst case, however, the value $|\mathbf{A}|^3$ in Eq. 4.3 ignores the fact that an algorithm is, by definition, applicable only once within a schedule and only if its input requirements are fulfilled. Therefore, the real cost of OPTIMALPIPELINESCHEDULING will be much lower in practice. Also, instead of scheduling all $|\mathbf{A}|$ single algorithms, the search space of possible schedules can usually be significantly reduced by scheduling the filtering stages that result from our method for ideal pipeline design (cf. Sect. 3.1). We give an example in the following case study and then come back to the practical benefits of OPTIMAL-PIPELINESCHEDULING in the discussion at the end of this section.

4.1.4 Case Study of Ideal Scheduling

We now apply the proposed solution to optimal scheduling to a concrete algorithm set for an information need in the context of our project INFEXBA (cf. Sect. 2.3) on two different text corpora. Our goal is to once give experimental evidence that different input texts may lead to different run-time optimal schedules. An analysis of the reasons behind follows in Sect. 4.2. Details on the source code used here is found in Appendix B.4.

Information Need. We consider the extraction of all forecasts on organizations with a time and a money entity. An example sentence that spans all relevant information types is the following: *"IBM will end the first-quarter 2011 with $13.2 billion of cash on hand and with generated free cash flow of $0.8 billion."*[4] For our input

---

[3]Notice that using more than one text as input does not require changes of OPTIMALPIPELINE-SCHEDULING, since we can simply assume that the texts are given in concatenated form.

[4]Taken from an IBM annual report, http://ibm.com/investor/1q11/press.phtml, accessed on June 15, 2015.

control from Sect. 3.5, the information need can be formalized as the scoped query $\gamma^* = Sentence[Forecast(Time, Money, Organization)]$.[5]

Algorithm Set. To produce the output sought for in γ^*, we use the entity recognition algorithms ETI, EMO, and ENE as well as the forecast event detector RFO. To fulfill their input requirements, we additionally employ three preprocessing algorithms, namely, SSE, STO_2, and TPO_1. All algorithms operate on the sentence level (cf. Appendix A for further information). During scheduling, we implicitly apply the lazy evaluation step from Sect. 3.1 to create filtering stages, i.e., each preprocessor is scheduled as late as possible in all pipelines. Instead of filtering stages, we simply speak of the algorithm set $\mathbf{A} = \{$ETI, EMO, ENE, RFO$\}$ in the following without loss of generality.

Text Corpora. As in Sect. 3.5, we consider both our REVENUE CORPUS (cf. Appendix C.1) and the CoNLL-2003 dataset (cf. Appendix C.4). For lack of alternatives to the employed algorithms, we rely on the German part of the CoNLL-2003 dataset this time. We process only the training sets of the two corpora. These training sets consist of 21,586 sentences (in case of the REVENUE CORPUS) and 12,713 sentences (CoNLL-2003 dataset), respectively.

Experiments. We run all pipelines $\Pi_i^{(j)}$, which are computed within the execution of OPTIMALPIPELINESCHEDULING, ten times on both text corpora using a 2 GHz Intel Core 2 Duo MacBook with 4 GB memory. For each pipeline, we measure the averaged overall run-time $t(\Pi_i^{(j)})$. In our experiments, all standard deviations were lower than 1.0 s on the REVENUE CORPUS and 0.5 s on the CoNLL-2003 dataset. Below, we omit them for a concise presentation. For similar reasons, we state only the number of sentences in the scopes $S(\Pi_i^{(j)})$ of all $\Pi_i^{(j)}$, instead of the sentences themselves.

Input Dependency of Pipeline Scheduling. Figure 4.4 illustrates the application of OPTIMALPIPELINESCHEDULING for the algorithm set $\mathbf{A}$ to the two considered corpora as trellis diagrams. The bold arrows correspond to the respective Viterbi paths, indicating the optimal pipeline $\Pi_i^{(j)}$ of each length j. Given all four algorithms, the optimal pipeline takes 48.25 s on the REVENUE CORPUS, while the one on the CoNLL-2003 dataset requires 18.17 s. ETI is scheduled first and ENE is scheduled last on both corpora, but the optimal schedule of EMO and RFO differs. This shows the input-dependency of run-time optimal scheduling.

One main reason lies in the selectivities of the employed text analysis algorithms: On the REVENUE CORPUS, 3813 sentences remain relevant after applying $\Pi_{EMO}^{(2)} = $ (ETI, EMO) as opposed to 2294 sentences in case of $\Pi_{RFO}^{(2)} = $ (ETI, RFO). Conversely, only 82 sentences are filtered after applying $\Pi_{EMO}^{(2)}$ to the CoNLL-2003

---

[5]We note here once that some of the implementations in the experiments in Chap. 4 do *not* use the exact input control approach presented in Chap. 3. Instead, the filtering of relevant portions of text is directly integrated into the employed algorithms. However, as long as only a single information need is addressed and only one degree of filtering is specified, there will be no conceptual difference in the obtained results.

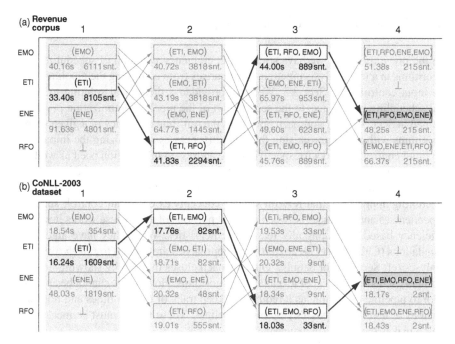

Fig. 4.4 Trellis illustrations of executing OPTIMALPIPELINESCHEDULING for the algorithm set **A** = {ETI, EMO, ENE, RFO} on the training set of **a** the REVENUE CORPUS and **b** the German CoNLL-2003 dataset. Below each pipeline $\Pi_i^{(j)}$, the run-time $t(\Pi_i^{(j)})$ is given in seconds next to the number of sentences (snt.) in $S(\Pi_i^{(j)})$. The bold arrows denote the Viterbi paths resulting in the run-time optimal pipelines (ETI, RFO, EMO, ENE) and (ETI, EMO, RFO, ENE), respectively.

dataset, whereas 555 sentences still need to be analyzed after $\Pi_{RFO}^{(2)}$. Altogether, each admissible pipeline $\Pi_i^{(4)}$ based on the complete algorithm set **A** classifies the same 215 sentences (1.0 %) of the REVENUE CORPUS as relevant, while not more than two sentences of the CoNLL-2003 dataset (0.01 %) are returned to address γ^*.[6] These values originate in different distributions of relevant information, as we discuss in detail in Sect. 4.2.

While the algorithms' selectivities impact the optimal schedule in the described case, the efficiency of scheduling ETI first primarily emanates from the low run-time of ETI. On the CoNLL-2003 dataset, for instance, the optimal pipeline $\Pi_{ENE}^{(4)}$ schedules ETI before EMO, although much less sentences remain relevant after $\Pi_{EMO}^{(1)}$ = (EMO) than after $\Pi_{ETI}^{(1)}$ = (ETI). Applying ETI and EMO in sequence is even faster than applying EMO only. This becomes important in case of parallelization, as we discuss in Sect. 4.6. Even more clearly, ENE alone takes 91.63 s on the REVENUE CORPUS and 48.03 s on the CoNLL-2003 dataset, which underlines the general efficiency impact of scheduling, when using an input control (cf. Sect. 3.5).

---

[6]As can be seen, the numbers of sentences at position 4 do not vary between the different pipelines for one corpus. This offers practical evidence for the commutativity of employing independent algorithms within an admissible pipeline (cf. Sect. 3.1).

4.1.5 Discussion of Ideal Scheduling

On the previous pages, we have stressed the efficiency potential of scheduling the algorithms in a text analysis pipeline, which arises from equipping the pipeline with the input control from Sect. 3.5. We have provided a theoretical solution to optimal scheduling and, hence, to the second part of the pipeline optimization problem defined in Sect. 3.1. Our approach optimizes the run-time efficiency of a given set of algorithms without compromising their effectiveness by maximizing the impact of the input control. It works irrespective of the addressed information need as well as of the language and other characteristics of the input texts to be processed.

For information extraction, both Shen et al. (2007) and Doan et al. (2009) present scheduling approaches that rely on similar concepts as our input control, such as dependencies and distances between relevant portions of text. These works improve efficiency based on empirically reasonable heuristics. While they have algebraic foundations (Chiticariu et al. 2010a), both approaches are limited to *rule-based* text analyses (cf. Sect. 2.4 for details). Our approach closes this gap by showing how to optimally schedule *any* set of text analysis algorithms. However, it cannot be applied prior to pipeline execution, as it requires to keep track of the run-times and relevant portions of texts of all possibly optimal pipelines. These values must be measured, which makes the approach expensive.

As such, the chosen dynamic programming approach is not meant to serve for practical text mining applications, although it still represents an efficient way to compute benchmarks for more or less arbitrary text analysis tasks.[7] Rather, it clarifies the theoretical background of empirical findings on efficient text analysis pipelines in terms of the underlying algorithmic and linguistic determinants. In particular, we have shown that the optimality of a pipeline depends on the run-times and selectivities of the employed algorithms on the processed input texts. In the next section, we investigate the characteristics of collections and streams of input texts that influence pipeline optimality. On this basis, we then turn to the development of efficient practical scheduling approaches.

4.2 The Impact of Relevant Information in Input Texts

The case study in the previous section already shows that the run-time optimality of an input-controlled pipeline depends on the given collection or stream of input texts. In the following, we provide both formal and experimental evidence that the reason behind lies in the distribution of relevant information in the texts, which

---

[7]Different from our input control, the dynamic progrmaming approach covers only our basic scenario from Sect. 1.2, where we seek for a *single* set of information types C. While relevant in practice, we skip the possibly technically complex extension to more than one set for lack of expected considerable insights. The integration of different pipelines sketched in the properties part of Sect. 3.3 indicates, though, what to pay attention to in the extension.

governs the portions of text filtered by the input control after each execution of an algorithm (cf. Sect. 3.5). Consequently, the determination of an optimal schedule requires to estimate the algorithms' selectivities, which we approach in Sect. 4.3. As above, this section reuses content from Wachsmuth and Stein (2012).

4.2.1 Formal Specification of the Impact

When we speak of relevant information in the book at hand, we always refer to information that can be used to address one or more information needs, each defined as a set of information types $\mathbf{C}$. Accordingly, with the *distribution* of relevant information, we mean the distribution of instances of each information type $C \in \mathbf{C}$ in the input texts to be processed. More precisely, what matters in terms of efficiency is the distribution of instances of all types in $\mathbf{C}$ found by some employed algorithm set, because this information decides what portions of the texts are *classified as relevant* and are, thus, filtered by the input control. We quantify this distribution in terms of density as opposed to relative frequency:

The *relative frequency* of an information type C in a collection or a stream of input texts $\mathbf{D}$ is the average number of instances of C found per portion of text in $\mathbf{D}$ (of some specified text unit type, cf. Sect. 3.4). This frequency affects the efficiency of algorithms that take instances of C as input. Although this effect is definitely worth analyzing, in the given context we are primarily interested in the efficiency impact of filtering. Instead, we therefore capture the *density* of C in $\mathbf{D}$, which we define as the fraction of portions of text in $\mathbf{D}$ in which instances of C are found.[8]

To illustrate the difference between frequency and density, assume that relations of a type *IsMarriedTo(Person, Person)* shall be extracted from a text D with two portions of text (say, sentences). Let three person names be found in the first sentence and none in the second one. Then the type *Person* has a relative frequency of 1.5 in D but a density of 0.5. The frequency affects the average number of candidate relations for extraction. In contrast, the density implies that relation extraction needs to take place on 50 % of all sentences only, which is what we are up to.

Now, consider the general case that some text analysis pipeline $\Pi = \langle \mathbf{A}, \pi \rangle$ is given to address an information need $\mathbf{C}$ on a text D. The density of each information type from $\mathbf{C}$ in D directly governs what portions of D are filtered by our input control after the execution of an algorithm in $\mathbf{A}$. Depending on the schedule π, the resulting run-times of all algorithms on the filtered portions of text then sum up to the run-time of Π. Hence, it might seem reasonable to conclude that the fraction of those portions of D, which pipeline Π classifies as relevant, impacts the run-time optimality of π. In fact, however, the optimality depends on the portions of D classified as *not* relevant, as follows from Theorem 4.2:

---

[8]Besides, an influencing factor of efficiency is the *length* of the portions of text, of course. However, we assume that, on average, all relative frequencies and densities equally scale with the length. Consequently, both can be seen as an implicit model of length.

Theorem 4.2. *Let $\Pi^* = \langle \mathbf{A}, \pi^* \rangle$ be run-time optimal on a text D under all admissible text analysis pipelines based on an algorithm set $\mathbf{A}$, and let $S(D) \subseteq D$ denote a scope containing all portions of D classified as relevant by Π^*. Let $S(D') \subseteq D'$ denote the portions of any other input text D' classified as relevant by Π^*. Then Π^* is also run-time optimal on $(D \backslash S(D)) \cup S(D')$.*

Proof. In the proof, we denote the run-time of a pipeline Π on an arbitrary scope S as $t_\Pi(S)$. By hypothesis, the run-time $t_{\Pi^*}(D)$ of $\Pi^* = \langle \mathbf{A}, \pi^* \rangle$ is optimal on D, i.e., for all admissible pipelines $\Pi' = \langle \mathbf{A}, \pi' \rangle$, we have

$$t_{\Pi^*}(D) \leq t_{\Pi'}(D). \qquad (4.4)$$

As known from Sect. 3.1, for a given input text D, all admissible text analysis pipelines based on the same algorithm set $\mathbf{A}$ classify the same portions $S(D) \subseteq D$ as relevant. Hence, each portion of text in $S(D)$ is processed by every algorithm in $\mathbf{A}$, irrespective of the schedule of the algorithms. So, the run-time of two pipelines $\Pi_1 = \langle \mathbf{A}, \pi_1 \rangle$ and $\Pi_2 = \langle \mathbf{A}, \pi_2 \rangle$ on $S(D)$ is always equal (at least on average):

$$t_{\Pi_1}(S(D)) = t_{\Pi_2}(S(D)) \qquad (4.5)$$

Since we do not put any constraints on D, Eq. 4.5 also holds for D' instead of D. Combining Eq. 4.5 with Ineq. 4.4, we can thus derive the correctness of Theorem 4.2 as follows:

$$
\begin{aligned}
t_{\Pi^*}((D \backslash S(D)) \cup S(D')) &= \quad t_{\Pi^*}(D) - t_{\Pi^*}(S(D)) + t_{\Pi^*}(S(D')) \\
&\overset{(4.4)}{\leq} t_{\Pi'}(D) - t_{\Pi^*}(S(D)) + t_{\Pi^*}(S(D')) \\
&\overset{(4.5)}{=} t_{\Pi'}(D) - t_{\Pi'}(S(D)) + t_{\Pi'}(S(D')) \\
&= \quad t_{\Pi'}((D \backslash S(D)) \cup S(D'))
\end{aligned}
$$

$\square$

Theorem 4.2 states that the portions of text $S(D)$ classified as relevant by a text analysis pipeline have no impact on the run-time optimality of the pipeline. Consequently, differences in the efficiency of two admissible pipelines based on the same algorithm set $\mathbf{A}$ must emanate from applying the algorithms in $\mathbf{A}$ to different numbers of irrelevant portions of texts. We give experimental evidence for this conclusion in the following.

4.2.2 Experimental Analysis of the Impact

In order to stress the impact of the distribution of relevant information, we now present controlled experiments that show how the run-time efficiency of a text analysis pipeline and its possible run-time optimality behave under changing densities of the relevant information types.

Pipelines. In the experiments, we employ the same algorithm set as we did at the end of Sect. 4.1. Again, we apply lazy evaluation in all cases, allowing us to consider the four algorithms ETI, EMO, ENE, and RFO only. Based on these, we investigate the efficiency of two pipelines, Π_1 and Π_2:

$$\Pi_1 = (\text{ETI, RFO, EMO, ENE}) \qquad \Pi_2 = (\text{EMO, ETI, RFO, ENE})$$

As shown in the case study of Sect. 4.1, Π_1 denotes the run-time optimal pipeline for the information need $\mathbf{C} = \{$*Forecast, Time, Money, Organization*$\}$ on the training set of the REVENUE CORPUS. In contrast, Π_2 represents an efficient alternative when given texts with few money entities.

Text Corpora. To achieve different distributions of the set of relevant information types $\mathbf{C}$, we have created artificially altered versions of the training set of the REVENUE CORPUS. In particular, we have modified the original corpus texts by randomly duplicating or deleting

(a) **relevant sentences**, which contain all relevant information types,
(b) **irrelevant sentences**, which miss at least one relevant type,
(c) **irrelevant sentences, which contain money entities**, but which miss at least one other relevant type.

In case (a) and (b), we created text corpora, in which the density of the whole set $\mathbf{C}$ is 0.01, 0.02, 0.05, 0.1, and 0.2, respectively. In case (c), it is not possible to obtain higher densities than a little more than 0.021 from the training set of the REVENUE CORPUS, because under that density, all irrelevant sentences with money entities have been deleted. Therefore, we restrict our view to five densities between 0.009 and 0.021 in that case.

Experiments. We processed all created corpora ten times with both Π_1 and Π_2 on a 2 GHz Intel Core 2 Duo MacBook with 4 GB memory. Due to the alterations, the corpora differ significantly in size. For this reason, we compare the efficiency of the pipelines in terms of the average run-times per sentence. Appendix B.4 outlines how to reproduce the experiments.

The Impact of the Distribution of Relevant Information. Figure 4.5 plots the run-times as a function of the density of $\mathbf{C}$. In line with Theorem 4.2, Fig. 4.5(a) conveys that changing the number of relevant sentences does not influence the absolute differences of the run-time of Π_1 and Π_2.[9] In contrast, the gap between the curves in Fig. 4.5(b) increases proportionally under growing density, because the two pipelines spend a proportional amount of time processing irrelevant portions of text. Finally, the impact of the distribution of relevant information becomes explicit in Fig. 4.5(c): Π_1 is faster on densities lower than about 0.018, but Π_2 outperforms Π_1 under a

---

[9]Minor deviations occur on the processed corpora, since we have changed the number of relevant sentences as opposed to the number of sentences that are classified as relevant.

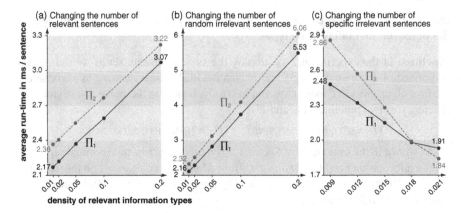

density of relevant information types

Fig. 4.5 Interpolated curves of the average run-times of the pipelines Π_1 = (ETI, RFO, EMO, ENE) and Π_2 = (EMO, ETI, RFO, ENE) under different densities of the relevant information types in modified training sets of the REVENUE CORPUS. The densities were created by duplicating or deleting **a** relevant sentences, **b** random irrelevant sentences, and **c** irrelevant sentences with money entities.

higher density (0.021).[10] The reason for the change in optimality is that, the more irrelevant sentences with money entities are deleted, the less portions of text are filtered after EMO, which favors the schedule of Π_2.

Altogether, we conclude that the distribution of relevant information can be decisive for the optimal scheduling of a text analysis pipeline. While there are other influencing factors, some of which trace back to the efficiency of the employed text analysis algorithms (as discussed in the beginning of this section), we have cancelled out many of these factors by only duplicating and deleting sentences from the REVENUE CORPUS itself.

4.2.3 Practical Relevance of the Impact

For specific text analysis tasks, we have already exemplified the efficiency potential of pipeline scheduling (Sect. 3.1) and the input dependency (Sect. 4.1). A general quantification of the practical impact of the distribution of relevant information is hardly possible, because it depends on the processed input texts and the employed algorithms. As an indicator of its relevance, however, we offer evidence here that distributions of information tend to vary much more significantly between different collections and streams of texts than the run-times of text analysis algorithms.

---

[10]The declining curves in Fig. 4.5(c) seem counterintuitive. The reason is that, in the news articles of the REVENUE CORPUS, sentences with money entities often contain other relevant information like time entities, too. So, while duplicating irrelevant sentences of this kind reduces the density of **C**, the average time to process these sentences is rather high.

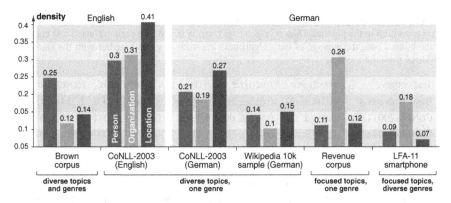

Fig. 4.6 Illustration of the densities of person, organization, and location entities in the sentences of two English and four German collections of texts. All densities are computed based on the results of the pipeline $\Pi_{\text{ENE}} = (\text{SSE}, \text{STO}_2, \text{TPO}_1, \text{PCH}, \text{ENE})$.

To obtain some degree of generality, we resort to standard information types from information extraction. In particular, we consider the three very common entity types *Person*, *Location*, and *Organization*, whose importance is underlined by their central role in the CoNLL-2003 SHARED TASK on named entity recognition (Tjong Kim Sang and Meulder 2003). Figure 4.6 compares the densities of these types in six text corpora that differ in language, topic diversity, and genre diversity among others. The shown values are computed based on the output information created by the pipeline $\Pi_{\text{ENE}} = (\text{SSE}, \text{STO}_2, \text{TPO}_1, \text{PCH}, \text{ENE})$. For details on the algorithms, the executed code, and all corpora, see Appendices A, B.4, and C.

For all three entity types, the observed values cover a wide spectrum, e.g. ranging from 0.07 to 0.41 in case of *Location*. In the classic BROWN CORPUS, which aims to serve as a representative sample of American English, person names are densest (0.25), while locations are of upmost importance in the mixed classic news paper articles from the CoNLL-2003 datasets of both given languages.[11] Compared to these, the densities in the processed sample of 10,000 articles from the German WIKIPEDIA appear small. One reason behind may be that WIKIPEDIA also covers topics where the considered entity types do not play a leading role. Finally, both our REVENUE CORPUS and the smartphone part of our LFA-11 CORPUS show an extraordinarily high proportion of sentences with organization names. Here, the comparably lower values of the LFA-11 CORPUS certainly result from the fact that it represents a web crawl of blog posts and, hence, also contains completely irrelevant texts. Altogether, Fig. 4.6 suggests that the distribution of relevant information can and does vary significantly in all respects in practice.

Now, Table 4.1 lists the run-times per sentence of all algorithms in Π_{ENE}. Especially because of different average sentence lengths in the six corpora, the run-times do

---

[11]Notice that the employed named entity recognition algorithm, ENE, has been trained on the CoNLL-2003 datasets, which partly explains the high densities in these corpora.

Table 4.1 The average run-time t in milliseconds per sentence and its standard deviation σ for every algorithm in the pipeline $\Pi_{ENE} = (SSE, STO_2, TPO_1, PCH, ENE)$ on each evaluated text corpus. In the bottom line, the average of each algorithm's run-time is given together with the standard deviation from the average.

Text corpus	$t(SSE) \pm \sigma$	$t(STO_2) \pm \sigma$	$t(TPO_1) \pm \sigma$	$t(PCH) \pm \sigma$	$t(ENE) \pm \sigma$
BROWN CORPUS	$0.041 \pm .002$	$0.055 \pm .001$	$0.955 \pm .008$	$1.070 \pm .008$	$2.254 \pm .028$
CoNLL-2003 (en)	$0.031 \pm .003$	$0.042 \pm .000$	$0.908 \pm .010$	$0.893 \pm .011$	$1.644 \pm .003$
CoNLL-2003 (de)	$0.045 \pm .003$	$0.057 \pm .001$	$1.121 \pm .006$	$0.977 \pm .007$	$2.626 \pm .005$
WIKIPEDIA 10k (de)	$0.053 \pm .001$	$0.059 \pm .000$	$1.031 \pm .009$	$1.059 \pm .008$	$2.612 \pm .021$
REVENUE CORPUS	$0.041 \pm .002$	$0.050 \pm .001$	$0.927 \pm .004$	$0.917 \pm .006$	$2.188 \pm .005$
LFA-11 smartphone	$0.042 \pm .003$	$0.054 \pm .001$	$1.039 \pm .009$	$0.967 \pm .008$	$2.338 \pm .009$
Average	$\mathbf{0.042 \pm .007}$	$\mathbf{0.053 \pm .006}$	$\mathbf{0.997 \pm .081}$	$\mathbf{0.980 \pm .072}$	$\mathbf{2.277 \pm .360}$

vary, e.g. between 0.042 ms and 0.059 ms in case of STO_2. However, the standard deviations of the run-times averaged over all corpora (bottom line of Table 4.1) all lie in an area of about 5 % to 15 % of the respective run-time. Compared to the measured densities in the corpora, these variations are apparently small, which means that the algorithms' run-times are affected from the processed input only little.[12]

So, to summarize, the evaluated text corpora and information types suggest that the run-times of the algorithms used to infer relevant information tend to remain rather stable. At the same time, the resulting distributions of relevant information may completely change. In such cases, the practical relevance of the impact outlined above becomes obvious, since, at least for algorithms with similar run-times, the distribution of relevant information will directly decide the optimality of the schedule of the algorithms.[13]

4.2.4 Implications of the Impact

This section has made explicit that the distribution of relevant information in the input texts processed by a text analysis pipeline (equipped with the input control from Sect. 3.5) impacts the run-time optimal schedule of the pipeline's algorithms.

---

[12]Of course, there exist algorithms whose run-time per sentence will vary more significantly, namely, if the run-times scale highly overproportionally in the length of the processed sentences, such as for syntactic parsers. However, some of the algorithms evaluated here at least have quadratic complexity, indicating that the effect of sentence length is limited.

[13]The discussed example may appear suboptimal in the sense that our entity recognition algorithm ENE relies on STANFORD NER (Finkel et al. 2005), which classifies persons, locations, and organizations jointly and, therefore, does not allow for scheduling. However, we merely refer to the standard entity types for illustration purposes, since they occur in almost every collection of texts. Besides, notice that joint approaches generally conflict with the first step of an ideal pipeline design, maximum decomposition, as discussed in Sect. 3.1.

This distribution can vary significantly between different collections and streams of texts, as our experiments have indicated. In contrast, the average run-times of the employed algorithms remain comparably stable. As a consequence, it seems reasonable to rely on run-time estimations of the algorithms, when seeking for an efficient schedule.

For given run-time estimations, we have already introduced a greedy pipeline scheduling approach in Sect. 3.3, which sorts the employed algorithms (or filtering stages, to be precise) by their run-time in ascending order. Our experimental results in the section at hand, however, imply that the greedy approach will fail to construct a near-optimal schedule under certain conditions, namely, when the densities of the information types produced by faster algorithms are much higher than of those produced by slower algorithms. Since reasonable general estimates of the densities seem infeasible according to our analysis, we hence need a way to infer the distribution of relevant information from the given input texts, in cases where run-time efficiency is of high importance (and, thus, optimality is desired).

A solution for large-scale text mining scenarios is to estimate the selectivities of the employed algorithms from the results of processing a sample of input texts. For information extraction, samples have been shown to suffice for accurate selectivity estimations in narrow domains (Wang et al. 2011). Afterwards, we can obtain a schedule that is optimal with respect to the estimations of both the run-times and the selectivities using our adaptation of the VITERBI ALGORITHM from Sect. 4.1. More efficiently, we can also directly integrate the estimation of selectivities in the scheduling process by addressing optimal scheduling as an informed search problem (Russell and Norvig 2009). In particular, the VITERBI ALGORITHM can easily be transformed into an A* best-first search (Huang 2008), which in our case then efficiently processes the sample of input texts.

In the next section, we propose an according best-first search scheduling approach, which uses a heuristic that is based on the algorithms' run-time estimations. We provide evidence that it works perfectly as long as the distribution of relevant information does not vary significantly in different input texts. In other cases, a schedule should be chosen depending on the text at hand for maintaining efficiency, as we discuss in Sects. 4.4 and 4.5.

4.3 Optimized Scheduling via Informed Search

We now develop a practical approach to the pipeline scheduling problem from Sect. 3.1 for large-scale scenarios. The approach aims to efficiently determine the run-time optimal schedule of a set of text analysis algorithms for a collection or a stream of input texts. To this end, it processes a sample of texts in an informed best-first search manner (Russell and Norvig 2009), relying on run-time estimations of the algorithms. Our evaluation indicates that such an *optimized scheduling* robustly finds a near-optimal schedule on narrow-domain corpora. In terms of efficiency, it outperforms the greedy pipeline linearization from Sect. 3.3 among others. The idea behind has been sketched in Wachsmuth et al. (2013a), from which we reuse some content. While Melzner (2012) examines the use of informed search for pipeline scheduling in his master's thesis, we fully revise his approach here. As such, this section denotes a new contribution of the book at hand.

4.3.1 Modeling Pipeline Scheduling as a Search Problem

We consider the problem of scheduling an algorithm set $\mathbf{A}$ with a defined partial schedule $\tilde{\pi}$. $\tilde{\pi}$ explicitly defines all ordering constraints between the algorithms in $\mathbf{A}$ that follow from their input and output information types. This is the situation resulting from our algorithm selection approach in Sect. 3.3. There, we have argued that scheduling should take almost zero-time in case of *ad-hoc* text mining, where a fast response time is of upmost priority in terms of efficiency. In contrast, we here target at *large-scale* text mining, where we seek to process a potentially huge collection or stream of texts as fast as possible. Under this goal, we claim (and offer evidence later on) that it makes sense to perform scheduling on a sample of texts, given that only relevant portions of text are processed (as our input control from Sect. 3.5 ensures). Instead of a sample, we speak of an input text D in the following without loss of generality.[14] Section 4.1 has revealed that it will often be too expensive to actually compute the optimal schedule. Therefore, we propose to address scheduling as an informed search problem in order to efficiently obtain an at least near-optimal schedule.

The term *informed search* (also often called *heuristic search*) denotes a general and fundamental technique from artificial intelligence that aims at efficiently finding solutions to problems by exploiting problem-specific knowledge (Russell and Norvig 2009). Informed search stepwise generates the nodes of a directed acyclic *search graph*, in which leaf nodes define solutions, while each path from the graph's root node to a leaf prescribes how to solve the given problem.[15] Accordingly, nodes correspond to partial solutions, and edges to actions that solve subproblems. For many informed search problems, an edge is associated to a *step cost* of performing the respective action. The aggregation of all step costs involved in the generation of a node results in the *path cost* of the associated partial solution, which is called *solution cost* in case of leaf nodes. A leaf node with minimum solution cost hence represents the optimal solution to the tackled problem.

For scheduling, we define each solution to be a text analysis pipeline $\langle \mathbf{A}, \pi \rangle$ with an admissible schedule π (cf. Sect. 3.1). In this regard, an optimal solution for an input text D is given by the run-time optimal pipeline $\langle \mathbf{A}, \pi^* \rangle$ on D under all admissible pipelines based on $\mathbf{A}$. For informed search, we let each node with depth j in the associated search graph denote a partial pipeline $\langle \mathbf{A}^{(j)}, \pi^{(j)} \rangle$, where $\mathbf{A}^{(j)}$ is a subset

---

[14]The input text D may e.g. denote the concatenation of all texts from the sample.

[15]Depending on the tackled problem, not all leaf nodes represent solutions. Also, sometimes the path to a leaf node represents the solution and not the leaf node itself.

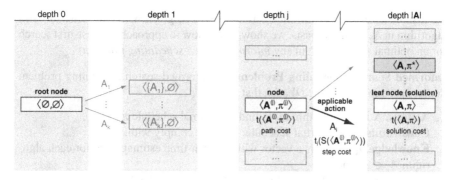

Fig. 4.7 Illustration of the nodes, actions, and costs of the complete search graph of the informed search for the optimal schedule π^* of an algorithm set **A**.

of **A** with j algorithms and $\pi^{(j)}$ is an admissible schedule. The graph's root is the empty pipeline $\langle \emptyset, \emptyset \rangle$, and each leaf a complete pipeline $\langle \mathbf{A}, \pi \rangle$. An edge represents the execution of an applicable algorithm $A_i \in \mathbf{A}$ on the currently relevant portions of D. Here, we define applicability exactly like in Sect. 4.1.[16] The run-time of A_i represents the step cost, while the path and solution costs refer to the run-times of partial and complete pipelines, respectively. Figure 4.7 illustrates all concepts in an abstract search graph. It imitates the trellis visualization from Fig. 4.3 in order to show the connection to the dynamic programming approach from Sect. 4.1.

However, the search graph will often be even much larger than the respective trellis (in terms of the number of nodes), since an algorithm set **A** can entail up to $|\mathbf{A}|$! admissible schedules. To efficiently find a solution, informed search aims to avoid to explore the complete search graph by following some *search strategy* that governs the order in which nodes of the search graph are generated.[17] The notion of being informed refers to the use of a *heuristic* within the search strategy. Such a heuristic relies on problem-specific or domain-specific knowledge specified beforehand, which can be exploited to identify nodes that may quickly lead to a solution. For scheduling, we consider one of the most common search strategies, named *best-first search*, which always generates the successor nodes of the node with the lowest *estimated solution cost* first. Best-first search operationalizes its heuristic in the form of a *heuristic function* $\mathcal{H}$, which estimates the cost of the cheapest path from a given node to a leaf node (Russell and Norvig 2009).

As mentioned above, the knowledge that we exploit for our heuristic consists in the average run-times of the employed algorithms, since the run-times tend to be rather stable among different collections or streams of texts (cf. Sect. 4.2). In particular,

---

[16]Again, we schedule single text analysis algorithms here for a less complex presentation. To significantly reduce the search space, it would actually be more reasonable to define the filtering stages from Sect. 3.1 as actions, as we propose in Wachsmuth et al. (2013a).

[17]In the given context, it is important not to confuse the efficiency of the search for a pipeline schedule and the efficiency of the schedule itself. Both are relevant, as both influence the overall efficiency of addressing a text analysis task. We evaluate their influence below.

we assume a vector $\mathbf{q}$ of run-time estimations to be given with one value for each algorithm in $\mathbf{A}$.[18] On this basis, we show below how to approach the best-first search for an optimal schedule π^* in any *informed search scheduling problem*:

Informed Search Scheduling Problem. An informed search scheduling problem denotes a 4-tuple $\langle \mathbf{A}, \tilde{\pi}, \mathbf{q}, D \rangle$ such that

1. **Actions.** $\mathbf{A}$ is an algorithm set to find an optimal schedule π^* for,
2. **Constraints.** $\tilde{\pi}$ is a partial schedule, π^* must comply with,
3. **Knowledge.** $\mathbf{q} \in \mathbb{R}^{|\mathbf{A}|}$ is a vector with one run-time estimation q_i for each algorithm $A_i \in \mathbf{A}$, and
4. **Input.** D is the input text, with respect to which π^* shall be optimal.

4.3.2 Scheduling Text Analysis Algorithms with k-best A* Search

The most widely used informed best-first search approach is *A* search*. A* search realizes the best-first search strategy by repeatedly performing two operations based on a so called *open list*, which contains all not yet expanded nodes, i.e., those nodes without generated successor nodes: First, it computes the estimated solution cost of all nodes on the open list. Then, it generates all successor nodes of the node with the minimum estimation. To estimate the cost of a solution that contains some node, A* search relies on an additive *cost function*, that sums up the path cost of reaching the node and the estimated cost from the node to a leaf node. The latter is obtained from the heuristic function $\mathscr{H}$. Given that $\mathscr{H}$ is *optimistic* (i.e., $\mathscr{H}$ never overestimates costs), it has been shown that the first leaf node generated by A* search denotes an optimal solution (Russell and Norvig 2009).

To adapt A* search for pipeline scheduling, we hence need a heuristic that, for a given partial pipeline $\langle \mathbf{A}^{(j)}, \pi^{(j)} \rangle$, optimistically estimates the run-time $t(\langle \mathbf{A}, \pi \rangle)$ of a complete pipeline $\langle \mathbf{A}, \pi \rangle$ that begins with $\langle \mathbf{A}^{(j)}, \pi^{(j)} \rangle$. As detailed in Sects. 3.1 and 4.1, a pipeline's run-time results from the run-times and the selectivities of the employed algorithms. While we can resort to the estimations $\mathbf{q}$ for the former, we propose to obtain information about the latter from processing an input text D. In particular, let $S(\tilde{\Pi})$ contain the relevant portions of D after executing a partial pipeline $\tilde{\Pi}$. Further, let $q(A)$ be the estimation of the average run-time per portion of text of an algorithm A in $\tilde{\Pi}$, and let $\mathbf{A}_i$ be the set of all algorithms that are applicable

---

[18]As in the method GREEDYPIPELINELINEARIZATION from Sect. 3.3, for algorithms without run-time estimations, we can at least rely on default values. GREEDYPIPELINELINEARIZATION can in fact be understood as a greedy best-first search whose heuristic function simply assigns the run-time estimation of the fastest applicable filtering stage to each node.

after $\tilde{\Pi}$. Then, we define the heuristic function $\mathcal{H}$ for estimating the cost of reaching a leaf node from some node $\tilde{\Pi}$ as:[19]

$$\mathcal{H}(\tilde{\Pi}, \mathbf{A}_i, \mathbf{q}) \;=\; |S(\tilde{\Pi})| \cdot \min\{q(A_i) \mid A_i \in \mathbf{A}_i\} \qquad (4.6)$$

The actually observed run-time $t(\tilde{\Pi})$ of $\tilde{\Pi}$ and the value of the heuristic function then sum up to the estimated solution cost $q(\tilde{\Pi})$. Similar to the dynamic programming approach from Sect. 4.1, we hence need to keep track of all run-times and filtered portions of text. By that, we implicitly estimate the selectivities of all algorithms in $\mathbf{A}$ on the input text D at each possible position in a pipeline based on $\mathbf{A}$.

Now, assume that each run-time estimation $q(A_i)$ is optimistic, meaning that the actual run-time $t_i(S(\tilde{\Pi}))$ of A_i exceeds $q(A_i)$ on all scopes $S(\tilde{\Pi})$. In this case, $\tilde{\Pi}$ is optimistic, too, because at least one applicable algorithm has to be executed on the remaining scope $S(\tilde{\Pi})$. In the end, however, the only way to guarantee optimistic run-time estimations consists in setting all of them to 0, which would render the defined heuristic $\mathcal{H}$ useless. Instead, we relax the need of finding an optimal schedule here to the need of optimizing the schedule with respect to the given run-time estimations $\mathbf{q}$. Consequently, the accuracy of the run-time estimations implies a tradeoff between the efficiency of the search and the efficiency of the determined schedule: The higher the estimations are set, the less nodes A* search will expand on average, but also the less probable it will return an optimal schedule, and vice versa. We analyze some of the effects of run-time estimations in the evaluation below.

Given an informed search scheduling problem $\langle \mathbf{A}, \tilde{\pi}, \mathbf{q}, D \rangle$ and the defined heuristic $\mathcal{H}$, we can apply A* search to find an optimized schedule. However, A* search may still be inefficient when the number of nodes on the open list with similar estimated solution costs becomes large. Here, this can happen for algorithm sets with many admissible schedules of similar efficiency. Each time a node is expanded, every applicable algorithm needs to process the relevant portions of text of that node, which may cause high run-times in case of computationally expensive algorithms. To control the efficiency of A* search, we introduce a parameter k that defines the maximum number of nodes to be kept on the open list. Such a k-best variant of A* search considers only the seemingly best k nodes for expansion, which improves efficiency while not guaranteeing optimality (with respect to the given run-time estimations) anymore.[20] In particular, k thereby provides another means to influence the efficiency-effectiveness tradeoff, as we also evaluate below. Setting k to ∞ yields a standard A* search.

---

[19]For simplicity, we assume here that there is one type of portions of text only (say, *Sentence*) without loss of generality. For other cases, we could distinguish between instances of the different types and respective run-time estimations in Eq. 4.6.

[20]k-best variants of A* search have already been proposed for other tasks in natural language processing, such as parsing (Pauls and Klein 2009).

K-BESTA*PIPELINESCHEDULING($\mathbf{A}, \tilde{\pi}, \mathbf{q}, D, k$)

  1: Pipeline Π_0 $\leftarrow \langle \emptyset, \emptyset \rangle$
  2: Scope $S(\Pi_0)$ $\leftarrow D$
  3: Run-time $t(\Pi_0)$ $\leftarrow 0$
  4: Algorithm set $\mathbf{A}_i$ $\leftarrow \{A_i \in \mathbf{A} \mid \nexists (A < A_i) \in \tilde{\pi}\}$
  5: Estimated run-time $q(\Pi_0) \leftarrow \mathscr{H}(\Pi_0, \mathbf{A}_i, \mathbf{q})$
  6: Pipelines $\boldsymbol{\Pi}_{\text{open}}$ $\leftarrow \{\Pi_0\}$

  7: **loop**
  8:    Pipeline $\langle \tilde{\mathbf{A}}, \pi^* \rangle \leftarrow \boldsymbol{\Pi}_{\text{open}}.\text{poll}(\arg\min_{\Pi \in \boldsymbol{\Pi}_{\text{open}}} (q(\Pi)))$
  9:    **if** $\tilde{\mathbf{A}} = \mathbf{A}$ **then return** $\langle \mathbf{A}, \pi^* \rangle$
10:    $\mathbf{A}_i \leftarrow \{A_i \in \mathbf{A} \setminus \tilde{\mathbf{A}} \mid \forall (A < A_i) \in \tilde{\pi}: A \in \tilde{\mathbf{A}}\}$
11:    **for each** Algorithm $A_i \in \mathbf{A}_i$ **do**
12:       Pipeline Π_i $\leftarrow \langle \tilde{\mathbf{A}} \cup \{A_i\}, \pi^* \cup \{(A < A_i) \mid A \in \tilde{\mathbf{A}}\}\rangle$
13:       Scope $S(\Pi_i)$ $\leftarrow S_i(S(\langle \tilde{\mathbf{A}}, \pi^* \rangle))$
14:       Run-time $t(\Pi_i)$ $\leftarrow t(\langle \tilde{\mathbf{A}}, \pi^* \rangle) + t_i(S(\langle \tilde{\mathbf{A}}, \pi^* \rangle))$
15:       Estimated run-time $q(\Pi_i) \leftarrow t(\Pi_i) + \mathscr{H}(\Pi_i, \mathbf{A}_i \setminus \{A_i\}, \mathbf{q})$
16:       $\boldsymbol{\Pi}_{\text{open}}$ $\leftarrow \boldsymbol{\Pi}_{\text{open}} \cup \{\Pi_i\}$
17:    **while** $|\boldsymbol{\Pi}_{\text{open}}| > k$ **do** $\boldsymbol{\Pi}_{\text{open}}.\text{poll}(\arg\max_{\Pi \in \boldsymbol{\Pi}_{\text{open}}} (q(\Pi)))$

Pseudocode 4.2: k-best variant of A* search for transforming a partially ordered text analysis pipeline $\langle \mathbf{A}, \tilde{\pi} \rangle$ into a pipeline $\langle \mathbf{A}, \pi^* \rangle$, which is nearly run-time optimal on the given input text D.

Pseudocode 4.2 shows our k-best A* search approach for determining an optimized schedule of an algorithm set $\mathbf{A}$ based on an input text D. The root node of the implied search graph refers to the empty pipeline Π_0 and to the complete input text $S(\Pi_0) = D$. Π_0 does not yield any run-time and, so, the estimated solution cost of Π_0 equals the value of the heuristic $\mathscr{H}$, which depends on the initially applicable algorithms in $\mathbf{A}_i$ (lines 1–5). Line 6 creates the set $\boldsymbol{\Pi}_{\text{open}}$ from Π_0, which represents the open list. In lines 7–17, the partial pipeline $\langle \tilde{\mathbf{A}}, \pi^* \rangle$ with the currently best estimated solution cost is iteratively polled from the open list (line 8) and expanded until it contains all algorithms and is, thus, returned. Within one iteration, line 10 first determines all remaining algorithms that are applicable after $\langle \tilde{\mathbf{A}}, \pi^* \rangle$ according to the partial schedule $\tilde{\pi}$. Each such algorithm A_i processes the relevant portions of text of $\langle \tilde{\mathbf{A}}, \pi^* \rangle$, thereby generating a successor node for the resulting pipeline Π_i and its associated portions of texts (lines 11–13).[21] The run-time and the estimated solution cost of Π_i are then updated, before Π_i is added to the open list (lines 14–16). After expansion, line 17 reduces the open list to the k currently best pipelines.[22]

---

[21] In the given pseudocode, we implicitly presume the use of the input control from Sect. 3.5, which makes the inclusion of filters (cf. Sect. 3.2) obsolete. Without an input control, applicable filters would need to be preferred in the algorithm set $\mathbf{A}_i$ for expansion over other applicable algorithms in order to maintain early filtering.

[22] Notice that, without line 17, Pseudocode 4.2 would correspond to a standard A* search approach that follows all possibly optimal search paths.

4.3.3 Properties of the Proposed Approach

The method K-BESTA*PIPELINESCHEDULING works irrespective of the algorithm set $\mathbf{A}$ to be applied and the input text D to be processed, given that an admissible total schedule can be derived from the partial schedule $\tilde{\pi}$ at all. While the impact of the method depends on the existence and exactness of the algorithms' run-time estimations, such estimations should often be easy to obtain according the observations made in Sect. 4.2.

Although our proposed approach to optimized scheduling applies to every pipeline $\langle \mathbf{A}, \tilde{\pi} \rangle$, the presented form of best-first search targets at pipelines that infer only a single set of information types $\mathbf{C}$ from input texts (similar to our optimal scheduling approach from Sect. 4.1). In particular, the heuristic in Eq. 4.6 implicitly assumes that there is one set of currently relevant portions of text only, which does not hold in tasks that refer to different information needs at the same time and respective disjunctive queries (cf. Sect. 3.4). To a wide extent, an extension of the heuristic to such tasks is straightforward, because the estimated costs on different portions of text simply sum up. However, it needs to account for cases where the minimum run-time estimation refers to an algorithm that produces information types for different information needs. This makes the resulting heuristic function quite complex and requires to be aware of the respective information needs underlying a given pipeline $\langle \mathbf{A}, \tilde{\pi} \rangle$, which is why we leave it out here for reasons of simplicity.

Similarly, our approach schedules single text analysis algorithms instead of complete filtering stages obtained from early filtering and lazy evaluation (cf. Sect. 3.1) merely to simplify the discussion. As already stated, a resort to filtering stages would, in general, allow for a more efficient search due to an often significantly reduced search space. In contrast, modeling the processed sample of texts as a single (concatenated) input text in fact proves beneficial, namely, it enables us to easily find the schedule that is fastest in total. If more than one text would be processed, different schedules might be found, which entails the additional problem of inferring the fastest schedule in total from the fastest schedules of all texts.

Correctness. Under the described circumstances, the standard A^* search variant of K-BEST A*PIPELINESCHEDULING (which emanates from setting k to ∞ or, alternatively, from skipping line 17 of Pseudocode 4.2) can be said to be correct in that it always finds an optimal solution, as captured by the following theorem. Like in the proof in Sect. 4.1, we refer to consistent algorithm sets without circular dependencies (cf. Sect. 3.3) here:[23]

Theorem 4.3. *Let* $\langle \mathbf{A}, \tilde{\pi}, \mathbf{q}, D \rangle$ *be an informed search scheduling problem with a consistent algorithm set* $\mathbf{A}$ *that has no circular dependencies. If all estimations in* $\mathbf{q}$ *are optimistic on each portion of the text* D, *then the pipeline* $\langle \mathbf{A}, \pi^* \rangle$ *returned by*

---

[23]Besides being correct, A^* search has also been shown to dominate other informed search approaches, meaning that it generates the minimum number of nodes to reach a leaf node (Russell and Norvig 2009). We leave out an according proof here for lack of relevance.

a call of K-BESTA*PIPELINESCHEDULING($\mathbf{A}$, $\tilde{\pi}$, $\mathbf{q}$, D, ∞) *is run-time optimal on* D *under all admissible pipelines based on* $\mathbf{A}$.

Proof. We only roughly sketch the proof, since the correctness of A* search has already often been shown in the literature (Russell and Norvig 2009). As clarified above, optimistic run-time estimations in $\mathbf{q}$ imply that the employed heuristic $\mathcal{H}$ is optimistic, too. When K-BESTA*PIPELINESCHEDULING returns a pipeline $\langle \mathbf{A}, \pi^* \rangle$ (pseudocode line 9), the estimated solution cost $q(\langle \mathbf{A}, \pi^* \rangle)$ of $\langle \mathbf{A}, \pi^* \rangle$ equals its run-time $t(\langle \mathbf{A}, \pi^* \rangle)$, as all algorithms have been applied. At the same time, no other pipeline on the open list has a lower estimated solution cost according to line 8. By definition of $\mathcal{H}$, all estimated solution costs are optimistic. Hence, no pipeline on the open list can entail a lower run-time than $\langle \mathbf{A}, \pi^* \rangle$, i.e., $\langle \mathbf{A}, \pi^* \rangle$ is optimal. Since algorithms from $\mathbf{A}$ are added to a pipeline on the open list in each iteration of the outer loop in Pseudocode 4.2, $\langle \mathbf{A}, \pi^* \rangle$ is always eventually found. □

Complexity. Given that K-BESTA*PIPELINESCHEDULING is correct, the question remains for what input sizes the effort of processing a sample of texts is worth spending in order to optimize the efficiency of a text analysis process. Naturally, this size depends on the efficiency of the method. Before we evaluate the method's run-time for different pipelines, collections of texts, and k-parameters, we derive its worst-case run-time in terms of the $\mathcal{O}$-calculus (Cormen et al. 2009) from its pseudocode. To this end, we again first consider A* search with k set to infinity.

Following the respective argumentation in Sect. 4.1, in the worst case the complete text D must be processed by each algorithm in $\mathbf{A}$, while all algorithms are always applicable and take exactly the same run-time $t_{\mathbf{A}}(D)$ on D. As a consequence, the schedule of a pipeline does not affect the pipeline's run-time and, so, the run-time is higher the longer the pipeline (i.e., the number of employed algorithms). Therefore, lines 7–17 generate the whole search graph except for the leaf nodes, because line 9 directly returns the pipeline of the first reached leaf node (which corresponds to a pipeline of length $|\mathbf{A}|$). Since all algorithms can always be applied, there are $|\mathbf{A}|$ pipelines of length 1, $|\mathbf{A}| \cdot (|\mathbf{A}| - 1)$ pipelines of length 2, and so forth. Hence, the number of generated nodes is

$$|\mathbf{A}| + |\mathbf{A}| \cdot (|\mathbf{A}| - 1) + \ldots + |\mathbf{A}| \cdot (|\mathbf{A}| - 1) \cdot \ldots \cdot 2 = \mathcal{O}(|\mathbf{A}|!) \qquad (4.7)$$

Mainly, a single node generation requires to measure the run-time of processing the input text as well as to estimate the remaining costs using the heuristic function $\mathcal{H}$. The latter depends on the number of algorithms in $\mathbf{A}_i$, which is bound by $|\mathbf{A}|$. Since $\mathcal{O}(|\mathbf{A}|!) \cdot |\mathbf{A}|$ is still $\mathcal{O}(|\mathbf{A}|!)$, the asymptotic worst-case run-time of K-BESTA*PIPELINESCHEDULING with $k = \infty$ is

$$t_{\text{A*PIPELINESCHEDULING}}(\mathbf{A}, D) = \mathcal{O}(|\mathbf{A}|! \cdot t_{\mathbf{A}}(D)) \qquad (4.8)$$

Avoiding this worst case is what the applied best-first search strategy aims for in the end. In addition, we can control the run-time with the parameter k. In particular,

k changes the products in Eq. 4.7. Within each product, the last factor denotes the number of possible expansions of a node of the respective length, while the multiplication of all other factors results in the number of such nodes to be expanded. This number is limited to k, which means that we can transform Eq. 4.7 into

$$|\mathbf{A}| + k \cdot (|\mathbf{A}| - 1) + \ldots + k \cdot 2 = \mathcal{O}\left(k \cdot |\mathbf{A}|^2\right) \qquad (4.9)$$

Like above, a single node generation entails costs that largely result from $t_\mathbf{A}(D)$ and at most $|\mathbf{A}|$. As a consequence, we obtain a worst-case run-time of

$$t_{\text{K-BESTA}^*\text{PIPELINESCHEDULING}}(\mathbf{A}, D) = \mathcal{O}\left(k \cdot |\mathbf{A}|^2 \cdot (t_\mathbf{A}(D) + |\mathbf{A}|)\right) \qquad (4.10)$$

In the following, we demonstrate how the run-time of optimized scheduling behaves in practice for different configurations.

4.3.4 Evaluation of Optimized Scheduling

We now evaluate our k-best A* search approach for optimized pipeline scheduling in different text analysis tasks related to our information extraction case study INFEXBA (cf. Sect. 2.3). In particular, on the one hand we explore in what scenarios the additional effort of processing a sample of input texts is worth being spent. On the other hand, we determine the conditions under which our approach achieves to find a run-time optimal pipeline based on a respective training set. Details on the source code used in the evaluation are given in Appendix B.4.

Corpora. As in Sect. 4.1, we conduct experiments on the REVENUE CORPUS described in Appendix C.1 and on the German dataset of the CoNLL-2003 SHARED TASK described in Appendix C.4. First, we process different samples of the training sets of these corpora for obtaining the algorithms' run-time estimations as well as for performing scheduling. Then, we execute the scheduled pipelines on the union of the respective validation and test sets in order to measure their run-time efficiency.

Queries. We consider three information needs of different complexity that we represent as queries in the form presented in Sect. 3.4:

$\gamma_1 = \textit{Financial(Money, Forecast(Time))}$
$\gamma_2 = \textit{Forecast(Time, Money, Organization)}$
$\gamma_3 = \textit{Forecast(Revenue(Resolved(Time), Money, Organization))}$

γ_1 and γ_2 have already been analyzed in Sects. 3.5 and 4.1, respectively. In contrast, we introduce γ_3 here, which we also rely on when we analyze efficiency under increasing heterogeneity of input texts in Sect. 4.5. γ_3 targets at revenue forecasts that contain resolvable time information, a money value, and an organization name. A simple example for such a forecast is *"Apple's annual revenues could hit $400* *billion by 2015"*. We require all information of an instance used to address any query to lie within a sentence, i.e., the degree of filtering is *Sentence* in all cases.

Pipelines. To address γ_1, γ_2, and γ_3, we assume the following pipelines to be given initially. They employ different algorithms from Appendix A:

$\Pi_1 = (\text{SSE}, \text{STO}_2, \text{TPO}_2, \text{ETI}, \text{EMO}, \text{RFO}, \text{RFI})$
$\Pi_2 = (\text{SSE}, \text{STO}_2, \text{TPO}_2, \text{PCH}, \text{ENE}, \text{EMO}, \text{ETI}, \text{RFO})$
$\Pi_3 = (\text{SSE}, \text{STO}_2, \text{TPO}_2, \text{PCH}, \text{ENE}, \text{EMO}, \text{ETI}, \text{NTI}, \text{RRE}_2, \text{RFO})$

Each pipeline serves as input to all evaluated approaches. The respective pipeline is seen as an algorithm set with a partial schedule, for which an optimized schedule can then be computed. The algorithms in Π_1 allow for only 15 different admissible schedules, whereas Π_2 entails 84, and Π_3 even 1638 admissible schedules.

Baselines. We compare our approach to three baseline approaches. All approaches are equipped with our input control from Sect. 3.5 and, thus, process only relevant portions of text in each analysis step. We informally define the three baselines by the rules they follow to obtain a schedule, when given a training set:

1. **Fixed baseline.** Do not process the training set at all. Remain with the schedule of the given text analysis pipeline.
2. **Greedy baseline.** Do not process the training set at all. Schedule the given algorithms according to their run-time estimation in an increasing and admissible order, as proposed in Sect. 3.3.
3. **Optimal baseline.** Process the training set with all possible admissible schedules by stepwise executing the given algorithms in a breadth-first search manner (Cormen et al. 2009). Choose the schedule that is most efficient on the training set.[24]

The standard baseline is used to highlight the general efficiency potential of scheduling when filtering is performed, while we analyze the benefit of processing a sample of texts in comparison to the greedy baseline. The last baseline is called "optimal", because it guarantees to find the schedule that is run-time optimal on a training set. However, its brute-force nature contrasts the efficient process of our informed search approach, as we see below.

Different from Chap. 3, we omit to construct filtering stages here (cf. Sect. 3.1), but we schedule the single text analysis algorithms instead. This may affect the efficiency of both the greedy baseline and our k-best A* search approach, thereby favoring the optimal baseline to a certain extent. Anyway, it enables us to simplify the analysis of the efficiency impact of optimized scheduling, which is our main focus in the evaluation.

Experiments. Below, we measure the absolute run-times of all approaches averaged over ten runs. We break these run-times down into the *scheduling time* on the training

---

[24]The optimal baseline generates the complete search graph introduced above. It can be seen as a simple alternative to the optimal scheduling approach from Sect. 4.1.

Table 4.2 Comparison between our 20-best A* search approach and the optimal baseline with respect to the scheduling time and execution time on the REVENUE CORPUS for each query γ and for five different numbers of training texts.

		20-best A* search		Optimal baseline	
γ	Training on	Scheduling time	Execution time	Scheduling time	Execution time
γ_1	1 text	**12.8 s** ± 0.1 s	13.7 s ± 0.8 s	14.3 s ± 0.1 s	**13.6 s** ± 0.5 s
	10 texts	**15.5 s** ± 0.1 s	13.5 s ± 0.3 s	18.3 s ± 0.0 s	**12.9 s** ± 0.1 s
	20 texts	**18.4 s** ± 0.2 s	12.7 s ± 0.3 s	22.3 s ± 0.1 s	**12.6 s** ± 0.3 s
	50 texts	**26.3 s** ± 0.6 s	**12.6 s** ± 0.3 s	37.0 s ± 0.4 s	**12.6 s** ± 0.2 s
	100 texts	**65.0 s** ± 1.3 s	13.2 s ± 0.2 s	117.3 s ± 3.3 s	**12.5 s** ± 0.2 s
γ_2	1 text	**20.4 s** ± 0.3 s	17.1 s ± 1.3 s	27.3 s ± 0.1 s	**16.5 s** ± 0.5 s
	10 texts	**25.0 s** ± 0.3 s	**15.1 s** ± 0.3 s	49.5 s ± 0.1 s	15.2 s ± 0.4 s
	20 texts	**30.6 s** ± 0.5 s	15.2 s ± 0.4 s	71.7 s ± 0.1 s	**15.0 s** ± 0.3 s
	50 texts	**44.0 s** ± 1.4 s	**14.7 s** ± 0.2 s	139.0 s ± 2.2 s	**14.7 s** ± 0.3 s
	100 texts	**98.4 s** ± 2.0 s	**15.7 s** ± 0.4 s	617.4 s ± 1.6 s	**15.7 s** ± 0.4 s
γ_3	1 text	**61.8 s** ± 0.6 s	**16.3 s** ± 0.8 s	448.1 s ± 6.2 s	17.6 s ± 0.7 s
	10 texts	**93.3 s** ± 1.5 s	15.9 s ± 0.8 s	824.9 s ± 8.7 s	**16.0 s** ± 0.5 s
	20 texts	**105.4 s** ± 2.7 s	15.7 s ± 0.3 s	1190.5 s ± 6.1 s	**15.5 s** ± 0.3 s
	50 texts	**169.4 s** ± 2.3 s	**15.4 s** ± 0.3 s	2488.6 s ± 10.9 s	16.9 s ± 0.8 s
	100 texts	**507.2 s** ± 10.4 s	**15.5 s** ± 0.3 s	15589.1 s ± 52.6 s	17.9 s ± 0.4 s

sets and the *execution time* on the combined validation and test sets in order to analyze and compare the efficiency of the approaches in detail. All experiments are conducted on a 2 GHz Intel Core 2 Duo Macbook with 4 GB memory.[25]

Efficiency Impact of k-best A* Search Pipeline Scheduling. First, we analyze the efficiency potential of scheduling a pipeline for each of the given queries with our k-best A* search approach in comparison to the optimal baseline. To imitate realistic circumstances, we use run-time estimations obtained on one corpus (the CoNLL-2003 dataset), but schedule and execute all pipelines on another one (the REVENUE CORPUS). Since it is not clear in advance, what number of training texts suffices to find an optimal schedule, we perform scheduling based on five different training sizes (with 1, 10, 20, 50, and 100 texts). In contrast, we delay the analysis of the parameter k of our approach to later experiments. Here, we set k to 20, which has reliably produced near-optimal schedules in some preliminary experiments.

Table 4.2 opposes the scheduling times and execution times of the two evaluated approaches as well as their standard deviations. In terms of scheduling time, the k-best

---

[25]Sometimes, both the optimal baseline and the informed search approaches return different pipelines in different runs of the same experiment. This can happen when the measured run-time of the analyzed pipelines are very close to each other. Since such behavior can also occur in practical applications, we simply average the run-times of the returned pipelines.

A* search approach significantly outperforms the optimal baseline for all queries and training sizes.[26] For γ_1, k exceeds the number of admissible schedules (see above), meaning that the approach equals a standard A* search. Accordingly, the gains in scheduling time appear rather small. Here, the largest difference is observed for 100 training texts, where informed search is almost two times as fast as the optimal baseline (65.0 vs. 117.3 s). However, this factor goes up to over 30 in case of γ_3 (e.g. 507.2 vs. 15589.1 s), which indicates the huge impact of informed search for larger search graphs. At the same time, it fully competes with the optimal baseline in finding the optimal schedule. Moreover, we observe that, on the REVENUE CORPUS, 20 training texts seem sufficient for finding a pipeline with a near-optimal execution time that deviates only slightly in different runs. We therefore restrict our view to this training size in the remainder of the evaluation.

Efficiency Impact of Optimized Scheduling. Next, we consider the question under what conditions it is worth spending the additional effort of processing a sample of input texts. In particular, we evaluate the method K-BESTA*PIPELINESCHEDULING for different values of the parameter k (1, 5, 10, 20, and 100) on the REVENUE CORPUS (with estimations obtained from the CoNLL-2003 dataset again) for all three queries. We measure the scheduling time and execution time for each configuration and compare them to the respective run-times of the three baselines.

Figure 4.8 shows the results separately for each query. At first sight, we see that the execution time of the fixed baseline is significantly worse than all other approaches in all cases, partly being even slower than the total time of both scheduling and execution of the k-best A* search approaches. In case of γ_1, the greedy baseline is about 13 % slower than the optimal baseline (14.2 vs. 12.6 s). In contrast, all evaluated k values result in the same execution time as the optimal baseline, indicating that the informed search achieves to find the optimal schedule.[27] Similar results are also observed for γ_2, except for much higher scheduling times. Consequently, 1-best A* search can be said to be most efficient with respect to γ_1 and γ_2, as it requires the lowest number of seconds for scheduling in both cases.

However, the results discussed so far render the processing of a sample of input texts for scheduling questionable, because the greedy baseline performs almost as good as the other approaches. The reason behind is that the run-times of the algorithms in Π_1 and Π_2 differ relatively more than the associated selectivities (on the REVENUE CORPUS). This situation turns out to be different for the algorithms in Π_3. For instance, the time resolver NTI is faster than some other algorithms (cf. Appendix A.2), but entails a very high selectivity, because of a low number of not resolvable time entities. In accordance with this fact, the bottom part of Fig. 4.8 shows that our approach clearly outperforms the greedy baselines when addressing query γ_3, e.g. by a factor of around 2 in case of $k = 20$ and $k = 100$. Also, it denotes an example where, the higher the value of k, the better the execution time of k-best A* search

---

[26]Partly, our approach improves over the baseline even in terms of execution time. This, however, emanates from a lower system load and not from finding a better schedule.

[27]Notice that the standard deviations in Fig. 4.8 reveal that the slightly better looking execution times of our k-best A* search approaches are not significant.

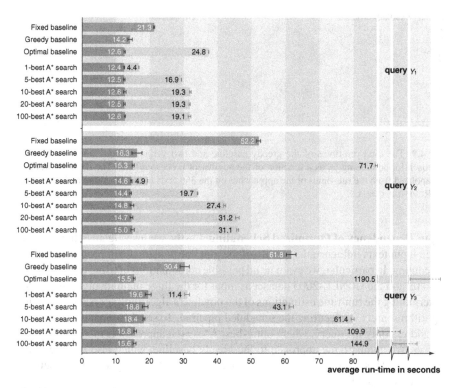

Fig. 4.8 Illustration of the execution times (medium colors, left) and the scheduling times (light colors, right) as well as their standard deviations (small black markers) of all evaluated approaches on the REVENUE CORPUS for each of the three addressed queries and 20 training texts (Color figure online).

(with respect to the evaluated values). This demonstrates the benefit of a real informed best-first search.

Still, it might appear unjustified to disregard the scheduling time when comparing the efficiency of the approaches. However, while we experiment with small text corpora, in fact we target at large-scale text mining scenarios. For these, Fig. 4.9 exemplarily extrapolates the total run-times of two k-best A* search approaches and the greedy baseline for γ_3, assuming that the run-times grow proportionally to those on the 366 texts of the validation and test set of the REVENUE CORPUS. Given 20 training texts, our approach actually saves time beginning at a number of 386 processed texts: There, the total run-time of 1-best A* search starts to be lower than the execution time of the greedy baseline. Later on, 5-best A* search becomes better, and so on. Consequently, our hypothesis already raised in Sect. 3.3 turns out to be true for this evaluation: Given that an information need must be addressed ad-hoc, a zero-time scheduling approach (like the greedy baseline) seems more reasonable, but when large amounts of text must be processed, performing scheduling based on a sample of texts is worth the effort.

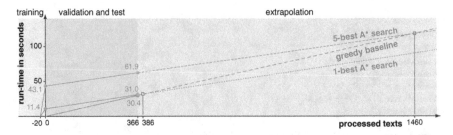

Fig. 4.9 The total run-times of the greedy baseline and two variants of our k-best A* search approach for addressing γ_3 as a function of the number of processed texts. The dashed parts are extrapolated from the run-times of the approaches on the 366 texts in the validation and test set of the REVENUE CORPUS.

Input Dependency of Optimized Scheduling. Lastly, we investigate in how far the given input texts influence the quality of the pipeline constructed through optimized scheduling. In particular, we evaluate all possible combinations of using the REVENUE CORPUS and the CoNLL-2003 dataset as input for the three main involved steps: (1) Determining the run-time estimations of the pipeline's algorithms, (2) scheduling the algorithms, and (3) executing the scheduled pipeline. To see the impact of the input, we address only the query, where our k-best A* search approach is most successful, i.e., γ_3. We compare the approach to the greedy baseline, which also involves step (1) and (3). This time, we leave both k and the number of training texts fixed, setting each of them to 20.

Table 4.3 lists the results for each corpus combination. A first observation matching our argumentation from Sect. 4.2 is that the efficiency impact of our approach remains stable under the different run-time estimations: The resulting execution times are exactly the same for the respective configurations on the CoNLL-2003 dataset and

Table 4.3 The average execution times in seconds with standard deviations of addressing the query γ_3 using the pipelines scheduled by our 20-best A* search approach and the greedy baseline depending on the corpora on which (1) the algorithms' run-time estimations are determined, (2) scheduling is performed (in case of 20-best A* search), and (3) the pipeline is executed.

Estimations on	Scheduling on	Execution on	20-best A* search	Greedy baseline
REVENUE	REVENUE	REVENUE	16.1 s ± 0.2 s	21.5 s ± 1.3 s
CoNLL-2003			**15.8 s ± 0.4 s**	30.4 s ± 1.3 s
REVENUE	CoNLL-2003		16.8 s ± 0.1 s	21.5 s ± 1.3 s
CoNLL-2003			17.0 s ± 0.2 s	30.4 s ± 1.3 s
REVENUE	REVENUE	CoNLL-2003	6.5 s ± 0.1 s	6.0 s ± 0.9 s
CoNLL-2003			6.5 s ± 0.1 s	8.2 s ± 0.5 s
REVENUE	CoNLL-2003		**5.1 s ± 0.0 s**	6.0 s ± 0.9 s
CoNLL-2003			**5.1 s ± 0.1 s**	8.2 s ± 0.5 s

are also very similar on the REVENUE CORPUS. In contrast, the greedy baseline is heavily affected by the estimations at hand. Overall, the execution times on the two corpora differ largely because only the REVENUE CORPUS contains many portions of text that are relevant for γ_3. The best execution times are 16.1 and 5.1 s, respectively, both achieved by the informed search approach. For the CoNLL-2003 dataset, however, we see that scheduling based on inappropriate training texts can have negative effects, as in the case of the REVENUE CORPUS, where the efficiency of 20-best A* search significantly drops from 5.1 to 6.5 s. In practice, this gets important when the input texts to be processed are heterogeneous, which we analyze in the following sections.

4.3.5 Discussion of Optimized Scheduling

This section has introduced our practical approach to optimize the schedule of a text analysis pipeline. Given run-time estimations of the employed algorithms, it aims to efficiently find a pipeline schedule that is run-time optimal on a sample of input texts. The approach can be seen as a modification of the dynamic programming approach from Sect. 4.1, which incrementally builds up and compares different schedules using informed best-first search. It is able to trade the efficiency of scheduling for the efficiency of the resulting schedule through a pruning of the underlying search graph down to a specified size k.

The presented realization of an informed best-first search in the method K-BEST-A*PIPELINESCHEDULING is far from optimized yet. Most importantly, it does not recognize nodes that are dominated by other nodes. E.g., if there are two nodes on the open list, which represent the partial pipelines (A_1, A_2) and (A_2, A_1), then we already know that one of these is more efficient for the two scheduled algorithms. A solution is to let nodes represent algorithm sets instead of pipelines, which works because all admissible schedules of an algorithm set entail the same relevant portions of text (cf. Sect. 3.1). In this way, the search graph becomes much smaller, still being a directed acyclic graph but not a tree anymore (as in our realization). Whereas we tested the efficiency of our approach against a breadth-first search approach (the optimal baseline), it would then be fairer to compete with the optimal solution from Sect. 4.1, which applies similar techniques. The efficiency of scheduling could be further improved by pruning the search graph earlier, e.g. by identifying very slow schedules on the first training texts (based on certain thresholds) and then ignoring them on the other texts. All such extensions are left to future work.

In our evaluation, the optimization of schedules has sped up pipelines by factor 4. When the employed algorithms differ more strongly in efficiency, even gains of more than one magnitude are possible, as exemplified in Sect. 3.1. Also, we have demonstrated that scheduling on a sample of texts provides large benefits over our greedy approach from Sect. 3.3, when the number of processed texts becomes large, which we focus on in this chapter. In contrast, as hypothesized in Chap. 3, the additional effort will often not be compensable in ad-hoc text mining scenarios.

While k-best A* search appears to reliably find a near-optimal schedule if the training and test texts are of similar kind, we have seen first evidence that the efficiency of the optimized schedules may significantly drop when the texts show variations, i.e., when the distribution of relevant information changes as discussed in Sect. 4.2. In the following, we consider situations where such changes are highly frequent, because the texts are of heterogeneous types or domains that cannot be fully anticipated. As a result, it does not suffice to choose a schedule based on a sample of texts, but we need to schedule algorithms depending on the text at hand.

4.4 The Impact of the Heterogeneity of Input Texts

The developed informed search approach appears perfectly appropriate to obtain efficient text analysis pipelines, when the distribution of relevant information in the input texts is rather stable. Conversely, in cases where the distribution significantly varies across texts, efficiency may be limited, because the optimality of a pipeline's schedule then depends on the input text at hand. In this section, we first outline effects of such *text heterogeneity* based on concrete examples. Then, we present a measure to quantify text heterogeneity and we compare the measure's behavior on different collections of texts. For that, we reuse a discussion from Wachsmuth et al. (2013b). Before we design an approach to maintain efficiency on heterogeneous texts in Sect. 4.5, we sketch how to decide in advance whether a fixed schedule suffices, partly based on considerations from Mex (2013).

4.4.1 Experimental Analysis of the Impact

To begin with, we exemplify possible efficiency effects caused by the variance of a collection or stream of texts regarding the distribution of relevant information. We have already seen differences between collections with respect to this distribution in Sect. 4.2. However, there may also be significant variations between the texts *within* a corpus, even in seemingly homogeneous narrow-domain corpora. To illustrate this, we refer to the experimental set-up from Sect. 4.1 again:

Algorithms and Corpora. We construct text analysis pipelines from the algorithm set $\mathbf{A} = \{$ETI, EMO, ENE, RFO$\}$ as well as some preprocessing algorithms that are always delayed according to the lazy evaluation paradigm from Sect. 3.1. These pipelines then process the training set of the CoNLL-2003 dataset or the REVENUE CORPUS, respectively (for more details, see Sect. 4.1).

Experiments. On each corpus, we measure the absolute run-times of all 12 admissible pipelines $\Pi_1, \ldots, \Pi_{12}$ based on $\mathbf{A}$, averaged over ten runs on a 2 GHz Intel Core 2 Duo MacBook with 4 GB memory (information on the source code is found in Appendix B.4). In addition, we count how often each pipeline performs best (on average) and we compare the pipelines' run-times to the *gold standard* (cf. Sect. 2.1), which we define here as the sum of the run-times that result from applying on each input text at hand the pipeline $\Pi^* \in \{\Pi_1, \ldots, \Pi_{12}\}$ that is most efficient on that text.

Optimality Under Heterogeneity. The results are listed in Table 4.4, ordered by the run-times on the CoNLL-2003 dataset. As known from Sect. 4.1, the pipeline (ETI, RFO, EMO, ENE) dominates the evaluation on the REVENUE CORPUS, taking only $t(\Pi_5) = 48.25$ s and being most efficient on 295 of the 752 texts. However, three other pipelines also do best on far more than a hundred texts. So, there is not one single optimal schedule at all. A similar situation can be observed for the CoNLL-2003 dataset, where the second fastest pipeline, Π_2, is still most efficient on 77 and the sixth fastest, Π_6, even on 96 of the 553 texts. While the best fixed pipeline, Π_1, performs well on both corpora, Π_2 and Π_6 fail to maintain efficiency on the REVENUE CORPUS, with e.g. Π_6 being almost 50% slower than the gold standard. Although the gold standard significantly outperforms all pipelines on both corpora at a very high confidence level (say, 3σ), the difference to the best fixed pipelines may seem acceptable. However, the case of Π_2 and Π_6 shows that a slightly different training set could have caused the optimized scheduling from Sect. 4.3 to construct a pipeline whose efficiency is not robust to changing distributions of relevant information. We

Table 4.4 The run-time $t(\Pi)$ with standard deviation σ of each admissible pipeline Π based on the given algorithm set **A** on both processed corpora in comparison to the gold standard. *#best* denotes the number of texts, Π is most efficient on.

Admissible pipeline Π	CoNLL-2003 dataset			REVENUE CORPUS		
	$t(\Pi)$	$\pm \sigma$	#best	$t(\Pi)$	$\pm \sigma$	#best
Π_1 = (ETI, EMO, RFO, ENE)	**18.17 s**	± 0.38 s	154	49.63 s	± 0.93 s	155
Π_2 = (ETI, EMO, ENE, RFO)	18.43 s	± 0.50 s	77	59.04 s	± 1.00 s	17
Π_3 = (EMO, ETI, RFO, ENE)	19.12 s	± 0.43 s	76	51.67 s	± 0.92 s	127
Π_4 = (EMO, ETI, ENE, RFO)	19.29 s	± 0.40 s	35	61.06 s	± 1.06 s	11
Π_5 = (ETI, RFO, EMO, ENE)	19.65 s	± 0.40 s	71	**48.25 s**	± 0.85 s	295
Π_6 = (EMO, ENE, ETI, RFO)	20.31 s	± 0.40 s	96	66.37 s	± 0.29 s	13
Π_7 = (ETI, RFO, ENE, EMO)	21.24 s	± 0.43 s	33	51.38 s	± 0.94 s	130
Π_8 = (ETI, ENE, RFO, EMO)	24.28 s	± 0.54 s	7	66.41 s	± 1.20 s	3
Π_9 = (ETI, ENE, EMO, RFO)	25.00 s	± 0.96 s	4	67.68 s	± 1.18 s	1
Π_{10} = (ENE, ETI, RFO, EMO)	49.74 s	± 0.98 s	0	97.25 s	± 1.63 s	0
Π_{11} = (ENE, ETI, EMO, RFO)	49.78 s	± 0.85 s	0	98.83 s	± 1.85 s	0
Π_{12} = (ENE, EMO, ETI, RFO)	50.05 s	± 1.09 s	0	99.61 s	± 1.61 s	0
gold standard	16.50 s	± 0.07 s	553	45.28 s	± 0.42 s	752

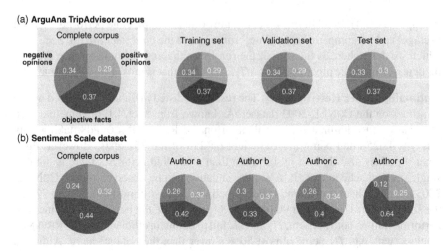

Fig. 4.10 Distribution of positive opinions, negative opinions, and objective facts in **a** our ARGUANA TRIPADVISOR CORPUS and its different parts as well as in **b** the SENTIMENT SCALE DATASET (Pang and Lee 2005) and its different parts. All distributions are computed based on the results of the pipeline (SSE, STO$_2$, TPO$_1$, PDU, CSB, CSP). See Appendices A and B.4 for details.

hypothesize that such a danger gets more probable the higher the text heterogeneity of a corpus.[28]

To deal with text heterogeneity, the question is whether and how we can anticipate it for a collection or a stream of texts. Intuitively, it appears reasonable to assume that text heterogeneity relates to the mixing of types, domains, or according text characteristics, as is typical for the results of an exploratory web search. However, the following example from text classification suggests that there is not only dimension that governs the heterogeneity. In text classification tasks, the information sought for is the final class information of each text. While the density of classes naturally will be 1.0 in all cases (given that different classes refer to the same information type), what may vary is the distribution of those information types that serve as input for the final classification. For instance, our sentiment analysis approach developed in the ARGUANA project (cf. Sect. 2.3) relies on the facts and opinions in a text. For our ARGUANA TRIPADVISOR CORPUS (cf. Appendix C.2) and for the SENTIMENT SCALE DATASET from Pang and Lee (2005), we illustrate the distribution of these types in Fig. 4.10.[29]

---

[28]Also, larger numbers of admissible schedules make it harder to find a robust pipeline, since they allow for higher efficiency gaps, as we have seen in the evaluation of Sect. 4.3.

[29]In Wachsmuth et al. (2014a), we observe that the distributions and positions of facts and opinions influence the *effectiveness* of sentiment analysis. As soon as a pipeline restricts some analysis to certain portions of text only (say, to positive opinions), however, the different distributions will also impact the efficiency of the pipeline's schedule.

As can be seen, the distribution of relevant information in the ARGUANA TRI-PADVISOR CORPUS remains nearly identical among its three parts.[30] The corpus compiles texts of the same type (user reviews) and domain (hotel), but different topics (hotels) and authors, suggesting that the type and domain play a more important role. This is supported by the different densities of facts, positive, and negative opinions in the SENTIMENT SCALE DATASET, which is comprised of more professional reviews from the film domain.[31] However, the four parts of the SENTIMENT SCALE DATASET show a high variation. Especially the distribution of facts and opinions in *Author d* deviates from the others, so the writing style of the texts seems to matter, too. We conclude that it does not suffice to know the discussed characteristics for a collection or a stream of texts in order to infer its heterogeneity. Instead, we propose to quantify the differences between the input texts as follows.

4.4.2 Quantification of the Impact

Since we consider text heterogeneity with the aim of achieving an efficient text analysis irrespective of the input texts at hand, we propose to quantify text heterogeneity with respect to the differences that actually impact the efficiency of a text analysis pipeline equipped with our input control from Sect. 3.5, namely, variations in the distribution of information relevant for the task at hand (as revealed in Sect. 4.2). That means, we see text heterogeneity as a task-dependent input characteristic.

In particular, we measure the heterogeneity of a collection or a stream of input texts D here with respect to the densities of all information types $C_1, \ldots, C_{|C|}$ in D that are referred to in an information need C. The reason is that an input-controlled pipeline analyzes only portions of text, which contain instances of all information types produced so far (cf. Sect. 3.5). As a consequence, differences in a pipeline's average run-time per portion of text result from varying densities of $C_1, \ldots, C_{|C|}$ in the processed texts.[32] So, the text heterogeneity of D can be quantified by measuring the variance of these densities in C. The outlined considerations give rise to a new measure that we call the *averaged deviation*:

Averaged Deviation. Let $C = \{C_1, \ldots, C_{|C|}\}$ be an information need to be addressed on a collection or a stream of input texts D, and let $\sigma_i(D)$ be the

---

[30] Since the distributions are computed based on the self-created annotations here, the values for the ARGUANA TRIPADVISOR CORPUS differ from those in Appendix C.2.

[31] In the given case, the density and relative frequency of each information type (cf. Sect. 4.2) are the same, since the information types define a partition of all portions of text.

[32] Notice that even without an input control the number of instances of the relevant information types can affect the efficiency, as outlined at the beginning of Sect. 4.2. However, the density of information types might not be the appropriate measure in this case.

standard deviation of the density of $C_i \in \mathbf{C}$ in $\mathbf{D}$, $1 \leq i \leq |\mathbf{C}|$. Then, the averaged deviation of $\mathbf{C}$ in $\mathbf{D}$ is

$$\mathscr{D}(\mathbf{C}|\mathbf{D}) \quad = \quad \frac{1}{|\mathbf{C}|} \cdot \sum_{i=1}^{|\mathbf{C}|} \sigma_i(\mathbf{D}) \qquad\qquad (4.11)$$

Given a text analysis task, the averaged deviation can be estimated based on a sample of texts. Different from other sampling-based approaches for efficiency optimizations, like (Wang et al. 2011), it does *not* measure the typical characteristics of input texts, but it quantifies how much these characteristics vary. By that, the averaged deviation reflects the impact of the input texts to be processed by a text analysis pipeline on the pipeline's efficiency, namely, the higher the averaged deviation, the more the optimal pipeline schedule will vary on different input texts.

To illustrate the defined measure, we refer to *Person*, *Location*, and *Organization* entities again, for which we have presented the densities in two English and four German text corpora in Sect. 4.2. Now, we determine the standard deviations of these densities in order to compute the associated averaged deviations (as always, see Appendix B.4 for the source code). Table 4.5 lists the results, ordered by increasing averaged deviation.[33] While the deviations behave quite orthogonal to the covered topics and genres, they seem connected to the quality of the texts in a corpus to some extent. Concretely, the REVENUE CORPUS and BROWN CORPUS (both containing a carefully planned choice of texts) show less heterogeneity than the random sample of WIKIPEDIA articles and much less than the LFA-11 web crawl of smartphone blog posts. This matches the intuition of web texts being heterogeneous. An exception is given by the values of the CoNLL-2003 datasets, though, which rather suggest that high deviations correlate with high densities (cf. Fig. 4.5). However, the LFA-11 corpus contradicts this, having the lowest densities but the second highest averaged deviation (18.4 %).

Altogether, the introduced measure does not clearly reflect any of the text characteristics discussed above. For efficiency purposes, it therefore serves as a proper solution to compare the heterogeneity of different collections or streams of texts with respect to a particular information need. In contrast, it does not help to investigate our hypothesis that the danger of losing efficiency grows under increasing text heterogeneity, because it leaves unclear what a concrete averaged deviation value actually means. For this purpose, we need to estimate how much run-time is wasted by relying on a text analysis pipeline with a fixed schedule.

---

[33] Some of the standard deviations of organization entities in Table 4.5 and the associated averaged deviations exceed those presented in Wachsmuth et al. (2013c). This is because there we use a modification of the algorithm ENE, which rules out some organization names.

Table 4.5 The standard deviations of the densities of person, organization, and location entities from Fig. 4.5 (cf. Sect. 4.2) as well as the resulting averaged deviations, which quantify the text heterogeneity in the respective corpora. All values are computed based on the results of the pipeline $\Pi_{\text{ENE}} = (\text{SSE}, \text{STO}_2, \text{TPO}_1, \text{PCH}, \text{ENE})$.

Text corpus	Topics	Genres	Person entities	Organization entities	Location entities	Averaged deviation
REVENUE CORPUS	focused	one	±11.1%	±16.0%	±10.9%	**12.7%**
BROWN CORPUS	diverse	diverse	±17.6%	±11.1%	±12.7%	**13.8%**
WIKIPEDIA 10k (de)	diverse	one	±15.9%	±14.1%	±16.0%	**15.3%**
CoNLL-2003 (de)	diverse	one	±18.4%	±18.1%	±16.6%	**17.7%**
LFA-11 smartphone	focused	one	±16.6%	±23.4%	±15.3%	**18.4%**
CoNLL-2003 (en)	diverse	diverse	±27.6%	±25.5%	±26.8%	**26.7%**

4.4.3 Practical Relevance of the Impact

For a single input text, our optimal solution from Sect. 4.1 determines the run-time optimal text analysis pipeline. However, most practical text analysis tasks require to process many input texts, which may entail different optimal pipelines, as the conducted experiments have shown. For this reason, we now develop an estimation of the efficiency loss of executing a pipeline with a fixed schedule on a collection or a stream of input texts as opposed to choosing the best pipeline schedule for each input text. The latter denotes the gold standard defined above.

To estimate the gold standard run-time, we adopt an idea from the master's thesis of Mex (2013) who analyzes the efficiency-effectiveness tradeoff of scheduling multi-stage classifiers. Such classifiers can be seen as a generalization of text analysis pipelines (for single information needs) to arbitrary classification problems. Mex (2013) sketches a method to compare the efficiency potential of different scheduling approaches in order to choose the approach whose potential lies above some threshold. While this method includes our estimation, we greatly revise the descriptions from Mex (2013) in order to achieve a simpler but also a more formal presentation.

We estimate the efficiency impact induced by text heterogeneity on a sample of texts $\mathbf{D}$ for a given algorithm set $\mathbf{A} = \{A_1, \ldots, A_m\}$. Technically, the impact can be understood as the difference between the run-time $t^*(\mathbf{D})$ of an optimal (fixed) pipeline $\Pi^* = \langle \mathbf{A}, \pi^* \rangle$ on $\mathbf{D}$ and the run-time $t_{\text{GS}}(\mathbf{D})$ of the gold standard GS. While we can measure the run-time of an (at least nearly) optimal pipeline using our scheduling approach from Sect. 4.3, the question is how to compute $t_{\text{GS}}(\mathbf{D})$. To actually obtain GS, we would need to determine the optimal pipeline for each single text in $\mathbf{D}$. In contrast, its run-time can be found much more efficiently, as shown in the following. For conciseness, we restrict our view to algorithm sets that have no interdependencies, meaning that all schedules of the algorithms are admissible. For other cases, a similar

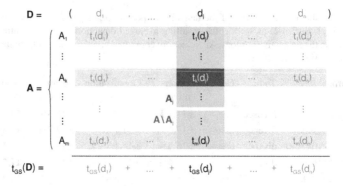

Fig. 4.11 Illustration of the computation of the gold standard run-time $t_{GS}(\mathbf{D})$ of an algorithm set $\mathbf{A} = \{A_1, \ldots, A_m\}$ on a sample of portions of texts $\mathbf{D} = (d_1, \ldots, d_n)$ for the simplified case that the algorithms in $\mathbf{A}$ have no interdependencies.

but more complex computation can be conducted by considering filtering stages (cf. Sect. 3.1) instead of single algorithms.

Now, to compute the run-time of GS for an algorithm set $\mathbf{A}$ without interdependencies, we consider the sample $\mathbf{D}$ as an ordered set of $n \geq 1$ portions of text $(d_1, \ldots, d_n)$. We process every $d_j \in \mathbf{D}$ with each algorithm $A_i \in \mathbf{A}$ in order to measure the run-time $t_i(d_j)$ of A_i on d_j and to determine whether A_i classifies d_j as relevant (i.e., whether d_j contains all required output information produced by A_i). As we know from Sect. 4.2, a portion of text can be disregarded as soon as an applied algorithm belongs to the subset $\mathbf{A}_j \subseteq \mathbf{A}$ of algorithms that classify d_j as irrelevant. Thus, we obtain the gold standard's run-time $t_{GS}(d_j)$ on d_j from only applying the fastest algorithm $A_k \in \mathbf{A}_j$, if such an algorithm exists:

$$t_{GS}(d_j) = \begin{cases} \min \{t_k(d_j) \mid A_k \in \mathbf{A}_j\} & \text{if } \mathbf{A}_j \neq \emptyset \\ \sum_{k=1}^{m} t_k(d_j) & \text{otherwise} \end{cases} \qquad (4.12)$$

As a matter of fact, the overall run-time of the gold standard on the sample of texts $\mathbf{D}$ results from summing up all run-times $t_{GS}(d_j)$:

$$t_{GS}(\mathbf{D}) = \sum_{j=1}^{n} t_{GS}(d_j) \qquad (4.13)$$

The computation of $t_{GS}(\mathbf{D})$ is illustrated in Fig. 4.11. Given $t_{GS}(\mathbf{D})$ and the optimal pipeline's run-time $t^*(\mathbf{D})$, we finally estimate the efficiency impact of text heterogeneity in the collection or stream of texts represented by the sample $\mathbf{D}$ as the fraction of run-time that can be saved through scheduling the algorithms depending on the input text, i.e., $1 - t^*(\mathbf{D})/t_{GS}(\mathbf{D})$.[34]

4.4.4   Implications of the Impact

In many text analysis tasks, the greedy scheduling approach from Sect. 3.3 and the optimized scheduling approach from Sect. 4.3 will successfully construct very efficient text analysis pipelines. However, the experiments in this section indicate that text heterogeneity can cause a significant efficiency loss, when relying on a pipeline with a fixed schedule. Moreover, performing scheduling on heterogeneous texts involves the danger of choosing a far from optimal schedule in the first place. We suppose that this danger becomes especially important where input texts come from different sources as in the world wide web. Moreover, streams of texts can undergo substantial changes, which may affect the distribution of relevant information and, hence, the efficiency of an employed pipeline.

In order to detect heterogeneity, we have introduced the averaged deviation as a first measure that quantifies how much input texts vary. While the measure reveals differences between collections and streams of texts, its current form (as given in Eq. 4.11) leaves unclear how to compare averaged deviation values across different information needs. One possible solution is to normalize the values. Such a normalization could work either in an external fashion with respect to a reference corpus or in an internal fashion with respect to the tackled task, e.g. to a situation where all admissible schedules of the given algorithms achieve the same efficiency. Here, we have taken another approach, namely, we have developed an estimation of the efficiency loss of tackling text analysis tasks with a fixed pipeline.

To put it the other way round, the estimated efficiency loss represents the optimization potential of choosing the schedule of a pipeline depending on the input text at hand. On this basis, a pipeline designer can decide whether it seems worth spending the additional effort of realizing such an adaptive scheduling. In the next section, we first present an according approach. Then, we evaluate the importance of adaptive scheduling for maintaining efficiency under increasing text heterogeneity.

4.5   Adaptive Scheduling via Self-supervised Online Learning

To maintain efficiency on heterogeneous collections and streams of input texts, we now present another approach to pipeline scheduling for large-scale scenarios. The

---

[34]In cases where performing an optimized scheduling in the first place seems too expensive, also $t^*(\mathbf{D})$ could be approximated from the run-times modeled in Fig. 4.11, e.g. by computing a weighted average of some lower bound $t(\text{LB})$ and upper bound $t(\text{UB})$. For instance, $t(\text{LB})$ could denote the lowest possible run-time when the first j algorithms of Π^* are fixed and $t(\text{LB})$ the highest on. The weighting then may follow from the average number of algorithms in $\mathbf{A}_j$. For lack of new insights, we leave out according calculations here.

idea is to adapt a pipeline to the input texts by predicting and choosing the run-time optimal schedule depending on the text. Since run-times can be measured during processing, the prediction can be learned self-supervised (cf. Sect. 2.1). Learning in turn works online, because each processed text serves as a new training instance (Witten and Frank 2005). We conduct several experiments in order to analyze when the approach is necessary in the sense of this chapter's introductory Darwin quote, i.e., when it avoids wasting a significant amount of time (by using a fixed schedule only). This section reproduces the main contributions from Wachsmuth et al. (2013b) but it also provides several additional insights.

4.5.1 Modeling Pipeline Scheduling as a Classification Problem

Given a collection or a stream of input texts $\mathbf{D}$ to be processed by an algorithm set $\mathbf{A}$, we aim for an *adaptive scheduling* of $\mathbf{A}$, which automatically determines and chooses the run-time optimal pipeline $\Pi^{*(D)} = \langle \mathbf{A}, \pi^{*(D)} \rangle$ for each input text $D \in \mathbf{D}$. Again, we refer to pipelines here that analyze only relevant portions of text, implying that a pipeline's schedule affect the pipeline's efficiency (cf. Sect. 4.1). Let $\Pi = \{\Pi_1, \ldots, \Pi_k\}$ be the set of candidate pipelines to choose from. Then our aim is to find a mapping $\mathbf{D} \to \Pi$ that minimizes the overall run-time of $\mathbf{A}$ on $\mathbf{D}$. I.e., we see pipeline scheduling as a text classification problem (cf. Sect. 2.1).

In this regard, the number of classes k has a general upper bound of $|\mathbf{A}|!$. To maximize the effectiveness of $\mathbf{A}$ on the information needs it addresses, however, we again consider only admissible pipelines (where the input constraints of all algorithms are met), as defined in Sect. 3.1. Moreover, there are possible ways to restrict Π to a reasonable selection. For instance, the results from the previous sections suggest that it e.g. may make sense to first determine optimized pipelines for different samples of input texts and then let each of these become a candidate pipeline. In the following, we simply expect some $k \leq |\mathbf{A}|!$ candidate pipelines to be given.

Now, the determination of an optimal pipeline $\Pi^{*(D)} \in \Pi$ for an input text $D \in \mathbf{D}$ requires to have information about D. For text classification, we represent this information in the form of a feature vector $\mathbf{x}$ (cf. Sect. 2.1). Before we can find $\mathbf{D} \to \Pi$, we therefore need a mapping $\mathbf{D} \to \mathbf{x}$, which in turn requires a preceding analysis of the texts in $\mathbf{D}$.[35] Let $\Pi_{pre} = \langle \mathbf{A}_{pre}, \pi_{pre} \rangle$ be the pipeline that realizes this text analysis. For distinction, we call Π_{pre} the *prefix pipeline* and each $\Pi \in \Pi$ a *main pipeline*. Under the premise that all algorithms from $\mathbf{A}_{pre} \cap \mathbf{A}$ have been removed from the main pipelines, the prefix pipeline can be viewed as the fixed first part of an overall pipeline, while each main pipeline denotes one of the possible second parts. The results of Π_{pre} for an input text $D \in \mathbf{D}$ lead to the feature values $\mathbf{x}^{(D)}$, which can then be used to choose a main pipeline $\Pi \in \Pi$ for D.

---

[35]We discuss the question what information to use and what features to compute later on.

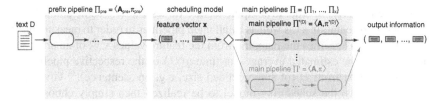

Fig. 4.12 Illustration of pipeline scheduling as a text classification problem. Given the results of a *prefix pipeline*, a learned *scheduling model* chooses one *main pipeline* for the input text D at hand.

Concretely, we propose to realize the mapping from feature values to main pipelines as a statistical model obtained through machine learning on a set of training texts $\mathbf{D}_T$. The integration of such a *scheduling model* into the overall pipeline is illustrated in Fig. 4.12. We formalize our aim of finding a mapping $\mathbf{D} \rightarrow \boldsymbol{\Pi}$ as an *adaptive scheduling problem*:

Adaptive Scheduling Problem. An adaptive scheduling problem denotes a 4-tuple $\langle \Pi_{pre}, \boldsymbol{\Pi}, \mathbf{D}_T, \mathbf{D} \rangle$ such that

1. **Prefix pipeline.** Π_{pre} is a pipeline to process each input text with,
2. **Main pipelines.** $\boldsymbol{\Pi}$ is a set of pipelines based on the same algorithm set, of which one is to be chosen to process each input text after Π_{pre},
3. **Training Set.** $\mathbf{D}_T$ is a set of texts for learning a scheduling model that maps a text to the main pipeline to be chosen for that text,
4. **Input.** $\mathbf{D}$ is a collection or a stream of texts to apply the model to.

4.5.2 Learning to Predict Run-Times Self-supervised and Online

The standard approach to address a text classification problem is to learn a classifier in a supervised manner on known training instances, i.e., on texts with known class values (cf. Sect. 2.1). Often, the creation of an according training set $\mathbf{D}_T$ requires a manual labeling of class values, making supervised learning cost-intensive. An adaptive scheduling problem consists in the prediction of the main pipelines with the lowest *run-times*, though. These run-times can be measured automatically, namely, by observing the execution of the pipelines. In case input texts are available, this enables the resort to self-supervised learning, which means to generate and learn from training instances without supervision (cf. Sect. 2.1), thus rendering manual labeling obsolete. Moreover, run-times denote numeric values from a metric scale. Instead of classifying the optimal schedule, we therefore propose to address adaptive scheduling problems with self-supervised statistical regression (cf. Sect. 2.1).

In particular, given a problem $\langle \Pi_{pre}, \boldsymbol{\Pi}, \mathbf{D}_T, \mathbf{D} \rangle$, we propose to learn one *regression model* $\mathscr{Y}(\Pi)$ on $\mathbf{D}_T$ for each main pipeline $\Pi \in \boldsymbol{\Pi}$. To this end, all texts in $\mathbf{D}_T$

are processed by Π_{pre} in order to compute feature values $\mathbf{x}^{(D)}$ (for some defined feature vector representation $\mathbf{x}$) as well as by all main pipelines in order to measure their run-times. $\mathscr{Y}(\Pi)$ specifies the mapping from the feature values $\mathbf{x}^{(D)}$ of an arbitrary input text D to the estimated average run-time $q(\Pi)$ of the respective pipeline Π per portion of text from D (of some defined size, e.g. one sentence).[36] Given the regression models, the scheduling model to be realized then simply chooses the main pipeline with the lowest prediction for each input text from $\mathbf{D}$.

A positive side effect of the self-supervised approach is that the feature values $\mathbf{x}^{(D)}$ of each input text D together with the observed run-time $t(\Pi)$ of a pipeline Π that processes D serve as a new training instance. Accordingly, the regression error is given by the difference between $q(\Pi)$ and $t(\Pi)$. As a consequence, the regression models can be updated in an *online learning* manner, incrementally processing and learning from one training instance at a time (Witten and Frank 2005). This, of course, works only for the regression model of the chosen pipeline $\Pi^{*(D)}$ whose run-time has been observed. Only an explicit training set $\mathbf{D}_T$ thus ensures that all regression models are trained sufficiently.[37] Still, the ability to continue learning online is desired, as it enables our approach not only to adapt to $\mathbf{D}_T$, but also to the collection or stream of input texts $\mathbf{D}$ while processing it.

4.5.3 Adapting a Pipeline's Schedule to the Input Text

Our considerations of addressing an adaptive scheduling problem $\langle \Pi_{pre}, \mathbf{\Pi}, \mathbf{D}_T, \mathbf{D} \rangle$ with self-supervised online learning allow us to adapt the schedule of a set of algorithms $\mathbf{A}$ to each processed input text. We operationalize the outlined approach in two phases:

1. **Training Phase.** On each text $D \in \mathbf{D}_T$, execute the prefix pipeline Π_{pre} and each main pipeline $\Pi \in \mathbf{\Pi}$. Update the regression model of each Π with respect to the results of Π_{pre} and the run-time $t(\Pi)$ of Π on D.
2. **Update Phase.** On each text $D \in \mathbf{D}$, execute Π_{pre} and predict a run-time $q(\Pi)$ for each $\Pi \in \mathbf{\Pi}$. Execute the main pipeline $\Pi^{*(D)}$ with the lowest prediction and update its regression model with respect to the results of Π_{pre} and the observed run-time $t(\Pi^{*(D)})$ of $\Pi^{*(D)}$ on D.

Pseudocode 4.3 shows our adaptive pipeline scheduling approach. Lines 1 and 2 initialize the regression model $\mathscr{Y}(\Pi)$ of each main pipeline Π. All regression models are then trained incrementally on each input text $D \in \mathbf{D}_T$ in lines 3–8. First, feature values are computed based on the results of Π_{pre} (lines 3 and 4). Then, the run-times

---

[36]By considering the run-time *per portion of text* (say, per sentence), we make the regression of a run-time independent from the length of the input text D at hand.

[37]In the evaluation below, the training set $\mathbf{D}_T$ simply constitutes a sample from $\mathbf{D}$.

ADAPTIVEPIPELINESCHEDULING(Π_{pre}, $\mathbf{\Pi}$, $\mathbf{D}_T$, $\mathbf{D}$)

1: **for each** Main Pipeline $\Pi \in \mathbf{\Pi}$ **do**
2:    Regression model $\mathscr{Y}(\Pi)$ ← INITIALIZEREGRESSIONMODEL()

3: **for each** Input text $D \in \mathbf{D}_T$ **do**
4:    Π_{pre}.process(D)
5:    Feature values $\mathbf{x}^{(D)}$ ← COMPUTEFEATUREVALUES(Π_{pre}, D)
6:    **for each** Main Pipeline $\Pi \in \mathbf{\Pi}$ **do**
7:      Run-time $t(\Pi)$ ← Π.process(D)
8:      UPDATEREGRESSIONMODEL($\mathscr{Y}(\Pi)$, $\mathbf{x}^{(D)}$, $t(\Pi)$)

9: **for each** Input text $D \in \mathbf{D}$ **do**
10:    Π_{pre}.process(D)
11:    Feature values $\mathbf{x}^{(D)}$ ← COMPUTEFEATUREVALUES(Π_{pre}, D)
12:    **for each** Main Pipeline $\Pi \in \mathbf{\Pi}$ **do**
13:      Estimated run-time $q(\Pi)$ ← $\mathscr{Y}(\Pi)$.predictRunTime($\mathbf{x}^{(D)}$)
14:    Main pipeline $\Pi^{*(D)}$ ← $\arg\min_{\Pi \in \mathbf{\Pi}} \left(q(\Pi) \right)$
15:    Run-time $t(\Pi^{*(D)})$ ← $\Pi^{*(D)}$.process(D)
16:    UPDATEREGRESSIONMODEL($\mathscr{Y}(\Pi^{*(D)})$, $\mathbf{x}^{(D)}$, $t(\Pi^{*(D)})$)

Pseudocode 4.3: Learning the fastest main pipeline $\Pi^{*(D)} \in \mathbf{\Pi}$ self-supervised for each input text D from a training set $\mathbf{D}_T$ and then predicting and choosing $\Pi^{*(D)}$ depending on the input text $D \in \mathbf{D}$ at hand while continuing learning online.

of all main pipelines on D are measured in order to update their regression models. Lines 9 to 16 process the input texts in $\mathbf{D}$. After feature computation (lines 9 and 10), the regression models are applied to obtain a run-time estimation $q(\Pi)$ for each main pipeline Π on the current input text D (Lines 11 to 13). The fastest-predicted main pipeline $\Pi^{*(D)}$ is then chosen to process D in lines 14 and 15. Finally, line 16 updates the regression model $\mathscr{Y}(\Pi^{*(D)})$ of $\Pi^{*(D)}$.

4.5.4 Properties of the Proposed Approach

Like the scheduling approaches introduced in preceding sections (cf. Sects. 3.3, 4.1, and 4.3), the proposed adaptive scheduling works for arbitrary text analysis algorithms and collections or streams of input texts. Moreover, it does not place any constraints on the information needs to be addressed, but works for any set of candidate main pipelines, which are equipped with our input control from Sect. 3.5 or which restrict their analyses to relevant portions of text in an according manner.

Different from the other scheduling approaches, however, the adaptive scheduling approach in Pseudocode 4.3 defines a method scheme rather than as a concrete method. In particular, we have neither talked at all about what features to be computed for the prediction of the run-times yet (pseudocode line 5), nor have we exactly specified how to learn the regression of run-times based on the features.

With respect to regression, the pseudocode suggests to apply a learning algorithm, which can process training instances individually as opposed to process all training instances as a batch (Witten and Frank 2005). Otherwise, the incremental update of the regression models in each iteration of the outer for-loops would be highly inefficient. In contrast, there exists no particular clue for how to represent a text for the purpose of pipeline run-time prediction. Generally, such a feature representation must be efficiently computable in order to avoid spending more time for the predictions than can be saved through scheduling later on. At the same time, it should capture characteristics of a text that precisely model the run-time complexity of the text. In our experiments below, we aim to fulfill these requirements with a number of task-independent features. Afterwards, we discuss the limitations of our approach and outline possible alternatives.

Correctness. As a consequence of the schematic nature of our approach, we cannot check its correctness in the algorithmic sense, i.e., whether it halts with the correct output (Cormen et al. 2009). Only the termination of ADAPTIVEPIPELINESCHEDULING is obvious (given that $\mathbf{D}_{tr}$ and $\mathbf{D}$ are finite). Anyway, in the end statistical approaches are hardly ever correct, as they generalize from sample data (cf. Sect. 2.1 for details).

Complexity. Because of the schematic nature, it is also not possible to compute the asymptotic worst-case run-time of ADAPTIVEPIPELINESCHEDULING. Instead, we roughly quantify the required run-times on $\mathbf{D}_T$ and $\mathbf{D}$ here. Besides the numbers of input texts in $\mathbf{D}_T$ and $\mathbf{D}$, Pseudocode 4.3 shows that further relevant input sizes are the number of input texts in $\mathbf{D}_T$ and $\mathbf{D}$ as well as the number of main pipelines in $\boldsymbol{\Pi}$. In contrast, the size of the prefix pipeline Π_{pre}, the feature vector $\mathbf{x}$, and each regression model $\mathscr{Y}(\Pi)$ of a main pipeline $\Pi \in \boldsymbol{\Pi}$ can be assumed as constant.

For the training set, let $t_{pre}(\mathbf{D}_T)$, $t_{fc}(\mathbf{D}_T)$, and $t_{reg}(\mathbf{D}_T)$ denote the times spent for Π_{pre}, feature computation, and the updates of regression models, respectively. In addition to these operations, each text is processed by every main pipeline in $\boldsymbol{\Pi}$. In the worst case, all main pipelines take the same run-time on each input text and, hence, the same run-time $t_{main}(\mathbf{D}_T)$ on $\mathbf{D}_T$. So, we estimate the training time of ADAPTIVEPIPELINESCHEDULING as

$$t_{\text{train}}(\mathbf{D}_T, \boldsymbol{\Pi}) \leq t_{pre}(\mathbf{D}_T) + t_{fc}(\mathbf{D}_T) + |\boldsymbol{\Pi}| \cdot \left(t_{main}(\mathbf{D}_T) + t_{reg}(\mathbf{D}_T) \right) \quad (4.14)$$

Correspondingly, we make the following estimate for the update phase of ADAPTIVEPIPELINESCHEDULING. Here, we do not differentiate between the run-times of a prediction and of the update of a regression model:

$$t_{\text{update}}(\mathbf{D}, \boldsymbol{\Pi}) \leq t_{pre}(\mathbf{D}) + t_{fc}(\mathbf{D}) + t_{main}(\mathbf{D}) + (|\boldsymbol{\Pi}|+1) \cdot t_{reg}(\mathbf{D}_T) \quad (4.15)$$

In the evaluation below, we do not report on the run-time of the training phase, since we have already exemplified in Sect. 4.3 how training time amortizes in large-scale scenarios. Inequality 4.14 stresses, though, that the training time grows linearly with the size of $\boldsymbol{\Pi}$. In principle, the same holds for the run-time of the update phase because of the factor $(|\boldsymbol{\Pi}|+1) \cdot t_{reg}(\mathbf{D}_T)$. However, our results presented next indicate that the regression time does not influence the overall run-time significantly.

4.5.5 Evaluation of Adaptive Scheduling

We now evaluate several parameters of our adaptive scheduling approach on text corpora of different heterogeneity. In the evaluation, we investigate the hypothesis that the impact of online adaptation on a pipeline's efficiency gets higher under increasing text heterogeneity. For this purpose, we rely on a controlled experiment setting that is described in the following. For information on the source code of the experiments, see Appendix B.4.

Text Analysis Task. We consider the extraction of all information that fulfills the query γ_3 = *Forecast(Revenue(Resolved(Time), Money, Organization))*, which we have already introduced in Sect. 4.3. As throughout this chapter, we address this task as a filtering task, meaning that only relevant portions of texts are processed in each step (cf. Sects. 3.4 and 3.5). Here, we set the degree of filtering to *Sentence*.

Corpora. For a careful analysis of our hypothesis, we need comparable collections or streams of input texts that refer to different levels of text heterogeneity. Most existing corpora for information extraction tasks are too small to create reasonable subsets of different heterogeneity like those used in the evaluations above, i.e., the REVENUE CORPUS (cf. Appendix C.1) and the CoNLL-2003 dataset (cf. Appendix C.4). An alternative is given by web crawls. Web crawls, however, tend to include a large fraction of completely irrelevant texts (as indicated by our analysis in Sect. 4.2), which conceals the efficiency impact of scheduling.

We therefore decided to create partly artificial text corpora $\mathbf{D}_0, \ldots, \mathbf{D}_3$ instead. $\mathbf{D}_0$ contains a random selection of 1500 original texts from the REVENUE CORPUS and the German CoNLL-2003 dataset. The other three consist of both original texts and artificially modified versions of these texts, where the latter are created by randomly duplicating one sentence, ensuring that each text is unique in every corpus: $\mathbf{D}_1$ is made up of the 300 texts from $\mathbf{D}_0$ with the highest differences in the density of the information types relevant for γ_3 as well as 1200 modified versions. Accordingly, $\mathbf{D}_2$ and $\mathbf{D}_3$ are created from the 200 and 100 highest-difference texts, respectively. Where not stated otherwise, we use the first 500 texts of each corpus for training and the remaining 1000 for testing (and updating regression models).

By resorting to modified duplicates, we limit our approach to a certain extent in learning features from the input texts. However, we gain that we can capture the impact of adaptive scheduling as a function of the text heterogeneity, quantified using the averaged deviation from Sect. 4.4. Table 4.6 lists the deviations of the densities of all relevant information types in the sentences of each of the four corpora.

Algorithms and Pipelines. To address the query γ_3, we rely on a set of nine text analysis algorithms (details on these are provided in Appendix A):

Table 4.6 The standard deviations of the densities of all information types from **C** in the four evaluated text corpora as well as the resulting averaged deviations. All values are computed from the results of a non-filtering pipeline based on **A**.

Text corpus	Time entities	Money entities	Organization entities	Statement events	Forecast events	Averaged deviation
D_0	±19.1%	±19.8%	±19.3%	±7.1%	±3.8%	**13.8%**
D_1	±22.5%	±19.1%	±21.6%	±7.8%	±5.9%	**15.4%**
D_2	±24.6%	±20.4%	±22.4%	±8.9%	±6.7%	**16.6%**
D_3	±25.9%	±22.3%	±25.0%	±10.6%	±8.5%	**18.5%**

$$\mathbf{A} = \{\text{STO}_1, \text{TPO}_1, \text{PCH}, \text{ETI}, \text{EMO}, \text{ENE}, \text{RRE}_2, \text{RFO}, \text{NTI}\}$$

In the prefix pipeline $\Pi_{pre} = (\text{STO}_1, \text{TPO}_1, \text{PCH})$, we employ the tokenizer STO_1, the part-of-speech tagger TPO_1, as well as the chunker PCH.[38] The remaining six algorithms become part of the main pipelines. While these algorithms allow for 108 admissible schedules, we restrict our view to only three main pipelines in order to allow for a concise presentation and a clear interpretation of the obtained results.[39] In particular, we have selected the following main pipelines Π_1, Π_2, and Π_3 based on some preliminary experiments. They target at very different distributions of relevant information while being comparably efficient:

$$\Pi_1 = (\text{ETI}, \text{RFO}, \text{EMO}, \text{RRE}_2, \text{NTI}, \text{ENE})$$
$$\Pi_2 = (\text{ETI}, \text{EMO}, \text{RFO}, \text{NTI}, \text{ENE}, \text{RRE}_2)$$
$$\Pi_3 = (\text{EMO}, \text{ETI}, \text{RFO}, \text{ENE}, \text{RRE}_2, \text{NTI})$$

Self-supervised Learning. For learning to predict the main pipeline's run-times, we represent all texts with features computed from the results of Π_{pre}. For generality, we consider only features that neither require a preceding run over the training set nor exploit knowledge about the given corpora and main pipelines. Our standard feature set consists of three types:

1. **Lexical statistics.** The average and maximum number of characters in a token and of the tokens in a sentence of the input text as well as the numbers of tokens and sentences.
2. **Algorithm run-times.** The run-time per sentence of each algorithm in Π_{pre}.
3. **Part-of-speech tags.** The frequency of all part-of-speech tags distinguished by the algorithm TPO_1.

---

[38]In Wachsmuth et al. (2013c), we state that the prefix pipeline in this evaluation consists of two algorithms only. This is because, we use a combined version of TPO_1 and PCH, there.

[39]The main benefit of considering all 108 main pipelines would be to know the overall efficiency potential of scheduling the algorithms in **A**. An according experiment can be found in Wachsmuth et al. (2013c), but it is omitted here, because according values have already been presented in different evaluations from Chaps. 3 and and this chapter.

In addition, we evaluate two further types in the feature analysis below, which attempt to capture general characteristics of entities:

4. **Chunk n-grams.** The frequency of each possible unigram and bigram of all chunk tags distinguished by PCH.
5. **Regex matches.** The frequencies of matches of a regular expression for arbitrary numbers and of a regular expression for upper-case words.

In order to allow for online learning, we trained linear regression models with the WEKA 3.7.5 implementation (Hall et al. 2009) of the incremental algorithm STOCHASTIC GRADIENT DESCENT (cf. Sect. 2.1). In all experiments, we let the algorithm iterate 10 epochs over the training set, while its learning rate was set to 0.01 and its regularization parameter to 0.00001.

Baselines. The aim of adaptive scheduling is to achieve optimal efficiency on collections or streams of input texts where no single optimal schedule exists. In this regard, we see the *optimal baseline* from Sect. 4.3, which determines the run-time optimal fixed pipeline (Π_{pre}, Π^*) on the training set and then chooses this pipeline for each test text, as the main competitor. Moreover, we introduce another baseline to assess whether adaptive scheduling improves over trivial non-fixed approaches:

Random baseline. Do not process the training set at all. For each test text, choose one of the fixed pipelines (pseudo-) randomly.

Gold Standard. Besides the baselines, we oppose all approaches to the *gold standard*, which knows the optimal main pipeline for each text beforehand. Together with the optimal baseline, the gold standard implies the optimization potential of adaptive scheduling on a given collection or stream of input texts (cf. Sect. 4.4).

Experiments. In the following, we present the results of a number of efficiency experiments. The efficiency is measured as the run-time in milliseconds per sentence, averaged over ten runs. For reproducability, all run-times and their standard deviations were saved in a file in advance. In the experiments, we then loaded the precomputed run-times instead of executing the pipelines.[40] We omit to report on effectiveness, as all main pipelines are equally effective by definition. The experiments were conducted on 2 GHz Intel Core 2 Duo MacBook with 4 GB memory.

Efficiency Impact of Adaptive Scheduling. We evaluate adaptive scheduling on the test sets of each corpus $D_0, \ldots, D_3$ after training on the respective training sets. Figure 4.13 compares the run-times of the main pipelines of our approach to those of the two baselines and the gold standard as a function of the averaged deviation. The shown confidence intervals visualize the standard deviations σ, which range from 0.029 to 0.043 ms.

---

[40]For lack of relevance in our discussion, we leave out an analysis of the effects of relying on precomputed run-times here. In Wachsmuth et al. (2013c), we offer evidence that the main effect is a significant reduction of the standard deviations of the pipelines' run-times.

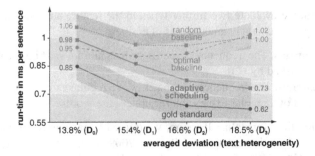

Fig. 4.13 Interpolated curves of the average run-times of the main pipelines of both baselines, of our adaptive scheduling approach, and of the gold standard under increasing averaged deviation, which represents the heterogeneity of the processed texts. The background areas denote the 95 % confidence intervals ($\pm 2\sigma$).

On the least heterogeneous corpus D_0, we achieve an average run-time of 0.98 ms per sentence through adaptive scheduling. This is faster than the random base-line (1.06 ms), but slower than the optimal baseline (0.95 ms) at a low confidence level. On all other corpora, our approach also outperforms the optimal baseline, providing evidence for the growing efficiency impact of adaptive scheduling under increasing text heterogeneity. At the averaged deviation of 18.5 % on D_3, adaptive scheduling clearly succeeds over both baselines, whose main pipelines take 37 % and 40 % more time on average, respectively. There, the optimal baseline does not choose the main pipeline, which performs best on the test set. This matches our hypothesis from Sect. 4.4 that higher text heterogeneity may cause a significant effi-ciency loss when relying on a fixed schedule.

Altogether, the curves in Fig. 4.13 emphasize that only our adaptive scheduling approach manages to stay close to the gold standard on all corpora. In this respect, one reason for the seemingly weak performance of our approach on D_0 lies in the low optimization potential of adaptive scheduling on that corpus: The optimal baseline takes only about 12 % more time on average than the gold standard (0.95 ms as opposed to 0.85 ms). This indicates very small differences in the main pipelines' run-times, which renders the prediction of the fastest main pipeline both hard and quite unnecessary. In contrast, D_3 yields an optimization potential of over 50 %. In the following, we analyze the effects of these differences in detail.

Run-time and Error Analysis. Figure 4.14 breaks down the run-times of the three fixed pipelines, our approach, and the gold standard on D_0 and D_3 according to Ineq. 4.15. On D_3, all fixed pipelines are significantly slower than our approach in terms of overall run-time. The overall run-time of our approach is largely caused by the prefix pipeline and the main pipelines, while the time spent for computing the above-mentioned standard feature types 1–3 (0.03 ms) and for the subsequent regression (0.01 ms) is almost negligible. This also holds for D_0 where our approach performs worse only than the optimal fixed pipeline (Π_{pre}, Π_1).

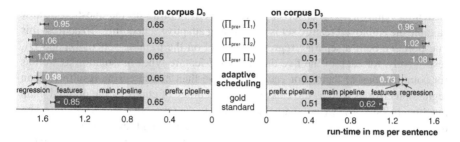

Fig. 4.14 The average run-times per sentence (with standard deviations) of the three fixed pipelines, our adaptive scheduling approach, and the gold standard on the test sets of D_0 and D_3. Each run-time is broken down into its different parts.

Table 4.7 The average *regression time* per sentence (including feature computation and regression), the mean *regression error*, and the *accuracy* of choosing the optimal pipeline for each input text in either D_0 or D_3 for different feature types.

#	Feature type	Regression error		Accuracy		Regression time	
		D_0	D_3	D_0	D_3	D_0	D_3
1	Lexical statistics	0.60 ms	0.78 ms	59 %	50 %	0.03 ms	0.02 ms
2	Average run-times	0.62 ms	1.34 ms	47 %	38 %	<0.01 ms	<0.01 ms
3	Part-of-speech tags	0.48 ms	0.69 ms	34 %	**58 %**	0.03 ms	0.02 ms
4	Chunk n-grams	0.58 ms	0.70 ms	43 %	**58 %**	0.04 ms	0.03 ms
5	Regex matches	0.46 ms	0.74 ms	44 %	27 %	0.16 ms	0.13 ms
1–3	**Standard features**	**0.45 ms**	0.69 ms	39 %	55 %	0.05 ms	0.04 ms
1–5	All features	**0.45 ms**	**0.54 ms**	47 %	42 %	0.19 ms	0.24 ms

(Π_{pre}, Π_1) is the fastest pipeline on 598 of the 1000 test texts from D_0, whereas (Π_{pre}, Π_2) and (Π_{pre}, Π_3) have the lowest run-time on 229 and 216 texts, respectively (on some texts, the pipelines are equally fast). In contrast, our approach takes Π_2 (569 times) more often than Π_1 (349) and Π_3 (82), which results in an accuracy of only 39 % for choosing the optimal pipeline. This behavior is caused by a mean regression error of 0.45 ms, which is almost half as high as the run-times to be predicted on average and, thus, often exceeds the differences between them. However, the success on D_3 does not emanate from lower regression errors, which are in fact 0.24 ms higher on average. Still, the accuracy is increased to 55 %. So, the success must result from larger differences in the main pipelines' run-times.

One reason behind can be inferred from the average run-time per sentence of Π_{pre} in Fig. 4.14, which is significantly higher on D_1 (0.65 ms) than on D_3 (0.51 ms). Since the run-times of all algorithms in Π_{pre} scale linearly with the number of input tokens, the average sentence length of D_0 must exceed that of D_3. Naturally, shorter sentences tend to contain less relevant information. Hence, many sentences can be discovered as being irrelevant after few analysis steps by a pipeline that schedules the respective text analysis algorithms early.

Learning Analysis. The observed regression errors bring up the question of how suitable the employed feature set is for learning adaptive scheduling. To address this question, we built a separate regression model on the training sets of D_0 and D_3, respectively, for each of the five distinguished feature types in isolation as well as for combinations of them. For each model, we then measured the resulting mean regression error as well as the classification accuracy of choosing the optimal main pipeline. In Table 4.7, we compare these values to the respective *regression time*, i.e., the run-time per sentence spent for feature computations and regression.

In terms of the mean regression error, the part-of speech tags and regex matches perform best among the single feature types, while the average run-times fail completely, especially on D_3 (1.34 ms). Still, the accuracy of the average run-times is far from worst, indicating that they sometimes provide meaningful information. The best accuracy is clearly achieved by the lexical statistics.[41] Obviously, none of the single feature types dominates the evaluation. The set of all features outperforms both the single types and the standard features in most respects. Nevertheless, we use the standard features in all other experiments, because they entail a regression time of only 0.04 to 0.05 ms per sentence on average. In contrast, the regex matches e.g. need 0.16 ms alone on D_0, which exceeds the difference between the optimal baseline and the gold standard on D_0 and, thus, renders the regex matches useless in the given setting.

The regex matches emphasize the need for efficiently computable features that we discussed above. While the set of standard features fulfills the former requirement, it seems as if none of the five feature types really captures the text characteristics relevant for adaptive scheduling.[42]

Alternatively, though, the features may also require more than the 500 training texts given so far. To rule out this possibility, we next analyze the performance of the standard features depending on the size of the training set. Figure 4.15 shows the main pipelines' run-times for nine training sizes between 1 and 5000. Since the training set of D_0 is limited, we have partly performed training on duplicates of the texts in D_0 (modified in the way sketched above) where necessary. Adaptive scheduling does better than the random baseline but not than the optimal baseline on all training sizes except for 1. The illustrated curve minimally oscillates in the beginning. After its maximum at 300 training texts (1.05 ms), it then declines monotonously until it reaches 0.95 ms at size 1000. From there, the algorithm mimics the optimal baseline, i.e., it chooses Π_1 on about 90% of the texts. While the observed learning behavior may partly result from overfitting the training set in consequence of using modified duplicates, it also underlines that the considered features simply do not suffice to always find the optimal pipeline for each text. Still, more training decreases the danger of being worse than without adaptive scheduling.

---

[41] The low inverse correlation of the mean regression error and the classification accuracy seems counterintuitive, but it indicates the limitations of these measures: E.g., a small regression error can still be problematic if run-times differ only slightly, while a low classification accuracy may have few negative effects in this case.

[42] We have also experimented with other task-independent features, especially further regular expressions, but their benefit was low. Therefore, we omit to report on them here.

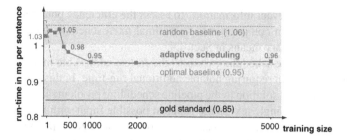

Fig. 4.15 The average run-time of the main pipelines of the two baselines, our adaptive scheduling approach, and the gold standard on the test set of D_0 as a function of the training size.

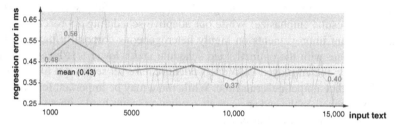

Fig. 4.16 The mean regression error for the main pipelines chosen by our adaptive scheduling approach on 15,000 modified versions of the texts in D_0 with training size 1. The values of the two interpolated learning curves denote the mean of 100 (light curve) and 1000 (bold curve) consecutive predictions, respectively.

In addition, our approach continues learning in its update phase, as we finally exemplify. Figure 4.16 plots two levels of detail of the learning curve of the employed regression models on 15,000 modified duplicates of the texts from D_0.[43] Here, only one text is used for an initial training. As the bold curve highlights, the mean regression error decreases on the first 4000 to 5000 texts to an area between 0.35 ms and 0.45 ms, where it stays most of the time afterwards. Although the light curve reveals many outliers, we conclude that online learning apparently works well.

4.5.6 Discussion of Adaptive Scheduling

In this section, we have developed a pipeline scheduling approach that aims to achieve optimal run-time efficiency for a set of text analysis algorithms (equipped with the input control from Sect. 3.5) on each input text. The approach automatically learns to adapt a pipeline's schedule to a processed text without supervision. It targets at text analysis tasks where the collection or stream of input texts is heterogeneous in

---

[43] The curves in Fig. 4.16 represent the differences between the predicted and the observed run-times of the main pipelines that are actually executed on the respective texts.

the distribution of relevant information. To assess the efficiency potential of such an adaptive scheduling in comparison to an optimal fixed schedule, we have already introduced the necessary means in Sect. 4.4.

Ideally, an adaptive scheduling chooses the fastest admissible main pipeline for each input text without requiring notable additional run-time. In this case, it denotes the ultimately optimal solution to the pipeline scheduling problem raised in Sect. 3.1: Since we consider a single text as the smallest possible input within a text analysis task (cf. Sect. 2.2), there is nothing better to be done to optimize a pipeline's efficiency without compromising its effectiveness. Hence, adaptive scheduling always proves beneficial, as it will at least achieve the efficiency of all other scheduling approaches.

Practically, both an accurate and an efficient prediction of the fastest admissible pipeline denote non-trivial challenges that we have not fully solved yet, as our experimental results emphasize: While our adaptive scheduling approach has provided significant improvements on highly heterogeneous corpora, it has failed to robustly compete with the optimal fixed schedule under lower text heterogeneity. Most obviously, the employed task-independent feature set seems not to suffice to accurately predict a pipeline's run-time. While there may be important features that we have overlooked, in the end an accurate prediction seems hard without exploiting knowledge about the relevant information types.

At least when given computationally expensive text analysis algorithms, one promising approach to include such knowledge is to employ cheap alternatives to these algorithms in the prefix pipeline (e.g. entity recognizers based on small lexicons). Such algorithms will often naturally help to estimate the selectivities of the expensive algorithms and, hence, result in more accucate run-time predictions. Aside from that, another way to reduce the prediction errors may be to iteratively schedule each text analysis algorithm separately. This would allow for more informed features in later predictions, but it would also make the learning of the scheduling much more complex. Moreover, the introductory example in Sect. 4.1 suggests that the first filtering stages in a pipeline tend to be most decisive for the pipeline's efficiency. Since the main purpose of this section is to show how to deal with text heterogeneity in general, we leave according and other extensions of our adaptive scheduling approach for future work.

As a result, we close the analysis of the pipeline scheduling problem here. Throughout this chapter, we have offered evidence that the optimization of a pipeline's design and execution in terms of efficiency can drastically speed up the realized text analysis process. The underlying goal in the context of this book is to enable text analysis pipelines to be used for large-scale text mining and, thus, to work on big data. The analysis of big data strongly relies on distributed and parallelized processing. In the following, we therefore conclude this chapter by discussing to what extent the developed scheduling approaches can be parallelized.

4.6 Parallelizing Execution in Large-Scale Text Mining

The approaches developed in this chapter aim to optimize the efficiency of sequentially executing a set of text analysis algorithms on a single machine. The next logical step is to parallelize the execution. Despite its obvious importance for both ad-hoc and large-scale text mining, the parallelization of text analysis pipelines is only discussed sporadically in the literature (cf. Sect. 2.4). In the following, we outline possible ways to parallelize pipelines and we check how well they integrate with our approaches. For a homogeneous machine setting, a reasonable parallelization appears straightforward, although some relevant parameters remain to be evaluated.

4.6.1 Effects of Parallelizing Pipeline Execution

When we speak of the *parallelization* of pipeline execution, we refer to the distribution of text analysis pipelines over different *machines*, each of which being able to execute text analysis algorithms. We consider the basic case of a homogeneous parallel system architecture, where all machines are comparably fast and where an algorithm is executed in the same way on each machine. In contrast, specialized hardware that executes certain algorithms faster is beyond the scope of this book.

In Sect. 2.4, we have already clarified that text analysis processes are very amenable to parallelization because different input texts are analyzed independently in most cases. In general, parallelization may have a number of purposes, as e.g. surveyed in Kumar et al. (1994). Not all of these target at the memory and processing power of an application. For instance, parallelization can also be used to introduce redundancy within an application, which allows a handling of machine breakdowns, thereby increasing the *fault tolerance* of an application. While we roughly discuss fault tolerance below, in the context of pipeline execution we are predominantly interested in the question to what extent the run-time efficiency of the pipelines resulting from our approaches scales under parallelization, i.e., whether it grows proportionally to the number of available machines. To this end, we qualitatively examine possible ways to parallelize pipeline execution with respect to different efficiency-related metrics.

In particular, we primarily focus on the *pipeline execution time*, i.e., the total run-time of all employed pipelines on the (possibly large) collection or stream of input texts. This run-time is connected to other metrics: First, some experiments in this chapter have indicated that the *memory consumption* of maintaining pipelines on a machine matters, namely, a high memory load lowers the efficiency of text analysis. Second, the impact of parallelization depends on the extent to which machine idle times are avoided. In this regard, *machine utilization* denotes the percentage of the overall run-time of a machine, in which it processes text. And third, the distribution of texts over a network causes communication overhead, which we indirectly capture

Table 4.8 Qualitative overview of the expected effects of the four distinguished types of parallelization with respect to each considered metric. The scale ranges from *very positive* [++] and *positive* [+] over *none or hardly any* [o] to *negative* [−] and *very negative* [− −].

Metric	Analysis pipelining	Analysis parallelization	Pipeline duplication	Schedule parallelization
Fault tolerance	−	−	++	+
Memory consumption	++	++	o	+
Machine utilization	−	− −	++	++
Network time	− −	−	o	−
Pipeline execution time	+	±	+	+
Scheduling time	++	++	++	++
Training time	+	+	++	++
Minimum response time	o	±	+	++

as the *network time*. We assume these three to be most important for the pipeline execution time and we omit to talk about others accordingly.

Aside from a scalable execution, parallelization can also be exploited to speed up pipeline scheduling. We analyze the effects of parallelization on the *scheduling time*, i.e., the time spent for an optimized scheduling on a sample of texts, as proposed in Sect. 4.3 (or for the optimal scheduling in Sect. 4.1) as well as on the *training time* of our adaptive scheduling approach from Sect. 4.5. Also, we look at the *minimum response time* of a pipeline, which we define as the pipeline's run-time on a single input text. The minimum response time becomes important in ad-hoc text mining, when first results need to be returned as fast as possible (cf. Sect. 3.3).

In the following, we examine four types of parallelization for the scenario that a single text analysis task is to be addressed on a network of machines with pipelines equipped with our input control from Sect. 3.5. All machines are uniform in speed and execute algorithms and pipelines in the same way. They can receive arbitrary input texts from other machines, analyze the texts, and return the produced output information. We assess the effects of each type on all metrics introduced above on a comparative scale from *very positive* [++] to *very negative* [− −]. Table 4.8 provides an overview of all effects.

To illustrate the different types, we consider three machines $\mu_0, \ldots, \mu_2$. μ_0 serves as the *master machine* that distributes input texts and aggregates output information. Given this setting, we schedule four sample algorithms related to our case study INFEXBA from Sect. 2.3: a time recognizer A_T, a money recognizer A_M, a forecast event detector A_F, and some segmentation algorithm A_S. Let the output of A_S be required by all others and let A_F additionally depend on A_T. Then, three admissible pipelines exist: (A_S, A_T, A_M, A_F), (A_S, A_T, A_F, A_M), and (A_S, A_M, A_T, A_F).

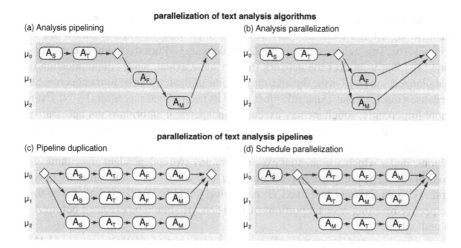

Fig. 4.17 The four considered ways of parallelizing four sample text analysis algorithms on three machines $\mu_0, \ldots, \mu_2$: **a** Different algorithms on different machines in sequence, **b** different algorithms on different machines in parallel where possible, **c** one schedule on different machines, **d** different schedules on different machines.

4.6.2 Parallelization of Text Analyses

One of the most classical ways of parallelizing a sequence of actions is to perform *pipelining* (Ramamoorthy and Li 1977). In the given context, this means to see the machines as an assembly line and, hence, to partition the algorithms employed in a pipeline over the machines. Such an *analysis pipelining* allows for parallel execution. When μ_2 in Fig. 4.17(a), for example, analyzes some input text, μ_1 can already process another text, and μ_0 a third one. While the fault tolerance of analysis pipelining is low as long as no redundancy is introduced [–], it significantly reduces memory consumption by maintaining only some algorithms on each machine [++]. However, a machine may have to wait for its predecessor to finish, negatively affecting its utilization [–]. In addition, input texts need to be sent from machine to machine, which implies high network times [– –]. Still, a parallel processing of input texts can often improve the pipeline execution time [+].

Partitioning the employed algorithms can significantly speed up the scheduling time of K-BESTA*PIPELINESCHEDULING [++], as the iterative search node expansion for each applicable algorithm (cf. Pseudocode 4.2) can easily be parallelized. Also, processing input texts in parallel benefits the training time of adaptive scheduling [+]. Conversely, the minimum response time cannot be reduced [o], as each text is still processed sequentially.[44]

---

[44]Notice that we assume homogeneous machines here. In case of machines, which are specialized for certain text analyses, analysis pipelining may entail more advantages.

Intuitively, it seems beneficial to extend the analysis pipelining by executing independent algorithms simultaneously, resulting in an *analysis parallelization* like in Fig. 4.17(b). This neither changes the fault tolerance [−] nor the memory consumption [++], but it reduces the network time to some extent, since communication is parallelized, too [−]. On the flipside, the machine utilization can be further decreased, because a machine may cause idle times on all its parallelized successors [− −]. Even more importantly, simultaneouly executing independent algorithms not necessarily reduces the pipeline execution time, but can even increase it for input-controlled pipelines [+/−]. Since this claim goes against intuition, we directly specify the conditions, under which a sequential execution of any two independent algorithms A_1 and A_2 should be preferred. In particular, let $t_1(D)$ and $t_2(D)$ be the run-times of A_1 and A_2 on an arbitrary input text D, respectively, and let $S_1(D)$ and $S_2(D)$ be the respective resulting relevant portions of D. Then, A_1 should be executed before A_2 if and only if

$$t_1(D) + t_2(S_1(D)) < t_2(D) + t_1(S_2(D)). \tag{4.16}$$

The same holds for exchanged roles of A_1 and A_2. We have seen an example that fulfills Ineq. 4.16 in the evaluation of Sect. 4.1, where the pipeline (ETI, EMO) outperforms the algorithm EMO alone. The danger of losing efficiency (which also exists for the minimum response time [+/−]) generally makes analysis parallelization questionable. While the scheduling time [++] and training time [+] behave in the same way as for analysis pipelining, other types of parallelization exist that come with only few notable drawbacks and with even more benefits, as discussed next.

4.6.3 Parallelization of Text Analysis Pipelines

Instead of deploying single algorithms on different machines, the execution of a text analysis pipeline can also be parallelized by simply deploying one duplicate of the complete pipeline on each machine, as shown in Fig. 4.17(c). The redundant nature of such a *pipeline duplication* is naturally optimal in terms of fault tolerance [++]. Not only because of its simplicity and fault tolerance, pipeline duplication is very prominent in large-scale text mining (cf. Sect. 2.4) and it denotes the built-in type of APACHE UIMA, called UIMA ASYNCHRONOUS SCALEOUT.[45] Most evidently, this type of parallelization provides a near 100 % machine utilization [++], because a machine can directly request the next input text from the master machine itself when the previous text has been processed. At the same time, the memory consumption per machine remains unaffected [o], and the network time stays low [o], since each text needs to be sent only once to a machine. Consequently, the pipeline execution time will largely scale [++].

---

[45]UIMA ASYNCHRONOUS SCALEOUT, http://uima.apache.org/doc-uimaas-what.html, accessed on June 15, 2015.

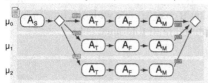
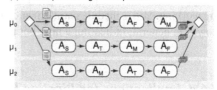

Fig. 4.18 Parallel processing of a single input text with four sample text analysis algorithms: **a** The master machine μ_0 segments the input text into portions of text, each of which is then processed on one machine. **b** All machines process the whole text, but schedule the algorithms differently.

As each machine employs all algorithms, the scheduling time can again be significantly improved through parallel search node expansions [++]. Similarly, the training time of adaptive scheduling scales well [++], because input texts can be processed on different machines (while centrally updating the mapping to be learned on the master machine). Moreover, pipeline duplication can reduce the minimum response time to some extent [+], even though all machines execute the employed pipeline in the same order. In particular, our input control allows the duplicated pipelines to process different portions of an input text simultaneously. To this end, the master machine needs to execute some kind of prefix pipeline, which segments the input text into single portions, whose size is constrained by the largest specified degree of filtering in the query to be addressed (cf. Sect. 3.4). The portions can then be distributed to the available machines. Figure 4.18(a) sketches such an input distribution for our four sample algorithms.

Pipeline duplication appears to be an almost perfect choice, at least when a single text analysis pipeline is given, as in the case of our optimized scheduling approach from Sect. 4.3. In contrast, the (ideally) even better adaptive scheduling approach from Sect. 4.5 can still cause a high memory consumption, because every machine needs to maintain all candidate schedules. A solution is to parallelize the schedules instead of the pipeline, as illustrated in Fig. 4.17(d). Such a *schedule parallelization* requires to store only a subset of the schedules on each machine, thereby reducing memory consumption [+]. The adaptive choice of a schedule (and, hence, of a machine) for an input text then must take place on the master machine. Consequently, idle times can occur, especially when the choice is very imbalanced. In order to ensure a full machine utilization [++], input texts may therefore have to be reassigned to other machines, which implies a negative effect on the network time [−]. So, we cannot generally determine whether schedule parallelization yields a better pipeline execution time than pipeline duplication or vice versa [++].

In terms of scheduling time [++] and training time [++], schedule parallelization behaves analog to pipeline duplication, whereas the distribution of schedules over machines will tend to benefit the minimum response time on a single input text more clearly [++]: Similar to Kalyanpur et al. (2011), a text can be processed by each machine simultaneously (cf. Fig. 4.18(b)). As soon as the first machine finishes, the execution can stop to directly return the produced output information. However, the full potential of such a massive parallelization is only achieved when all machines are working. Still, schedule parallelization makes it easy to cope with machine break-downs in general, indicating a high but not optimal fault tolerance [+].

4.6.4 Implications for Pipeline Robustness

Altogether, our qualitative analysis suggests that a parallelized pipeline execution in a homogeneous machine setting is straightforward, in principle. An easy-to-manage and effective solution is to replicate the employed pipeline on each available machine (called pipeline duplication here). The potential of other parallelization types (e.g. schedule parallelization) comes with significantly increased management complexity. Of course, we cannot actually quantify the scalability of a pipeline's execution time for the distinguished types by now, because the impact of the overhead from memory load, communication, and idle times depends on the network and task parameters of the given setting. Nevertheless, we skip an evaluation of these parameters, because we do not expect to get considerable scientific insights from it.[46] For similar reasons, we omit to investigate other scenarios that are relevant for practical text mining applications, such as the parallel execution of several text analysis tasks at the same time.

Once again, this section has emphasized the benefit of equipping a pipeline with an input control for the pipeline's run-time efficiency. While the process-oriented view of text analysis from Sect. 3.2 enables ad-hoc text mining, the formalization of text analysis as a filtering task underlying the input control (cf. Sect. 3.4) is the core idea that gives rise to large-scale text mining. Together with the scheduling approaches developed in this chapter, the two views create the ability to combine ad-hoc and large scale text mining. For instance, given a large pool of text analysis algorithms, a search engine could construct a pipeline for an ad-hoc information need, optimize the pipeline's efficiency on a sample of input texts, and then process a large collection or a stream of input texts with the optimized pipeline.

As we motivated in Chap. 1, however, sophisticated pipelines will only find their way into practical text mining applications, when they consistently achieve to produce high-quality information on all (or at least most) input texts. In Chap. 5, we approach such a pipeline robustness through a focus on the overall structure of the input texts (as opposed to their content) during analysis. The approach aims especially at tasks from the area of text classification where a result captures an input text as a whole. In this regard, the optimization of efficiency through filtering seems counterproductive, because the less portions of texts are filtered the less output information is produced. In the end, though, the only consequence is that the efficiency impact of filtering will be limited in respective cases.

---

[46]In exemplary tests with the main pipeline in our project ARGUANA (cf. Sect. 2.3), pipeline duplication on five machines reduced the pipeline execution time by factor 3.

Chapter 5
Pipeline Robustness

In making a speech one must study three points: first, the means of producing persuasion; second, the style, or language, to be used; third, the proper arrangement of the various parts of the speech.

– Aristotle

Abstract The ultimate purpose of text analysis pipelines is to infer new information from unknown input texts. To this end, the algorithms employed in pipelines are usually developed on known training texts from the anticipated domains of application (cf. Sect. 2.1). In many applications, however, the unknown texts significantly differ from the known texts, because a consideration of all possible domains within the development is practically infeasible (Blitzer et al. 2007). As a consequence, algorithms often fail to infer information effectively, especially when they rely on features of texts that are specific to the training domain. Such missing *domain robustness* constitutes a fundamental problem of text analysis (Turmo et al. 2006; Daumé and Marcu 2006). The missing robustness of an algorithm directly reduces the robustness of a pipeline it is employed in. This in turn limits the benefit of pipelines in all search engines and big data analytics applications, where the domains of texts cannot be anticipated. In this chapter, we present first substantial results of an approach that improves robustness by relying on novel structure-based features that are invariant across domains.

Section 5.1 discusses how to achieve ideal domain independence in theory. Since the domain robustness problem is very diverse, we then focus on a specific type of text analysis tasks (unlike in Chaps. 3 and 4). In particular, we consider tasks that deal with the classification of argumentative texts, like sentiment analysis, stance recognition, or automatic essay grading (cf. Sect. 2.1). In Sect. 5.2, we introduce a shallow model of such tasks, which captures the sequential overall structure of argumentative texts on the pragmatic level while abstracting from their content. For instance, we observe that review argumentation can be represented by the flow of local sentiment. Given the model, we demonstrate that common flow patterns exist in argumentative texts (Sect. 5.3). Our hypothesis is that such patterns generalize well across domains. In Sect. 5.4, we learn common flow patterns with a supervised variant of clustering. Then, we use each pattern as a single feature for classifying argumentative texts

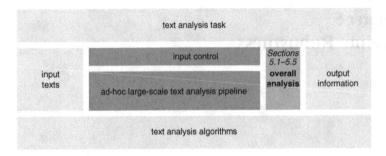

Fig. 5.1 Abstract view of the overall approach of this book (cf. Fig. 1.5). The main contribution of this chapter is represented by the *overall analysis*.

from different domains. Our results for sentiment analysis indicate the robustness of modeling overall structure (other tasks are left for future work). In addition, we can visually make results more intelligible based on the model (Sect. 5.5). Altogether, this chapter realizes the overall analysis within the approach of this book, highlighted in Fig. 5.1. Both robustness and intelligibility benefit the use of pipelines in ad-hoc large-scale text mining.

5.1 Ideal Domain Independence for High-Quality Text Mining

In this section, we discuss how to achieve an ideal domain independence of text analysis pipelines in order to enable high-quality text mining on arbitrary input texts. First, we outline the domain dependence problem of text analysis. Then, we argue that a pipeline's domain robustness is mainly affected by three factors: the training texts the pipeline is developed on, the features of the texts it relies on, and the way it analyzes the features. For most text analysis tasks, no silver bullet exists, which optimally handles these factors. In the book at hand, we focus on what features to rely on and we restrict our view to tasks that aim at classifying argumentative texts.

5.1.1 The Domain Dependence Problem in Text Analysis

Several tasks from information extraction and text classification have been successfully tackled with text analysis pipelines (cf. Chap. 2). The algorithms employed in pipelines are mostly developed based on a set of known training texts. These texts are analyzed manually or automatically in order to find rules or statistics about certain features of the texts that help to generally infer the output information (in terms of classes, annotations, etc.) to be inferred by the respective algorithm from input texts (cf. Sect. 2.1 for details). Such a corpus-based development often results in

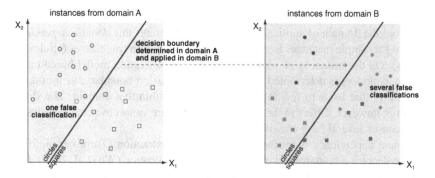

Fig. 5.2 Illustration of the domain dependence of text analysis for a two-class classification task: Applying the decision boundary from *domain A* in some *domain B* with a different feature distribution (here, for x_1 and x_2) often works badly.

high effectiveness when the training texts are representative for the input texts the algorithm shall process later on, i.e., for the algorithm's domain of application.

The notion of *domains* is common in related areas like software engineering, where it captures two respects: (1) The specific concepts of some problem area and (2) shared software requirements and functionalities that are key software reuse (Harsu 2002). While, to our knowledge, no clear definition of domains exists in text analysis, here the term is used rather in the first respect, namely, to capture common properties of a set of texts.

Many authors refer to domains in terms of topics, such as Li et al. (2012a). However, domains are also distinguished according to other schemes, e.g. with respect to genres or styles (Blitzer et al. 2007). In our project ARGUANA, we analyzed the sentiment of reviews (cf. Sect. 2.3), while some related approaches rather target at the comment-like texts from TWITTER[1] (Mukherjee and Bhattacharyya 2012). Also, the combination of a topic and a genre can make up a domain, as in our study of language functions (Wachsmuth and Bujna 2011). Others differentiate between authors Pang and Lee (2005) or even see languages as a special case of domains (Prettenhofer and Stein 2011). In the end, the domain scheme depends on the addressed task.

What the texts from a specific domain share, in general, is that they are assumed to be drawn from the same underlying feature distribution (Daumé and Marcu 2006), meaning that similar feature values imply similar output information. Given a training set with texts from a single domain, it is therefore not clear whether found rules or statistics about a feature represent properties of texts that are generally helpful to infer output information correctly or whether they refer to properties that occur only within the specific domain at hand.[2] Either way, an algorithm can rely on the feature when being applied to any other set of texts from that domain.

In practice, however, the domain of application is not always the same as the training domain. Since different domains yield different feature distributions, an algorithm

---

[1] TWITTER, http://www.twitter.com, accessed on June 15, 2015.

[2] In software engineering terms, the latter could be seen as some *domain-specific language*.

that relies on domain-specific features is likely to fail to achieve high effectiveness on texts from the domain of application. Figure 5.2 illustrates this *domain dependence* problem for sample instances from a classification task with two classes (circles and squares): On the instances of some domain A, a classification model based on the features x_1 and x_2 is determined (visualized as a decision boundary, as introduced in Sect. 2.1) that leads to few false classifications within that domain. The shown domain B, however, differs in the distribution of feature values over the two classes, which causes several false classifications.

Domain dependence is intrinsic to information extraction (Turmo et al. 2006) and also denotes a fundamental problem in text classification (Wu et al. 2010). E.g., the rule-based extraction of absolute money information in our project INFEXBA required the existence of currency names or symbols close to numeric values (cf. Sect. 2.3). This works well on news articles, but it may fail when money information is extracted from informal texts like blog posts. Similarly, we investigated word-based features for statistical sentiment analysis in ARGUANA that included topic-specific words like "cheap", usually indicating positive sentiment in hotel reviews. In some other domains (say, film), cheap rather has the opposite polarity.[3]

As the examples suggest, domain-specific features can be very discriminative within a domain. However, the consequence of relying on them is that training needs to take place directly in the domain of application in order to achieve effectiveness. This is not only cost-intensive but sometimes also infeasible, namely, when training data from that domain is too scarce. Moreover, the use of according algorithms in the wild (where the domains of input texts are unknown beforehand) naturally appears problematic, rendering their benefit for search engines and big data analytics applications questionable. In the following, we therefore discuss ways to overcome domain dependence and to thereby obtain *domain independence*.

5.1.2   Requirements of Achieving Pipeline Domain Independence

The domain independence of a text analysis pipeline follows from the domain independence of the algorithms employed in the pipeline, as it refers to the performed analyses. According to the discussion above, the development of each algorithm can be seen as deriving a model from a set of training texts that maps features of input texts to output information. To obtain an ideally domain-independent algorithm for a given text analysis task, we argue that three requirements must be fulfilled:

---

[3] According to Blitzer et al. (2008), domain dependence occurs in nearly every application of machine learning. As exemplified, it is not restricted to statistical approaches, though.

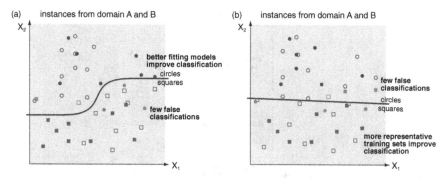

Fig. 5.3 Illustration of two ways of improving the decision boundary from Fig. 5.2 for the domains A and B as a whole: **a** Choosing a model that better fits the task. **b** Choosing a training set (open icons) that represents both domains.

a. **Optimal fitting** of the model complexity to the text analysis task,
b. **optimal representativeness** of the training set with respect to all possible input texts, and
c. **optimal invariance** of the features across all domains of application.[4]

A general assumption behind every text analysis task is that some unknown target function exists, which defines the correct output information for each input text (cf. Sect. 2.1). The model derived from the training texts can be seen as an approximation of the target function for the task at hand. Such a model may both overfit and underfit the training data (Montavon et al. 2012). An *overfitting* model does not only capture relevant but also irrelevant properties of the training texts (including noise) rather than generalizing from the texts. I.e., the model complexity is too high. *Underfitting* in turn means to generalize too much by assuming a too simple model, thus failing to capture certain relevant properties of input texts. Both overfitting and underfitting weaken the effectiveness of an algorithm on new input texts. In contrast, an *optimal fitting* perfectly approximates the complexity of the target function and, hence, will work on all input texts as effectively as possible based on the considered training texts and features.

To give an example, the instances from domains A and B in Fig. 5.2 as a whole suggest that the shown decision boundary underfits the target function. In particular, the function does not seem to be linear with respect to x_1 and x_2. As an alternative, Fig. 5.3(a) sketches that an appropriate sigmoid-like decision boundary better fits the classification task across domains, causing only few falsely classified instances.

Optimal fitting is always desired in text analysis, because it implies that the derivation of the model from the training texts is done appropriately. Unfortunately, there is no general way of choosing the right model complexity for a text analysis task at hand. While approaches to avoid overfitting and underfitting exist (Montavon et al. 2012),

---

[4]The terms used here come from the area of machine learning (Hastie et al. 2009). However, our argumentation largely applies to rule-based text analysis approaches as well.

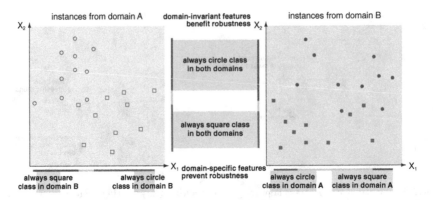

Fig. 5.4 Illustration of the different domain invariance of the features x_1 and x_2 with respect to the instances from domains A and B: Only for x_2, the distribution of values over the circle and square remains largely invariant across the domains.

in the end the appropriateness of a model depends on the training set it is derived from. This directly leads to requirement of *optimal representativeness*.

The used training set governs the distribution of values of the considered features and, hence, the quality of the derived model. According to learning theory (cf. Sect. 2.1), the best model is obtained when the training set is optimally representative for the domain of application. The representativeness prevents the model from incorrectly generalizing from the training data. Given different domains of application, the training texts should, thus, optimally represent all texts irrespective of their domains (Sapkota et al. 2014). Figure 5.3(b) shows an alternative training set (open icons) for the sample instances from domains A and B that adresses this requirement. As for optimal fitting, it leads to a decision boundary, which causes fewer false classifications than the one shown in Fig. 5.2. Among others, we observe such behavior in Wachsmuth and Bujna (2011) after training on a random crawl of blog posts instead of a focused collection of reviews.

Optimal representativeness is a primary goal of corpus design (Biber et al. 1998). Besides the problem of how to achieve representativeness, an optimally representative training set can only be built when enough training texts are given from different domains. This contradicts one of the basic scenarios that motivates the need for domain robustness, namely, that enough data is given from some source domain, but only few from a target domain. The domain adaptation approaches summarized in Sect. 2.4 deal with this scenario by learning the shift in the feature distribution between domains or by aligning features from the source and the target domain. Hence, they require at least some data from the target domain for training and, so, need to assume the domains of application in advance.

The question is how to develop domain-independent text analysis algorithms without knowing the domains of application. Since an algorithm cannot adapt to the target domains in this scenario, the only way seems to derive a model from the training texts that already refrains from any domain dependence in the first place.

This leads to our notion of *optimal invariance* of features. We call a set of features (optimally) *domain-invariant* in a given text analysis task, if the distribution of their values remains the same (with respect to the output information sought for) across all possible domains of applications. Accordingly, *strongly domain-invariant* features entail similar distributions across domains. For illustration, Fig. 5.4 emphasizes the strong domain invariance of the feature x_2 in the sample classification task: In both domains, high values of x_2 always refer to instances of the circle class, and low values to the square class, which benefits domain robustness. Only the medium values show differences between the domains. In contrast, x_1 is very domain-specific. The distribution of its values is almost contrary for the two domains.

The intuition behind domain invariance is that the respective features capture properties of the task to be addressed only and not of the domain of application. As a consequence, the resort to domain-invariant features simplifies the above-described requirement of optimal representativeness. In particular, it limits the need to consider all domains of application since the feature distribution remains stable across domains. Ideally, a training set then suffices, which is representative in terms of the distribution of features with respect to the task in a single domain.

In practice, optimal invariance will often not be achievable, because a differentiation between task-specific and domain-specific properties of texts requires to know the target function. Still, we believe that strongly domain-invariant features can be found for many text analysis tasks. While the domain invariance of a certain set of features cannot be proven, the robustness of an algorithm based on the features can at least be evaluated using test sets from different domains of application. Such research has already been done for selected tasks. For instance, Menon and Choi (2011) give experimental evidence that features based on function words robustly achieve high effectiveness in authorship attribution across domains.

Domain-invariant features benefit the domain independence of text analysis algorithms and, consequently, the domain independence of a pipeline that employs such algorithms. That being said, we explicitly point out that the best set of features in terms of domain invariance is not necessarily the best in terms of effectiveness. In the case of the figures above, for instance, the domain-specific feature x_1 may still add to the overall classification accuracy, when used appropriately. Hence, domain-invariant features do not solve the general problem of achieving optimal effectiveness in text analysis, but they help to robustly maintain the effectiveness of a text analysis pipeline when applying the pipeline to unknown texts.

To conclude, none of the described requirements can be realized perfectly in general, preventing ideal domain independence in practice. Still, approaches to address each requirement exist. The question is whether general ways can be found to overcome domain dependence, thereby improving pipeline robustness in ad-hoc large-scale text mining. For a restricted setting, we consider this question in the remainder of this chapter.

5.1.3 Domain-Independent Features of Argumentative Texts

The domain dependence of text analysis algorithms and pipelines is manifold and widely discussed in the literature (cf. Sect. 2.4). Different from the problems of optimizing pipeline design and pipeline efficiency that we tackled in Chaps. 3 and 4, domain dependence can hardly be addressed irrespective of the text analysis task at hand, as it is closely connected to the actual analysis of natural language text and to the domain scheme relevant in the task. Therefore, it seems impossible to approach domain dependence comprehensively within one book chapter.

Instead, we restrict our view to the requirement of optimally invariant features here, which directly influences possible solutions to optimal representativeness and optimal fitting, as sketched above. To enable high-quality text mining, we seek for invariant features that, at the same time, achieve high effectiveness in the addressed text analysis task. Concretely, we focus on tasks that deal with the classification of *argumentative texts* like essays, transcripts of political speeches, scientific articles, or reviews, since they seem particularly viable for the development of domain-invariant features: In general, an argumentative text represents a written form of monologi-cal argumentation. For our purposes, such *argumentation* can be seen as a regulated sequence of text with the goal of providing persuasive arguments for an intended con-clusion (cf. Sect. 2.4 for details). This involves the identification of facts about the topic being discussed as well as the structured presentation of pros and cons (Besnard and Hunter 2008). As such, argumentative texts resemble the type of speeches Aristotle refers to in the quote at the beginning of this chapter.

Typical tasks that target at argumentative texts are sentiment analysis, stance recognition, and automatic essay grading among others (cf. Sect. 2.1). In such tasks, domains are mostly distinguished in terms of topic, like different product types in reviews or different disciplines of scientific articles. Moreover, argumentative texts share common linguistic characteristics in terms of their structure (Trosborg 1997). Now, according to Aristotle, the arrangement of the parts of a speech (i.e., the *overall structure* of the speech) plays an important role in making a speech. Putting both together, it therefore seems reasonable that the following two-fold hypothesis holds for many tasks that deal with the classification of argumentative texts, where overall structure can be equated with *argumentation structure*:

1. **Impact of Structure.** The class of an argumentative text is often decided by its overall structure.
2. **Invariance of Structure.** Features that capture the overall structure of argumentative texts are often strongly domain-invariant.

The first part of the hypothesis is important, since it suggests that structure-based features actually help to effectively address a given task. If the second part turns out to be true, we can in fact achieve a domain-robust classification of argumentative texts. We investigate both parts in this chapter.

5.2   A Structure-Oriented View of Text Analysis

To investigate whether a focus on the analysis of overall structure benefits the domain robustness of pipelines for the classification of argumentative texts, we now model the units and relations in such texts that make up overall structure from an argumentation perspective. Our shallow model is based on the intuition that many people organize their argumentation largely sequentially. The model allows viewing text analysis as the task to classify the argumentation structure of input texts, as we exemplify for the sentiment analysis of reviews. This section partly reuses content and follows the discussion of Wachsmuth et al. (2014a), but the model developed here aims for more generality and wider applicability in text analysis.

5.2.1   Text Analysis as a Structure Classification Task

Not only sentiment analysis, but also several other non-standard text classification tasks (cf. Sect. 2.1) directly or indirectly deal with structure. As an obvious example, automatic essay grading explicitly rates argumentative texts, mostly targeting at structural aspects (Dikli 2006). In genre identification, a central concept is the form of texts (Stein et al. 2010). Some genre-related tasks explicitly aim at argumentative texts, such as language function analysis (cf. Sect. 2.3). Criteria in text quality assessment of WIKIPEDIA articles and the like often measure structure (Anderka et al. 2012), while readability has been shown to be connected to discourse (Pitler and Nenkova 2008). Arun et al. (2009) rely on structural clues like patterns of unconsciously used function words in authorship attribution, and similar patterns have been successfully exploited for plagiarism detection (Stamatatos 2011).[5]

According to our hypothesis from Sect. 5.1, we argue that in these and related tasks the class of an argumentative text is often decided by the structure of its argumentation rather than by its content, while the content adapts the argumentation to the domain at hand. For the classification of argumentative texts, we reinterpret the basic scenario from Sect. 1.2 in this regard by viewing text analysis as a *structure classification task*:

Structure Classification Task. Given a collection or a stream of argumentative input texts **D**, process **D** in order to infer class information of some type C from each text based on the argumentation structure of the text.

This reinterpretation differs more significantly from the definition in Sect. 1.2 than those in Sects. 3.2 and 3.4, because here the type of output information to be

---

[5]On a different level, overall structure also play a role in sequence labeling tasks like named entity recognition (cf. Sect. 2.3). There, many approaches analyze the *syntactic* structure of a sentence for the decision whether some candidate text span denotes an entity.

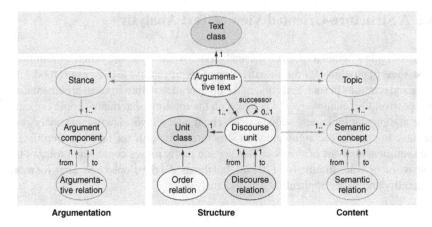

Fig. 5.5 The proposed metamodel of the *structure* of an argumentative text (center) and its connection to the *argumentation* (left) and the *content* (right) of the text.

produced is much more restricted (i.e., text-level class information).[6] As such, the reinterpretation may seem unnecessarily limiting. We apply it merely for a more focused discussion, though. Accordingly, it should not be misunderstood as an exclusive approach to respective tasks. Apart from that, the reinterpretation appears rather vague, because it leaves open what is exactly meant by argumentation structure. In the following, we present a metamodel that combines different concepts from the literature to define such structure for argumentative texts in a granularity that we argue is promising to address text classification.

Figure 5.5 shows the ontological metamodel with all presented concepts. Similar to the information-oriented view of text analysis in Sect. 3.4, the ontology is not used in terms of a knowledge base, but it serves as an analogy to the process-oriented view in Sect. 3.2. We target at the center part of the model, which defines the overall structure of argumentative texts, i.e., their argumentation structure. In some classification tasks, structure may have to be analyzed in consideration of the content referred to in the argumentation of a text. An example in this regard is stance recognition, where the topic of a stance is naturally bound to the content. First, we thus introduce the left and right part. Given the topic is known or irrelevant, however, a focus on structure benefits domain robustness, as we see later on.

5.2.2 Modeling the Argumentation and Content of a Text

As stated in Sect. 5.1, an argumentative text can be seen as the textual representation of an argumentation. An argumentation aims to give persuasive arguments for some

---

[6]Notice, though, that *all* single text classification tasks target at the inference of information of one type C only, which remains implicit in the basic scenario from Sect. 1.2.

conclusion. In the hotel reviews analyzed in our project ARGUANA (cf. Sect. 2.3), for instance, authors often justify the score they assign to the reviewed hotel by sharing their experiences with the reader. According to Stab and Gurevych (2014a), most argumentation theories agree that an argumentation consists in a composition of *argument components* (like a claim or a premise) and *argumentative relations* between the components (like the support of a claim by a premise). In contrast, the concrete types of components and relations differ. E.g., Toulmin (1958) further divides premises into grounds and backings (cf. Sect. 2.4 for details). The conclusion of an argumentation may or may not be captured explicitly in an argument component itself. It usually corresponds to the *stance* of the author of the text with respect to the topic being discussed.

The *topic* of an argumentative text sums up what the content of the text is all about, such as the stay at some specific hotel in case of the mentioned reviews. The topic is referred to in the text directly or indirectly by talking about different semantic concepts. We use the generic term *semantic concept* here to cover entities, attributes, and similar, like a particular employee of a hotel named John Doe or like the hotel's staff in general. *Semantic relations* may exist between the concepts, e.g. John Doe works for the reviewed hotel. As the examples show, the relevant concrete types of both semantic concepts and semantic relations are often domain-specific, similar to what we observed for annotation types in Sect. 3.2.

An actual understanding of the arguments in a text would be bound to the contained semantic concepts and relations. In contrast, we aim to determine only the class of an argumentative text given some classification scheme here. Such a *text class* represents meta information about the text, e.g. the sentiment score of a review or the name of its author. As long as the meta information does not relate to the topic of a text, loosing domain independence by analyzing content-related structure seems unnecessary.

Stab and Gurevych (2014a) present an annotation of the structure of argumentative texts (precisely, of persuasive essays) that relates to the defined concepts. They distinguish major claims (i.e., conclusions), claims, and premises as argumentation components as well as support and attack as argumentative relations. Such annotation schemes serve research on the mining of arguments and their interactions (cf. Sect. 2.4). The induced structure may also prove beneficial for text classification, though, especially when the given classification scheme targets at the purpose of argumentation (as in the case of stance recognition). However, we seek for a model that can be applied to several classification tasks. Accordingly, we need to abstract from concrete classification tasks in the first place.

5.2.3 Modeling the Argumentation Structure of a Text

For the classification of argumentative texts, we propose to model the pragmatics side of overall structure, i.e., how relevant information is arranged in a text in order to justify the intended conclusion. To this end, we compose abstract concepts in the center part of our metamodel in Fig. 5.5 that relate to the *information structure* of argumentative texts. Information structure defines how information is packaged within and across sentences and builds, in turn, upon *discourse structure* (cf. Sect. 2.4).

The most recognized model of the discourse structure of a text is the *rhetorical structure theory* (Mann and Thompson 1988). Like in that theory, we consider discourse structure as a connection of text parts that are related through interpretable *discourse relations* (also called *rhetorical relations*). In total, Mann and Thompson (1988) distinguish 23 concrete relation types that are irrespective of the given task or domain. Among these, some of the most frequent are e.g. contrast, elaboration, and summary. With respect to the connected parts, we follow Carlson et al. (2001) who have introduced the widely-adopted notion of (elementary) *discourse units* as the minimal building blocks a text is composed of. In the information-structural view, such a unit captures a single piece of information relevant within the discourse, normally packed within a clause or a sentence (Gylling 2013).

The question is how to model the relevant information in a discourse unit while abstracting from the unit's content. Our assumption is that each discourse unit plays a role in the argumentation structure of the text it belongs to with respect to the given classification task. In Fig. 5.5, we capture the role in terms of a *unit class* that can be assigned to a discourse unit. Concrete unit classes are not domain-specific but task-specific. In Sect. 5.3 below, for instance, we model the local sentiment polarity of a discourse unit for the classification of the global sentiment score of the respective text. Local sentiment may also help to infer the stance of an author with respect to some topic, whereas the language function of a text rather emanates from the local language functions in the text (Wachsmuth and Bujna 2011).[7] In some tasks, unit classes are ordinal or metric, so there exists an *order relation* for the unit classes (say, *Positive > Objective > Negative* for local sentiment).

Altogether, we model the overall structure of an argumentative text D for text classification based on the defined concepts in a shallow manner (a discussion of the shallow model follows at the end of this section). In particular, we consider an argumentative text as a sequence of $n \geq 1$ discourse units $d_1, \ldots, d_n$, where each discourse unit d_i has a unit class $C_U(d_i)$ from a task-specific scheme. Moreover, we take the simplifying view that every two subsequent discourse units d_i and d_{i+1} are connected by a discourse relation of some concrete type C_R. For this reason, we do not speak of the nucleus and satellite of a discourse relation, like Mann and Thompson (1988), but we simply specify the relation to be directed, either as $C_R(d_i, d_{i+1})$ or as $C_R(d_{i+1}, d_i)$. Figure 5.6 visualizes the resulting metamodel of overall structure that emanates from the abstract concepts. In the following, we exemplify how to instantiate the metamodel for a concrete task.[8]

---

[7] As the examples demonstrate, the scheme of unit classes can, but needs not necessarily, be related to the scheme of the text class to be inferred.

[8] Besides different namings, the metamodel can be seen as a generalization of the review argumentation model from Wachsmuth et al. (2014a). However, we emphasize here that the semantic concepts contained in a discourse unit do not belong to the structure.

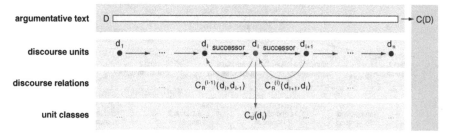

Fig. 5.6 Visualization of our model of the structure of an argumentative text D for finding its text class $C(D)$ in some task. D is represented as a sequence of $n \geq 1$ discourse units. Each unit d_i has a task-specific unit class and discourse relations of some concrete types to its predecessor d_{i-1} and its successor d_{i+1} if existing.

5.2.4 Defining a Structure Classification Task Ontology

The instantiation of the structure part of the metamodel in Fig. 5.5 entails two steps: Given a classification task to be addressed on a set of argumentative texts, the first step is to derive a concrete model for that task from the metamodel. Such a derivation can be understood as defining a *structure classification task ontology* that instantiates the abstract concepts of structure:

Structure Classification Task Ontology. A structure classification task ontology Ω denotes a 2-tuple $\langle C_U^{(\Omega)}, \mathbf{C}_R^{(\Omega)} \rangle$ such that

1. **Unit Classes.** $C_U^{(\Omega)}$ is a set of concrete unit classes and
2. **Relation Types.** $\mathbf{C}_R^{(\Omega)}$ is a set of concrete types of discourse relations.

Once a structure classification task ontology has been defined, the second step is to actually model the structure of each text, i.e., to create individuals of the concepts in the concrete model.

The considered types of unit classes and discourse relations decide what information to use for analyzing overall structure in the task at hand. In contrast, the defined ontology does not distinguish concrete types of discourse units, since they can be assumed task-independent. While also discourse relations are task-independent (as mentioned), different subsets of the 23 relation types from the rhetorical structure theory may be beneficial in different tasks or even other relation types, such as those from the PENN DISCOURSE TREEBANK (Carlson et al. 2001).

As an example, we illustrate the two instantiation steps for the sentiment analysis of reviews, as tackled in our project ARGUANA (cf. Sect. 2.3). Reviews comprise a positional argumentation, where an author collates and structures a choice of statements (i.e., facts and opinions) about a product or service in order to inform intended recipients about his or her beliefs (Besnard and Hunter 2008). The conclusion of a review is often not explicit, but it is quantified in terms of an overall sentiment rating. For example, a review from the hotel domain may look like the following:

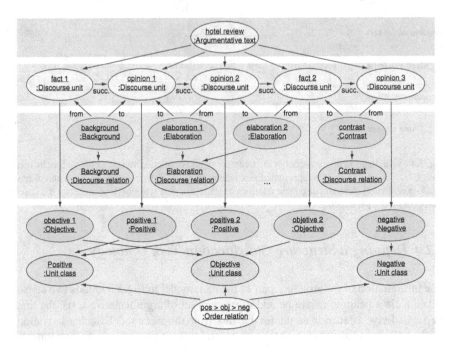

Fig. 5.7 Instantiation of the structure part of the metamodel from Fig. 5.5 with concrete concepts of discourse relations and unit classes as well as with individuals of the concepts for the example hotel review discussed in the text.

> We spent one night at that hotel. Staff at the front desk was very nice, the room was clean and cozy, and the hotel lies in the city center... but all this never justifies the price, which is outrageous!

Five statements can be identified in the review: A fact on the stay, followed by two opinions on the staff and the room, another fact on the hotel's location, and a final opinion on the price. Although there are more positive than negative statements, the argumentation structure of the review reveals a negative *global sentiment*, i.e., the overall sentiment to be inferred in the sentiment analysis of reviews.

In simplified terms, the argumentation structure is given by a sequential composition of statements with *local sentiments* on certain aspects of the hotel. Figure 5.7 models the argumentation structure of the example review as an instance of our metamodel from Fig. 5.5: Each statement represents a discourse unit whose unit class corresponds to a local sentiment. Here, we cover the positive and negative polarities of opinions as well as the objective nature of a fact as classes of local sentiment. They entail the order relation already mentioned above. The five statements are connected by four discourse relations. The discourse relations in turn refer to three from whatever number of discourse relation types.

What Fig. 5.7 highlights is the sequence information induced by our shallow structure-oriented view of text analysis. In particular, according to this view an argumentative text implies both a sequence of unit classes and a sequence of discourse relations. In the remainder of this chapter, we examine in how far such sequences can be exploited in features for an effective and domain-robust text analysis. However, Fig. 5.7 also illustrates that the representation of a text as an instance of the defined metamodel is tedious and space-consuming. Instead, we therefore prefer visualizations in the style of Fig. 5.6 from here on.

5.2.5 Discussion of the Structure-Oriented View

The metamodel presented in this section defines an abstract view of text analysis dedicated to tasks that deal with the classification of argumentative texts. At its heart, it represents the overall structure of a text on the pragmatic level, namely, as a sequence of interrelated discourse units of certain types. For a classification task at hand, we propose to instantiate the metamodel and to then derive features from the resulting concrete model. Since the metamodel defines a significant abstraction, some information in and about argumentative texts is covered only implicitly if at all, such as lexical and syntactic properties. When it comes to the computation of features, missing information can still be integrated with the structural information derived from the model, though, if needed. The same holds for information related to the argumentation and content part of the metamodel.

The main goal of this chapter is to develop more domain-robust text classification approaches. In this regard, our resort to discourse structure in the metamodel for supporting domain independence follows related research. For instance, Ó Séaghdha and Teufel (2014) hypothesize (and provide evidence to some extent) that the language used in a text to convey discourse function is independent of the topical content of the text. Moreover, as argued, the question of how to represent discourse structure is largely independent from the text analysis tasks being addressed.

On the contrary, the concrete unit classes to be chosen for the discourse units strongly depend on the given task and they directly influence the effectiveness of all approaches based on the respective model. In particular, the assumption behind is that the composition of unit classes in a text reflects argumentation structure on an abstraction level that helps to solve the task. What makes the choice even more complex is that a text analysis algorithm is required, in general, to infer the unit classes of discourse units, since the unit classes are usually unknown beforehand. Such an algorithm may be domain-dependent again, which then shifts the domain robustness problem from the text level to the unit level instead of overcoming it. At least, the shift may go along with a reduction of the problem, as in the case of modeling local sentiment *polarities* to reflect global sentiment *scores*. Also, later on we discuss what types of fully or nearly domain-independent unit classes can be used to model argumentation structure and when.

At first sight, the shallow nature of our model of argumentation structure has shortcomings. Especially, the limitation that discourse relations always connect neighboring discourse units makes an identification of deeper non-sequential interactions of the arguments in a text hard. Such interactions are in the focus of many approaches related to argumentation mining (cf. Sect. 2.4). For text classification, however, we argue that the shallow model should be preferred over deeper models (as far as the abstraction in our model proves useful): Under our hypothesis from Sect. 5.1, the overall structure of an argumentative text is decisive for its class in several text classification tasks. By relying on a more abstract representation of these argumentation structures, the search space of possible patterns in the structures is reduced and, hence, common patterns can be found more reliably. In the next section, we provide evidence for the impact of such patterns.

5.3 The Impact of the Overall Structure of Input Texts

As discussed in Sect. 5.1, one way to improve a pipeline's domain robustness is to analyze features of input texts only, whose distribution stays strongly invariant across domains. For the classification of argumentative texts, this section motivates our hypothesis that features, which capture overall structure, qualify as candidates for achieving such invariance. We present revised versions of empirical findings from Wachsmuth and Bujna (2011) and Wachsmuth et al. (2014b): First, we give evidence that many commonly used features generalize across domains only fairly. Based on the model from Sect. 5.2, we then demonstrate that patterns in the overall structure of argumentative texts exist, which are decisive for classification. Their domain invariance is examined afterwards in Sect. 5.4.

5.3.1 Experimental Analysis of Content and Style Features

Standard approaches to text classification map an input text to a vector of lexical and shallow syntactic features, from which class information is inferred with supervised learning (cf. Sect. 2.1). Many common features represent either the content of a text, focusing on the distribution of words and semantic concepts, or they capture its style, relying on lexical characteristics or syntactic patterns (Stamatatos 2009). While such features are effective for narrow-domain texts with explicit class information (Joachims 2001; Pang et al. 2002), we now provide experimental evidence that they tend to be insufficient for classifying out-of-domain texts:

Tasks and Domains. We consider two tasks that deal with the classification of argumentative texts, sentiment analysis and language function analysis. In terms of sentiment, we distinguish positive, negative, and neutral polarities for the hotel reviews (H) of our English ARGUANA TRIPADVISOR CORPUS (cf. Appendix C.2) and for the film reviews (F) of the English SENTIMENT SCALE DATASET (cf. Appendix C.4). Similarly, we classify the language functions of each input text from both the *music* (M) and the *smartphone* (S) part of our German LFA- 11 corpus (cf. Appendix C.3) as being predominantly personal, commercial, or informational.

Preprocessing. Each text is split into sentences and tokens, the latter enriched with part-of-speech and phrase chunk tags. For these annotations, we rely on the respective language-specific versions of the algorithms SSE, STO_2, TPO_1, and PCH. Details on the algorithms are found in Appendix A.

Features. Based on the annotations, we evaluate the following 15 feature types. Each type comprises a number of single features (given in brackets).[9] For exact parameters of the feature types, see Appendix B.4. With respect to the information they capture, the 15 types can be grouped into five sets:

1. Word features, namely, the distribution of frequent *token 1-grams* (324–425 features), *token 2-grams* (112–217), and *token 3-grams* (64–310),
2. class features, namely, the distribution of *class-specific words* (8–83) that occur three times as often in one class as in every other (Lee and Myaeng 2002), some lexicon-based *sentiment scores* (6), and the distribution of subjective *sentiment words* (123–363). The two latter rely on SENTIWORDNET (Baccianella et al. 2010), which is available for English only.
3. part-of-speech (POS) features, namely, the distribution of *POS 1-grams* (43–52), *POS 2-grams* (63–178), and *POS 3-grams* (69–137),
4. phrase features, namely, the distribution of *chunk 1-grams* (8–16), *chunk 2-grams* (24–74), and *chunk 3-grams* (87–300), and
5. stylometry features common in authorship attribution (Stamatatos 2009), namely, the distribution of *character 3-grams* (200–451) and of the most frequent *function words* (100) as well as *lexical statistics* (6) like the number of tokens in the text and in a sentence on average.

Experiments. Given the two domains for each of the two considered tasks, we create classifiers for all feature types in isolation using supervised learning. Concretely, we separately train one linear multi-class support vector machine from the LIBSVM integration of WEKA (Chang and Lin 2011; Hall et al. 2009) on the training set of each corpus, optimizing parameters on the respective validation set.[10] Then, we measure the accuracy of each feature type on the test sets of the corpora in the associated task in two scenarios: (1) when training is performed in-domain on the training set of the corpus, and (2) when training is performed on the training set of the other domain.[11] The results are listed in Table 5.1 for each possible combination A2B of a training domain A and a test domain B.

---

[9]The numbers of features vary depending on the processed training set, because only distributional features with some minimum occurrence are considered (cf. Sect. 2.1).

[10]The SENTIMENT SCALE DATASET is partitioned into four author datasets (cf. Sect. C.4). Here, we use the datasets of author c and d for training, b for validation, and a for testing.

[11]Research on domain adaptation often compares the accuracy of a classifier in its training domain to its accuracy in some other test domain (i.e., $A2A$ vs. $A2B$), because training data from the test domain is assumed to be scarce. However, this leaves unclear whether an accuracy change may be caused by a varying difficulty of the task at hand across domains. For the analysis of domain invariance, we therefore put the comparison of different training domains for the same test domain (i.e., $A2A$ vs. $B2A$) in the focus here.

Table 5.1 Accuracy of 15 common feature types in experiments with 3-class sentiment analysis and 3-class language function analysis for eight different scenarios A2B. A is the domain of the training texts, and B the domain of the test texts, with A, B ∈ {*hotel* (H), *film* (F), *music* (M), *smartphone* (S)}. The two right-most columns shows the minimum observed accuracy of each feature type and the maximum loss of accuracy points caused by training out of the test domain.

Feature type	Sentiment polarity (en)				Language function (de)				Min	Max
	H2H	F2H	F2F	H2F	M2M	S2M	S2S	M2S	acc'y	loss
Token 1-grams	64%	44%	42%	30%	71%	54%	67%	42%	30%	−25
Token 2-grams	50%	46%	40%	**65%**	51%	48%	69%	20%	20%	−49
Token 3-grams	25%	40%	40%	37%	42%	49%	66%	27%	25%	−39
Class-specific words	43%	40%	24%	24%	78%	**67%**	61%	24%	24%	−37
Sentiment scores	61%	49%	43%	27%	n/a	n/a	n/a	n/a	27%	−16
Sentiment words	60%	45%	39%	28%	n/a	n/a	n/a	n/a	27%	**−15**
POS 1-grams	57%	44%	39%	36%	72%	53%	58%	40%	36%	−19
POS 2-grams	53%	48%	41%	36%	68%	54%	64%	40%	36%	−24
POS 3-grams	44%	41%	40%	23%	57%	49%	57%	**55%**	23%	−17
Chunk 1-grams	51%	46%	37%	28%	55%	53%	57%	30%	28%	−27
Chunk 2-grams	56%	43%	39%	33%	62%	50%	57%	31%	31%	−26
Chunk 3-grams	54%	44%	41%	33%	60%	55%	58%	37%	33%	−21
Character 3-grams	53%	**51%**	38%	24%	62%	52%	63%	39%	24%	−24
Function words	60%	44%	43%	37%	79%	61%	62%	49%	37%	−18
Lexical statistics	43%	38%	40%	40%	52%	18%	34%	48%	18%	−34
All features	**65%**	40%	**49%**	40%	**81%**	59%	**73%**	48%	**40%**	−25

Limited Domain Invariance of all Feature Types. The token 1-grams perform comparably well in the in-domain scenarios (H2H, F2F, M2M, and S2S), but their accuracy significantly drops in the out-of-domain scenarios with a loss of up to 25% points. The token 2-grams and 3-grams behave inconsistent in these respects, indicating that their distribution is not learned on the given corpora. Anyway, the minimum observed accuracy of all word features lies below 33.3%, i.e., below chance in three-class classification. The class features share this problem, but they seem less domain-dependent as far as available in the respective scenarios. While the sentiment scores and the sentiment words work well in three of the four sentiment analysis scenarios, the class-specific words tend to be more discriminative for language functions with one exception: In M2S, they fail, certainly because only 11 class-specific words have been found in the music training set.

While similar observations can be made for many of the remaining feature types, we restrict our view to the best results, all of which refer to features that capture style: In terms of domain robustness, the part-of-speech features are the best group in our experiments with a maximum loss of 17–24 points. Especially the POS 1-grams turn out to be beneficial across domains, achieving high accuracy in a number

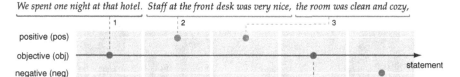

Fig. 5.8 Illustration of capturing the structure of a sample hotel review as a local sentiment flow, i.e., the sequence of local sentiment in the statements of the review.

of scenarios and always improving over chance. Only the function words do better with an accuracy of at least 37 % and a loss of at most 18 points, when trained out of the domain of application. At the same time, the function words yield the best accuracy value under all single feature types with 79 % in case of M2M.

The reasonable benefit of function words across domains matches results from the above-mentioned related work in authorship attribution (Menon and Choi 2011). However, Table 5.1 also conveys that neither the function words nor any other of the 15 content and style feature types seem strongly domain-invariant. In addition, the bottom line of the table makes explicit that these types do not suffice to achieve high quality in the evaluated classification tasks, although the combination of features at least performs best in all in-domain scenarios. For out-of-domain scenarios, we hence need to find features that are both effective and domain-robust.

5.3.2 Statistical Analysis of the Impact of Task-Specific Structure

In order to achieve high effectiveness across domains, features are needed that model text properties, which are specific to the task being addressed and not to the domain of application. In the chapter at hand, we focus on the classification of argumentative texts. To obtain domain-invariant features for such texts, our hypothesis is that we can exploit their sequential argumentation structure, as captured in our model from Sect. 5.2. Before we turn to the question of domain invariance, however, we first provide evidence that such structure can be decisive for text classification. For this purpose, we refer to the sentiment analysis of hotel reviews again.

As stated in Sect. 5.2, the argumentation structure of a review can be represented by the sequence of local sentiment classes in the review. We distinguish between positive (*pos*), negative (*neg*), and objective (*obj*). Following Mao and Lebanon (2007), we call the sequence the *local sentiment flow*. For instance, the local sentiment flow of the example review from Sect. 5.2 is visualized in Fig. 5.8. It can be seen as an instance of the structure classification task ontology from Sect. 5.2, in which discourse relations are ignored. Not only in the example review, the local sentiment

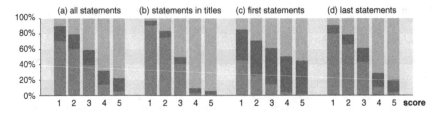

Fig. 5.9 a The fractions of positive opinions (upper part of the columns), objective facts (center part), and negative opinions (lower part) in the texts of the ARGUANA TRIPADVISOR CORPUS, separated by the sentiment scores between 1 and 5 of the reviews they refer to. **b–d** The respective fractions for statements at specific positions in the reviews.

flow of a review impacts the review's global sentiment, as we now demonstrate. For a careful distinction between the frequency and the composition of local sentiment, we hypothesize three dependencies:

1. The global sentiment of a review correlates with the ratio of positive and negative opinions in the review.
2. The global sentiment of a review correlates with the polarity of opinions at certain positions of the review.
3. The global sentiment of a review depends on the review's local sentiment flow.

To test the hypotheses, we statistically analyze our ARGUANA TRIPADVISOR CORPUS, which contains 2100 reviews from the hotel domain.[12] As detailed in Appendix C.2, each review has a title and a body and it has been manually segmented into facts, positive opinions, and negative opinions that are annotated as such. Since the corpus is balanced with respect to the reviews' global sentiment scores between 1 (worst) and 5 (best), we can directly measure correlations between local and global sentiment in the corpus.

Figure 5.9(a) illustrates that hypothesis 1 turns out to be true statistically for our corpus, matching the intuition that, the larger the fraction of positive opinions, the better the sentiment score, and vice versa: On average, a hotel review with score 1 is made up of 71 % negative and 9.4 % positive opinions. This ratio decreases strictly monotonously under increasing scores down to 5.1 % negative and 77.5 % positive opinions for score 5. The impact of the frequency of local sentiment is obvious. Interestingly, the fraction of facts remains stable close to 20 % at the same time.

For the second hypothesis, we compute the distributions of opinions and facts in the review's titles as well as in the first and last statements of the review's bodies. In comparison with Fig. 5.9(a), the results for the title distributions in Fig. 5.9(b) show much stronger gaps in the above-mentioned ratio with a rare appearance of facts, suggesting that the sentiment polarity of the title of a hotel review often reflects the review's global sentiment polarity. Conversely, Fig. 5.9(c) shows that over 40 % of all first statements denote facts, irrespective of the sentiment score. This number may

---

[12]For information on the source code of the statistical analysis, see Appendix B.4.

Table 5.2   The 13 most frequent sentiment change flows in the ARGUANA TRIPADVISOR CORPUS and their distribution over all possible global sentiment scores.

#	Sentiment change flow	Frequency	Score 1	Score 2	Score 3	Score 4	Score 5
1	(pos)	7.7%	1.9%	3.1%	7.5%	31.1%	**56.5%**
2	(obj)	5.3%	3.6%	13.6%	20.0%	**33.6%**	29.1%
3	(neg)	3.5%	**58.9%**	30.1%	9.6%	1.4%	–
4	(pos, obj, pos)	3.0%	–	–	6.5%	35.5%	**58.1%**
5	(obj, pos)	2.7%	–	1.8%	7.0%	31.6%	**59.6%**
6	(pos, neg, pos)	2.1%	–	15.9%	11.4%	**56.8%**	15.9%
7	(obj, pos, obj, pos)	1.9%	–	–	5.1%	35.8%	**59.0%**
8	(pos, neg)	1.7%	11.1%	**36.1%**	33.3%	19.4%	–
9	(neg, obj, neg)	1.7%	**88.9%**	8.3%	2.8%	–	–
10	(obj, pos, neg, pos)	1.5%	–	3.2%	**32.3%**	**32.3%**	**32.3%**
11	(neg, pos, neg)	1.5%	35.5%	**51.6%**	12.9%	–	–
12	(obj, neg, obj, neg)	1.1%	**77.3%**	18.2%	4.5%	–	–
13	(obj, neg)	1.1%	**83.3%**	16.7%	–	–	–

originate in the introductory nature of first statements. It implies a limited average impact of the first statement on a hotel review's global sentiment. So, both the titles and first statements support the second hypothesis. In contrast, the distributions in Fig. 5.9(d) do not differ clearly from those in Fig. 5.9(a). A possible explanation is that the last statements often summarize reviews. However, they may also simply reflect the average.

The impact of local sentiment at certain positions indicates the importance of structural aspects of a review. Yet, it does not allow drawing inferences about a review's overall structure. Therefore, we now come to the third hypothesis, which refers to local sentiment flows. For generality, we do not consider a review's title as part of its flow, since many reviews have no title—unlike in the ARGUANA TRIP-ADVISOR CORPUS. Our method to test the hypothesis is to first determine sentiment flows that represent a significant fraction of all reviews in the corpus. Then, we compute how often these patterns cooccur with each sentiment score.

We do not determine the exact local sentiment flows, though, due to the varying lengths of reviews: The only five local sentiment flows that represent at least 1 % of the ARGUANA TRIPADVISOR CORPUS are trivial without any change in local sentiment, e.g. *(pos, pos, pos, pos)* or *(obj)*. In principle, a solution is to length-normalize the flows. We return to this in the context of our overall analysis in Sect. 5.4.[13] From an argumentation perspective, length normalization appears hard to grasp. Instead, we move from local sentiment to changes in local sentiment here. More precisely, we

---

[13] Alternatively, Mao and Lebanon (2007) propose to ignore the objective facts. Our according experiments did not yield new insights except for a higher frequency of trivial flows. For lack of relevance, we omit to present results on local sentiment flows here, but they can be easily reproduced using the provided source code (cf. Appendix B.4).

combine consecutive statements with the same local sentiment, thereby obtaining local sentiment segments. We define the *sentiment change flow* of a review as the sequence of all such segments in the review's body.[14] In case of the example in Fig. 5.8, e.g., the second and third statement have the same local sentiment. Hence, they refer to the same segment in the sentiment change flow, *(obj, pos, obj, neg)*.

In total, our corpus contains reviews with 826 different sentiment change flows. Table 5.2 lists all those with a frequency of at least 1 %. Together, they cover over one third (34.8 %) of all texts. The most frequent flow, *(pos)*, represents the 161 (7.7 %) fully positive hotel reviews, whereas the best global sentiment score 5 is indicated by flows with objective facts and positive opinions (table lines 4, 5, and 7). Quite intuitively, *(neg, pos, neg)* and *(pos, neg, pos)* denote typical flows of reviews with score 2 and 4, respectively. In contrast, none of the listed flows clearly indicates score 3. The highest correlation is observed for *(neg, obj, neg)*, which results in score 1 in 88.9 % of the cases.

The outlined cooccurrences offer strong evidence for the hypothesis that the global sentiment of a review depends on the review's local sentiment flow. Even more, they imply the expected effectiveness (in the hotel domain) of a single feature based on a sentiment change flow. In particular, the frequency of a flow can be seen as the recall of any feature that applies only to reviews matching the flow. Correspondingly, the distribution of a flow over the sentiment scores shows what precision the feature would achieve in predicting the scores. However, Table 5.2 also reveals that all found flows cooccur with more than one score. Thus, we conclude that sentiment change flows do not decide global sentiment alone. This becomes explicit for *(obj, pos, neg, pos)*, which is equally distributed over scores 3–5.

5.3.3 Statistical Analysis of the Impact of General Structure

The representation of argumentation structure by local sentiment flows appears rather specific for sentiment analysis. Now, we analyze whether the more task-independent concepts of our structure-oriented model from Sect. 5.2 help in sentiment analysis, too. For this purpose, we repeat parts of the last experiment for the *discourse relation flow* of a review, i.e., the sequence of discourse relation types in the review's body. In case of the example review from Figs. 5.7 and 5.8, the discourse relation flow would be *(background, elaboration, elaboration, contrast)*. Based on another analysis of the ARGUANA TRIPADVISOR CORPUS (that can be reproduced with the same source code used above), we investigate two hypotheses, one about the distribution and one about the structure of discourse relations:

1. The global sentiment of a review correlates with the frequency of certain types of discourse relations in the review.
2. The global sentiment of a review depends on the review's discourse relation flow.

---

[14]In Wachsmuth et al. (2014b), we name these sequences *argumentation flows*. In the given more general context, we prefer a more task-specific naming in order to avoid confusion.

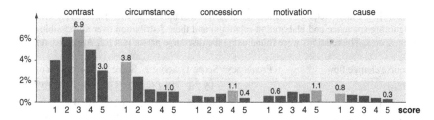

Fig. 5.10 The fractions of five types of discourse relations under all discourse relations, separated by the sentiment scores between 1 and 5 of the reviews they refer to. The discourse relations were found using the algorithm PDR (cf. Appendix A.1).

Unlike local sentiment, discourse relations are not annotated in the ARGUANA TRIPADVISOR CORPUS. Instead, we processed all texts with our heuristic discourse parser PDR. PDR distinguishes a subset of 10 discourse relation types from the rhetorical structure theory (cf. Appendix A.1 for details). Based on the output of PDR, we have computed the distributions of each discourse relation type over the sentiment scores of the reviews in the corpus in order to check for evidence for the first hypothesis. For brevity, Fig. 5.10 shows only the results of those types that occur in the discourse change flows, which we discuss below.

Figure 5.10 stresses that, in terms of sentiment analysis, one of the most important discourse relation types is the *contrast* between discourse units: Quite intuitively, medium reviews (those with sentiment score 3) yield the largest fraction of contrast relations (6.9%). This is more than twice as high as the fraction in the score 5 reviews (3.0%) on average. A sign of rather negative sentiment in hotel reviews seems the resort to *causes*, which are often used to justify statements. Interestingly, *circumstance* relations (like when or where something happened) even more behave in this way; they cooccur 3.8 times as often with score 1 than with score 4 or 5. Conversely, *motivation* relations (e.g. indicated by second person voice) appear more frequently in medium and positive hotel reviews, and *concession* (e.g. indicated by the connective "although") play a particular role in score 4 reviews.

The outlined correlations between frequencies of discourse relations and global sentiment support hypothesis 1. The remaining question is whether the overall structure of discourse relations in the text is decisive, as captured by hypothesis 2. Analog to above, we again consider changes in the discourse relation flows, resulting in *discourse change flows*, which would be *(background, elaboration, contrast)* for our example review. However, not coincidentally, we have left out both *elaboration* and *sequence* in Fig. 5.10. Together, these two types make up over 80% of all discourse relations found by PDR, rendering it hard to find common flows with other (potentially more relevant) types. Thus, we ignore *elaboration* and *sequence* relations in the determination of the most frequent discourse change flows.

Table 5.3 shows the distributions of sentiment scores for all such 12 discourse change flows that represent at least 1% of the reviews in the ARGUANA TRIP-ADVISOR CORPUS each and 44.6% of the corpus reviews in total. The flows are

Table 5.3 The 12 most frequent discourse change flows in the ARGUANA TRIPADVISOR CORPUS (when ignoring sequence and elaboration relations) and their distribution over all possible global sentiment scores. The relations were found using the discourse parser PDR (cf. Appendix A).

Discourse change flow	Frequency	Score 1	Score 2	Score 3	Score 4	Score 5
(contrast)	25.2%	15.7%	**28.1%**	25.5%	18.3%	12.5%
(circumstance)	3.7%	**44.2%**	29.9%	5.2%	10.4%	10.4%
(contrast, circumstance)	1.9%	**35.0%**	22.5%	22.5%	10.0%	10.0%
(circumstance, contrast)	1.5%	**37.5%**	21.9%	12.5%	15.6%	12.5%
(contrast, circumstance, contrast)	1.0%	**45.0%**	25.0%	15.0%	10.0%	5.0%
(concession)	2.6%	16.4%	12.7%	**30.9%**	27.3%	12.7%
(contrast, concession)	1.4%	**30.0%**	23.3%	13.3%	26.7%	6.7%
(concession, contrast)	1.3%	17.9%	21.4%	**28.6%**	25.0%	7.1%
(motivation)	2.4%	15.7%	5.9%	17.6%	19.6%	**41.2%**
(contrast, motivation)	1.3%	14.3%	17.9%	**35.7%**	14.3%	17.9%
(motivation, contrast)	1.0%	**27.3%**	22.7%	22.7%	13.6%	13.6%
(cause)	1.3%	11.1%	**33.3%**	11.1%	25.9%	18.5%

grouped according to the contained discourse relation types. This is possible because only *contrast* cooccurs with other types in the listed flows, certainly due to the low frequency of the others.

About every fourth review (25.2%) contains only *contrast* relations (except for sequences and elaborations). Compared to Fig. 5.10, such reviews differ from an average review with contrast relations, having their peak at score 2 (28.1%). Similar observations can be made for *(cause)*. The found flows with *circumstance* relations suggest that discourse change flows do not influence sentiment scores: No matter if a contrast is expressed before or after a circumstance, the respective review tends to be negative mostly. However, this is different for *concession* and *motivation* relations. E.g., a motivation in isolation leads to score 4 and 5 in over 60% of the cases, whereas the flow *(contrast, motivation)* most often cooccurs with score 3. *(motivation, contrast)* even speaks for a negative review on average. An explanation might be that readers shall be warned right from the beginning in case of negative hotel experiences, while recommendations are rather made at the end.

Altogether, the correlations between scores and flows in Table 5.3 are not as clear as for the sentiment change flows. While the existence of certain discourse relations obviously affects the global sentiment of the hotel reviews, their overall structure seems sometimes but not always decisive for the sentiment analysis of reviews.

5.3.4 Implications of the Invariance and Impact

Features that model the content of a text are extensively used in text classification (Aggarwal and Zhai 2012). In case of argumentative texts, many approaches also rely on style features (Stamatatos 2009). In this section, we have first offered evidence for the domain dependence of typical content and style features in the classification of argumentative texts. As an alternative, we have then analyzed two ways to capture the overall structure of such texts (reviews, specifically): sentiment change flows and discourse change flows. The former relies on task-specific information, while the latter capture discourse structure. We argue that both can be seen as shallow models of argumentation structure that abstract from content.

The revealed existence of patterns in the sentiment change flows and discourse change flows of hotel reviews that cooccur with certain sentiment scores demonstrates the impact of modeling argumentation structure. In addition, the abstract nature of the two types of flows brings up the possibility that the found or similar *flow patterns* generalize well across domains. For these reasons, we hence concretize our hypothesis from Sect. 5.1 by supposing that features, which are based on according flow patterns, help to achieve (1) domain robustness and (2) high effectiveness in text analysis tasks that deal with the classification of argumentative texts.

Different from the sentiment analysis of reviews, however, at least the resort to local sentiment flows does not generalize well to all such tasks. E.g., scientific articles only sporadically contain sentiment at all, making respective features useless for classification. Still, we assume that local sentiment flows have correspondences in other classification tasks, which hence allow for corresponding *unit class flows*. To this end, our structure-oriented view from Sect. 5.2 needs to be concretized adequately for the task at hand. A few examples for such instantiations have already been sketched in Sect. 5.2. The discourse change flows may be more generally beneficial, but the experiments above suggest that the impact of analyzing discourse structure also may be lower than of analyzing task-specific unit classes.

As motivated, the focus on argumentation structure targets at the development of text analysis algorithms, which improve the robustness and intelligibility of the pipeline they are employed in. In this regard, we investigate the benefits of modeling such structure in Sects. 5.4 and 5.5. Since the two types of change flows in the form considered here still depend on the length of the analyzed texts to some extent, they may not be optimal for cross-domain text analysis, though. Below, we therefore introduce a novel alternative way of identifying typical overall structures of argumentative texts. It allows computing the similarity between arbitrary texts and, hence, does not require to detect exactly the same patterns across domains.

Either way, our analysis of the ARGUANA TRIPADVISOR CORPUS in this section shows that structure-based features are not always decisive for text classification. To enable high-quality text mining, a combination with other feature types may thus be required. Candidates have already been presented, namely, some of the content and style features as well as the distribution of unit classes and discourse relations. We evaluate below how their integration affects domain robustness and effectiveness.

5.4 Features for Domain Independence via Supervised Clustering

Based on our structure-oriented model from Sect. 5.2, we now develop statistical features that aim for an effective classification of argumentative texts across domains. First, we learn a set of common patterns of the overall structure of such texts through supervised clustering. In the sense of the overall analysis from Fig. 5.1, we then use each such flow pattern as a similarity-based feature for text classification. We detail and evaluate an according analysis for sentiment scoring, reusing content from Wachsmuth et al. (2014a). Our results suggest that the considered flow patterns learned in one domain generalize to other domains to a wide extent.

5.4.1 Approaching Classification as a Relatedness Problem

As motivated in Sect. 5.2, we propose to address the classification of argumentative texts as a structure classification task, where we refer to the overall structure of the texts. To the best of our knowledge, no approach to explicitly capture overall structure has been presented in the surrounding field so far (cf. Sect. 2.4). Even local sentiment flows (Mao and Lebanon 2007), which define the starting point of some analyses in this chapter, capture sentiment at different positions of a text only: Each flow value is represented by an individual feature. Hence, classification algorithms will naturally tend to assign positive weights to all values (or proceed accordingly if no weights are used), thereby disregarding the flow as a whole.

In contrast, we now develop a novel feature type that achieves to make the overall structure of argumentative texts measurable by addressing structure classification as a *relatedness problem*, i.e., by computing how similar the overall structure of a text is to a common set of known patterns of overall structure. The idea behind resembles *explicit semantic analysis* (Gabrilovich and Markovitch 2007), which measures the semantic relatedness of texts. Explicit semantic analysis represents the meaning of a text as a weighted vector of semantic concepts, where each concept is derived from a WIKIPEDIA article. The relatedness of two texts then corresponds to the similarity of their vectors, e.g. measured using the cosine distance (cf. Sect. 2.1).

Since we target at overall structure, we rely on our model from Sect. 5.2 instead of semantic concepts. In particular, in line with our analyses from Sect. 5.3, we propose to capture the overall structure of an argumentative text in terms of a specific unit class flow or of the discourse relation flow of a text. From here on, we summarize all concrete types of unit classes (e.g. local sentiments, language functions, etc.) and the discourse relation type under the term *flow type*, denoted as C_f. Hence, every *flow* can be seen as a sequence of instances of the respective type:

Flow. The flow $\mathbf{f}$ of a text of some concrete flow type C_f denotes the sequence of instances of C_f in the text.

Based on flows, we define *flow patterns* to capture the overall structure we seek for:

Flow Pattern. A flow pattern $\mathbf{f}^*$ denotes the average of a set of similar length-normalized flows $F = \{\mathbf{f}_1, \ldots, \mathbf{f}_{|F|}\}$, $|F| \geq 1$, of some concrete flow type.

Analog to deriving semantic concepts from WIKIPEDIA articles, we determine a set of flow patterns $F^* = \{\mathbf{f}_1^*, \ldots, \mathbf{f}_{|F^*|}^*\}$, $|F^*| \geq 1$, of some flow type $C_{\mathbf{f}}$ from a training set of argumentative texts. Unlike the semantic concepts, however, we aim for common patterns that represent more than one text. Therefore, we construct F^* from flow clusters that cooccur with text classes. Each pattern is then deployed as a single feature, whose value corresponds to the similarity between the pattern and a given flow. The resulting feature vectors can be used for statistical approaches to text classification, i.e., for learning to map flows to text classes (cf. Sect. 2.1). In the following, we detail the outlined process and we exemplify it for sentiment scoring.

5.4.2 Learning Overall Structures with Supervised Clustering

We assume to be given a set of training texts $\mathbf{D}_T$ and an associated set C_T containing the text class of each text in $\mathbf{D}_T$. To obtain common flow patterns of some flow type $C_{\mathbf{f}}$, we first need to determine the respective flow of each text in $\mathbf{D}_T$. Usually, instances of $C_{\mathbf{f}}$ are not annotated beforehand. Consequently, a text analysis pipeline $\Pi_{\mathbf{f}}$ is required that can infer $C_{\mathbf{f}}$ from $\mathbf{D}_T$.[15] The output of $\Pi_{\mathbf{f}}$ directly leads to the flows. As an example, Fig. 5.11(a) depicts flows of two types for the sample text from Sect. 5.3: the local sentiment flow already shown in Fig. 5.8 as well as the discourse relation flow of the sample text with all occurring types of discourse relations including *elaboration* (unlike the discourse change flows in Sect. 5.3).

The length of a flow follows from the number of discourse units in a text (cf. Sect. 5.2), which varies among input texts in most cases. To assess the similarity of flows, we thus convert each flow into a length-normalized version. The decision what length to be used resembles the optimal fitting problem sketched in Sect. 5.1: Short normalized versions may oversimplify long flows, losing potentially relevant flow type information. Long versions may capture too much noise in the flows. A reasonable normalized length should therefore be chosen in dependence of the expected average or median length of the texts to be represented.

Besides the length, normalization brings up the question of whether and how to interpolate values, at least in case of ordinal or metric flow types. For instance, local sentiment could be interpreted as a numeric value between 0.0 (negative) and 1.0 (positive) with 0.5 meaning objective or neutral. In such cases, an interpolation seems beneficial, e.g. for detecting similarities between flows like *(1.0, 0.5, 0.0)* and *(1.0, 0.0)*. For illustration, Fig. 5.11(b) shows normalized versions of the flows from Fig. 5.11(a). There, some non-linear interpolation is performed for the local

---

[15] In the evaluation at the end of this section, we present results on the extent to which the effectiveness of inferring $C_{\mathbf{f}}$ affects the quality of the features based on the flow patterns.

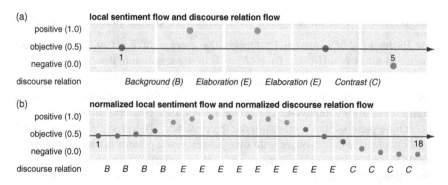

Fig. 5.11 a Illustration of the local sentiment flow and the discourse relation flow of the sample text from Sect. 5.3. **b** Length-normalized versions of the two flows for length 18 (local sentiment) and 17 (discourse relations), respectively.

sentiment values, while the nominal discourse relation types are duplicated for lack of reasonable alternatives. The chosen normalized lengths are exemplary only.

Once the set of all normalized flows F has been created from $\mathbf{D}_T$, flow patterns can be derived. As usual for feature computations (cf. Sect. 2.1), however, it may be reasonable to discard rare flows before (say, flows that occur only once in the training set) in order to avoid capturing noise.

Now, our hypothesis behind flow patterns is that similar flows entail the same or, if applicable, similar text classes. Here, the similarity of two length-normalized flows is measured in terms of some similarity function (cf. Sect. 2.1). For instance, the (inverse) Manhattan distance may capture the similarity of the metric local sentiment flows. In case of discourse relation flows, we can at least compute the fraction of matches. With respect to the chosen similarity function, flows that construct the same pattern should be as similar as possible and flows that construct different patterns as dissimilar as possible. Hence, it seems reasonable to partition the set F using clustering (cf. Sect. 2.1) and to derive flow patterns from the resulting clusters.

In particular, we propose to perform *supervised clustering*, which can be understood as a clustering variant, where we exploit knowledge about the training text classes to ensure that all obtained clusters have a certain *purity*. In accordance with the original purity definition (Manning et al. 2008), here purity denotes the fraction of those flows in a cluster, whose text class equals the majority class in the cluster. This *standard purity* assumes exactly one correct class for each flow, implying that a flow alone decides the class, which is not what we exclusively head for (as discussed in Sect. 5.2). At least larger classification schemes speak for a *relaxed purity* definition. For example, our results for sentiment scores between 1 and 5 in Sect. 5.3 suggest to also see the dominant neighbor of the majority score as correct. Either way, based on any measure of purity, we define *supervised flow clustering*:

Supervised Flow Clustering. Given a set of flows F with known classes, determine a clustering $\mathbf{F} = \{F_1, \ldots, F_{|\mathbf{F}|}\}$ of F with $\bigcup_{i=1}^{|\mathbf{F}|} F_i = F$ and $F_i \cap F_j = \emptyset$ for $F_i \neq F_j \in \mathbf{F}$, such that the purity of each $F_i \in \mathbf{F}$ lies above some threshold.

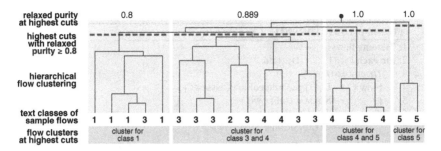

Fig. 5.12 Illustration of hierarchically clustering a set of 20 sample flows, represented by their associated text classes between 1 and 5. The example relaxed purity threshold of 0.8 leads to cuts in the hierarchy that create four flow clusters.

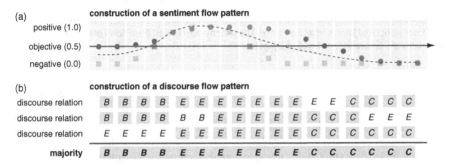

Fig. 5.13 Sketch of the construction of **a** a *sentiment flow pattern* (dashed curve) from two length-normalized sample local sentiment flows (circles and squares) and **b** a *discourse flow pattern* (bold) from three according discourse relation flows.

We seek for clusters with a high purity, as they indicate specific classes, which matches the intuition behind the flow patterns to be derived. At the same time, the number of clusters should be small in order to achieve a high average cluster size and, thus, a high commonness of the flow patterns. An easy way to address both requirements is to rely on a hierarchical clustering (cf. Sect. 2.1), where we can directly choose a flat clustering $\mathbf{F}$ with a desired number $|\mathbf{F}|$ of clusters through cuts at appropriate nodes in the binary tree of the associated hierarchy. To minimize the number of clusters, we then search for all cuts closest to the tree's root that create clusters whose purity lies above the mentioned threshold. Figure 5.12 exemplifies the creation for the relaxed purity defined above and a threshold of 0.8.

The centroid of each flow cluster, i.e., the mean of all contained flows, finally becomes a flow pattern, if it is made up of some minimum number of flows. Figure 5.13(a) sketches the resulting construction of a *sentiment flow pattern* for two sample local sentiment flows of normalized length. Since we consider local sentiment as a metric classification scheme here, each value of the flow pattern can in fact represent the average of the flow values. In contrast, for nominal flow types, a possible alternative is to use the majority flow type in according patterns.

DETERMINEFLOWPATTERNS($\mathbf{D}_T$, C_T, C_f, Π_f)

1: Training flows $F \leftarrow \emptyset$
2: **for each** $i \in \{1, \ldots, |\mathbf{D}_T|\}$ **do**
3:     Π_f.process($\mathbf{D}_T[i]$)
4:     Flow $\mathbf{f} \leftarrow \mathbf{D}_T[i]$.getOrderedFlowClasses($C_f$)
5:     $\mathbf{f} \quad\quad \leftarrow$ NORMALIZEFLOW($\mathbf{f}$)
6:     $F \quad\quad \leftarrow F \cup \{\langle \mathbf{f}, C_T[i]\rangle\}$
7: $F \quad\quad\quad \leftarrow$ RETAINSIGNIFICANTFLOWS(F)
8: Flow patterns $F^* \leftarrow \emptyset$
9: Clusters $\mathbf{F} \leftarrow$ PERFORMSUPERVISEDFLOWCLUSTERING(F)
10: $\mathbf{F} \quad\quad\quad \leftarrow$ RETAINSIGNIFICANTFLOWCLUSTERS($\mathbf{F}$)
11: **for each** Cluster $F_i \in \mathbf{F}$ **do** $F^* \leftarrow F^* \cup F_i$.getCentroid()
12: **return** F^*

Pseudocode 5.1: Determination of a common set of flow patterns F^* from a set of training texts $\mathbf{D}_T$ and their associated known text classes C_T. The patterns are derived from flows of the type C_f whose instances are in turn inferred with the pipeline Π_f.

Figure 5.13(b) illustrates this for a *discourse flow pattern* derived from three sample discourse relation flows.

Altogether, the high-level process of deriving common flow patterns from a training set $\mathbf{D}_T$ is summarized in Pseudocode 5.1. There, lines 1–7 determine the set of training flows F. To this end, a given text analysis pipeline Π_f infers instances of the flow type C_f from all texts in $\mathbf{D}_T$ (line 3). Next, the sequences of instances in each text is converted into a normalized flow $\mathbf{f}$ (lines 4 and 5). In combination with the associated text class $C_T[i]$, $\mathbf{f}$ is stored as a training flow (line 6). Once all such flows have been computed, only those are retained that occur some significant number of times (line 7). The flow patterns F^* are then found by performing the presented clustering method (line 9) and retaining only clusters of some significant minimum size (line 10). Each pattern is given by the centroid of a cluster (line 11).

5.4.3 Using the Overall Structures as Features
for Classification

Although we use the notion of an overall analysis as a motivation, our goal is not to develop a new text classification method. Rather, we propose the derived flow patterns as a new feature type to be used for classification. Typically, text classification is approached with supervised learning, i.e., by deriving a classification model from the feature representations of training texts with known classes. The classification model then allows classifying the representations of unknown texts (cf. Sect. 2.1).

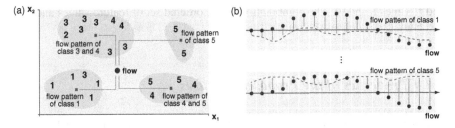

Fig. 5.14 Two illustrations of measuring the similarity (here, the inverse Manhattan distance) of an unknown flow to the flow patterns resulting from the clusters in Fig. 5.12: **a** 2D plot of the distance of the flow's vector to the cluster centroids. **b** Distances of the values of the flow to the values of the respective patterns.

CREATETRAININGFEATUREVECTORS($\mathbf{D}_T$, C_T, $C_\mathbf{f}$, $\Pi_\mathbf{f}$, F^*)

1: Training vectors $X \leftarrow \emptyset$
2: **for each** $i \in \{1, \ldots, |\mathbf{D}_T|\}$ **do**
3:     $\Pi_\mathbf{f}$.process($\mathbf{D}_T[i]$)
4:     Flow $\mathbf{f} \leftarrow \mathbf{D}_T[i]$.getOrderedFlowClasses($C_\mathbf{f}$)
5:     $\mathbf{f}$ $\leftarrow$ NORMALIZEFLOW($\mathbf{f}$)
6:     Feature values $\mathbf{x}^{(i)} \leftarrow \emptyset$
7:     **for each** Flow Pattern $\mathbf{f}^* \in F^*$ **do**
8:         Feature value $x^{(i)}$ $\leftarrow$ COMPUTESIMILARITY($\mathbf{f}, \mathbf{f}^*$)
9:         $\mathbf{x}^{(i)}$ $\leftarrow \mathbf{x}^{(i)} \| x^{(i)}$
10:     X $\leftarrow X \cup \{\langle \mathbf{x}^{(i)}, C_T[i] \rangle\}$
11: **return** X

Pseudocode 5.2: Creation of a training feature vector for every text from a training set $\mathbf{D}_T$ with associated text classes C_T. Each feature value denotes the similarity of a flow pattern from F^* to the text's flow of type $C_\mathbf{f}$ (inferred with the pipeline $\Pi_\mathbf{f}$).

After the set of common flow patterns F^* has been determined, the next step is hence to compute one training feature vector for each text from the above-processed sets $\mathbf{D}_T$ and $C_\mathbf{f}$. In order to capture the overall structure of a text, we measure the similarity of its normalized flow to each flow pattern in F^* using the same similarity function as for clustering (see above). As a result, we obtain a feature vector with one similarity value for each flow pattern. Figure 5.14 sketches two views of the similarity computations for a sample flow: On the left, the vector view with the cluster centroids that represent the flow patterns, mapped into two dimensions (for illustration purposes) that correspond to the positions in the flow. And, on the right, the flow view with the single values of the flows and flow patterns.

Pseudocode 5.2 shows how to create a vector for each text in $\mathbf{D}_T$ given the flow patterns F^*. Based on the normalized flow $\mathbf{f}$ of a text (lines 3–5), one feature value is computed for each flow pattern $\mathbf{f}^* \in F^*$ by measuring the similarity between $\mathbf{f}$

and $\mathbf{f}^*$ (lines 8 and 9). The combination of the ordered set of feature values and the text class $C_T[i]$ defines the vector (line 10).[16]

5.4.4 Properties of the Proposed Features

In general, the introduced feature type itself is applicable to arbitrary tasks from the area of text classification (a discussion of a transfer to other tasks follows at the end of this section). It works irrespective of the type, language, or other properties of the input texts being processed, since it outsources the specific analysis of producing the flow type C_f to the employed text analysis pipeline Π_f. Nevertheless, our feature type explicitly aims to serve for approaches to the classification of argumentative texts, because it relies on our hypothesis that the overall structure of a text is decisive for the class of a text, which will not hold for all text classification tasks, e.g. not for topic detection (cf. Sect. 2.1). While the feature type can cope with all flow types as exemplified, we have indicated that nominal flow types restrict its flexibility.

Correctness. Similar to the adaptive scheduling approach in Sect. 4.5, the two presented pseudocodes (Pseudocodes 5.1 and 5.2) define method schemes rather than concrete methods. As a consequence, again we cannot prove correctness here. Anyway, the notion of correctness generally does not really make much sense in the context of feature computations (cf. Sect. 2.1).

In particular, besides the flow type C_f that is defined as part of the input, both the realized processes in general and the flow patterns in specific are schematic in that they imply a number of relevant parameters:

1. **Normalization.** How to normalize flows and what normalized length to use.
2. **Similarity.** How to measure the similarity of flows and clusters.
3. **Purity.** How to measure purity and what purity threshold to ensure.
4. **Clustering.** How to perform clustering and what clustering algorithm to use.
5. **Significance.** How often a flow must occur to be used for clustering, and how large a cluster must be to be used for pattern construction.

For some parameters, reasonable configurations may be found conceptually in regard of the task at hand. Others should rather be found empirically.

With respect to the question of how to perform clustering, we have clarified that the benefit of a supervised flow clustering lies in the construction of common flow patterns that cooccur with certain text classes. A regular unsupervised clustering may also achieve commonness, but it may lose the cooccurrences. Still, there are scenarios where the unsupervised variant can make sense, e.g. when rather few input texts with classes are available, but a large number of unknown texts. Then, semi-supervised

---

[16]For clarity, we have included the computation of flows both in Pseudocode 5.1 and in Pseudocode 5.2. In practice, the flow of each text can be maintained during the whole process of feature determination and vector creation and, thus, needs to be computed only once.

learning could be conducted (cf. Sect. 2.1) where flow patterns are first derived from the unknown texts and cooccurrences thereafter from the known texts.

Although we see the choice of a concrete clustering algorithm as part of the realization, above we propose to resort to hierarchical clustering in order to be able to easily find flow clusters with some minimum purity. An alternative would be to directly compute a flat clustering and then retain only pure clusters. While such an approach provides less control about the obtained flow patterns, it may significantly improve run-time: Many flat clustering algorithms scale linearly with the number of objects to be clustered, whereas most common hierarchical clustering algorithms are at least quadratic (Manning et al. 2008). This brings us to the computational complexity of using flow patterns as features for text classification as described. As far as possible, we now estimate the asymptotic run-time of the schematic pseudocodes in terms of the $\mathcal{O}$-calculus (Cormen et al. 2009).

The main input size of DETERMINEFLOWPATTERNS in Pseudocode 5.1 is the number of texts in $\mathbf{D}_T$ (both the number of flows in F and the number of clusters in $\mathbf{F}$ are restricted by $|\mathbf{D}_T|$). The complexity of two operations of the method cannot be quantified asympotically, namely, the analysis of the pipeline $\Pi_\mathbf{f}$ in line 3 and the computation of a clustering $\mathbf{F}$ in line 9. We denote their overall run-times on $\mathbf{D}_T$ as $t_\mathbf{f}(\mathbf{D}_T)$ and $t_\mathbf{F}(\mathbf{D}_T)$, respectively. The run-times of all remaining operations on the flows and clusters depend on the length of the flows only. In the worst case, the length of all flows is the same but different from the normalized length. We denote this length as $|\mathbf{f}_{max}|$ here. The remaining operations are executed either at most once for each text (like normalization) or once for all texts (like retaining significant flows), resulting in the run-time $\mathcal{O}(|\mathbf{D}_T| \cdot |\mathbf{f}_{max}|)$. Altogether, we thus estimate the run-time of DETERMINEFLOWPATTERNS as:

$$t_{\text{DETERMINEFLOWPATTERNS}}(\mathbf{D}_T) \;=\; t_\mathbf{f}(\mathbf{D}_T) + t_\mathbf{F}(\mathbf{D}_T) + \mathcal{O}(|\mathbf{D}_T| \cdot |\mathbf{f}_{max}|) \qquad (5.1)$$

In terms of asymptotic run-times, CREATETRAININGFEATUREVECTORS (cf. Pseudocode 5.2) differs only in two respects from DETERMINEFLOWPATTERNS: First, no clustering takes place there, and second, similarities need to be computed between each text and every flow pattern. Under the reasonable assumption that the normalized length of the flows and flow patterns is constant, however, the second difference does not play a role asymptotically. Hence, the run-time of CREATETRAININGFEATUREVECTORS is:

$$t_{\text{CREATETRAININGFEATUREVECTORS}}(\mathbf{D}_T) \;=\; t_\mathbf{f}(\mathbf{D}_T) + \mathcal{O}(|\mathbf{D}_T| \cdot |\mathbf{f}_{max}|) \qquad (5.2)$$

In practice, the most expensive operation will often be the clustering in DETERMINEFLOWPATTERNS for larger numbers of input texts.[17] The goal of this chapter is not to optimize efficiency, which is why we do not evaluate run-times in the following experiments, where we employ the proposed features in an overall analysis. We

---

[17]If the flow of each text from $\mathbf{D}_T$ is computed only once during the whole process (see above), Ineq. 5.2 would even be reduced to $\mathcal{O}(|\mathbf{D}_T| \cdot |\mathbf{f}_{max}|)$.

return to the efficiency of feature computation, when we discuss the overall analysis in the context of ad-hoc large-scale text mining at the end of this section.

5.4.5 Evaluation of Features for Domain Independence

A comprehensive evaluation of the effectiveness and domain robustness of flow patterns in the classification of argumentative texts would require to analyze several classification tasks, flow types, and domains. As an initial step, we now investigate the sentiment scoring of reviews. We use local sentiment as the flow type, which appears promising according to the results in Sect. 5.3. To stress the domain dependence problem of text classification, we look at two highly different topical review domains, *hotel* (H) and *film* (F). For information on the source code of the evaluation, see Appendix B.4. Descriptions and effectiveness estimations of all algorithms mentioned in the following are found in Appendix A.

Argumentative Texts. Our experiments are based on two English review corpora: First, our ARGUANA TRIPADVISOR CORPUS (cf. Appendix C.2) with 2100 hotel reviews and an average review length of 14.8 subsentence-level discourse units (produced with the algorithm PDU). And second, the SENTIMENT SCALE DATASET (cf. Appendix C.4) with about 5000 film reviews and an average length of 36.1 discourse units, where we assume each sentence to denote one unit. The former is split into training, validation, and test texts. The latter consists of four separated datasets, one for each review author (*a, b, c* and *d*). We preprocess all reviews with the algorithms SSE, STO$_2$, and POS$_1$. For generality, we ignore the reviews' titles, since our features target at arbitrary argumentative texts, including those without a title.

Text Classes. Each given hotel review has a sentiment score between 1 (worst) and 5 (best). The film reviews come with two sentiment scales. We rely on the scale from 0 (worst) to 2 (best), so we can logically map the scale of the hotel reviews to the scale of the film reviews for a domain transfer. In particular, scores 1 and 2 are mapped to 0, score 3 to 1, and score 4 and 5 to 2.

Unit Classes. We distinguish the three local sentiment classes already used above, namely, *positive* (1.0), *objective* (0.5), and *negative* (0.0). For both domains, we trained the algorithms CSB and CSP to first classify the subjectivity of the discourse units and then the polarity of the subjective discourse units. The hotel reviews contain ground-truth local sentiment annotations, i.e., every discourse unit is annotated as an objective fact, a positive opinion, or a negative opinion. For training CSB and CSP in the film domain, we additionally acquired the SUBJECTIVITY DATASET and the SENTENCE POLARITY DATASET (cf. Appendix C.4). The resulting distributions of local sentiment in the two review corpora have already been shown in Fig. 4.10 (Sect. 4.4). They give a hint on how different the evaluated domains are.

Flows. Based on either the ground-truth or the self-created annotations, we computed the local sentiment flow of each review. To construct sentiment flow patterns, all flows were length-normalized with non-linear interpolation and subsequent sampling. We used length 30 in case of the hotel reviews and length 60 in case of the film reviews, in order to represent most of the original flows without loss.

Flow Patterns. For supervised clustering, we have developed a basic agglomerative hierarchical clusterer. After some tests with different settings, we decided to measure flow and cluster similarity using group-average link clustering (Manning et al. 2008) based on the Manhattan distance between the normalized flows. In terms of purity, we resort to the relaxed purity for the sentiment scale of the hotel reviews and the standard purity for the film reviews, both with a threshold of 0.8. The centroids of all resulting clusters with at least three flows become a sentiment flow pattern.

Features. Given the unit classes and the normalized flow of each review, we computed features for the prediction of the review's sentiment score. Besides the flow patterns, we examine a selection of features in the sense of baselines that participated in our experiments in Sect. 5.3 or that are derived from the obtained results. For a concise presentation, we combine some of them in the following feature types, each of which comprising a number of single features (given in brackets).[18]

1. **Content and style features** (1026 to 2071 features). The distributions of word and part-of-speech 1-grams, 2-grams, and 3-grams as well as of all character 3-grams in the text. Lexical statistics of the text and six word-based average sentiment scores (cf. Sect. 5.3).
2. **Local sentiment distributions** (50 to 80 features). The frequencies of all local sentiment classes in the text, of series of the same class, and of changes from one class to another. Also, the local sentiment at specific positions like the first and last two units, the average local sentiment, and the original local sentiment flow from Mao and Lebanon (2007).
3. **Discourse relation distributions** (64 to 78 features). The distribution of all ten discourse relation types extracted by our heuristic discourse parser PDR as well as of frequent combinations of a relation type and the local sentiment classes it relates, e.g. *contrast(positive, negative)*.[19]
4. **Sentiment Flow Patterns** (16 to 86 features). The similarity of the normalized flow of the text to each flow pattern, as proposed above.

Experiments. Based on the four feature types, we evaluate the accuracy of a supervised classification of sentiment scores within and across domains. Concretely, we use different combinations of the employed corpora to train and test the algorithm CSS on subsets of all feature types. CSS learns a mapping from feature values to scores using a linear support vector machine (cf. Appendix A.1 for details). To this end, we

---

[18] As in Sect. 5.3, the numbers of features vary depending on the training set, because we take only those features whose frequency in the training texts exceeds some specified threshold (cf. Sect. 2.1). For instance, a word unigram is taken into account only if it occurs in at least 5 % of the hotel reviews or 10 % of the film reviews, respectively.

[19] In Wachsmuth et al. (2014a), we also evaluate the local sentiment on specific domain concepts in the given text. For lack of relevance, we leave out respective experiments here.

first processed the respective training set to determine the concrete features of each type. Then, we computed values of these features for each review. In the in-domain tasks, we optimized the cost parameter of CSS during training. For the classification across domains, we relied on the default parameter value, because an optimization with respect to the training domain does not make sense there. After training, we measure accuracy on the respective test set.

In case of the hotel reviews, we trained and optimized CSS on the training set and the validation set of the ARGUANA TRIPADVISOR CORPUS, respectively. On the film reviews, we performed 10-fold cross-validation (cf. Sect. 2.1) separately on the dataset of each review author, averaged over five runs. By that, we can directly compare our results to those of Pang and Lee (2005) who published the SENTI-MENT SCALE DATASET. In particular, we consider their best support vector machine approach here, called *ova*.[20]

Effectiveness Within Each Domain. First, we report on the in-domain tasks. For the hotel domain, we provide accuracy values both with respect to the sentiment scale from 1 to 5 and with respect the mapped scale from 0 to 2. In addition, we compare the theoretically possible accuracy to the practically achieved accuracy by opposing the results on the ground-truth local sentiment annotations of the ARGUANA TRIP-ADVISOR CORPUS to those on our self-created annotations. For the film domain, we can refer only to self-created annotations. All results are listed in Table 5.4.

In the 5-class scenario on the ground-truth annotations of the hotel reviews, the local sentiment distributions and the sentiment flow patterns are best under all single feature types with an accuracy of 52 % and 51 %, respectively. Combining all types boosts the accuracy to 54 %. Using self-created annotations, however, it significantly drops down to 48 %. The loss of feature types 2–4 is even stronger, making them perform slightly worse than the content and style features (40 %–42 % vs. 43 %). These results seem not to match with Wachsmuth et al. (2014a), where the regression error of the argumentation features remains lower on the self-created annotations. The reason behind can be inferred from the 3-class hotel results, which demonstrate the effectiveness of modeling argumentation for sentiment scoring: There, all argumentation feature types outperform feature type 1. This indicates that at least the polarity of their classified scores is often correct, thus explaining the low regression errors.

On all four film review datasets, the sentiment flow patterns classify scores most accurately among the argumentation feature types, but their effectiveness still remains limited.[21] The content and style features dominate the evaluation, which again gives evidence for the effectiveness of such features within a domain (cf. Sect. 5.3).

---

[20]We evaluate only the *classification* of scores for a focused discussion. In general, a more or less metric scale like sentiment scores suggests to use *regression* (cf. Sect. 2.1), as we have partly done in Wachsmuth et al. (2014a). Moreover, since our evaluation does not aim at achieving maximum effectiveness in the first place, for simplicity we do not explicitly incorporate knowledge about the neighborship between classes here, e.g. that score 1 is closer to score 2 than to score 3. An according approach has been proposed by Pang and Lee (2005).

[21]We suppose that the reason behind mainly lies in the limited accuracy of 74 % of our polarity classifier CSP in the film domain (cf. Appendix A.2), which reduces the impact of all features that rely on local sentiment.

Table 5.4 Accuracy of all evaluated feature types in 5-class and 3-class sentiment analysis on the test hotel reviews of the ARGUANA TRIPADVISOR CORPUS based on ground-truth annotations (*Corpus*) or on self-created annotations (*Self*) as well as in 3-class sentiment analysis on the film reviews of author *a, b, c* and *d* in the SENTIMENT SCALE DATASET. The bottom line compares our approach to Pang and Lee (2005).

| # | Feature type | Hotel (5-class) | | Hotel (3-class) | | Film (3-class) | | | |
		Corpus	Self	Corpus	Self	a	b	c	d
1	Content and style features	43 %	43 %	59 %	59 %	**69 %**	57 %	72 %	58 %
2	Local sentiment distributions	52 %	42 %	76 %	70 %	50 %	48 %	62 %	51 %
3	Discourse relation distibutions	48 %	41 %	76 %	65 %	50 %	47 %	61 %	50 %
4	**Sentiment flow patterns**	51 %	40 %	73 %	63 %	52 %	49 %	63 %	51 %
2–4	Argumentation feature types	51 %	44 %	76 %	**71 %**	53 %	48 %	65 %	51 %
1–4	All four feature types	**54 %**	**48 %**	**78 %**	70 %	68 %	**57 %**	72 %	58 %
	ova (Pang and Lee 2005)	–	–	–	–	62 %	**57 %**	**73 %**	**62 %**

Compared to *ova*, our classifier based on all feature types is significantly better on the reviews of author *a* and a little worse on two other datasets (*c* and *d*).

We conclude that the proposed feature types are competitive, achieving similar effectiveness than existing approaches. In the in-domain task, the sentiment flow patterns do not fail, but they also do not excel. Their main benefit lies in their strong domain invariance, as we see next.

Effectiveness Across Domains. We now offer evidence for our hypothesis from Sect. 5.1 that features like the sentiment flow patterns, which capture overall structure, improve the domain robustness of classifying argumentative texts. For this purpose, we apply the above-given classifiers trained in one domain to the reviews of the other domain. Different from Wachsmuth et al. (2014a), we consider not only the transfer from the hotel to the film domain, but also the other way round.

For the transfer to the hotel domain, Fig. 5.15 shows the accuracy loss of each feature type resulting from employing either of the four film datasets instead of hotel reviews for training (given in percentage points). With a few exceptions, feature types 1–3 fail in these out-of-domain scenarios. Most significantly, the content and style features lose 13 (F_a2H) to 19 % points (F_b2H), but the local sentiment and discourse relation distributions seem hardly more robust. As a consequence, the accuracy of all four feature types in combination is compromised severely. At the same time, the sentiment flow patterns maintain effectiveness across domains, losing only 4–10 points through out-of-domain training. This supports our hypothesis. Still, the local sentiment distributions compete with the sentiment flow patterns in the resulting accuracy on the hotel reviews.

However, this is different when we exchange the domains of training and application. According to Fig. 5.16, the local sentiment distributions denote the second

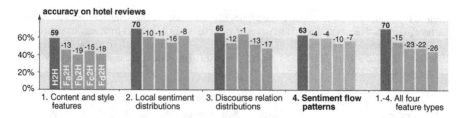

Fig. 5.15 Accuracy of the four evaluated feature types and their combination on the test hotel reviews in the ARGUANA TRIPADVISOR CORPUS based on self-created annotations with training either on the training hotel reviews (H2H) or on the film reviews of author a, b, c, or d in the SENTIMENT SCALE DATASET (F_a2H, F_b2H, F_c2H, and F_d2H).

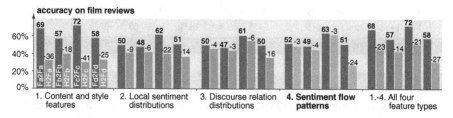

Fig. 5.16 Accuracy of the four evaluated feature types and their combination on the film reviews of author a, b, c, and d in the SENTIMENT SCALE DATASET in 10-fold cross-validation on these reviews (F_a2F_a, F_b2F_b, F_c2F_c, and F_d2F_d) or with training on the training hotel reviews of the ARGUANA TRIPADVISOR CORPUS ($H2F_a$, $H2F_b$, $H2F_c$, and $H2F_d$).

worst feature type when training them on the hotel reviews. Their accuracy is reduced by up to 22 % points ($H2F_c$), resulting in values around 40 % on all film datasets. Only the content and style features seem more domain-dependent with drastic drops between 18 and 41 points. In contrast, the accuracy of the discourse relation distributions and especially of the sentiment flow patterns provide further evidence for the truth of our hypothesis. They remain almost stable on three of the film datasets. Only in scenario $H2F_d$, they also fail with the sentiment flow patterns being worst. Apparently, the argumentation structure of the film review author d, which is reflected by the found sentiment flow patterns, differs from the others.

Insights into Sentiment Flow Patterns. For each sentiment score, Fig. 5.17(a) plots the most common of the 38 sentiment flow patterns that we found in the training set of the ARGUANA TRIPADVISOR CORPUS (based on self-created annotations). As depicted, the patterns are constructed from the local sentiment flows of up to 226 texts. Below, Figs. 5.17(b–c) show the respective patterns for author c and d in the SENTIMENT SCALE DATASET. One of the 75 patterns of author c results from 155 flows, whereas all 41 patterns of author d represent at most 16 flows.

With respect to the shown sentiment flow patterns, the film reviews yield less clear sentiment but more changes of local sentiment than the hotel reviews. While there

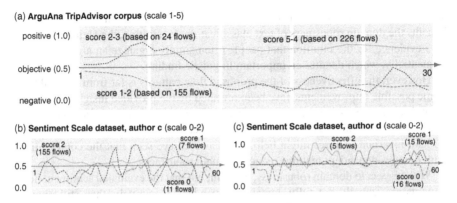

Fig. 5.17 a The three most common sentiment flow patterns in the training set of the ARGUANA TRIPADVISOR CORPUS, labeled with their associated sentiment scores. **b–c** The according sentiment flow patterns for all scores of the texts of author *c* and *d* in the SENTIMENT SCALE DATASET.

appears to be some similarity in the overall argumentation structure between the hotel reviews and the film reviews of author *c*, two of the three patterns of author *d* contain only little clear sentiment at all, especially in the middle parts. We have already indicated the disparity of the author *d* dataset in Fig. 4.10 (Sect. 4.4). In particular, 73 % of all discourse units in the ARGUANA TRIPADVISOR CORPUS are classified as positive or negative opinions, but only 37 % of the sentences of author *d*. The proportions of the three other film datasets at least range between 58 % and 67 %. These numbers also serve as a general explanation for the limited accuracy of the argumentation feature types 1–3 in the film domain.

A solution to improve the accuracy and domain invariance of modeling argumentation structure might be to construct flow patterns from the subjective statements only or from the changes of local sentiment, which we leave for future work. Here, we conclude that our novel feature type does not yet solve the domain dependence problem of classifying argumentative texts, but our experimental sentiment scoring results suggest that it denotes a promising step towards more domain robustness.

5.4.6 Discussion of Features for Domain Independence

In this section, we have pursued the main goal of this chapter, i.e., to develop a novel feature type for the classification of argumentative texts whose distribution is strongly domain-invariant across the domains of the texts. The feature type relies on our structure-oriented view of text analysis from Sect. 5.2. For the first time, it captures the overall structure of an argumentative text by measuring the similarity of the flow of the text to a set of learned flow patterns. Our evaluation of sentiment scoring supports the hypothesis from Sect. 5.1 that such a focus on overall structure benefits the domain robustness of text classification. In addition, the obtained results give evidence for the intuition that people often simply organize an argumentation sequentially, which denotes an important linguistic finding.

However, the effectiveness of the proposed flow patterns is far from optimal yet. Some possible improvements have been revealed by the provided insight into sentiment flow patterns. Also, a semi-supervised learning approach on large numbers of texts (as sketched above) may result in more effective flow patterns. Besides, further domain-invariant features might help, whereas we have seen that the combination with domain-dependent features reduces domain robustness.

With respect to domain robustness, we point out that the evaluated sentiment flow patterns are actually not fully domain-independent. Concretely, they still require a (possibly domain-specific) algorithm that can infer local sentiment from an input text, although this seems at least a somewhat easier problem. To overcome domain dependence, a solution may be to build patterns from more general information. For instance, Sect. 5.3 indicates the benefit of discourse relations in this regard. Within one language, another approach is to compute flow patterns based on the function words in a text, which can be understood as an evolution of the function word n-grams used in tasks like plagiarism detection (Stamatatos 2011).

Apparently, even the evaluated sentiment scoring task alone implies several directions of research on flow patterns. Investigating all of them would greatly exceed the scope of this book. In general, further classification tasks are viable for analyzing the discussed or other flow types, particularly those that target at argumentative texts. Some are mentioned in the preceding sections, like automatic essay grading or language function analysis. Moreover, while we restrict our view to text classification here, other text analysis tasks may profit from modeling overall structure.

In the area of information extraction, common approaches to tasks like named entity recognition or relation extraction already include structural features (Sarawagi 2008). There, overall structure must be addressed on a different level (e.g. on the sentence level). A related approach from relation extraction is to classify candidate entity pairs using *kernel functions*. Kernel functions measure the similarity between graphs such as dependency parse trees, while being able to integrate different feature types. Especially *convolutional kernels* aim to capture structural information by looking at similar graph substructures (Zhang et al. 2006). Such kernels have also proven beneficial for tasks like semantic role labeling (cf. Sect. 2.2).

As in the latter cases, the deeper the analysis, the less shallow patterns of overall structure will suffice. With respect to argumentative texts, a task of increasing prominence that emphasizes the need for more complex models is a full argumentation analysis, which seeks to understand the arguments in a text and their interactions (cf. Sect. 2.4 for details). In the context of ad-hoc large-scale text mining, we primarily aim for comparably shallow analyses like text classification. Under this goal, the resort to unit class flows and discourse relation flows provides two advantages: On one hand, the abstract nature of the flows reduces the search space of possible patterns, which facilitates the determination of patterns that are discriminative for certain text classes (as argued at the end of Sect. 5.2). On the other hand, computing flows needs much less time than complex analyses like parsing (cf. Sect. 2.1). This becomes decisive when processing big data.

Our analysis of Pseudocodes 5.1 and 5.2 indicates that the scalability of our feature type rises and falls with the efficiency of two operations: (1) Computing flows and (2) clustering them. The first depends on the effort of inferring all flow type instances for the flow patterns (including preprocessing steps). The average run-times of the algorithms CSB and CSP employed here give a hint of the increased complexity of performing sentiment scoring in this way (cf. Appendix A.2). Other flow types may be much cheaper to infer (like function words), but also much more expensive. Discourse relations, for instance, are often obtained through parsing. Still, efficient alternatives exist (like our lexicon-based algorithm PDR), indicating the usual tradeoff between efficiency and effectiveness (cf. Sect. 3.1). With respect to the second (clustering), we have discussed that our hierarchical approach may be too slow for larger numbers of training texts and we have outlined flat clusterers as an alternative. Nevertheless, clustering tends to represent the bottleneck of the feature computation and, thus, of the training of an according algorithm.

Anyway, training time is not of upmost importance in the scenario we target at, where we assume the text analysis algorithms to choose from to be given in advance (cf. Sect. 1.2). This observation conforms with our idea of an overall analysis from Sect. 1.3: The determination of features takes place within the development of an algorithm A_T that produces instances of a set of text classes C_T. At development time, A_T can be understood as an overall analysis: It denotes the last algorithm in a pipeline Π_T for inferring C_T while taking as input all information produced by the preceding algorithms in Π_T. Once A_T is given, it simply serves as an algorithm in the set of all available algorithms. In the end, our overall analysis can hence be seen as a regular text analysis algorithm for cross-domain usage. Besides the intended domain robustness, such an analysis provides the benefit that its results can be explained, as we finally sketch in Sect. 5.5.

5.5 Explaining Results in High-Quality Text Mining

A text analysis pipeline that robustly achieves sufficient effectiveness irrespective of the domain of the input texts qualifies for being used in search engines and big data analytics applications. Still, the end user acceptance of an according application may be limited, if erroneous analysis results cannot be explained (Lim and Dey 2009). In this section, we outline that both general knowledge about a text analysis process and specific information of our feature type from Sect. 5.4 allow for automatic result explanations. A first user study based on a prototypical sentiment scoring application indicates the intelligibility of the explanations. We conclude that intelligibility denotes the final building block of high quality in text mining.

5.5.1 Intelligible Text Analysis through Explanations

The *intelligibility* of an application can be seen as the application's ability to make transparent what information it has from where and what it does with that information (Bellotti and Edwards 2001). One way to approach intelligibility is to automatically provide explanations to the user of an application. We use the term *explanation* to refer to a (typically visual) presentation of information about the application's behavior. The goal of intelligibility and, thus, of giving explanations is to increase a user's acceptance of an application. The acceptance is largely affected by the *trust* a user has in the correctness of the presented information as well as by the user's *understanding* of how the results of an application have come up (Lim and Dey 2009). At the same time, the *speed* in which users can process the information provided via an interface always matters (Gray and Fu 2001).

In the context of text analysis pipelines, an understanding of the reasons behind results is not trivial, because the results often emerge from a process with several complex and uncertain decisions about natural language (Das Sarma et al. 2011). We hypothesize that intelligibility can be supported by explaining this process. Below, we show how to generally explain arbitrary text analysis processes, reusing ideas from our approach to ad-hoc pipeline construction (cf. Sect. 3.3). Especially in the area of text classification, the decisive step is the mapping from features to a text class, though. While most approaches output only a class label (cf. Sect. 2.4 for details), we can use the flow patterns from Sect. 5.4 to intuitively explain a classification decision, as we sketch afterwards.[22]

In the discussion, we follow Kulesza et al. (2013) who analyze the benefit of explanations of an application depending on their soundness and completeness. Here, *soundness* describes how truthful the presented information reflects what the application does, whereas *completeness* refers to the extent to which the information reflects all relevant aspects of the application. The authors found that explanations, which are both highly sound and highly complete, are most trusted by users. Still, such explanations entail the danger that important information is overlooked. According to the results of the authors, a reduced completeness tends to maintain trust, but it often causes a slower and worse understanding of what is happening. Reducing soundness enables simplification, thus often speeding up the understanding, but it lowers the trust for lack of enough information.

5.5.2 Explanation of Arbitrary Text Analysis Processes

We consider the scenario that a text analysis pipeline $\Pi = \langle \mathbf{A}, \pi \rangle$ has processed an input text to produce instances of a set of information types $\mathbf{C}$ (in terms of annotations

---

[22]Besides explanations, a common approach to improve intelligibility in tasks like information extraction, which we do not detail here, is to support verifiability, e.g. by linking back to the source documents from which the returned results have been inferred.

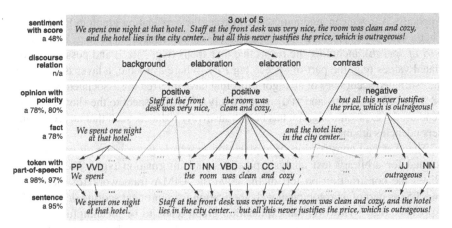

Fig. 5.18 Illustration of an explanation graph for the sentiment score of the sample text from Sect. 5.2. The dependencies between the different types of output information as well as the accuracy estimations (*a*) are derived from knowledge about the text analysis pipeline that has produced the output information.

with features, cf. Sect. 3.2). The goal is to automatically explain the text analysis process realized to create some target instance of any information type from **C**. For this goal, we now outline how to reuse the partial order induced by the interdependencies of the algorithms in **A**, which we exploited in Sect. 3.3.

In particular, we propose to construct a directed acyclic *explanation graph* that illustrates the process based on the produced information. Each node in the graph represents an annotation with its features. The root node corresponds to the target instance. An edge between two nodes denotes a dependency between the respective annotations. Here, we define that an annotation of type $C_1 \in$ **C** depends on an annotation of type $C_2 \in$ **C**, if the annotations overlap and if the algorithm in **A**, which produces C_1 as output, requires C_2 as input. In addition to the dependencies, every node is assigned properties of those algorithms in **A** that have been used to infer the associated annotation types and features, e.g. quality estimations. Only nodes belong to the graph the target instance directly or indirectly depends on.

As an example, let the following pipeline Π_{sco} be given to assign a sentiment score to the sample text from Sect. 5.2:

$$\Pi_{sco} = (\text{SSE, STO}_2, \text{TPO}_1, \text{PDU, CSB, CSP, PDR, CSS})$$

CSS classifies sentiment scores based on the local sentiment flow of a text derived from the output of CSB and CSP as well as discourse relations between local sentiments extracted with PDR (cf. Sect. 5.4). Using the input and output types of the eight employed algorithms listed in Appendix A.1 and the estimations of their quality from

Appendix A.2, we can automatically construct the explanation graph in Fig. 5.18.[23]
There, each layer subsumes the instances of one information type (e.g. *token with part-of-speech*), including the respective text spans (e.g. *"We"*) and possibly associated values (e.g. the part-of-speech tag *PP*). Where available, a layer is assigned the estimated accuracies of all algorithms that have inferred the associated type (e.g. 98 % and 97 % of STO_2 and TPO_1, respectively).[24] With respect to the shown dependencies, the explanation graph has been transitively reduced, such that no redundant dependencies are maintained.

The sketched construction of explanation graphs is generic, i.e., it can be performed for arbitrary text analysis pipelines and information types. We have realized the construction on top of the APACHE UIMA framework (cf. Sects. 3.3 and 3.5) as part of a prototypical web application for sentiment scoring described in Appendix B.3.[25] However, an explanation graph tends to be meaningful only for pipelines with deep hierarchical interdependencies. This typically holds for information extraction rather than text classification approaches (cf. Sect. 2.2), but the given example emphasizes that according pipelines also exist within text classification.

In terms of an external view of text analysis processes, explanation graphs are quite sound and complete. Only few information about a process is left out (e.g., although not common, annotations sometimes depend on annotations they do not overlap with). Still, the use of explanation graphs in the presented form may not be adequate for explanations, since some contained information is rather technical (e.g. part-of-speech tags). While such details might increase the trust of users with a computational linguistics or similar background, their benefit for average users seems limited. In our prototype, we thus simplify explanation graphs. Among others, we group different part-of-speech tags (e.g. *common noun (NN)* and *proper noun (NE)*) under meaningful terms (e.g. *noun*) and we add edges between independent but fully overlapping nodes (cf. Appendix B.3 for examples). The latter reduces soundness, but it makes the graph more easy to conceive. Besides, Fig. 5.18 indicates that explanation graphs can become very large, which makes their understanding hard and time-consuming. To deal with the size, our prototype reduces completeness by displaying only the first layers in an overview graph and the others in a detail graph. Nevertheless, long texts make the resort to explanation graphs questionable.

In terms of an internal view, the expressiveness of explanation graphs is rather low because of their generic nature. Concretely, an explanation graph provides no information about how the explained target instance emanates from the annotations it depends on. As mentioned above, the decisive step of most text classification approaches (and also many information extraction algorithms) is the feature computation, which remains implicit in an explanation graph. General information in this

---

[23]For clarity, we omit the text span in case of discourse relations in Fig. 5.18. Relation types can easily be identified, as only they point to the information they are dependent on.

[24]Although Π_{sco} employs PDU, Fig. 5.18 contains no discourse unit annotations. This is because each discourse unit is classified as being a fact or an opinion by CSB afterwards.

[25]In APACHE UIMA, the algorithms' interdependencies can be inferred from the descriptor files of the employed primitive analysis engines. For properties like quality estimations, we use a fixed notation in the description field of a descriptor file, just as we do for the expert system from Sect. 3.3.

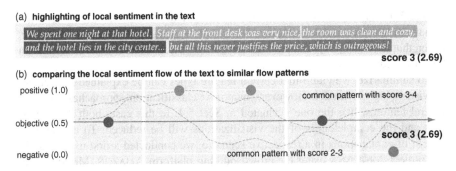

Fig. 5.19 Two possible visual explanations for the sentiment score of the sample text from Fig. 5.3 based on our model from Sect. 5.2: **a** Highlighting all local sentiment. **b** Comparison to the most similar sentiment flow patterns.

respect could be specified via according properties of the employed algorithm, say *"features: lexical and shallow syntactic"* in case of CSB. For input-specific information, however, the actually performed text analysis must be explained. This is easy for our overall analysis from Sect. 5.4, as we discuss next.

5.5.3 Explanation of the Class of an Argumentative Text

We now close our investigation of the classification of argumentative texts by exemplifying how to explain a determined text class based on our structure-oriented model from Sect. 5.2. For the related explicit semantic analysis, Gabrilovich and Markovitch (2007) point out that an important benefit of modeling the natural concepts from WIKIPEDIA as individual features is that the approach can be easily explained to users. Similarly, we argue that the unit class flows introduced in Sect. 5.3 and the flow patterns from Sect. 5.4 provide all information needed to automatically create intuitive explanations in argumentation-related tasks.

For illustration, Fig. 5.19 shows two exemplary ways of using the information captured in our model to visually explain the sentiment score of a sample text, which should be 3 out of 5 here (or a little less than 3 in case of real-valued scores). Many other visualizations are possible, e.g. a combination of a text and a flow similar to Fig. 5.8 (cf. Sect. 5.2).

The highlighted text in Fig. 5.19(a) aims to increase the speed of conceiving that positive and negative sentiment is quite balanced. Given that the underlying scoring approach is restricted to the distribution of local sentiment (maybe complemented with lexical features), the abstraction of reflecting global sentiment by the length of positive and negative text spans seems sound and not very incomplete. In contrast, Fig. 5.19(b) puts more focus on structure. By comparing the local sentiment flow of the text to common flow patterns, it directly visualizes the feature type developed in Sect. 5.4. If few patterns are much more similar to the flow than all others, the visualization serves as a sound and rather complete explanation of that feature type. Given that a user believes the patterns are correct, there should hence be no reason for mistrusting such an explanation.

To summarize, we claim that certain feature types can be explained adequately by visualizing our model. However, many text classification approaches combine several features, like the one evaluated in Sect. 5.4. In this case, both the soundness and the completeness of the visualizations will be reduced. To analyze the benefit of explanations in a respective scenario, we conducted a first user study in our project ARGUANA using the crowdsourcing platform AMAZON MECHANICAL TURK[26], where so called workers can be requested to perform tasks. The workers are paid a small amount of money if the results of the tasks are approved by the requester. For a concise presentation, we only roughly outline the user study here.

The goal of the study was to examine whether explanations (1) help to assess the sentiment of a text and (2) increase the speed of assessing the sentiment. To this end, each task asked a worker to classify the sentiment score of 10 given reviews from the ARGUANA TRIPADVISOR CORPUS (cf. Appendix C.2), based on presented information of exactly one of the following three types that we obtained from our prototypical web application (cf. Appendix B.3):

1. **Plain text.** The review in plain text form.
2. **Highlighted text.** The highlighted review text, as exemplified in Fig. 5.19(a).
3. **Plain text + local sentiment flow.** The review in plain text form with the associated local sentiment flow shown below the text.[27]

For each type, all 2100 reviews of the ARGUANA TRIPADVISOR CORPUS were classified by three different workers. To prevent flawed results, two check reviews with unambiguous sentiment (score 1 or 5) were put among every 10 reviews. We accepted only tasks with correctly classified check reviews and we reassigned rejected tasks to other workers. Altogether, this resulted in an approval rate of 93.1 %, which indicates the quality of the conducted crowdsourcing. Table 5.5 lists the aggregated classification results separately for the reviews of each possible sentiment score (in the center) as well as the seconds required by a worker to perform a task, averaged over all tasks and over the fastest 25 % of the tasks (on the right).

The average score of a TRIPADVISOR hotel review lies between 3 and 4 (cf. Appendix C.2). As Table 5.5 shows, these "weak" sentiment scores were most accurately assessed by the workers based on the plain text, possibly because the focus on the text avoids a biased reading in this case. In contrast, the highlighted text seems to help to assess the other scores. At least for score 2, also the local sentiment flow proves beneficial. In terms of the required time, the highlighted text clearly dominates the study. While type 3 speeds up the classification with respect to the fastest 25 %, it entails the highest time on average. The latter result is not unexpected, because of the complexity of understanding two instead of one visualization.

---

[26]AMAZON MECHANICAL TURK, http://www.mturk.com, accessed on June 15, 2015.

[27]Unfortunately, flow patterns were omitted, since they are not visualized in our application.

Table 5.5 The average sentiment score classified by the AMAZON MECHANICAL TURK workers for all reviews in the ARGUANA TRIPADVISOR CORPUS of each score between 1 and 5 depending on the presented information as well as the time the users took for classifying 10 reviews averaged over all tasks or over the fastest 25 %, respectively.

#	Presented information	1	2	3	4	5	All tasks	Fastest 25 %
1	Plain text	1.7	2.5	**3.1**	**3.9**	4.3	488.5 s	216.9 s
2	Highlighted text	**1.6**	**2.2**	2.8	3.8	**4.4**	**361.7 s**	**85.8 s**
3	Plain text + local sentiment flow	1.7	**2.2**	2.8	3.7	4.3	775.0 s	182.6 s

5.5.4 Implications for Ad-Hoc Large-Scale Text Mining

This section has roughly sketched that knowledge about a text analysis process and information obtained within the process can be used to improve the intelligibility of the pipeline that realizes the process. In particular, both our process-oriented view of text analysis from Sect. 3.2 and our structure-oriented view from Sect. 5.2 can be operationalized to automatically provide explanations for a pipeline's results.

The presented explanation graphs give general explanations of text analysis processes that come at no cost (except for the normally negligible time of constructing them). They can be derived from arbitrary pipelines. For a deeper insight into the reasons behind some result, we argue that more specific explanations are needed that rely on task-specific information. We have introduced two exemplary visual explanations in this regard for the sentiment scoring of argumentative texts. At least the intelligibility of highlighting local sentiment has been underpinned in a first user study, whereas we leave an evaluation of the explanatory benefit of flow patterns for future work. In the end, the creation of explanations requires research in the field of information visualization, which is beyond the scope of this book.

Altogether, this chapter has made explicit the difficulty of ensuring high quality in text mining. Concretely, we have revealed the domain dependence of the text analysis pipelines executed to infer certain information from input texts as a major problem. While we have successfully addressed one facet of improving the domain robustness of pipelines to a certain extent, our findings indicate that perfect robustness will often be impossible to achieve. In accordance with that, our experiments have underlined the fundamental challenge of high effectiveness in complex text analysis tasks (cf. Sect. 2.1). Although approaches to cope with limited effectiveness exist, like the exploitation of redundancy (cf. Sect. 2.4), the effectiveness of an employed text analysis pipeline will always affect the correctness of the results of the associated text mining application. Consequently, we argue that the intelligibility of a text analysis process is of particular importance, as it may increase the end user acceptance of erroneous results.

Moreover, in the given context of ad-hoc large-scale text mining (cf. Sect. 1.2), the correctness of results can be verified at least sporadically because of the sheer amount of processed data. Hence, a general trust in the quality of a text analysis pipeline seems necessary. Under this premise, intelligibility denotes the final building block of high-quality text mining aside from a robust effectiveness and a robust efficiency of the performed analyses.

Chapter 6
Conclusion

We can only see a short distance ahead, but we can see plenty there that needs to be done.

– Alan Turing

Abstract The ability of performing text mining ad-hoc in the large has the potential to essentially improve the way people find information today in terms of speed and quality, both in everyday web search and in big data analytics. More complex information needs can be fulfilled immediately, and previously hidden information can be accessed. At the heart of every text mining application, relevant information is inferred from natural language texts by a text analysis process. Mostly, such a process is realized in the form of a pipeline that sequentially executes a number of information extraction, text classification, and other natural language processing algorithms. As a matter of fact, text mining is studied in the field of computational linguistics, which we consider from a computer science perspective in this book.

Besides the fundamental challenge of inferring relevant information effectively, we have revealed the automatic design of a text analysis pipeline and the optimization of a pipeline's run-time efficiency and domain robustness as major requirements for the enablement of ad-hoc large-scale text mining. Then, we have investigated the research question of how to exploit knowledge about a text analysis process and information obtained within the process to approach these requirements. To this end, we have developed different models and algorithms that can be employed to address information needs ad-hoc on large numbers of texts. The algorithms rely on classical and statistical techniques from artificial intelligence, namely, planning, truth maintenance, and informed search as well as supervised and self-supervised learning. All algorithms have been analyzed formally, implemented as software, and evaluated experimentally.

In Sect. 6.1, we summarize our main findings and their contributions to different areas of computational linguistics. We outline that they have both scientific and practical impact on the state of the art in text mining. However, far from every problem of ad-hoc large-scale text mining has been solved or even approached at all in this book. In the words of Alan Turing, we can therefore already see plenty there that needs to be done in the given and in new directions of future research (Sect. 6.2). Also, some of our main ideas may be beneficial for other problems from computer science or even from other fields of application, as we finally sketch at the end.

6.1 Contributions and Open Problems

This book presents the development and evaluation of approaches that exploit knowledge and information about a text analysis process in order to effectively address information needs from information extraction, text classification, and comparable tasks ad-hoc in an efficient and domain-robust manner.[1] In this regard, our high-level contributions refer to an automatic pipeline design, an optimized pipeline efficiency, and an improved pipeline robustness, as motivated in Chap. 1. After introducing relevant foundations, basic definitions, and case studies, Chap. 2 has summarized that several successful related approaches exist, which address similar problems as we do. Still, we claim that the findings of this book improve the state of the art for different problems, as we detail in the following.[2]

6.1.1 Enabling Ad-Hoc Text Analysis

In Chap. 3, we have first discussed how to design a text analysis pipeline that is optimal in terms of efficiency and effectiveness. Given a formal specification of available text analysis algorithms, which has become standard in software frameworks for text analysis (cf. Sect. 2.2), we can define an information need to be addressed and a quality prioritization to be met in order to allow for a fully automatic pipeline construction. We have realized an according engineering approach with partial order planning (and a subsequent greedy linearization), implemented in a prototypical expert system for non-expert users (cf. Appendix B.1). After showing the correctness and asymptotic run-time complexity of the approach, we have offered evidence that pipeline construction takes near-zero time in realistic scenarios.

To our knowledge, we are thereby the first to enable ad-hoc text analysis for unanticipated information needs and input texts.[3] Some minor problems of our approach remain for future work, like its current limitation to single information needs. Most of these are of technical nature and should be solvable without restrictions (see the discussions in Sects. 3.2 and 3.3 for details). Besides, a few compromises had to be made due to automation, especially the focus on either effectiveness or efficiency during the selection of algorithms to be employed in a pipeline. Similarly, the flipside of constructing and executing a pipeline ad-hoc is the missing opportunity of evaluating the pipeline's quality before using it.

---

[1]Here, addressing an information need means to return all information found in given input texts that is relevant with respect to a defined query or the like (cf. Sect. 2.2).

[2]As clarified in Sect. 1.4, notice that many findings attributed to this book here have already been published with different co-authors in papers of the author of this book.

[3]The notion of unanticipated information needs refers to *combinations* of information types that may have never been sought for before. Still, algorithms that can infer the *single* types from input texts need to be either given in advance or created on-the-fly.

6.1.2 Optimally Analyzing Text

Our main finding regarding an optimal pipeline design in Chap. 3 refers to an often overseen optimization potential: By restricting all analyses to those portions of input texts that may be relevant for the information need at hand, much run-time can be saved while maintaining effectiveness. Such an input control can be efficiently operationalized for arbitrary text analysis pipelines with assumption-based truth maintenance based on the dependencies between the information types to be inferred. Different from related approaches, we thereby assess the relevance of portions of text formally. We have proven the correctness of this approach, analyzed its worst-case run-time, and realized it in a software framework on top of the industry standard APACHE UIMA (cf. Appendix B.2).

Every pipeline equipped with our input control is able to process input texts optimally in that all unnecessary analyses are avoided. Alternatively, it can also trade its run-time efficiency for its recall by restricting analysis to even smaller portions of text. In our experiments with information extraction, only roughly 40 % to 80 % of an input text needed to be processed by an employed algorithm on average. At the same time, the effort of maintaining relevant portions of text seems almost negligible. The benefit of our approach will be limited in tasks where most portions of text are relevant, as is often the case in text classification. Also, the input restriction does not work for some algorithms, namely those that do not stepwise process portions of a text separately (say, sentence by sentence). Still, our approach comes with hardly any notable drawback, which is why we argue in favor of generally equipping all pipelines with an input control.

6.1.3 Optimizing Analysis Efficiency

The use of an input control gives rise to the efficiency impact of optimizing the schedule of a text analysis pipeline, as we have comprehensively investigated in Chap. 4. We have shown formally and experimentally that, in theory, optimally scheduling a pipeline constitutes a dynamic programming problem, which depends on the run-times of the employed algorithms and the distribution of relevant information in the input texts. Especially the latter may vary significantly, making other scheduling approaches more efficient in practice. In order to decide what approach to take, we provide a first measure of the heterogeneity of texts with regard to this distribution. Under low heterogeneity, an optimal fixed schedule can reliably and efficiently be determined with informed best-first search on a sample of input texts. This approach, the proof of its correctness, and its evaluation denote new contributions of this book.[4] For higher heterogeneity, we have developed an adaptive approach that learns online

---

[4]The approach is correct given that we have optimistic estimations of the algorithms' run-times. Then, it always finds a schedule that is optimal on the sample (cf. Sect. 4.3).

and self-supervised what schedule to choose for each text. Our experiments indicate that we thereby achieve being close to the theoretically best solution in all cases.

With our work on the optimization of efficiency, we support the applicability of text analysis pipelines to industrial-scale data, which is still often disregarded in research. The major gain of optimizing a pipeline's schedule is that even computationally expensive analyses like dependency parsing can be conducted in little time, thus often allowing for more effective results. In our experiments, the run-time of information extraction was improved by up to factor 16 over naive approaches and by factor 2 over our greedy linearization named above. These findings conform with related research while being more generally applicable. In particular, all our scheduling approaches apply to arbitrary text analysis algorithms and to input texts of any type and language. They target at large-scale scenarios, where spending additional time for analyzing samples of texts is worth the effort, like in big data analytics. Conversely, when the goal is to respond to an information need ad-hoc, the greedy linearization should be preferred.

Some noteworthy aspects of pipeline optimization remain unaddressed here. First, although our input control handles arbitrary pipelines, we have considered only single information needs (e.g. forecasts with time information). An extension to combined needs (e.g. forecasts and declarations) will be more complicated, but is straightforward in principle as sketched. Next, we evaluated our approaches on large datasets, but not in real big data scenarios. Among others, big data requires to deal with huge memory consumption. While we are confident that such challenges even increase the impact of our approaches on a pipeline's efficiency, we cannot ultimately rule out the possibility that they revert some achieved efficiency gains. Similarly, streams of input texts have been used for motivation in this book, but their analysis is left for future work. Finally, an open problem refers to the limited accuracy of predicting pipeline run-times within adaptive scheduling, which prevents an efficiency impact of the approach on real data of low heterogeneity. Possible solutions have been discussed in Sect. 4.5. We do not deepen them in this book, since we have presented successful alternatives for low heterogeneity (cf. Sect. 4.3).

6.1.4 Robustly Classifying Text

In Chap. 5, we have turned our view to the actual analysis performed by a pipeline. In particular, we have investigated how to improve the domain robustness of an effective text analysis in tasks that deal with the classification of argumentative texts (like reviews or essays). Our general idea is that a focus on the overall structure instead of the content of respective texts benefits robustness. For reviews, we have found that common overall structures exist, which cooccur with certain sentiment. Here, overall structure is modeled as a sequential flow of either local sentiments or discourse relations, which can be seen as shallow representations of concepts from argumentation theory. Using a supervised variant of clustering, we have determined common flow patterns in the reduced search space of shallow overall structures. We exploit the patterns as features for machine learning approaches to text classification. In sentiment scoring experiments, these features have turned out to be strongly invariant across reviews from very different domains (hotel and film), losing less than five percentage points of accuracy in the majority of out-of-domain tasks.

Our approach contributes to research on domain-robust text classification. It targets at non-standard classification tasks where the structure of a text matters. Due to our restriction to the classification of review sentiment, however, we cannot assess yet as to whether our findings generalize to other tasks. Moreover, while our robustness results are very promising, the effectiveness of the considered features is still improvable. We have discussed possible improvements in Sect. 5.4, such as the use of other information in the flow or the resort to semi-supervised learning.

Besides text classification, our findings also give linguistic insights into the way people argue in argumentative texts. On the one hand, the sequential flows we found model overall structure from a human perspective and, thus should be intuitively understandable, such as *(positive, negative, positive)*. On the other hand, different from all existing approaches we know, the developed feature type captures the structure of a text in overall terms. We believe that these results open the door to new approaches in other areas of computational linguistics, especially in those related to argumentation. We detail the implications of our approach in the following.

6.2 Implications and Outlook

With respect to our research question from Sect. 1.3, the contributions of this book emphasize that a text analysis process can be improved in different respects using knowledge about the process (like formal algorithm specifications) as well as information obtained within the process (like observed algorithm run-times). Although we have omitted to fully integrate all our single approaches, we now discuss in how far their combination enables ad-hoc large-scale text mining, thereby coming back to our original motivation of enhancing today's information search from Sect. 1.1. Then, we close this book with an outlook on arising research questions in the concerned research field as well as in both more and less related fields.

6.2.1 Towards Ad-Hoc Large-Scale Text Mining

As we have stressed in Sect. 1.3, the overall problem approached in this book aims to make the design and execution of text analysis pipelines more intelligent. Our underlying motivation is to enable search engines and big data analytics to perform ad-hoc large-scale text mining, i.e., to return high-quality results inferred from large numbers of texts in response to information needs stated ad-hoc. The output of pipelines is structured information, which defines the basis for the results to be returned. Therefore, we have addressed the requirements of (1) designing pipelines automatically, (2) optimizing their efficiency, and (3) improving their robustness, as summarized above. The fundamental effectiveness problem of text analysis remains challenging and the definition of "large-scale" is not clear in general. Anyway, as far as we got, our findings underline that we have successfully enabled ad-hoc text mining, significantly augmented capabilities in large-scale text mining, and at least provided an important step towards high-quality text mining.

However, not all single approaches are applicable or beneficial in every text analysis scenario. In particular, the optimization of efficiency rather benefits information extraction, while our approach to pipeline robustness targets at specific text classification tasks. The latter tends to be slower than standard text classification approaches, but it avoids performing deep analyses. In contrast, all approaches from Chaps. 3 and 4 fit together perfectly. Their integration will even solve remaining problems. For instance, the restriction of our pipeline construction approach to single information needs is easy to manage when given an input control (cf. Sect. 3.3). Moreover, there are scenarios where all approaches have an impact. E.g., a sentiment analysis based only on the opinions of a text allows for automatic design, optimized scheduling, and the classification of overall structure. In addition, we have given hints in Sect. 5.4 on how to transfer our robustness approach to further tasks.

We realized all approaches on top of the standard software framework for text analysis, APACHE UIMA. A promising step still to be taken is their deployment in widely-recognized platforms and tools. In Sect. 3.5, we have already argued that a native integration of our input control within APACHE UIMA would minimize the effort of using the input control while benefiting the efficiency of many text analysis approaches based on the framework. Similarly, applications like U-COMPARE, which serves for the development and evaluation of pipelines (Kano et al. 2010), may in our view greatly benefit from including the ad-hoc pipeline construction from Sect. 3.3 or the scheduling approaches from Sects. 4.3 and 4.5. We leave these and other deployments for future work. The same holds for some important aspects of using pipelines in practical applications that we have analyzed only roughly here, such as the parallelization of pipeline execution (cf. Sect. 4.6) and the explanation of pipeline results (cf. Sect. 5.5). Both fit well to the approaches we have presented, but still require more investigation.

We conclude that our contributions do not fully enable ad-hoc large-scale text mining yet, but they define essential building blocks for achieving this goal. The decisive question is whether academia and industry in the context of information search will actually evolve in the direction suggested in this book. While we can only guess, the superficial answer may be "no", because there are too many possible variations of this direction. A more nuanced view on today's search engines and the lasting hype around big data, however, reveals that the need for automatic, efficient, and robust text mining technologies is striking: Chiticariu et al. (2010b) highlight their impact on enterprise analytics, and Etzioni (2011) stresses the importance of directly returning relevant information as search results (cf. Sect. 2.4 for details). Hence, we are confident that our findings have the potential of improving the future of information search. In the end, leading search engines show that this future has already begun (Pasca 2011).

6.2.2 Outside the Box

This book deals with the analysis of natural language texts from a pure text mining perspective merely. As a last step, we now give an outlook on the use of our approaches for other tasks from computational linguistics, from other areas of computer science, and even from outside these fields.

In computational linguistics, one of the most emerging research areas of the last years is argumentation mining (Habernal et al. 2014). IBM claims that debating technologies, which can automatically construct and oppose pro and con arguments, will be the "next big thing" after their famous question answering tool WATSON.[5] With our work on argumentation structure, we contribute to the development of such technologies. Our analysis of the overall structure of argumentative texts may, for instance, be exploited to retrieve the candidates for argument identification. Also, it may be adapted to assess the quality of an argumentation. The flow patterns at the heart of our approach imply several future research directions themselves and may possibly be transferred to other text analysis tasks, as outlined at the end of Sect. 5.4. For a deeper analysis of argumentation, other ways to capture argumentation structure than flow patterns are needed. E.g., deep syntactic parsing (Ballesteros et al. 2014) and convolutional kernels (Moschitti and Basili 2004) could be used to learn tree-like argumentation structures.

The derivation of an appropriate model that generates certain sequential information from example sequences (like the flows) is addressed in data mining. A common approach to detect system anomalies is to search for sequences of discrete events that are improbable under a previously learned model of the system (Aggarwal 2013). While recent work emphasizes the importance of time information for anomaly detection (Klerx et al. 2014), the relation to our computation of similarities between flows in a text remains obvious. This brings up the question whether the two approaches can benefit from each other, which we leave for future work.

Aside from text analysis, especially our generic approaches to pipeline design and execution are transferable to other problems. While we have seen in Sect. 4.6 that our scheduling approaches relate to but do not considerably affect the classical pipelining problem from computer architecture (Ramamoorthy and Li 1977), many other areas of computer science deal with pipeline architectures and processes.

An important example is computer graphics, where the creation of a 2D raster from a 3D scene to be displayed on a screen is performed in a rendering pipeline (Angel 2008). Similar to our input control, pipeline stages like clipping decide what parts of a scene are relevant for the raster. While the ordering of the high-level rendering stages is usually fixed, stages like a shader compose several programmable steps whose schedule strongly impacts rendering efficiency (Arens 2014). A transfer of our approaches to computer graphics seems possible, but it might put other parameters in the focus, since the execution of a pipeline is parallelized on a specialized graphics processing unit.

---

[5]IBM DEBATING TECHNOLOGIES project, http://researcher.ibm.com/researcher/view_group.php?id=5443, accessed on June 15, 2015.

Another related area is software engineering. Among others, recent software testing approaches deal with the optimization of test plans (Güldali et al. 2011). Here, an optimized scheduling can speed up detecting some defined number of failures or achieving some defined code coverage. Accordingly, approaches that perform an assembly-based method engineering based on situational factors and a repository of services (Fazal-Baqaie et al. 2013) should, in principle, be viable to automation with an adaptation of the pipeline construction from Sect. 3.3. Further possible applications reach down to basic compiler optimization operations like list scheduling (Cooper and Torczon 2011). The use of information obtained from training input is known in profile-guided compiler optimization (Hsu et al. 2002) where such information helps to improve the efficiency of program execution, e.g. by optimizing the scheduling of checked conditions in if-clauses.

Even outside computer science, our scheduling approaches may prove beneficial. An example from the real world is an authentication of paintings or paper money, which runs through a sequence of analyses with different run-times and numbers of found forgeries. Also, we experience in everyday life that scheduling affects the efficiency of solving a problem. For instance, the number of slices needed to cut some vegetable into small cubes depends on the ordering of the slices and the form of the vegetable. Moreover, the abstract concept of adaptive scheduling from Sect. 4.5 should be applicable to every performance problem where (1) different solutions to the problem are most appropriate for certain situations or inputs and (2) where the performance of a solution can be assessed somehow.

Altogether, we summarize that possible continuations of the work described in this book are manifold. We hope that our findings will inspire new approaches of other researchers and practitioners in the discussed fields and that they might help anyone who encounters problems like those we approached. With this in mind, we close the book with a translated quote from the German singer Andreas Front:[6]

> What you learn from that is up to you, though.
> I hope at least you have fun doing so.

---

[6] *"Was Du daraus lernst, steht Dir frei. Ich hoffe nur, Du hast Spaß dabei."* from the song "Spaß dabei", http://andreas-front.bplaced.net/blog/, accessed on December 21, 2014.

Appendix A
Text Analysis Algorithms

The evaluation of the design and execution of text analysis pipelines requires the resort to concrete text analysis algorithms. Several of these algorithms are employed in the experiments and case studies of our approaches to enable ad-hoc large-scale text mining from Chaps. 3–5. Some of them have been developed by the author of this book, while others refer to existing software libraries. In this appendix, we give basic details on the functionalities and properties of all employed algorithms and on the text analyses they perform. First, we describe all algorithms in a canonical form (Appendix A.1). Then, we present evaluation results on their efficiency and effectiveness as far as available (Appendix A.2). Especially, the measured run-times are important in this book, because they directly influence the efficiency impact of our pipeline optimization approaches, as discussed.

A.1 Analyses and Algorithms

In Chaps. 3–5, we refer to every employed text analysis algorithm mostly in terms of its three letter acronym (used as the algorithm's name) and the concrete text analysis it realizes. The first letter of each acronym stands for the type of text analysis it belongs to, and the others abbreviate the concrete analysis. The types have been introduced in Sect. 2.1. Now, we sketch all covered text analyses and we describe for each employed algorithm (1) how it performs the respective analysis, (2) what information it requires and produces, and (3) what input texts it is made for. An overview of the algorithms' input and output types is given in Table A.1.

We rely on a canonical form of algorithm description, but we also point out specific characteristics where appropriate. For an easy look-up, in the following we list the algorithms in alphabetical order of their names and, by that, also in alphabetical order of the text analysis types. All algorithms are realized as APACHE UIMA analysis engines (cf. Sect. 3.5). These analysis engines come with our software described in Appendix B. In case of algorithms that are taken from existing software libraries, wrappers are provided.

Table A.1 The required input types $\mathbf{C}^{(in)}$ and the produced output types $\mathbf{C}^{(out)}$ of all text analysis algorithms referred to in this book. Bracketed input types indicate the existence of variations of the respective algorithm with and without these types.

Name	Input types $\mathbf{C}^{(in)}$	Output types $\mathbf{C}^{(out)}$
CLF	Sentence, Token.partOfSpeech, (Time), (Money)	LanguageFunction.class
CSB	DiscourseUnit, Token.partOfSpeech	Opinion, Fact
CSP	Opinion, Token.partOfSpeech	Opinion.polarity
CSS	Sentence, Token.partOfSpeech, Opinion.polarity, Fact, (Product), (ProductFeature)	Sentiment.score
ENE	Sentence, Token.partOfSpeech/.chunk	Person, Location, Organization
EMO	Sentence	Money
ETI	Sentence	Time
NTI	Sentence, Time	Time.start, Time.end
PCH	Sentence, Token.partOfSpeech/.lemma	Token.chunk
PDE$_1$	Sentence, Token.partOfSpeech/.lemma	Token.parent/.role
PDE$_2$	Sentence, Token.partOfSpeech/.lemma	Token.parent/.role
PDR	Sentence, Token.partOfSpeech, Opinion.polarity	DiscourseRelation.type
PDU	Sentence, Token.partOfSpeech	DiscourseUnit
RFO	Sentence, Token.partOfSpeech /.lemma, Time	Forecast.time
RFI	Money, Forecast	Financial.money/.forecast
RFU	Token, Organization, Time	Founded.organization/.time
RRE$_1$	Sentence, Token	Revenue
RRE$_2$	Sentence, Token, Time, Money	Revenue
RTM$_1$	Sentence, Revenue, Time, Money	Revenue.time/.money
RTM$_2$	Sentence, Revenue, Time, Money, Token.partOfSpeech/.lemma./.parent/.role	Revenue.time/.money
SPA	–	Paragraph
SSE	–	Sentence
STO$_1$	–	Token
STO$_2$	Sentence	Token
TLE	Sentence, Token	Token.lemma
TPO$_1$	Sentence, Token	Token.partOfSpeech/.lemma
TPO$_2$	Sentence, Token	Token.partOfSpeech

A.1.1 Classification of Text

The classification of text is one of the central text analysis types the approaches in this book focus on. It assigns a class from a predefined scheme to each given text. In our experiments and case studies in Chap. 5, we deal with the classification of both whole texts and portions of text.

Language Functions. Language functions target at the question why a text was written. On an abstract level, most texts can be seen as being predominantly expressive, appellative, or informative (Bühler 1934). For product-related texts, we concretized this scheme with a personal, a commercial, and an informational class (Wachsmuth and Bujna 2011).

CLF (Wachsmuth and Bujna 2011) is a statistical classifier, realized as a linear multiclass support vector machine from the LIBSVM integration of WEKA (Chang and Lin 2011; Hall et al. 2009). It assigns a language function to a text based on different word, n-gram, entity, and part-of-speech features (cf. Sect. 5.3). CLF operates on the text level, requiring sentences, tokens and, if given, time and money entities as input and producing language functions with assigned class values. It has been trained on German texts from the music domain and the smartphone domain, respectively.

Subjectivity. Subjectivity refers to the sentiment-related question whether a text or a portion of text is subjective (Pang and Lee 2004). Opinions are subjective, while facts (including false ones) are seen as objective.

CSB (self-implemented[1]) is a statistical classifier, realized as a linear support vector machine from the LIBSVM integration of WEKA (Chang and Lin 2011; Hall et al. 2009). It classifies the subjectivity of discourse units based on the contained words, part-of-speech tags, scores from SENTIWORD-NET (Baccianella et al. 2010), and similar. CSB operates on the discourse unit level, requiring discourse units and tokens with part-of-speech as input and producing either one *Fact* or one *Opinion* annotation for each discourse unit. It has been trained on English reviews from the hotel domain and the film domain, respectively.

Sentiment Polarity. The classification of a text or a portion of text as having either a positive or a negative polarity with respect to some topic is one of the most common forms of sentiment analysis (Pang et al. 2002).

CSP (self-implemented) is a statistical classifier, realized as a linear support vector machine from the LIBSVM integration of WEKA (Chang and Lin 2011; Hall et al. 2009). Analog to CSB, it classifies the polarities of opinions based on the contained words, part-of-speech tags, scores from SENTIWORD-NET (Baccianella et al. 2010), and similar. CSP operates on the opinion level, requiring opinions and tokens with part-of-speech as input and producing the polarity feature of each opinion. It has been trained on English reviews from the hotel domain and the film domain, respectively.

Sentiment Scores. Sentiment is also often classified as an ordinal or metric score from a predefined scale (Pang and Lee 2005). Such sentiment scores e.g. represent the overall ratings of web user reviews.

CSS (Wachsmuth et al. 2014a) is a statistical score predictor, realized as a linear multi-class support vector machine with probability estimates and normalization from the LIBSVM integration of WEKA (Chang and Lin 2011; Hall et al. 2009). It assigns a score to a text based on a combination of word, part-of-speech, local sentiment, discourse relation, and domain concept features. CSS operates on the text level, requiring sentences, opinions, and tokens with part-of-speech as input and producing sentiment annotations with scores. It has been trained on English texts from the hotel domain and the film domain, respectively.

---

[1]Notice that all algorithms marked as *self-implemented* have been used in some of our publications, but have not been described in detail there.

A.1.2 Entity Recognition

According to Jurafsky and Martin (2009), the term *entity* is used not only to refer to names that represent real-world entities, but also to specific types of numeric information, like money and time expressions.

Money. In terms of money information, we distinguish absolute mentions (e.g. *"300 million dollars"*), relative mentions (e.g. *"by 10 %"*), and combinations of absolute and relative mentions.

EMO (self-implemented) is a rule-based money extractor that uses lexicon-based regular expressions, which capture the structure of money entities. EMO operates on the sentence level, requiring sentence annotations as input and producing money annotations. It works only on German texts and it targets at news articles.

Named Entities. In some of our experiments and case studies, we deal with the recognition of person, organization, and location names. These three named entity types are in the focus of widely recognized evaluations, such as the CoNLL-2003 SHARED TASK (Tjong et al. 2003).

ENE (Finkel et al. 2005) is a statistical sequence labeling algorithm, realized as a conditional random field in the software library STANFORD NER[2] that sequentially tags words as belonging to an entity of some type or not. ENE operates on the sentence level, requiring tokens with part-of-speech and chunk information as input and producing person, location, and organization annotations. It can been trained for different languages, including English and German, and it targets at well-formatted texts like news articles.

Time. Similar to money entities, we consider text spans that represent periods of time (e.g. *"last year"*) or dates (e.g. *"07/21/69"*) as time entities.

ETI (self-implemented) is a rule-based time extractor that, analog to EMO, uses lexicon-based regular expressions, which capture the structure of time entities. ETI operates on the sentence level, requiring sentence annotations as input and producing time annotations. It works only on German texts, and it targets at news articles.

A.1.3 Normalization and Resolution

Normalization denotes the conversion of information (usually, of an entity) into a machine-processable form. Resolution means the identification of different references of an entity in a text that belong to the same real-world entity (Cunningham

---

[2]STANFORD NER, http://nlp.stanford.edu/software/CRF-NER.shtml, accessed on June 15, 2015.

2006). The only type of information to be resolved in our experiments is time information (in Sects. 4.3 and 4.5).

Resolved Time. For our purpose, we define resolved time information to consist
of a start date and an end date, both of the form *YYYY-MM-DD*. Ahn et al. (2005)
distinguish fully qualified, deictic, and anaphoric time information in a text. For
normalization, some information must be resolved, e.g. *"last year"* may require the
date the respective text was written on.

NTI (self-implemented) is a rule-based time normalizer that splits a time entity into
  atomic parts, identifies missing information, and then seeks for this information
  in the surrounding text. NTI operates on the text level, requiring sentence and time
  annotations as input and producing normalized start and end dates as features of
  time annotations. It works on German texts only and it targets at news articles.

A.1.4 Parsing

In natural language processing, parsing denotes the syntactic analysis of texts or
sentences in order to identify relations between their different parts. In dependency
parsing, a part is a single word, while constituency parsing targets at hierarchically
structured phrases in sentences (Jurafsky and Martin 2009). Similarly, the discourse
structure of a text, detailed in Sect. 5.2, can be parsed (Marcu 2000). While a parser
typically outputs a tree structure, also shallow approaches exist that segment a text
into their parts, as in the case of phrase chunking (also called shallow parsing).

Chunks. Chunks represent the top-level phrases of a sentence (Jurafsky and
Martin 2009). Mostly, at least noun, verb, and prepositional phrases are distinguished.
Chunks are usually annotated as tags of tokens. E.g., the noun phrase *"the moon
landing"* might be encoded as *(B-NP, I-NP, I-NP)* where *B-NP* denotes the start and
each *I-NP* some other part. Chunks often serve as input to named entity recognition.

PCH (Schmid 1995) is a statistical phrase chunker, realized as a decision-tree classifier in the TT4J wrapper of the software library TREETAGGER.[3] PCH operates
  on the sentence level, requiring tokens as input and producing the chunk tag
  features of the tokens. It has been trained on a number of languages, including
  English and German, and it targets at well-formatted texts like news articles.

Dependency Parse Trees. The dependency parse tree of a sentence or similar is
often used for features in relation extraction. It defines how the contained tokens
syntactically depend on each other. Each token is represented by one node. Usually,
the root node corresponds to the main verb. The tree structure can be defined on the
token level by assigning a parent node to each node except for the root. In addition,
a token is usually assigned a label that defines the role of the subtree it represents.

---

[3]TT4J, http://reckart.github.io/tt4j/, accessed on June 15, 2015.

PDE₁ (Bohnet 2010) is a variant of the statistical dependency parser PDE₂ given below, realized in the MATE TOOLS[4] as a combination of a linear support vector machine and a hash kernel. It uses several features to identify only dependency parse trees without crossing edges (unlike PDE₂). PDE₁ operates on the sentence level, requiring sentences and tokens with part-of-speech and lemma as input and producing the parent and dependency role of each token. It has been trained on German texts and it targets at well-formatted texts like news articles.

PDE₂ (Bohnet 2010) is a statistical dependency parser, realized in the above-mentioned MATE TOOLS as a combination of a linear support vector machine and a hash kernel. It uses several features to identify dependency parse trees, including those with crossing edges. PDE₂ operates on the sentence level, requiring sentences and tokens with part-of-speech and lemma as input and producing the parent and dependency role of each token. It has been trained on a number of languages, including English and German, and it targets at well-formatted texts like news articles.

Discourse Units and Relations. Discourse units are the minimum building blocks in the sense of text spans that make up the discourse of a text. Several types of discourse relations may exist between discourse units, e.g. 23 types are distinguished by the widely-followed rhetorical structure theory (Mann and Thompson 1988).

PDR (self-implemented) is a rule-based discourse relation extractor that mainly relies on language-specific lexicons with discourse connectives to identify 10 discourse relation types, namely, *background, cause, circumstance, concession, condition, contrast, motivation, purpose, sequence,* and *summary.* PDR operates on the discourse unit level, requiring discourse units and tokens with part-of-speech as input and producing typed discourse relation annotations. It is implemented for English only and it targets at less-formatted texts like web user reviews.

PDU (self-implemented) is a rule-based discourse unit segmenter that analyzes commas, connectives (using language-specific lexicons), verb types, ellipses, etc. to identify discourse units in terms of main clauses with all their subordinate clauses. PDU operates on the text level, requiring sentences and tokens with part-of-speech as input and producing discourse unit annotations. It is implemented for English and German, and it targets at less-formatted texts like web user reviews.

A.1.5 Relation Extraction and Event Detection

In Sect. 3.4, we argue that all relations and events can be seen as relating two or more entities, often being represented by a span of text. Mostly, they are application-

---

[4]MATE TOOLS, http://code.google.com/p/mate-tools/, accessed on June 8, 2015.

specific (cf. Sect. 3.2). In this book, we consider relations and events in the context of our case study INFEXBA from Sect. 2.3.[5]

Financial Events. In Sect. 3.5, financial events denote a specific type of forecasts (see below) that are associated to money information.

RFI (self-implemented) is a rule-based event detector that naively assumes each portion of text with a money entity and a forecast event to represent a financial event. RFI can operate on arbitrary text unit levels, requiring money and forecast annotations as input and producing financial event annotations that relate the respective money entities and forecast events. It works on arbitrary texts of any language.

Forecast Events. A forecast is assumed here to be any sentence about the future with time information.

RFO (self-implemented) is a statistical event detector, realized as a linear support vector machine from the LIBSVM integration of WEKA (Chang and Lin 2011; Hall et al. 2009). It classifies candidate sentences with time entities using several types of information, including part-of-speech tags and occurring verbs. RFO operates on the sentence level, requiring sentences, tokens with part-of-speech and lemma as input and producing forecast annotations with set time features. It is implemented for German texts only and it targets at news articles.

Founded Relations. A founded relation between an organization entity and a time entity means that the respective organization was founded at the respective point in time or in the respective period of time.

RFU (self-implemented) is a rule-based relation extractor that assumes candidate pairs within the same portion of text to be related if the portion contains indicator words of the founded relation (from a language-specific lexicon). RFU can operate on arbitrary text unit levels, requiring organization and money annotations as input and producing founded relation annotations with features for the associated entities. It is implemented for both German and English texts of any kind.

Statement on Revenue Events. According to (Wachsmuth et al. 2010), we define a statement on revenue as a portion of text with information about the development of the revenues of a company or branch over time.

RRE₁ (Wachsmuth et al. 2010) is a rule-based event detector that uses a language-specific lexicon with terms indicating revenue to classify which sentences

---

[5]In the evaluation of ad-hoc pipeline construction in Sect. 3.3, we partly refer to algorithms for the recognition of biomedical events. Since the construction solely relies on formal properties of the algorithms, we do not consider the algorithms' actual implementations and, therefore, omit to talk about them here. The properties can be found in the respective APACHE UIMA descriptor files that come with our expert system (cf. Appendix B.1).

report on revenue. RRE_1 operates on the sentence level, requiring sentences and tokens as input and producing statement on revenue annotations. It is implemented for German texts only and it targets at news articles.

RRE_2 (Wachsmuth et al. 2010) is a statistical event detector, realized as a linear support vector machine from the LIBSVM integration of WEKA (Chang and Lin 2011; Hall et al. 2009). It classifies candidate sentences with time and money entities using several types of information, including language-specific lexicons. RRE_2 operates on the sentence level, requiring sentences, tokens, time entities, and money entities as input and producing statement on revenue annotations. It is implemented for German texts only and it targets at news articles.

Time/Money Relations. The relations between time and money entities that we consider here all refer to according pairs where both entities belong to the same statement on revenue.

RTM_1 (self-implemented) is a rule-based relation extractor that extracts the closest pairs of time and money entities (in terms of the number of characters). It operates on the sentence level, requiring sentences, time and money entities as well as statements on revenue as input and producing the time and money features of the latter. RTM_1 works on arbitrary texts of any language.

RTM_2 (self-implemented) is a statistical relation extractor, realized as a linear support vector machine from the LIBSVM integration of WEKA (Chang and Lin 2011; Hall et al. 2009). It classifies relations between candidate pairs of time and money entities based on several types of information. RTM_2 operates on the sentence level, requiring sentences, tokens with all annotation features, time and money entities, as well as statements on revenue as input and producing the time and money features of the latter. It works for German texts only and it targets at news articles.

A.1.6 Segmentation

Segmentation means the sequential partition of a text into single units. In this book, we restrict our view to lexical and shallow syntactic segmentations in terms of the following information types.

Paragraphs. We define a paragraph here syntactically to be a composition of sentences that ends with a line break.

SPA (self-implemented) is a rule-based paragraph splitter that looks for line breaks, which indicate paragraph ends. SPA operates on the character level, requiring only plain text as input and producing paragraph annotations. It works on arbitrary texts of any language.

Sentences. Sentences segment the text into basic meaningful grammatical units.

SSE (self-implemented) is a rule-based sentence splitter that analyzes whitespaces, punctuation and quotation marks, hyphenation, ellipses, brackets, abbreviations (based on a language-specific lexicon), etc. SSE operates on the character level, requiring only plain text as input and producing sentence annotations. It is implemented for German and English and it targets both at well-formatted texts like news articles and at less-formatted texts like web user reviews.

Tokens. In natural language processing, tokens denote the atomic lexical units of a text, i.e., words, numbers, symbols, and similar.

STO$_1$ (APACHE UIMA[6]) is a rule-based tokenizer that simply looks for whitespaces and punctuation marks. STO$_1$ operates on the character level, requiring only plain text as input and producing token and sentence annotations. It works on arbitrary texts of all those languages, which use the mentioned character types as word and sentence delimiters.

STO$_2$ (self-implemented) is a rule-based tokenizer that analyzes whitespaces, special characters, abbreviations (based on a language-specific lexicon), etc. STO$_2$ operates on the sentence level, requiring sentences as input and producing token annotations. It is implemented for German and English and it targets both at well-formatted texts like news articles and at less-formatted texts like web user reviews.

A.1.7 Tagging

Under the term tagging, we finally subsume text analyses that add information to segments of a text, here to tokens in particular.

Lemmas. A lemma denotes the dictionary form of a word (in the sense of a lexeme), such as *"be"* for *"am"*, *"are"*, or *"be"* itself. Lemmas are of particular importance for highly inflected languages like German and they serve, among others, as input for many parsers (see above).

TLE (Björkelund et al. 2010) is a statistical lemmatizer, realized as a large margin classifier in the above-mentioned MATE TOOLS, that uses several features to find the shortest edit script between the lemmas and the words. TLE operates on the sentence level, requiring tokens as input and producing the lemma features of the tokens. It has been trained on a number of languages, including English and German, and it targets at well-formatted texts like news articles.

Part-of-speech Tags. Parts of speech are the linguistic categories of tokens. E.g., in *"Let the fly fly!"*, the first *"fly"* is a noun and the second a verb. Mostly, more specific

---

[6]UIMA WHITESPACE TOKENIZER, http://uima.apache.org/sandbox.html, accessed on June 8, 2015.

part-of-speech tags are assigned to tokens, like common nouns as opposed to proper nouns. Although some universal part-of-speech tagsets have been proposed (Petrov et al. 2012), most approaches rather rely on language-specific tagsets, such as the widely-used STTS TAGSET[7] for German consisting of 53 different tags.

TPO$_1$ (Schmid 1995) is a statistical part-of-speech tagger, realized with the same decision-tree classifier of the TREETAGGER as PCH above. TPO$_1$ operates on the sentence level, requiring sentences and tokens as input and producing both part-of-speech and lemma features of the tokens. It has been trained on a number of languages, including English and German, and it targets at well-formatted texts like news articles.

TPO$_2$ (Björkelund et al. 2010) is a statistical part-of-speech tagger, realized as a large margin classifier in the above-mentioned MATE TOOLS, that uses several features to classify part-of-speech. TPO$_2$ operates on the sentence level, requiring sentences and tokens as input and producing part-of-speech features of tokens. It has been trained on a number of languages, including English and German, and it targets at well-formatted texts like news articles.

A.2 Evaluation Results

The impact of the approaches developed in Chaps. 3–5 is affected by the efficiency and/or the effectiveness of the employed text analysis algorithms. In particular, both the algorithm selection of ad-hoc pipeline construction (Sect. 3.3) and the informed search pipeline scheduling (Sect. 4.3) rely on run-time estimations of the algorithms, the former also on effectiveness estimations. The efficiency gains achieved by our input control from Sect. 3.5 and by every scheduling approach from Chap. 4 result from differences in the actually observed algorithm run-times. And, finally, the effectiveness and robustness of our features for text classification in Sect. 5.4 depends on the effectiveness of all algorithms used for preprocessing. For these reasons, we have evaluated the efficiency and effectiveness of all employed algorithms as far as possible. Table A.2 shows all results that we provide here with reference to the text corpora they were computed on. The corpora are described in Appendix C.

A.2.1 Efficiency Results

In terms of efficiency, Table A.2 shows the average run-time per sentence of each algorithm. We measured all run-times in either five or ten runs on a 2 GHz Intel Core 2 Duo MacBook with 4 GB RAM, partly using the complete respective corpus, partly its training set only.

---

[7]STTS TAGSET, http://www.sfs.uni-tuebingen.de/resources/stts-1999.pdf, accessed on June 15, 2015.

As can be seen, there is a small number of algorithms whose run-times greatly exceed those of the others. Among these, the most expensive are the two dependency parsers, PDE_1 and PDE_2. Common dependency parsing approaches are of cubic computational complexity with respect to the number of tokens in a sentence (Covington 2001), although more efficient approaches have been proposed recently (Bohnet and Kuhn 2012). Still, the importance of employing dependency parsing for complex text analysis tasks like relation extraction is obvious (and, here, indicated by the different F_1-scores of RTM_1 and RTM_2). The use of such algorithms particularly emphasizes the benefit of our pipeline optimization approaches, as exemplified in the case study of Sect. 3.1.

Besides, we point out that, while we argue in Sect. 4.2 that algorithm run-times remain comparably stable across corpora (compared to distributions of relevant information), a few outliers can be found in Table A.2. Most significantly, RRE_2 has an average run-time per sentence of 0.81 ms on the REVENUE CORPUS, but only 0.05 ms on the CONLL-2003 dataset. The reason behind is that the latter contains only a very small fraction of candidate statements on revenue that contain both a time and a money entity. Consequently, the observed differences rather give another indication of the benefit of filtering only relevant portions of text.

A.2.2 Effectiveness Results

The effectiveness values in Table A.2 were obtained on the test sets of the specified corpora in all cases except for those on the SENTIMENT SCALE DATASET, the SUBJECTIVITY DATASET, and the SENTENCE POLARITY DATASET. The latter are computed using 10-fold cross-validation in order to make them comparable to (Pang and Lee 2005). All results are given in terms of the quality criteria, we see as most appropriate for the respective text analyses (cf. Sect. 2.1 for details). For lack of required ground-truth annotations, we could not evaluate the effectiveness of some algorithms, such as PDR. Also, for a few algorithms, we analyzed a small subset of the REVENUE CORPUS manually to compute their precision (ETI and EMO) or accuracy (SSE and STO_2). With respect to the effectiveness of the algorithms from existing software libraries, we refer to the according literature.

We have added information on the number of classes where accuracy values do not refer to a two-class classification task. In case of CSS on the SENTIMENT SCALE DATASET, we specify an interval for the accuracy values, because they vary depending on which of the four datasets of the corpus is analyzed (cf. Appendix C.4). The perfect effectiveness of PDU on the ARGUANA TRIPADVISOR CORPUS is due to the fact that PDU is exactly the algorithm used to create the discourse unit annotations of the corpus (cf. Appendix C.2).

Table A.2 Evaluation results on the run-time efficiency (in milliseconds per sentence) and the effectiveness (as precision p, recall r, F_1-score f_1, and accuracy a) of all text analysis algorithms referred to in this book on the specified text corpora.

Name	Efficiency	Effectiveness	Evaluation on
CLF	0.65 ms/snt.	a 82 % (3 classes)	LFA-11 CORPUS (music)
	0.53 ms/snt.	a 69 % (3 classes)	LFA-11 CORPUS (smartphone)
CSB	22.31 ms/snt.	a 78 %	ARGUANA TRIPADVISOR CORPUS
	–	a 91 %	SUBJECTIVITY DATASET
CSP	6.96 ms/snt.	a 80 %	ARGUANA TRIPADVISOR CORPUS
	–	a 74 %	SENTENCE POLARITY DATASET
CSS	0.53 ms/snt.	a 48 % (5 classes)	ARGUANA TRIPADVISOR CORPUS
	0.86 ms/snt.	a 57 %–72 % (3 classes)	SENTIMENT SCALE DATASET
EMO	0.68 ms/snt.	p 0.99, r 0.95, f_1 0.97	REVENUE CORPUS
	0.59 ms/snt.	–	CoNLL-2003 (de)
ENE	2.03 ms/snt.	$cf.$ Finkel et al. (2005)	REVENUE CORPUS
	2.03 ms/snt.		CoNLL-2003 (de)
ETI	0.36 ms/snt.	p 0.91, r 0.97, f_1 0.94	REVENUE CORPUS
	0.39 ms/snt.	–	CoNLL-2003 (de)
NTI	1.21 ms/snt.	–	REVENUE CORPUS
	0.39 ms/snt.	–	CoNLL-2003 (de)
TCH	0.97 ms/snt.	$cf.$ Schmid (1995)	REVENUE CORPUS
	0.88 ms/snt.		CoNLL-2003 (de)
PDE_1	166.14 ms/snt.	$cf.$ Bohnet (2010)	REVENUE CORPUS
PDE_2	54.61 ms/snt.		REVENUE CORPUS
PDR	0.11 ms/snt.	–	ARGUANA TRIPADVISOR CORPUS
PDU	0.13 ms/snt.	a 100.0 %	ARGUANA TRIPADVISOR CORPUS
RFI	<0.01 ms/snt.	–	REVENUE CORPUS
	<0.01 ms/snt.	–	CoNLL-2003 (de)
RFO	0.27 ms/snt.	a 93 %	REVENUE CORPUS
	0.27 ms/snt.	–	CoNLL-2003 (de)
RFU	0.01 ms/snt.	p 0.71	REVENUE CORPUS
	0.01 ms/snt.	p 0.88	CoNLL-2003 (de)
RRE_1	0.03 ms/snt.	p 0.86, r 0.93, f_1 0.89	REVENUE CORPUS
RRE_2	0.81 ms/snt.	p 0.87, r 0.93, f_1 0.90	REVENUE CORPUS
	0.05 ms/snt.	–	CoNLL-2003 (de)
RTM_1	0.02 ms/snt.	p 0.69, r 0.88, f_1 0.77	
RTM_2	10.41 ms/snt.	p 0.75, r 0.88, f_1 0.81	REVENUE CORPUS
SPA	<0.01 ms/snt.	–	REVENUE CORPUS
	<0.01 ms/snt.	–	CoNLL-2003 (de)
SSE	0.04 ms/snt.	a 95 %	REVENUE CORPUS
	0.04 ms/snt.	–	CoNLL-2003 (de)
STO_1	0.04 ms/snt.	–	REVENUE CORPUS
STO_2	0.06 ms/snt.	a 98 %	REVENUE CORPUS
	0.06 ms/snt.	–	CoNLL-2003 (de)
TLE	11.12 ms/snt.	$cf.$ Björkelund et al. (2010)	REVENUE CORPUS
TPO_1	0.94 ms/snt.	$cf.$ Schmid (1995)	REVENUE CORPUS
	0.97 ms/snt.		CoNLL-2003 (de)
TPO_2	10.75 ms/snt.	$cf.$ Björkelund et al. (2010)	REVENUE CORPUS

Appendix B
Software

The optimization of pipeline design and execution that we discuss in the book at hand provides practical benefits only when working fully automatically. In the context of the book, prototypical software applications were developed that allow the usage and evaluation of all parts of our approach to enable ad-hoc large-scale text mining. This appendix presents how to work with these applications, all of which are given in the form of open JAVA source code. In Appendix B.1, we begin with the expert system for ad-hoc pipeline construction from Sect. 3.3. Then, Appendix B.2 sketches how to use our software framework that realizes the input control presented in Sect. 3.5. Our prototypical web application for sentiment scoring and explanation is described in Appendix B.3. Finally, we outline how to reproduce the results of all experiments and case studies of this book using the developed applications. All source code comes together with instructions and some sample text analysis algorithms and pipelines. It is split into different projects that we refer to below. As of end of 2014, the code should be accessible at least for some years at http://is.upb.de/?id=wachsmuth (under *Software*).[8]

B.1 An Expert System for Ad-hoc Pipeline Construction

In this appendix, we detail the usage of the expert system PIPELINE XPS, presented in Sect. 3.3. The expert system was implemented by Rose (2012) as part of his master's thesis. It provides a graphical user interface for the specification of text analysis tasks and quality prioritizations. On this basis, PIPELINE XPS constructs and executes a text analysis pipeline ad-hoc.

---

[8] In case you encounter problems with the link, please contact the author of this book.

B.1.1 Getting Started

Installation. The expert system refers to the project *XPS* of the provided software. By default, its annotation task ontology (cf. Sect. 3.2) comprises the algorithms and information types of the *EfXTools* project. When using the integrated development environment ECLIPSE[9], JAVA projects can be created with the respective top-level folders as root directories. Otherwise, an according procedure has to be performed.

General Information. Our expert system can be seen as a first prototype, which still may have some bugs and which tends not to be robust to wrong inputs and usage. Therefore, the instructions presented here should be followed carefully.

Launch. Before the first launch, one option has to be adjusted if not using WINDOWS as the operating system: In the file *./XPS/conf/xps.properties*, the line starting with `xps.treeTaggerModel`, which belongs to the operating system at hand, must be commented in, while the respective others must be commented out. The file *Main.launch* in the folder *XPS* can then be run in order to launch the expert system. At first start, no annotation task ontology is present in the system. After pressing `OK` in response to the appearing popup window, a standard ontology is imported. When starting again, the main window *Pipeline XPS* should appear as well as an *Explanations* window with the message *Pipeline XPS has been started*.

User Interface. Figure B.1 shows the user interface of the prototype from Rose (2012). A user first sets the directory of an input text collection to be processed and chooses a quality prioritization. Then, the user specifies an information need by repeatedly choosing annotation types with active features (cf. Sect. 3.2).[10] The addition of *types to filter* beneath does not replace the on-the-fly creation of filters from the pseudocode in Fig. 3.1, but it defines the value constraints.[11] Once all is set, pressing *Start XPS* leads to the ad-hoc construction and execution of a pipeline. Afterwards, explanations and results are given in separate windows. We rely on this user interface in our evaluation of ad-hoc pipeline construction in Sect. 3.3. In the following, we describe how to interact with the user interface in more detail.

---

[9]ECLIPSE, http://www.eclipse.org, accessed on June 15, 2015.

[10]According to the pseudocode described in Sect. 3.3, the expert system constructs pipelines for single information needs only. An integration with the input control from Sect. 3.5 (cf. Appendix B.2) would allow handling different information needs at the same time, but this is left for the future.

[11]Different from our model in Sect. 3.2, the user interface separates the specifications of information types and value constraints. Still, these inputs are used equally in both cases.

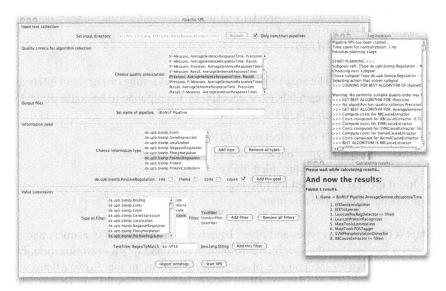

Fig. B.1 Screenshot of the prototypical user interface of our expert system PIPELINE XPS that realizes our approach to ad-hoc pipeline construction and execution.

B.1.2 Using the Expert System

The PIPELINE XPS user interface in Fig. B.1 is made up of the following areas, each of which including certain options that can or have to be set in order to start pipeline construction and execution:

Input Text Collection. Via the button *Browse*, a directory with the input texts to be processed (e.g., given as XMI files) can be set. If the checkbox *Only construct pipelines* is activated, pipeline execution will be disabled. Instead, an APACHE UIMA aggregate analysis engine is then constructed and stored in terms of an according descriptor file in the directory *./XPS/temp/*.

Quality Criteria for Algorithm Selection. According to Sect. 3.3, a quality prioritization needs to be chosen from the provided choice. Exactly those prioritizations are given that are illustrated in the quality model in Fig. 3.11, although the namings slightly differ in the expert system.

Output Files. In the area *Output files*, a name for the pipeline to be constructed can be specified. This name becomes the file name of the associated APACHE UIMA analysis engine descriptor file.

Information Needs. To set the information need **C** to be addressed by the pipeline, the following three steps need to be performed once for each information type $C \in \mathbf{C}$:

1. Select a type from the list and click on the *Add type* button.

2. Choose attributes for the added type by marking the appearing checkboxes (if the added type has attributes at all).
3. Press the button *Add this type*.

Value Constraints. The area *Value constraints* allows setting one or more filters that represent the value constraints to be checked by the pipeline to be constructed. For each filter, the following needs to be done:

1. In the *Type to filter* list, select the type to be filtered.
2. Select one of the appearing attributes of the selected type.
3. Select one of the three provided filters.
4. Insert the text to be used for filtering.
5. Press the button *Add this filter*.

Start XPS. When all types and filters have been set, *Start XPS* constructs and executes a pipeline for the specified information need and quality prioritization. Log output is shown in the console of ECLIPSE as well as in the *Explanations* window. A *Calculating results...* window appears where all results are shown when the pipeline execution is finished. In addition, the results are written to a file *./XPS/pipelineResults/resultOfPipeline-<pipelineName><timestamp>.txt*. All created pipeline descriptor files can be found in the *./XPS/temp/* directory, while the filter descriptor files are stored in *./XPS/temp/filter/*.

Import Ontology. By default, a sample ontology with a specified type system, an algorithm repository, and the built-in quality model described in Sect. 3.3 are set as the annotation task ontology to rely on. When pressing the button *Import ontology*, a window appears where an APACHE UIMA type system descriptor file can be selected as well as a directory in which to look for the analysis engine descriptor files (i.e., the algorithm repository). After pressing *Import Ontology Information*, the respective information is imported into the annotation task ontology and PIPELINE XPS is restarted.[12]

B.1.3 Exploring the Source Code of the System

XPS and *EfXTools* denote largely independent JAVA projects. In case the default ontology is employed, though, the former accesses the source code and the APACHE UIMA descriptor files of the latter. In the following, we give some information on both projects. For more details, see Appendix B.4.

---

[12]In case other analysis engines are imported, errors may occur in the current implementation. The reason is that there is a hardcoded blacklist of analysis engine descriptor files that can be edited in the class *de.upb.mrose.xps.application.ExpertSystemFrontendData* (ECLIPSE compiles this class automatically when starting the expert system the next time.

XPS. The source code *XPS* consists of four main packages: All classes related to the user interface of PIPELINE XPS belong to the package *de.upb.mrose.xps.application*, while the management of annotation task ontologies and their underlying data model are realized by the classes in the packages *de.upb.mrose.xps.knowledgebase* and *de.upb.mrose.xps.datamodel*. Finally, *de.upb.mrose.xps.problemsolver* is responsible for the pipeline construction. Besides, some further packages handle the interaction with classes and descriptors specific to APACHE UIMA. For details on the architecture and implementation of the expert system, we refer to (Rose 2012).

EfXTools. *EfXTools* is the primary software project containing text analysis algorithms and text mining applications developed within our case study INFEXBA described in Sect. 2.3. A large fraction of the source code and associated files is not relevant for the expert system, but partly plays a role in other experiments and case studies (cf. Appendix B.4 below). The algorithms used by the expert system can be found in all sub-packages of the package *de.upb.efxtools.ae*. The related APACHE UIMA descriptor files are stored in the folders *desc*, *desc38*, *desc76*, where the two latter represent the algorithm repositories evaluated in Sect. 3.3. Text corpora like the REVENUE CORPUS (cf. Appendix C.1) are given in the folder *data*.

Libraries. The folder *lib* of *XPS* contains the following freely available JAVA libraries, which are needed to compile the associated source code:[13]

APACHE JENA, http://jena.apache.org
APACHE LOG4J, http://logging.apache.org/log4j/2.x/
APACHE LUCENE, http://lucene.apache.org
APACHE XERCES, http://xerces.apache.org
JGRAPH, http://sourceforge.net/projects/jgraph
STAX, http://stax.codehaus.org
TAGSOUP, http://ccil.org/~cowan/XML/tagsoup
WOODSTOX, http://woodstox.codehaus.org

Similarly, the algorithms in *EFXTools* are based on the following libraries:

APACHE COMMONS, http://commons.apache.org/pool/
APACHE UIMA, http://uima.apache.org
ICU4J, http://site.icu-project.org
LIBSVM, http://www.csie.ntu.edu.tw/~cjlin/libsvm
MATE TOOLS, http://code.google.com/p/mate-tools
STANFORDNER, http://nlp.stanford.edu/ner/
TREETAGGER, http://www.ims.uni-stuttgart.de/projekte/corplex/TreeTagger/
TT4J, http://reckart.github.io/tt4j/
WEKA, http://www.cs.waikato.ac.nz/~ml/weka/

---

[13] All libraries accessed on June 15, 2015. The same holds for the libraries in *EFXTools*.

B.2 A Software Framework for Optimal Pipeline Execution

In this appendix, we sketch how to use the FILTERING FRAMEWORK introduced in Sect. 3.5. The framework was implemented by the author of this book as an extension of the APACHE UIMA framework. It allows equipping arbitrary text analysis pipelines with an input control. I.e., it automatically ensures that each algorithm employed in a pipeline analyzes only portions of input texts that are relevant for a specified information need, thus achieving an optimal pipeline execution.

B.2.1 Getting Started

Installation. The FILTERING FRAMEWORK corresponds to the project *IE-as-a-Filtering-Task* of the provided software. When using the above-mentioned integrated development environment ECLIPSE, a JAVA project can simply be created taking the respective folder as the root directory.

Overview. *IE-as-a-Filtering-Task* subsumes six folders:

 src The source code, consisting of the framework as well as some sample algorithms and applications.
 conf Lexica and models used by the algorithms.
 data Some sample text corpora.
 desc The descriptors of the APACHE UIMA analysis engines of the sample algorithms as well as of the associated type system.
 doc The javadoc documentation of the source code.
 lib The APACHE UIMA library used by the framework as well as other libraries for the algorithms.

Quick Start. For a first try of the framework, the class *QuickStartApplication* in the source code package *efxtools.sample.application* can be executed with the JAVA virtual machine parameters $-\texttt{Xmx1000m} -\texttt{Xms1000m}$. This starts the extraction of relevant information for the query γ_3^* on the REVENUE CORPUS (cf. Sect. 3.5). During the processing of the corpus, some output is printed to the console. After processing, the execution terminates. All results are printed to the console.

B.2.2 Using the Framework

The source code of the FILTERING FRAMEWORK has been designed with a focus on easy integration and minimal additional effort. In order to use the framework for applications, the following needs to be done:

Application. Within an application based on APACHE UIMA, only the following two additional lines of code are needed. They define the scoped query and create the scope TMS (cf. Sect. 3.5 for details):

```
AScopedQuery query =
  new EfXScopedQuery(myTypeSystem, myQueryString);
ScopeTMS.createScopeTMS(query, myAggregateAEDesc);
```

Here, both the application-specific type system `myTypeSystem` and the aggregate analysis engine description `myAggregateAEDesc` are available through the APACHE UIMA framework. In the provided implementation, the scoped query is given as a text string `myQueryString` that is parsed in the class *EfXScopedQuery* of the FILTERING FRAMEWORK. Example queries can be found in the sample applications in the package *efxtools.sample* (details on the source code follow below).

Analysis Engines. The determination, generation, and filtering of scopes are automatically called from the method `process(JCas)` that is invoked by the APACHE UIMA framework on every primitive analysis engine for each text. For this purpose, the abstract class *FilteringAnalysisEngine* in the package *efxtools.filtering* overrides the process method and instead offers a method `process(JCas, Scope)`. While it is still possible to use regular primitive analysis engines in the FILTERING FRAMEWORK, every analysis engine that shall restrict its analysis to scopes of a text should inherit from *FilteringAnalysisEngine* and implement the new method.[14] Typically, with only minor changes a regular primitive analysis engine can be converted into a filtering analysis engine. For examples, see the provided sample algorithms.

Analysis Engine Descriptors. In order to ensure a correct annotation and filtering, it is important to thoroughly define the input and output capabilities of all employed primitive and aggregate analysis engines. Examples can be found in the subdirectories of the directory *desc*.

B.2.3 Exploring the Source Code of the Framework

The source code of the FILTERING FRAMEWORK in the folder *src* contains two main packages, *efxtools.filtering* and *efxtools.sample*. The former consists of the actual framework classes, whereas the latter contains a number of sample algorithms and applications, including those that are used in the experiments in Sect. 3.5.

The Filtering Framework. The classes in *efxtools.filtering* realize the assumption-based truth maintenance system described in Sect. 3.5. Most of these nine classes implement the classes in Fig. 3.19 and are named accordingly. The code was carefully documented with javadoc comments to make it easily understandable.

---

[14]In its prototypical form, the framework checks only the existence of annotation types during filtering while ignoring whether possibly required features have been set explicitly. For some specific queries, this may prevent the framework from performing filtering as much as would be possible.

Sample Algorithms. The package *efxtools.sample.ae* contains a selection of the algorithms from Appendix A. These algorithms have been slightly modified such that they rely on an input control. As such, they represent examples of how to realize a *FilteringAnalysisEngine* in the FILTERING FRAMEWORK.

Sample Applications. *efxtools.sample.application* contains a number of applications that illustrate the use of the FILTERING FRAMEWORK. In particular, the package contains classes for the four queries addressed in the experiments in Sect. 3.5. Information on how to reproduce the associated results is given in Appendix B.4.

Libraries. The folder *lib* contains the following freely available JAVA libraries, which are needed to run and compile the provided source code:[15]

APACHE COMMONS, http://commons.apache.org/pool/
APACHE UIMA, http://uima.apache.org
LIBSVM, http://www.csie.ntu.edu.tw/~cjlin/libsvm
STANFORDNER, http://nlp.stanford.edu/ner/
TREETAGGER, http://www.ims.uni-stuttgart.de/projekte/corplex/TreeTagger/
TT4J, http://reckart.github.io/tt4j/
WEKA, http://www.cs.waikato.ac.nz/~ml/weka/

B.3 A Web Application for Sentiment Scoring and Explanation

This appendix describes the prototypical web application for predicting and explaining sentiment scores that we refer to in Sect. 5.5. The application was developed within the project ARGUANA (acknowledgments are given below). It can be accessed at http://www.arguana.com.

B.3.1 Getting Started

The web application accesses a webservice to predict a sentiment score between 1 (worst) and 5 (best) for an English input text. The webservice realizes the output analysis from Chap. 5, including the use of the feature type developed in Sect. 5.4 and the creation of explanation graphs from Sect. 5.5. While any input text can be entered by a user, the application targets at the analysis of hotel reviews.

---

[15] All libraries accessed on June 15, 2015. For the FILTERING FRAMEWORK, only APACHE UIMA is required. The other libraries are used for the sample algorithms and applications.

Before prediction, the application processes the entered text with a pipeline of several text analysis algorithms. In addition to the feature types considered in the evaluation of Sect. 5.4, it also extracts hotel names and aspects and it derives features from the combination of local sentiment and the found names and aspects. Unlike the evaluated sentiment scoring approach, prediction is then performed using supervised regression (cf. Sect. 2.1). Afterwards, the application provides different visual explanations of the prediction, as described in the following.

B.3.2 Using the Application

Figure B.2 shows the user interface of the application consisting of the following five areas. Only the first area is shown in the beginning, while the others are displayed after an input text has been analyzed.

Input Text to Be Analyzed. Here, a user can enter an arbitrary input text. After choosing either the shortened or the full *overview graph style* (see below), pressing *Analyze* sends the input text to the webservice.

Analyzed Text. When the webservice has returned its results, this area shows a segmentation of the input text into numbered discourse units. Each discourse unit is marked as being a fact (dark background), a positive opinion (light background), or a negative opinion (medium background).

Global Sentiment. Here, the predicted sentiment score is visualized in the form of a star rating with a more exact but still rounded value given in brackets.

Local Sentiment Flow. This area depicts the local sentiment flow of the input text as defined in Sect. 5.3. In addition, each value of the flow is labeled with the hotel names and aspects found in the associated discourse unit. By clicking on one of the values, a detail view of the explanation graph is displayed in the area below, as illustrated in Fig. B.3.

Explanation Graph. In the bottom area, a variant of the explanation graph sketched in Fig. 5.18 from Sect. 5.5 is visualized. In particular, the graph aggregates discourse relations, facts (marked as objective), and opinions all in the same layer. Moreover, the visualization pretends that the facts and opinions depend on the found hotel names and aspects (labeled as products and product features) to achieve a more simple graph layout. Given that the full overview graph style has been selected, the explanation graph includes tokens with simplified part-of-speech tags as well as sentences besides the outlined information. Otherwise, the tokens and sentences are shown in the mentioned detail view only.

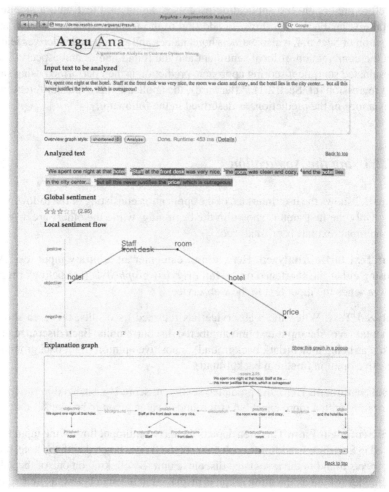

Fig. B.2 Screenshot of the main user interface of the prototypical web application for the prediction and explanation of the sentiment score of an input text.

B.3.3 Exploring the Source Code of the Application

The source code of the application can be found in the project *ArguAna*, except for the source code of the user interface, which is not part of the provided software. The packages *com.arguana.explanation* and *com.arguana.server* contain the source code of the creation of explanation graphs and the webservice, respectively. All employed algorithms can be found in the subpackages of *com.arguana.efxtools.ae*, whereas the used text analysis pipeline is represented by the descriptor file *HotelTextScoreRegressionPipeline.xml* in the folder *desc/aggregate-ae*.

Fig. B.3 Screenshot of the detail view of the explanation graph of a single discourse unit in the prototypical web application.

B.3.4 Acknowledgments

The development of the application was funded by the GERMAN FEDERAL MINISTRY OF EDUCATION AND RESEARCH (BMBF) as part of the project ARGUANA described in Sect. 2.3. The application's user interface was implemented by the RESOLTO INFOR-MATIK GMBH[16], based in Herford, Germany. The source code for predicting scores and creating explanation graphs was developed by the author of this book together with a research assistant from the WEBIS GROUP[17] of the BAUHAUS UNIVERSITÄT WEIMAR, Martin Trenkmann. The latter also realized the webservice underlying the application.

B.4 Source Code of All Experiments and Case Studies

Finally, we now shortly present how to reproduce all experiments and case studies described in this book. First, we give basic information on the provided software and the processed text corpora. Then, we point out how to perform an experiment or case study and where to find additional information.

B.4.1 Software

As already stated at the beginning of Appendix B, the provided software is split into different projects. These projects have been created in different periods of time between 2009 and 2014. As the book at hand does not primarily target at the publi-cation of software, the projects (including all source code and experiment data) are not completely uniform and partly overlap. In case, any problems are encountered when reproducing certain results, please contact the author of this book.

Three of the projects have already been described in Appendices B.1 and B.2, namely, *EfXTools*, *XPS*, and *IE-as-a-Filtering-Task*. Also, the fourth and last project

---

[16]RESOLTO INFORMATIK GMBH, http://www.resolto.com, accessed on June 15, 2015.

[17]WEBIS GROUP, http://www.webis.de, accessed on June 15, 2015.

has been mentioned (in Appendix B.3). It is given in the top-level folder *ArguAna* of the provided software. *ArguAna* contains all algorithms and applications from our case study ARGUANA (cf. Sect. 2.3) that are relevant for this book. This folder is organized similar to those of the projects *EfXTools* and *IE-as-a-Filtering-Task*.

Depending on the experiment or case study at hand, source code of one of the four projects has to be executed in order to reproduce the according results. More details are given after the following notes on the processed corpora.

B.4.2 Text Corpora

The top-level folder *corpora* consists of the three text corpora that we created ourselves and that are described in Appendix C.1 to C.3. Each of them already comes in the format that is required to reproduce the experiments and case studies.

For the processed existing corpora (cf. Appendix C.4), we provide conversion classes within the projects. In particular, the CoNLL-2003 dataset can be converted (1) into XMI files with the class *CoNLLToXMIConverter* in the package *de.upb.efxtools.application.convert* found in the project *EfXTools* and (2) into plain texts with the class *CoNLL03Converter* in *efxtools.sample.application* of *IE-as-a-Filtering-Task*. For the SENTIMENT SCALE DATASET and the related sentence subjectivity and polarity datasets, three accordingly named XMI conversion classes can be found in the package *com.arguana.corpus.creation* of *ArguAna*. Finally, the BROWN CORPUS is converted using the class *BrownCorpusToPlainTextConverter* from the package *de.upb.efxtools.application.convert* in *EfXTools*.

B.4.3 Experiments and Case Studies

Instructions and Results. Detailed descriptions on how to reproduce the results of all experiments and case studies are given in the top-level folder *experiments*. This folder has one sub-folder for each section of the book at hand, which presents an evaluation or similar. Every sub-folder includes one or more plain text instruction files that contain a step-by-step description on how to reproduce the respective results and what classes of which of the four projects to use for this purpose.[18] In many cases, parameter configurations for the respective experiments and case studies can be found in the files below the instructions. Also, further relevant information is given where necessary.

Besides the instruction files, every sub-folder contains a folder *results* with files that show the output of the executed classes, the tested parameters, or any other result information. In case of machine learning experiments conducted in the WEKA

---

[18]For sections with different separated experiments, another level of sub-folders is added.

toolkit (Hall et al. 2009), there is also a folder *arff-files* that contains all feature files of the evaluated text corpora.

Example. As an example, browse through the sub-folder *experiments_4_3* and open the file *instructions.txt*. At the top, this files shows the three steps needed to perform any of the experiments on the informed search scheduling approach from Sect. 4.3 as well as some additional notes. Below, an overview of the parameters to be set in the associated JAVA class is given as well as the concrete parameter specifications of each experiment. In the folder *results*, several plain text files can be found that are named according to the table or figure from Sect. 4.3 the respective results appear in. In addition, the file *algorithm-run-time-estimations.txt* gives an overview of the run-time estimations, the informed search strategy relies on.

Memory. Some of the text analysis algorithms employed in the experiments require a lot of heap space during execution, mostly because of large machine learning models. As a general rule, we propose to allocate 2 GB heap space in all experiments and case studies. If ECLIPSE is used to compile and run the respective code, memory can be assigned to every class with a main method under `Run... > Run Configurations`. In the appearing window, insert the virtual machine arguments $-\text{Xmx2000m} -\text{Xms2000m}$ in the tab *Arguments*. In case a class is run from the console, type the following to achieve the same effect: `javac < myClass > .java` $-\text{Xmx2000m} -\text{Xms2000m}$.

Run-times. Depending on the experiment, the reproduction of results may take anything between a few seconds and several hours. Notice that many of our experiments measure run-times themselves. During their execution, nothing else should be done with the executing system (as far as possible) in order to ensure accurate measurements. This includes the deactivation of energy saving modes, screen savers, and so on. Moreover, all run-time experiments include a warm-up run, ignored in the computation of the results, because pipelines based on APACHE UIMA tend to be somewhat slower in the beginning.

Appendix C
Text Corpora

The development and evaluation of text analysis algorithms and pipelines nearly always relies on text corpora, i.e., collections of texts with known properties (cf. Sect. 2.1 for details). For the approach to enable ad-hoc large-scale text mining discussed in the book at hand, we processed and analyzed three text corpora that we published ourselves as well as a few existing text corpora often used by researchers in the field. This appendix provides facts and descriptions on each employed corpus that are relevant for the understanding of the case studies and experiments in Chaps. 3 – 5. We begin with our corpora in Appendices C.1–C.3, the REVENUE CORPUS, the ARGUANA TRIPADVISOR CORPUS, and the LFA-11 CORPUS. Afterwards, we shortly outline the other employed corpora (Appendix C.4).

C.1 The Revenue Corpus

First, we outline the corpus that is used most often in this book to evaluate the developed approaches, the REVENUE CORPUS. The REVENUE CORPUS consists of 1128 German online business news articles, in which different types of statements on revenue are manually annotated together with all information needed to make them machine-processable. The purpose of the corpus is to investigate both the structure of sentences on financial criteria and the distribution of associated information over the text. The corpus was introduced in Wachsmuth et al. (2010), from which we reuse some content, but we provide more details here. It is free for scientific use and can be downloaded at http://infexba.upb.de.

C.1.1 Compilation

The REVENUE CORPUS consists of 1128 German news articles from the years 2003 to 2009. These articles were manually selected from 29 source websites by four

Table C.1 Numbers of texts from the listed websites in the complete REVENUE CORPUS as well as in its training set and in the union of its validation and test set.

Source websites	Training set	Validation and test set	Complete corpus
http://www.produktion.de	127	12	139
http://www.heise.de	127	12	139
http://www.golem.de	117	12	129
http://www.wiwo.de	112	11	123
http://www.boerse-online.de	100	11	111
http://www.spiegel.de	93	11	104
http://www.capital.de	76	11	87
http://www.tagesschau.de	–	73	73
http://www.finanzen.net	–	37	37
http://www.vdma.org	–	37	37
http://de.news.yahoo.com	–	37	37
http://www.faz.net	–	19	19
http://www.vdi.de	–	16	16
http://www.zdnet.de	–	13	13
http://www.handelsblatt.com	–	13	13
http://www.zvei.org	–	11	11
http://www.sueddeutsche.de	–	7	7
http://boerse.ard.de	–	7	7
http://www.it-business.de	–	5	5
http://www.manager-magazin.de	–	5	5
http://www.sachen-machen.org	–	5	5
http://www.swissinfo.ch	–	4	4
http://www.hr-online.de	–	1	1
http://nachrichten.finanztreff.de	–	1	1
http://www.tognum.com	–	1	1
http://www.pcgameshardware.de	–	1	1
http://www.channelpartner.de	–	1	1
http://www.cafe-future.net	–	1	1
http://www.pokerzentrale.de	–	1	1
Total	**752**	**188 each**	**1128**

employees of a company from the semantic technology field (see acknowledgments below). Table C.1 lists the distribution of websites in the corpus. As shown, we created a split of the corpus, in which two third of the texts constitute the training set and one sixth refers to the validation and test set each. In order to simulate the conditions of developing and applying text analysis algorithms, the training texts were randomly chosen from the seven most represented websites only, while the validation and test data both cover all 29 sources. As a result, the training set of the corpus consists of

Table C.2 Distribution of statements on revenues in the different parts of the REVENUE CORPUS, separated into the distributions of forecasts and of declarations.

Type	Training set		Validation set		Test set		Complete	
Forecasts	306	(22.4%)	113	(31.2%)	104	(30.0%)	523	(25.2%)
Declarations	1060	(77.6%)	249	(68.8%)	243	(70.0%)	1552	(74.8%)
All statements	1366	(100.0%)	362	(100.0%)	347	(100.0%)	2075	(100.0%)

752 texts with a total of 21,586 sentences, while the validation and test set sum up to 188 texts each with 5751 and 6038 sentences, respectively.

C.1.2 Annotation

In each text of the REVENUE CORPUS, annotations of text spans are given on the event level and on the entity level, as sketched in the following.

Event Level. Every sentence with explicit time and money information that represents a statement on the revenue of an organization or market is annotated as either a *forecast* or a *declaration*. If a sentence comprises more than one such statement on revenue, it is annotated multiple times.

Entity Level. In each statement, the *time expression* and the *monetary expression* are marked as such (relative money information is preferred over absolute information in case they are separated). Accordingly, the *subject* is marked within the sentence if available, otherwise its last mention in the preceding text. The same holds for optional entities, namely, a possible *referenced point* a relative time expression refers to, a *trend* word that indicates whether a relative monetary expression is increasing or decreasing, and the *author* of a statement. All annotated entities are linked to the statement on revenue they belong to. Only entities that belongs to a statement are annotated.

Table C.2 gives an overview of the 2075 statements on revenue annotated in the corpus. The varying distributions of forecasts and declarations give a hint that the validation and test set differ significantly from the training set.

Example

Figure C.1 shows a sample text from the REVENUE CORPUS with one statement on revenue, a forecast. Besides the required time and monetary expressions, the forecast spans an author mention and a trend indicator of the monetary expression. Other relevant information is spread across a text, namely, the organization the forecast is about as well as a reference date needed to resolve the time expression.

> *Loewe AG: Vorläufige Neun-Monats-Zahlen*
> **Reference point**
> *Kronach, 6. November 2007 --- Das Ergebnis vor Zinsen und Steuern (EBIT) des Loewe Konzerns konnte in den ersten*
> **Organization**
> *9 Monaten 2007 um 41% gesteigert werden. Vor diesem Hintergrund hebt die Loewe AG ihre EBIT-Prognose für das*
> **Author   Time expression**
> *laufende Geschäftsjahr auf 20 Mio. Euro an. Beim Umsatz strebt Konzernchef Rainer Hecker für das Gesamtjahr ein*
> **Trend   Monetary expression   Forecast**
> *höher als ursprünglich geplantes Wachstum von 10% auf ca. 380 Mio. Euro an. (...)*

Fig. C.1 Illustration of a sample text from the REVENUE CORPUS. Each statement on revenue that spans a time expression and a monetary expression is manually marked either as a forecast or as a declaration. Also, different types of information needed to process the statement are annotated.

Annotation Process

Two employees of the above-mentioned company manually annotated all texts from the corpus. They were given the following main guideline:

> Search for sentences in the text (including its title) that contain statements about the revenues of an organization or market with explicit time and money information. Annotate each such sentence as a forecast (if it is about the future) or as a declaration (if about the past). Also, annotate the following information related to the statement:

- **Author.** The person who made the statement (if given).
- **Money.** The money information in the statement (prefer relative over absolute information in case they are separated).
- **Subject.** The organization or market, the statement is about (annotate a mention in the statement if given, otherwise the closest in the preceding text).
- **Trend.** A word that makes explicit whether the revenues increase or decrease (if given).
- **Time.** The time information in the statement.
- **Reference point.** A point in time, the annotated time information refers to (if given).

In addition, each information type to be annotated was explained in detail and exemplified for a number of cases below the guideline. After the annotation of the first texts, we clarified possible misunderstandings with the employees and, then, added some further examples. Afterwards, the employees annotated the remaining texts. Annotations were created with the CAS EDITOR[19] provided by APACHE UIMA.

Inter-Annotator Agreement. Each text is annotated only once. To compute inter-annotator agreement, however, a preceding pilot study with respect to the annotation of statements on revenue yielded substantial agreement, as indicated by the value 0.79 of the measure Cohen's Kappa (Fleiss 1981).

---

[19]CAS EDITOR, http://uima.apache.org/toolsServers, accessed on June 8, 2015.

C.1.3 Files

The REVENUE CORPUS comes as a packed tar.gz archive (6 MB compressed; 32 MB uncompressed). The content of each contained news article is given as unicode plain text with appended source URL for access to the HTML source code. Annotations are specified in an XMI file preformatted for APACHE UIMA.

C.1.4 Acknowledgments

The creation of the REVENUE CORPUS was funded by the GERMAN FEDERAL MINISTRY OF EDUCATION AND RESEARCH (BMBF) as part of the project INFEXBA, described in Sect. 2.3. The corpus was planned by the author of this book together with a research assistant from the above-mentioned WEBIS GROUP of the BAUHAUS UNIVERSITÄT WEIMAR, Peter Prettenhofer. The described process of manually selecting and annotating the texts in the corpus was conducted by the RESOLTO INFORMATIK GMBH, also named above.

C.2 The ArguAna TripAdvisor Corpus

In this appendix, we describe the compilation, annotation, and formatting of the ARGUANA TRIPADVISOR CORPUS, i.e., a collection of 2,100 manually annotated hotel reviews, balanced with respect to the reviews' overall ratings. In addition, nearly 200,000 further reviews are provided without manual annotations. The text corpus serves for the development and evaluation of approaches that analyze the sentiment and argumentation of web user reviews. This appendix reuses content from Wachsmuth et al. (2014b), where we extensively present the design of the corpus. While we largely restrict our view to facts about the corpus here, more details on the reasons behind some design decisions are found in that publication. The corpus is free for scientific use and available at http://www.arguana.com.

C.2.1 Compilation

The ARGUANA TRIPADVISOR CORPUS is based on a highly balanced subset of a dataset originally used for aspect-level rating prediction (Wang et al. 2010). The original dataset contains nearly 250,000 crawled English hotel reviews from the travel website TRIPADVISOR[20] that refer to 1850 hotels from over 60 locations. Each review comprises a text, a set of numerical ratings, and some metadata. The quality of the

---

[20]TRIPADVISOR, http://www.tripadvisor.com, accessed on June 18, 2015.

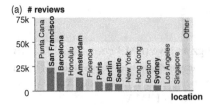
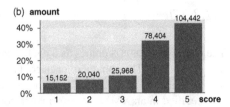

Fig. C.2 a Distribution of the locations of the reviewed hotels in the original dataset from Wang et al. (2010). The ARGUANA TRIPADVISOR CORPUS contains 300 annotated texts of each of the seven marked locations. **b** Distribution of the overall scores of the reviews in the original dataset.

Table C.3 The number of reviewed hotels of each location in the complete ARGUANA TRIP-ADVISOR CORPUS and in its three parts as well as the number of reviews for each sentiment score between 1 and 5 and in total.

Set	Location	Hotels	Score 1	Score 2	Score 3	Score 4	Score 5	Σ
Training	Amsterdam	10	60	60	60	60	60	300
	Seattle	10	60	60	60	60	60	300
	Sydney	10	60	60	60	60	60	300
Validation	Berlin	44	60	60	60	60	60	300
	San Francisco	10	60	60	60	60	60	300
Test	Barcelona	10	60	60	60	60	60	300
	Paris	26	60	60	60	60	60	300
Complete	**All seven**	**120**	**420**	**420**	**420**	**420**	**420**	**2100**

texts is not perfect in all cases, certainly due to crawling errors: Some line breaks have been lost, which hides a number of sentence boundaries and, sporadically, also word boundaries. The distributions of locations and overall ratings in the original dataset is illustrated in Fig. C.2. Since the reviews of the covered locations are crawled more or less randomly, the distribution of overall ratings can be assumed to be representative for TRIPADVISOR in general.

Our sampled subset consists of 2100 reviews balanced with respect to both location and overall rating. In particular, we selected 300 reviews of seven of the 15 most-represented locations in the original dataset each, 60 for every overall rating between 1 (worst) and 5 (best). This supports an optimal training for machine learning approaches to rating prediction. Moreover, the reviews of each location cover at least 10, but as few as possible hotels, which is beneficial for opinion summarization approaches.

To counter location bias, we provide a corpus split with a training set containing the reviews of three locations, and both a validation set and a test set with two of the other locations. Table C.3 lists details about the balanced compilation and the split.

Table C.4 Statistics of the tokens, sentences, manually classified statements, and manually annotated product features in the ARGUANA TRIPADVISOR CORPUS.

Type	Total	Average $\pm \sigma$	Median	Min	Max
Tokens	442615	210.77 ± 171.66	172	3	1823
Sentences	24162	11.51 ± 7.89	10	1	75
Statements	**31006**	**14.76 ± 10.44**	**12**	**1**	**96**
Facts	6303	3.00 ± 3.65	2	0	41
Positive opinions	11786	5.61 ± 5.20	5	0	36
Negative opinions	12917	6.15 ± 6.69	4	0	52
Product features	**24596**	**11.71 ± 10.03**	**10**	**0**	**180**

C.2.2 Annotation

The reviews in the dataset from (Wang et al. 2010) have a title and a body and they
include different ratings and metadata. We maintain all this information as text-level
and syntax-level annotations in the ARGUANA TRIPADVISOR CORPUS. In addition,
the corpus is enriched with annotations of local sentiment at the discourse level and
domain concepts at the entity level:

Text Level. Each review comes with optional ratings for seven hotels aspects: *value,
room, location, cleanliness, front desk, service,* and *business service.* We interpret the
mandatory overall rating as a global *sentiment score.* All ratings are integer values
between 1 and 5. In terms of metadata, the *ID* and *location* of the reviewed hotel, the
username of the *author,* and the *date* of creation are given.

Syntax Level. In every review text, the title and body are annotated as such and they
are separated by two line breaks.

Discourse Level. All review texts are segmented into *statements* that represent single
discourse units. A statement is a main clause together with all its dependent subordinate clauses (and, hence, a statement spans at most a sentence). Each statement is
classified as being an objective *fact,* a *positive opinion,* or a *negative opinion.*

Entity Level. Two types of domain concepts are marked as *product features* in
all texts: (1) *hotel aspects,* like those rated on the text level but also others like
atmosphere, and (2) everything that is called an *amenity* in the hotel domain, e.g.
facilities like a coffee maker or wifi as well as services like laundry.

Table C.4 lists the numbers of corpus annotations together with some statistics.
The corpus includes 31,006 classified statements and 24,596 product features. On
average, a text comprises 14.76 statements and 11.71 product features. A histogram of
the length of all reviews in terms of the number of statements is given in Fig. C.3(a),
grouped into intervals. As can be seen, over one third of all texts spans less than
10 statements (intervals 0–4 and 5–9), whereas less than one fourth spans 20 or

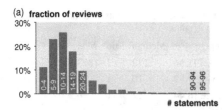
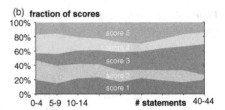

Fig. C.3 **a** Histogram of the number of statements in the texts of the ARGUANA TRIPADVISOR CORPUS, grouped into intervals. **b** Interpolated curves of the fraction of sentiment scores in the corpus depending on the numbers of statements.

| title: | *great* **location**, *bad* **service** | sentiment score: 2 of 5 |

body: *stayed at the darling harbour holiday inn.* *The* **location** *was great, right there at China town, restaurants everywhere, the monorail station is also nearby.* *Paddy's market is like 2 mins walk.* **Rooms** *were however very small.* *We were given the 1st floor* **rooms,** *and we were right under the monorail track,* *however* **noise** *was not a problem.* **Service** *is terrible.* **Staffs** *at the* **front desk** *were* **impatient,** *I made an enquiry about* **internet access** *from the* **room** *and the person on the phone was rude and unhelpful.* *Very shocking and unpleasant encounter.*

Fig. C.4 Illustration of a review from the ARGUANA TRIPADVISOR CORPUS. Each review text has a title and a body. It is segmented into discourse-level statements that are manually classified as *positive opinions* (light background), *negative opinions* (medium), and objective *facts* (dark). Also, manual annotations of domain concepts are provided (marked in bold).

more. Figure C.3(b) visualizes the distribution of sentiment scores for all intervals that cover at least 1 % of the corpus. Most significantly, the fraction of reviews with sentiment score 3 increases under higher numbers of statements.

Example

Figure C.4 illustrates the main annotations of a sample review from the corpus. Each text has a specified title and body. In this case, the body spans nine mentions of product features, such as *"location"* or *"internet access"*. It is segmented into 12 facts and opinions. The facts and opinions reflect the review's rather negative sentiment score 2 while e.g. highlighting that the internet access was not seen as negative. Besides, Fig. C.4 exemplifies the typical writing style often found in web user reviews like those from TRIPADVISOR: A few grammatical inaccuracies (e.g. inconsistent capitalization) and colloquial phrases (e.g. *"like 2 mins walk"*), but easily readable.

Annotation Process

The classification of all statements in the texts of the ARGUANA TRIPADVISOR CORPUS was performed using crowdsourcing, while experts annotated the product features. Before, the segmentation of the texts into statements was done automatically using the algorithm PDU (cf. Appendix A). The manual annotation process is summarized in the following.

Crowdsourcing Annotation. The statements were classified using the crowdsourcing platform AMAZON MECHANICAL TURK that we already relied on in Sect. 5.5. The task we assigned to the workers here involved the classification of a random selection of 12 statements. After some preliminary experiments with different task descriptions, the main guideline given to the workers was the following:

> When visiting a hotel, are the following statements positive, negative, or neither?

Together with the guideline, three notes were provided: (1) to choose *"neither"* only for facts, not for unclear cases, (2) to pay attention to subtle statements where sentiment is expressed implicitly or ironically, and (3) to pick the most appropriate answer in controversial cases. The different cases were illustrated using a carefully chosen set of example statements.

The workers were allowed to work on the 12 statements of a task at most 10 minutes and were paid $0.05 in case of approval. To assure quality, the tasks were assigned only to workers with over 1000 approved tasks and an average approval rate of at least 80 % on AMAZON MECHANICAL TURK. Moreover, we always put two hidden check statements with known and unambiguous classification among the statements in order to recognize faked or otherwise flawed answers. The workers were informed that tasks with incorrectly classified check statements are rejected. Rejected tasks were reassigned to other workers. For a consistent annotation, we assigned each statement to three workers and then applied majority voting to obtain the final classifications. Altogether, 328 workers performed 14,187 tasks with an approval rate of 72.8 %. On average, a worker spent 75.8 s per task.

Expert Annotation. Two experts with linguistic background annotated product features in the corpus based on the following guideline:

> Read through each review. Mark all product features of the reviewed hotel in the sense of hotel aspects, amenities, services, and facilities.

In addition, we specified (1) to omit attributes of product features, e.g. to mark *"location"* instead of *"central location"* and *"coffee maker"* instead of *"in-room coffee maker"*, (2) to omit guest belongings, and (3) not to mark the word *"hotel"* or brands like *"Bellagio"* or *"Starbucks"*. Analog to above, we illustrated the guidelines with the help of some example annotations. After an initial annotation of 30 reviews, we discussed and revised the annotations produced so far with each expert. Then, the experts annotated the rest of the corpus, taking about 5 min per text on average.

Inter-Annotator Agreement. In case of crowdsourcing, we measured the inter-annotator agreement for all statements in terms of Fleiss' Kappa (Fleiss 1981). The obtained value of 0.67 is usually interpreted as substantial agreement. In detail, 73.6 % of the statements got the same classification from all three workers and 24.7 % had a 2:1 vote (4.8 % with opposing opinion polarity). The remaining 1.7 % mostly refer to controversial statements, such as *"nice hotel, overpriced"* or *"It might not be* *the Ritz"*. We classified these statements ourselves in the context of the associated review. To measure the agreement of the product feature annotations, 633 statements were annotated by two experts. In 546 cases, both experts marked exactly the same spans in the statements as product features. Assuming a chance agreement probability of 0.5, this results in the value 0.73 of Cohen's Kappa (Fleiss 1981), which again means substantial agreement.

C.2.3 Files

The ARGUANA TRIPADVISOR CORPUS comes as a packed ZIP archive (8 MB compressed; 28 MB uncompressed), which contains XMI files preformatted for the APACHE UIMA framework just as for the REVENUE CORPUS in Appendix C.1. Moreover, we converted all those 196,865 remaining reviews of the dataset from Wang et al. (2010), which have a correct text and a correct overall rating between 1 and 5, into the same format without manual annotations but with all TRIPADVISOR metadata. This unannotated dataset (265 MB compressed; 861 MB uncompressed) can be used both for semi-supervised learning techniques (cf. Sect. 2.1) and for large-scale evaluations of rating prediction or similar. We attached some example applications and a selection of the text analysis algorithms from Appendix A to the corpus. The applications and algorithms can be executed to conduct the analyses from Sect. 5.3, thereby demonstrating how to process the corpus.

C.2.4 Acknowledgments

The creation of the ARGUANA TRIPADVISOR CORPUS was funded by the GERMAN FEDERAL MINISTRY OF EDUCATION AND RESEARCH (BMBF) as part of the project ARGUANA, described in Sect. 2.3. The corpus was planned by the author of this book together with a research assistant from the above-mentioned WEBIS GROUP of the BAUHAUS UNIVERSITÄT WEIMAR, Tsvetomira Palarkska. The latter then compiled the texts of the corpus and realized and supervised the crowdsourcing annotation process. The expert annotations were added by one assistant from the UNIVERSITY OF PADERBORN and one employee of the RESOLTO INFORMATIK GMBH.

C.3 The LFA-11 Corpus

Besides the REVENUE CORPUS and the ARGUANA TRIPADVISOR CORPUS, we use a third self-created corpus in some experiments of this book, the LFA-11 CORPUS. The LFA-11 CORPUS is a collection of 4806 manually annotated product-related texts. The corpus consists of two separate parts, which refer to different high-level topics, namely, music and smartphones. It serves as a linguistic resource for the development and evaluation of approaches to language function analysis (cf. Sect. 2.3) and sentiment analysis. In the following, we reuse and extend content from Wachsmuth and Bujna (2011), where the LFA-11 CORPUS has originally been presented. The corpus is free for scientific use and can be downloaded at http://infexba.upb.de.

C.3.1 Compilation

The LFA-11 CORPUS contains 2713 texts from the music domain as well as 2093 texts from the smartphone domain. The texts of these topical domains come from different sources and are of very different quality and style:

The music collection is made up of user reviews, professional reviews, and promotional texts from a social network platform, selected by employees of a company from the digital asset management industry (see acknowledgments below). These texts are well-written and of homogeneous style. On average, a music texts span 9.4 sentences with 23.0 tokens on average, according to the output of our algorithms SSE and STO$_2$ (cf. Appendix A.1). In contrast, the texts in the smartphone collection are blog posts. These posts were retrieved via queries on a self-made APACHE LUCENE[21] index, which was built for the SPINN3R CORPUS.[22] SPINN3R aims at crawling and indexing the whole blogosphere. Hence, the texts in the smartphone collection vary strongly in quality and writing style. They have an average length of 11.8 sentences but only 18.6 tokens per sentence.

C.3.2 Annotation

All texts of the LFA-11 CORPUS are annotated on the text level with respect to three classification schemes:

Text Level. First, the *language function* of each text is annotated as being predominantly personal, commercial, or informational (cf. Sect. 2.3).[23] Second, the texts are classified with respect to their sentiment polarity, where we distinguish positive, neutral, and negative sentiment. And third, the *relevance* with respect to the topic of the corpus part the text belongs to (music or smartphones) is annotated as being given (true) or not (false).

In the corpus texts, all three annotations are linked to a *metadata* annotation that provides access to them. Some texts were annotated twice for inter-annotator agree-

---

[21] APACHE LUCENE, http://lucene.apache.org, accessed on June 15, 2015.

[22] SPINN3R CORPUS, http://www.spinn3r.com, accessed on June 15, 2015.

[23] The language function annotation is called *Genre* in the corpus texts. Language functions can be seen as a single aspect of genres (Wachsmuth and Bujna 2011).

Table C.5 Distributions of the text-level classes in the three sets of the two topical parts of the LFA-11 CORPUS for the three annotated types.

Topic	Type	Class	Training set		Validation set		Test set	
music	Language function	personal	521	(38.5%)	419	(61.7%)	342	(50.4%)
		commercial	127	(9.4%)	72	(10.6%)	68	(10.0%)
		informational	707	(52.2%)	188	(27.7%)	269	(39.6%)
	Sentiment	positive	1003	(74.0%)	558	(82.2%)	514	(75.7%)
		neutral	259	(19.1%)	82	(12.1%)	115	(16.9%)
		negative	93	(6.9%)	39	(5.7%)	50	(7.4%)
	Topic relevance	true	1327	(97.9%)	673	(99.1%)	662	(97.5%)
		false	28	(2.1%)	6	(0.9%)	17	(2.5%)
smartphone	Language function	personal	546	(52.1%)	279	(53.3%)	302	(57.7%)
		commercial	90	(8.6%)	36	(6.9%)	28	(5.4%)
		informational	411	(39.3%)	208	(39.8%)	193	(36.9%)
	Sentiment polarity	positive	205	(19.6%)	110	(21.0%)	84	(16.1%)
		neutral	738	(70.5%)	343	(65.6%)	359	(68.6%)
		negative	104	(9.9%)	70	(13.4%)	80	(15.3%)
	Topic relevance	true	561	(53.6%)	307	(58.7%)	287	(54.9%)
		false	486	(46.4%)	216	(41.3%)	236	(45.1%)

[...] How did Alex ask recently when he saw the Kravitz' latest best-of collection: Is it his own liking, the voting on his website or the chart position what counts? Good question. However, in our case, there is nothing to argue about: 27 songs, all were number one. The Beatles. Biggest Band on the Globe. [...]	*[...] The sitars sound authentically Indian. In combination with the three-part harmonious singing and the jingle-jangle of the rickenbacker guitars, they create an oriental flair without losing their Beatlesque elegance. If that doesn't make you smile! [...]*	*[...] "It's All Too Much"? No, no, still okay, though an enormous hype was made about the seemingly new Beatles song for decades. The point is that exactly this song "Hey Bulldog" has already been published several times, most recently on a reprint of ``Yellow Submarine'' in the year 1987. [...]*
Language function: personal **Sentiment polarity:** neutral **Topic relevance:** true	**Language function:** commercial **Sentiment polarity:** positive **Topic relevance:** true	**Language function:** informational **Sentiment polarity:** neutral **Topic relevance:** true

Fig. C.5 Translated excerpts from three texts of the music part of the LFA-11 CORPUS, exemplifying one instance of each language function. Notice that the translation to English may have affected the indicators of the annotated classes.

ment purposes (see the annotation process below). These texts have two annotations of each type. We created splits for each topic with half of the texts in the training set and each one fourth in the validation set and test set, respectively. Table C.5 show the class distributions of language functions, sentiment polarities, and topic relevance. The distributions indicate that the training, validation, and test sets differ significantly from each other. In case of double-annotated texts, we used the annotation of the second employee to compute the distributions. So, the exact frequencies of the different classes depend on which annotations are used.

Example

Figure C.5 shows excerpts from three texts of the music collection, one out of each language function class. The excerpts have been translated to English for convenience purposes. The neutral sentiment of the personal text might seem inappropriate, but the given excerpt is misleading in this respect.

Annotation Process

The classification of all texts of the LFA-11 CORPUS was performed by two employees of the mentioned company based on the following guidelines:

Read through each text of the two collections. First, tag the text as being predominantly personal, commercial, or informational with respect to the product discussed in the text:

- **personal.** Use this annotation if the text seems not to be of commercial interest, but probably represents the personal view on the product of a private individual.
- **commercial.** Use this annotation if the text is of obvious commercial interest. The text seems to predominantly aim at persuading the reader to buy or like the product.
- **informational.** Use this annotation if the text seems not to be of commercial interest with respect to the product. Instead, it predominantly appears to be informative in a journalistic manner.

Second, tag the sentiment polarity of the text:

- **neutral.** Use this annotation if the text either reports on the product without making any positive or negative statement about it or if the texts is neither positive nor negative, but rather close to the midth between positive and negative.
- **negative.** Use this annotation if the text reports on the product in a positive way from an overall viewpoint.
- **positive.** Use this annotation if the text reports on the product in a negative way from an overall viewpoint.

Finally, decide whether the text is relevant (true) or irrelevant (false) with respect to the topic of the collection (music or smartphones).

As for the corpora described above, we provided a set of examples to illustrate each language function, sentiment polarity, and relevance class. After the annotation of a sample of texts, we clarified misunderstandings with the employees and we added some insightful examples.

Inter-Annotator Agreement. About 20 % of the music texts and 40 % of the smartphone texts were tagged twice. The resulting inter-annotator agreement values 0.78 (music) and 0.67 (smartphone) of Cohen's Kappa (Fleiss 1981) for the language function annotations constitute substantial agreement. Especially 0.67 is far from perfect, which can make an accurate text classification hard. Under consideration of the hybridity of language functions (cf. Sect. 2.3), both kappa values appear to be quite high, though.

C.3.3 Files

The LFA-11 CORPUS comes as a packed tar.gz archive (5 MB compressed; 35 MB uncompressed). Both the music and the smartphone texts are stored in a standard UTF-8 encoded XMI file together with their annotations, preformatted for the APACHE UIMA framework.

C.3.4 Acknowledgments

The creation of the LFA-11 CORPUS was also funded by the GERMAN FEDERAL MINISTRY OF EDUCATION AND RESEARCH (BMBF) as part of the project INFEXBA, described in Sect. 2.3. Both parts of the corpus were planned by the author of this book together with a research assistant from the above-mentioned WEBIS GROUP, Peter Prettenhofer. The latter gathered the texts of the smartphone collection, whereas the music texts were selected by the company DIGITAL COLLECTIONS VERLAGSGE-SELLSCHAFT MBH[24], based in Hamburg, Germany. This company also conducted the described annotation process.

C.4 Used Existing Text corpora

Finally, we provide basic information on all collections of texts referred to in this book that have not been created by ourselves. Concretely, we summarize the main facts about the purpose and compilation of each collection as well as about the given annotations as far as available. Also, we provide references to where the collection can be accessed.

C.4.1 CoNLL-2003 Dataset (English and German)

The CoNLL-2003 dataset (Tjong Kim Sang and Meulder 2003) serves for the development and evaluation of approaches to the CoNLL-2003 SHARED TASK on language-independent named entity recognition. It consists of an English part and a German part. The English part contains 1393 news stories with different topics. It is split into 946 training texts (12,705 sentences), 216 validation texts (3466 sentences), and 231 test texts (3684 sentences). The German part contains 909 mixed newspaper articles, split into 553 training texts (12,705 sentences), 201 validation texts (3068 sentences), and 155 test texts (3160 sentences). In all texts of both parts, every mention of a *person* name, a *location* name, and an *organization* name are manually annotated as an

---

[24]DIGITAL COLLECTIONS, http://www.digicol.de, accessed on June 8, 2015.

entity of the respective type. Besides, there is a type *Misc* that covers entities, which do not belong to these three types.

We process the English part in the experiments with our input control in Sect. 3.5 and the German part to evaluate all our scheduling appraoches in Sects. 4.1, 4.3, and 4.5. Both parts are analyzed in terms of their distribution of relevant information (Sects. 4.2 and 4.4). The CoNLL-2003 dataset is not freely available. For information on how to obtain this corpus, see the website of the CoNLL-2003 SHARED TASK, http://www.cnts.ua.ac.be/conll2003/ner (accessed on June 15, 2015).

C.4.2 Sentiment Scale Dataset (and Related Datasets)

The SENTIMENT SCALE DATASET (Pang and Lee 2005) is a collection of texts that has been widely used to evaluate approaches to the prediction of sentiment scores. It consists of 5006 reviews from the film domain and comes with two sentiment scales. In particular, each review is assigned one integer score in the range [0, 3] and one in the range [0, 2]. On average, a review has 36.1 sentences. The dataset is split into four text corpora according to the four authors of the reviews: 1770 reviews of *author a* (Steve Rhodes), 902 reviews of *author b* (Scott Renshaw), 1307 reviews of *author c* (James Berardinelli), and 1027 reviews of *author d* (Dennis Schwartz).

We first analyze the SENTIMENT SCALE DATASET in terms of its distribution of relevant information in Sect. 4.4. Later, we process the dataset in the feature experiments in Sect. 5.3 and in the evaluation of our overall analysis (Sect. 5.4), where we rely on the three-class sentiment scale. In the performed experiments, we discarded three reviews of *author a* and five reviews of *author c* due to encoding problems. The SENTIMENT SCALE DATASET can be downloaded (accessed on June 8, 2015) at http://www.cs.cornell.edu/people/pabo/movie-review-data.

In addition to the SENTIMENT SCALE DATASET, we also process the SUBJECTIVITY DATASET from (Pang and Lee 2004) and the SENTENCE POLARITY DATASET from (Pang and Lee 2005) in Sect. 5.4 in order to develop classifiers for sentence sentiment. Both are also freely available at the mentioned website. The SUBJECTIVITY DATASET contains 10,000 sentences, half of which are classified as subjective and half as objective. Similarly, the SENTENCE POLARITY DATASET contains 5331 positive and 5331 negative sentences. The sentences from these two datasets are taken from film reviews.

C.4.3 Brown Corpus

The widely used BROWN CORPUS (Francis 1966) was introduced in the 1960s as a standard text collection of present-day American English. It consists of 500 prose text samples of about 2000 words each. The samples are excerpts from texts that were printed in the year 1961 and that were written by native speakers of American

English as far as determinable. They cover a wide range of styles and varieties of prose. At a high level, they can be divided into informative prose (374 samples) and imaginative prose (126 samples).

We process the BROWN CORPUS in Sects. 4.2 and 4.4 to show how relevant information is distributed across texts and collections of texts. The BROWN CORPUS is free for non-commercial purposes and can be downloaded (accessed on June 15, 2015) at http://www.nltk.org/nltk_data.

C.4.4 Wikipedia Sample

The German WIKIPEDIA sample that we experiment with consists of the first 10,000 articles from the WIKIMEDIA[25] dump from March 9, 2013, ordered according to their internal page IDs. The complete dump contains over 3 million WIKIPEDIA pages, from which 1.8 million pages represent articles that are neither empty nor stubs or simple lists.

As in the case of the BROWN CORPUS, we process the WIKIPEDIA sample in Sects. 4.2 and 4.4 to show how relevant information is distributed across texts and collections of texts. The dump we rely on is outdated and not available anymore. However, similar dumps from later dates can be downloaded (accessed on June 15, 2015) at http://dumps.wikimedia.org/dewiki.

---

[25]WIKIMEDIA, http://dumps.wikimedia.org, accessed on October 20, 2014.

References

Aggarwal, C.C.: Outlier Analysis. Springer, New York (2013)

Aggarwal, C.C., Zhai, C.: A survey of text classification algorithms. In: Aggarwal, C.C., Zhai, C. (eds.) Mining Text Data, pp. 163–222. Springer, New York (2012)

Agichtein, E.: Scaling information extraction to large document collections. Bull. IEEE Comput. Soc. Tech. Comm. Data Eng. **28**, 3–10 (2005)

Agichtein, E., Gravano, L.: Querying text databases for efficient information extraction. In: Proceedings of the 19th International Conference on Data Engineering, pp. 113–124 (2003)

Ahn, D., Adafre, S.F., de Rijke, M.: Extracting temporal information from open domain text: a comparative exploration. J. Digit. Inf. Manag. **3**(1), 14–20 (2005)

Al-Rfou', R., Skiena, S.: SpeedRead: a fast named entity recognition pipeline. In: Proceedings of the 24th International Conference on Computational Linguistics, pp. 51–66 (2012)

Alvarez, I., Martin, S.; Explaining a result to the end-user: a geometric approach for classification problems. In: Proceedings of the IJCAI 2009 Workshop on Explanation Aware Computing, pp. 102–109 (2009)

Ananiadou, S., McNaught, J.: Text Mining for Biology and Biomedicine. Artech House Inc., Norwood (2005)

Ananiadou, S., Thompson, P., Nawaz, R.: Enhancing search: events and their discourse context. In: Gelbukh, A. (ed.) CICLing 2013, Part II. LNCS, vol. 7817, pp. 318–334. Springer, Heidelberg (2013)

Anderka, M., Stein, B., Lipka, N.: Predicting quality flaws in user-generated content: the case of wikipedia. In: 35th International ACM Conference on Research and Development in Information Retrieval, pp. 981–990 (2012)

Angel, E.: Interactive Computer Graphics: A Top-Down Approach Using OpenGL, 5th edn. Addison-Wesley Publishing Company, Boston (2008)

Arens, S.: A dataflow-based shader framework for visualizing dissections of the heart using individual patient data. Dissertation, University of Paderborn (2014)

Arun, R., Suresh, V., Veni Madhavan, C.E.: Stopword graphs and authorship attribution in text corpora. In: Proceedings of the 2009 IEEE International Conference on Semantic Computing, pp. 192–196 (2009)

Baader, F., Calvanese, D., McGuinness, D.L., Nardi, D., Patel-Schneider, P.F. (eds.): The Description Logic Handbook: Theory, Implementation, and Applications. Cambridge University Press, New York (2003)

Baccianella, S., Esuli, A., Sebastiani, F.: SentiWordNet 3.0: an enhanced lexical resource for sentiment analysis and opinion mining. In: Proceedings of the Seventh International Conference on Language Resources and Evaluation, pp. 2200–2204 (2010)

Ballesteros, M., Bohnet, B., Mille, S., Wanner, L.: Deep-syntactic parsing. In: Proceedings of the 25th International Conference on Computational Linguistics. Technical papers, pp. 1402–1413 (2014)

Bangalore, S.: Thinking outside the box for natural language processing. In: Gelbukh, A. (ed.) CICLing 2012, Part I. LNCS, vol. 7181, pp. 1–16. Springer, Heidelberg (2012)

Banko, M., Cafarella, M.J., Soderland, S., Broadhead, M., Etzioni, O.: Open information extraction from the web. In: Proceedings of the 20th International Joint Conference on Artificial Intelligence, pp. 2670–2676 (2007)

Batista, G.E.A.P.A., Prati, R.C., Monard, M.C.: A study of the behavior of several methods for balancing machine learning training data. SIGKDD Explor. Newslett. 6(1), 20–29 (2004)

Bellotti, V., Edwards, K.: Intelligibility and accountability: human considerations in context-aware systems. Hum.-Comput. Interact. 16(2–4), 193–212 (2001)

Beringer, S.: Effizienz und Effektivität der Integration von Textklassifikation in Information-Extraction-Pipelines. Master's thesis, University of Paderborn, Paderborn, Germany (2012)

Besnard, P., Hunter, A.: Elements of Argumentation. The MIT Press, Cambridge (2008)

Biber, D., Conrad, S., Reppen, R.: Corpus Linguistics: Investigating Language Structure and Use. Cambridge University Press, Cambridge (1998)

Björkelund, A., Bohnet, B., Hafdell, L., Nugues, P.: A high-performance syntactic and semantic dependency parser. In: Proceedings of the 23rd International Conference on Computational Linguistics: Demonstrations, pp. 33–36 (2010)

Blitzer, J., Dredze, M., Pereira, F.: Biographies, bollywood, boom-boxes and blenders: domain adaptation for sentiment classification. In: Proceedings of the 45th Annual Meeting of the Association for Computational Linguistics, pp. 440–447 (2007)

Blitzer, J., Crammer, K., Kulesza, A., Pereira, F., Wortman, J.: Learning bounds for domain adaptation. In: Platt, J., Koller, D., Singer, Y., Roweis, S. (eds.) Advances in Neural Information Processing Systems, vol. 21, pp. 105–134. MIT Press, Cambridge (2008)

Bohnet, B.: Very high accuracy and fast dependency parsing is not a contradiction. In: Proceedings of the International Conference on Computational Linguistics, pp. 89–97 (2010)

Bohnet, B., Kuhn, J.: The best of both worlds: a graph-based completion model for transition-based parsers. In: Proceedings of the 13th Conference of the European Chapter of the Association for Computational Linguistics, pp. 77–87 (2012)

Bohnet, B., Burga, A., Wanner, L.: Towards the annotation of penn treebank with information structure. In: Proceedings of the Sixth International Joint Conference on Natural Language Processing, Nagoya, Japan, pp. 1250–1256 (2013)

Bühler, K.: Sprachtheorie. Die Darstellungsfunktion der Sprache. Verlag von Gustav Fischer, Jena, Germany (1934)

Buschmann, F., Meunier, R., Rohnert, H., Sommerlad, P., Stal, M.: Pattern-oriented Software Architecture: A System of Patterns. Wiley, New York (1996)

Cafarella, M.J., Downey, D., Soderland, S., Etzioni, O.: KnowItNow: fast, scalable information extraction from the web. In: Proceedings of the Conference on Human Language Technology and Empirical Methods in Natural Language Processing, pp. 563–570 (2005)

Cardie, C., Ng, V., Pierce, D., Buckley, C.: Examining the role of statistical and linguistic knowledge sources in a general-knowledge question-answering system. In: Proceedings of the Sixth Applied Natural Language Processing Conference, pp. 180–187 (2000)

Carlson, L., Marcu, D., Okurowski, M.E.: Building a discourse-tagged corpus in the framework of rhetorical structure theory. In: Proceedings of the Second SIGdial Workshop on Discourse and Dialogue, vol. 16, pp. 1–10 (2001)

Cha, S.-H.: Comprehensive survey on distance/similarity measures between probability density functions. Int. J. Math. Models Methods Appl. Sci. 1(4), 300–307 (2007)

Chang, C.-C., Lin, C.-J.: LIBSVM: a library for support vector machines. ACM Trans. Intell. Syst. Technol. **2**, 27:1–27:27 (2011)

Chapelle, O., Schlkopf, B., Zien, A.: Semi-Supervised Learning. The MIT Press, Cambridge (2006)

Chenlo, J.M., Hogenboom, A., Losada, D.E.: Rhetorical structure theory for polarity estimation: an experimental study. Data Knowl. Eng. **94**(B), 135–147 (2014)

Chinchor, N., Lewis, D.D., Hirschman, L.: Evaluating message understanding systems: an analysis of the third message understanding conference (MUC-3). Comput. Linguist. **19**(3), 409–449 (1993)

Chiticariu, L., Krishnamurthy, R., Li, Y., Raghavan, S., Reiss, F.R., Vaithyanathan, S.: SystemT: an algebraic approach to declarative information extraction. In: Proceedings of the 48th Annual Meeting of the Association for Computational Linguistics, pp. 128–137 (2010a)

Chiticariu, L., Li, Y., Raghavan, S., Reiss, F.R.: Enterprise information extraction: recent developments and open challenges. In: Proceedings of the 2010 International Conference on Management of Data, pp. 1257–1258 (2010b)

Choi, Y., Breck, E., Cardie, C.: Joint extraction of entities and relations for opinion recognition. In: Proceedings of the 2006 Conference on Empirical Methods in Natural Language Processing, pp. 431–439 (2006)

Cooper, K.D., Torczon, L.: Engineering a Compiler. Morgan Kaufmann, Burlington (2011)

Cormen, T.H., Leiserson, C.E., Rivest, R.L., Stein, C.: Introduction to Algorithms, 3rd edn. MIT Press, Cambridge (2009)

Covington, M.A.: A fundamental algorithm for dependency parsing. In: Proceedings of the 39th Annual ACM Southeast Conference, pp. 95–102 (2001)

Cowie, J., Lehnert, W.: Information extraction. Commun. ACM **39**(1), 80–91 (1996)

Cui, H., Sun, R., Li, K., Kan, M.-Y., Chua, T.-S.: Question answering passage retrieval using dependency relations. In: Proceedings of the 28th Annual International ACM SIGIR Conference on Research and Development in Information Retrieval, pp. 400–407 (2005)

Cunningham, H.: Information extraction, automatic. Encycl. Lang. Linguist. **4**, 665–677 (2006)

Sarma, A.D., Jain, A., Bohannon, P.: Building a generic debugger for information extraction pipelines. In: Proceedings of the 20th ACM International Conference on Information and Knowledge Management, pp. 2229–2232 (2011)

Daumé III, H., Marcu, D.: Domain adaptation for statistical classifiers. J. Artif. Intell. Res. **26**(1), 101–126 (2006)

Davenport, T.H.: Enterprise Analytics: Optimize Performance, Process, and Decisions through Big Data. FT Press, Upper Saddle River (2012)

Dezsényi, C., Dobrowiecki, T.P., Mészáros, T.: Adaptive document analysis with planning. Multi-Agent Syst. Appl. **IV**, 620–623 (2005)

Dikli, S.: An overview of automated scoring of essays. J. Technol. Learn. Assess. **5**(1), 1–36 (2006)

Dill, S., Eiron, N., Gibson, D., Gruhl, D., Guha, R., Jhingran, A., Kanungo, T., Rajagopalan, S., Tomkins, A., Tomlin, J.A., Zien, J.Y.: SemTag and seeker: bootstrapping the semantic web via automated semantic annotation. In: Proceedings of the 12th International Conference on World Wide Web, pp. 178–186 (2003)

Doan, A.H., Naughton, J.F., Ramakrishnan, R., Baid, A., Chai, X., Chen, F., Chen, T., Chu, E., DeRose, P., Gao, B., Gokhale, C., Huang, J., Shen, W., Vuong, B.-Q.: Information extraction challenges in managing unstructured data. SIGMOD Rec. **37**(4), 14–20 (2009)

Downey, D., Etzioni, O., Soderland, S.: A probabilistic model of redundancy in information extraction. In: Proceedings of the 19th International Joint Conference on Artificial Intelligence, pp. 1034–1041 (2005)

Duggan, G.B., Payne, S.J.: Text skimming: the process and effectiveness of foraging through text under time pressure. J. Exp. Psychol.: Appl. **15**(3), 228–242 (2009)

Dunlavy, D.M., Shead, T.M., Stanton, E.T.: ParaText: scalable text modeling and analysis. In: Proceedings of the 19th ACM International Symposium on High Performance Distributed Computing, pp. 344–347 (2010)

Egner, M.T., Lorch, M., Biddle, E.: UIMA GRID: distributed large-scale text analysis. In: Proceedings of the Seventh IEEE International Symposium on Cluster Computing and the Grid, pp. 317–326 (2007)

Etzioni, O.: Search needs a shake-up. Nature **476**, 25–26 (2011)

Fader, A., Soderland, S., Etzioni, O.: Identifying relations for open information extraction. In: Proceedings of the 2011 Conference on Empirical Methods in Natural Language Processing, pp. 1535–1545 (2011)

Fazal-Baqaie, M., Luckey, M., Engels, G.: Assembly-based method engineering with method patterns. In: Software Engineering 2013 Workshopband, pp. 435–444 (2013)

Ferrucci, D., Lally, A.: UIMA: an architectural approach to unstructured information processing in the corporate research environment. Nat. Lang. Eng. **10**(3–4), 327–348 (2004)

Finkel, J.R., Grenager, T., Manning, C.D.: Incorporating non-local information into information extraction systems by Gibbs sampling. In: Proceedings of the 43rd Annual Meeting of the Association for Computational Linguistics, pp. 363–370 (2005)

Finkel, J.R., Manning, C.D., Ng, A.Y.: Solving the problem of cascading errors: approximate Bayesian inference for linguistic annotation pipelines. In: Proceedings of the 2006 Conference on Empirical Methods in Natural Language Processing, pp. 618–626 (2006)

Fleiss, J.L.: Statistical Methods for Rates and Proportions, 2nd edn. Wiley, New York (1981)

Forman, G., Kirshenbaum, E.: Extremely fast text feature extraction for classification and indexing. In: Proceedings of the 17th ACM Conference on Information and Knowledge Management, pp. 1221–1230 (2008)

Fox, M.S., Smith, S.F.: ISIS: a knowledge-based system for factory scheduling. Expert Syst. **1**, 25–49 (1984)

Francis, W.N.: A Standard Sample of Present-day English for Use with Digital Computers. Brown University (1966)

Gabrilovich, E., Markovitch, S.: Computing semantic relatedness using wikipedia-based explicit semantic analysis. In: Proceedings of the 20th International Joint Conference on Artifical Intelligence, pp. 1606–1611 (2007)

Gildea, D., Jurafsky, D.: Automatic labeling of semantic roles. Comput. Linguist. **28**(3), 245–288 (2002)

Glorot, X., Bordes, A., Bengio, Y.: Domain adaptation for large-scale sentiment classification: a deep learning approach. In: Proceedings of the 28th International Conference on Machine Learning, pp. 97–110 (2011)

Gottron, T.: Content extraction - identifying the main content in HTML documents. Ph.D. thesis, Universität Mainz (2008)

Gray, W.D., Fu, W.-T.: Ignoring perfect knowledge in-the-world for imperfect knowledge in-the-head. In: Proceedings of the SIGCHI Conference on Human Factors in Computing Systems, pp. 112–119 (2001)

Gruber, T.R.: A translation approach to portable ontology specifications. Knowl. Acquis. **5**(2), 199–220 (1993)

Gruhl, D., Chavet, L., Gibson, D., Meyer, J., Pattanayak, P., Tomkins, A., Zien, J.: How to build a WebFountain an architecture for very large-scale text analytics. IBM Syst. J. **43**(1), 64–76 (2004)

Güldali, B., Funke, H., Sauer, S., Engels, G.: TORC: test plan optimization by requirements clustering. Softw. Qual. J. 1–29 (2011)

Gupta, R., Sarawagi, S.: Domain adaptation of information extraction models. SIGMOD Rec. **37**(4), 35–40 (2009)

Gylling, M.: The structure of discourse: a corpus-based cross-linguistic study. Dissertation, Copenhagen Business School (2013)

Habernal, I., Eckle-Kohler, J., Gurevych, I.: Argumentation mining on the web from information seeking perspective. In: Frontiers and Connections between Argumentation Theory and Natural Language Processing (2014, to appear)

Hagen, M., Stein, B., Rüb, T.: Query session detection as a cascade. In: 20th ACM International Conference on Information and Knowledge Management (CIKM 2011), pp. 147–152 (2011)

Hajič, J., Ciaramita, M., Johansson, R., Kawahara, D., Martí, M.A., Màrquez, L., Meyers, A., Nivre, J., Padó, S., Štěpánek, J., Straňák, P., Surdeanu, M., Xue, N., Zhang, Y.: The CoNLL-2009 shared task: syntactic and semantic dependencies in multiple languages. In: Proceedings of the Thirteenth Conference on Computational Natural Language Learning: Shared Task, pp. 1–18 (2009)

Hall, M., Frank, E., Holmes, G., Pfahringer, B., Reutemann, P., Witten, I.H.: The WEKA data mining software: an update. SIGKDD Explor. **11**(1), 10–18 (2009)

Harsu, M.: A Survey on Domain Engineering. Tampere University of Technology (2002)

Hastie, T., Tibshirani, R., Friedman, J.: The Elements of Statistical Learning: Data Mining, Inference and Prediction, 2nd edn. Springer, New York (2009)

Hayes-Roth, B.: A blackboard architecture for control. Artif. Intell. **26**(3), 251–321 (1985)

Hearst, M.A.: Untangling text data mining. In: Proceedings of the 37th Annual Meeting of the Association for Computational Linguistics on Computational Linguistics, pp. 3–10 (1999)

Hearst, M.A.: Search User Interfaces. Cambridge University Press, Cambridge (2009)

Hinrichs, E., Hinrichs, M., Zastrow, T.: WebLicht: web-based LRT services for German. In: Proceedings of the ACL 2010 System Demonstrations, pp. 25–29 (2010)

Hollingshead, K., Roark, B.: Pipeline iteration. In: Proceedings of the 45th Annual Meeting of the Association for Computational Linguistics, pp. 952–959 (2007)

Horrocks, I.: Ontologies and the semantic web. Commun. ACM **51**(12), 58–67 (2008)

HP Labs: Annual Report (2010). http://www.hpl.hp.com/news/2011/jan-mar/pdf/HPL_AR_2010_web.pdf. Accessed 12 July 2013

Hsu, W.C., Chen, H., Yew, P.C., Chen, H.: On the predictability of program behavior using different input data sets. In: Sixth Annual Workshop on Interaction between Compilers and Computer Architectures, pp. 45–53 (2002)

Huang, L.: Advanced dynamic programming in semiring and hypergraph frameworks. In: COLING 2008: Advanced Dynamic Programming in Computational Linguistics: Theory, Algorithms and Applications - Tutorial Notes, pp. 1–18 (2008)

Ioannidis, Y.: Query optimization. In: Handbook for Computer Science. CRC Press (1997)

Jackson, P.: Introduction to Expert Systems, 2nd edn. Addison-Wesley Longman Publishing Co. Inc., Boston (1990)

Jean-Louis, L., Besançon, R., Ferret, O.: Text Segmentation and graph-based method for template filling in information extraction. In: Proceedings of the 5th International Joint Conference on Natural Language Processing, pp. 723–731 (2011)

Joachims, T.: A statistical learning model of text classification for support vector machines. In: Proceedings of the 24th Annual International ACM SIGIR Conference on Research and Development in Information Retrieval, pp. 128–136 (2001)

Jurafsky, D.: Pragmatics and computational linguistics. In: Horn, L.R., Ward, G. (eds.) Handbook of Pragmatics, pp. 578–604. Blackwell, Oxford (2003)

Jurafsky, D., Martin, J.H.: Speech and Language Processing: An Introduction to Natural Language Processing, Speech Recognition, and Computational Linguistics, 2nd edn. Prentice-Hall, Upper Saddle River (2009)

Kalyanpur, A., Patwardhan, S., Boguraev, B., Lally, A., Chu-Carroll, J.: Fact-based question decomposition for candidate answer re-ranking. In: Proceedings of the 20th ACM International Conference on Information and Knowledge Management, pp. 2045–2048 (2011)

Kano, Y.: Kachako: towards a data-centric platform for full automation of service selection, composition, scalable deployment and evaluation. In: Proceedings of the IEEE 19th International Conference on Web Services, pp. 642–643 (2012)

Kano, Y., Dorado, R., McCrohon, L., Ananiadou, S., Tsujii, J.: U-Compare: an integrated language resource evaluation platform including a comprehensive UIMA resource library. In: Proceedings of the Seventh International Conference on Language Resources and Evaluation, pp. 428–434 (2010)

Kelly, J.E., Hamm, S.: Smart Machines: IBM's Watson and the Era of Cognitive Computing. Columbia University Press, New York (2013)

Kim, J.-D., Wang, Y., Takagi, T., Yonezawa, A.: Overview of genia event task in BioNLP shared task 2011. In: Proceedings of the BioNLP Shared Task 2011 Workshop, pp. 7–15 (2011)

Büning, H.K., Lettmann, T.: Propositional Logic: Deduction and Algorithms. Cambridge University Press, New York (1999)

Klerx, T., Anderka, M., Büning, H.K., Priesterjahn, S.: Model-based anomaly detection for discrete event systems. In: Proceedings of the 26th IEEE International Conference on Tools with Artificial Intelligence, pp. 665–672 (2014)

Krikon, E., Carmel, D., Kurland, O.: Predicting the performance of passage retrieval for question answering. In: Proceedings of the 21st ACM International Conference on Information and Knowledge Management, pp. 2451–2454 (2012)

Krishnamurthy, R., Li, Y., Raghavan, S., Reiss, F., Vaithyanathan, S., Zhu, H.: SystemT: a system for declarative information extraction. SIGMOD Rec. 37(4), 7–13 (2009)

Kulesza, T., Stumpf, S., Wong, W.-K., Burnett, M.M., Perona, S., Ko, A., Oberst, I.: Why-oriented end-user debugging of naive Bayes text classification. ACM Trans. Interact. Intell. Syst. 1(1), 2:1–2:31 (2011)

Kulesza, T., Stumpf, S., Burnett, M.M., Yang, S., Kwan, I., Wong, W.-K.: Too much, too little, or just right? ways explanations impact end users' mental models. In: IEEE Symposium on Visual Languages and Human-Centric Computing, pp. 3–10 (2013)

Kumar, V., Grama, A., Gupta, A., Karypis, G.: Introduction to Parallel Computing: Design and Analysis of Algorithms. Benjamin-Cummings Publishing Co., Inc., Redwood City (1994)

Kushmerick, N.: Wrapper induction for information extraction. Dissertation, University of Washington (1997)

Lambrecht, K.: Information Structure and Sentence Form: Topic, Focus, and the Mental Representations of Discourse Referents. Cambridge University Press, New York (1994)

Lee, Y.-B., Myaeng, S.H.: Text genre classification with genre-revealing and subject-revealing deatures. In: Proceedings of the 25th Annual International ACM SIGIR Conference on Research and Development in Information Retrieval, pp. 145–150 (2002)

Lewis, D.D., Tong, R.M.: Text filtering in MUC-3 and MUC-4. In: Proceedings of the 4th Conference on Message Understanding, pp. 51–66 (1992)

Lewis, D.D., Yang, Y., Rose, T.G., Li, F.: RCV1: a new benchmark collection for text categorization research. J. Mach. Learn. Res. 5, 361–397 (2004)

Li, L., Jin, X., Long, M.: Topic correlation analysis for cross-domain text classification. In: Proceedings of the 26th AAAI Conference on Artificial Intelligence, pp. 998–1004 (2012a)

Li, Q., Anzaroot, S., Lin, W.-P., Li, X., Ji, H.: Joint inference for cross-document information extraction. In: Proceedings of the 20th ACM International Conference on Information and Knowledge Management, pp. 2225–2228 (2011)

Li, Y., Chiticariu, L., Yang, H., Reiss, F.R., Carreno-fuentes, A.: WizIE: a best practices guided development environment for information extraction. In: Proceedings of the ACL 2012 System Demonstrations, pp. 109–114 (2012b)

Lim, B.Y., Dey, A.K.: Assessing demand for intelligibility in context-aware applications. In: Proceedings of the 11th International Conference on Ubiquitous Computing, pp. 195–204 (2009)

Lipka, N.: Modeling non-standard text classification tasks. Dissertation, Bauhaus-Universität Weimar (2013)

Luís, T., de Matos, D.M.: High-performance high-volume layered corpora annotation. In: Proceedings of the Third Linguistic Annotation Workshop, pp. 99–107 (2009)

Mann, W.C., Thompson, S.A.: Rhetorical structure theory: toward a functional theory of text organization. Text 8(3), 243–281 (1988)

Manning, C.D., Schütze, H.: Foundations of Statistical Natural Language Processing. MIT Press, Cambridge (1999)

Manning, C.D., Raghavan, P., Schütze, H.: Introduction to Information Retrieval. Cambridge University Press, New York (2008)

Mao, Y., Lebanon, G.: Isotonic conditional random fields and local sentiment flow. Adv. Neural Inf. Process. Syst. 19, 961–968 (2007)

Marcu, D.: The Theory and Practice of Discourse Parsing and Summarization. MIT Press, Cambridge (2000)

Marler, R.T., Arora, J.S.: Survey of multi-objective optimization methods for engineering. Struct. Multidiscip. Optim. **26**(6), 369–395 (2004)

McCallum, A.: Joint inference for natural language processing. In: Proceedings of the Thirteenth Conference on Computational Natural Language Learning, p. 1 (2009)

Melzner, T.: Heuristische Suchverfahren zur Laufzeitoptimierung von Information-Extraction-Pipelines. Master's thesis, University of Paderborn, Paderborn, Germany (2012)

Menon, R., Choi, Y.: Domain independent authorship attribution without domain adaptation. In: Proceedings of the International Conference Recent Advances in Natural Language Processing 2011, pp. 309–315 (2011)

Mesquita, F., Schmidek, J., Barbosa, D.: Effectiveness and efficiency of open relation extraction. In: Proceedings of the 2013 Conference on Empirical Methods in Natural Language Processing, pp. 447–457 (2013)

Mex, D.: Efficiency and effectiveness of multi-stage machine learning algorithms for text quality assessment. Master's thesis, University of Paderborn, Paderborn, Germany (2013)

Meyer, D., Leisch, F., Hornik, K.: The support vector machine under test. Neurocomputing **55**(1–2), 169–186 (2003)

Minton, S., Bresina, J., Drummond, M.: Total-order and partial-order planning: a comparative analysis. J. Artif. Intell. Res. **2**(1), 227–262 (1995)

Mitchell, T.M.: Machine Learning, 1st edn. McGraw-Hill, Inc., New York (1997)

Mochales, R., Moens, M.-F.: Argumentation mining. Artif. Intell. Law **19**(1), 1–22 (2011)

Montavon, G., Orr, G.B., Müller, K.-R. (eds.): Neural Networks: Tricks of the Trade, Reloaded, 2nd edn. Springer, Heidelberg (2012)

Moschitti, A., Basili, R.: Complex linguistic features for text classification: a comprehensive study. In: McDonald, S., Tait, J.I. (eds.) ECIR 2004. LNCS, vol. 2997, pp. 181–196. Springer, Heidelberg (2004)

Mukherjee, S., Bhattacharyya, P.: Sentiment analysis in twitter with lightweight discourse analysis. In: Proceedings of the 24th International Conference on Computational Linguistics, pp. 1847–1864 (2012)

Nédellec, C., Vetah, M.O.A., Bessières, P.: Sentence filtering for information extraction in genomics, a classification problem. In: Siebes, A., De Raedt, L. (eds.) PKDD 2001. LNCS (LNAI), vol. 2168, pp. 326–337. Springer, Heidelberg (2001)

Ng, V.: Supervised noun phrase coreference research: the first fifteen years. In: Proceedings of the 48th Annual Meeting of the Association for Computational Linguistics, pp. 1396–1411 (2010)

Nivre, J.: An efficient algorithm for projective dependency parsing. In: Proceedings of the 8th International Workshop on Parsing Technologies, pp. 149–160 (2003)

Ó Séaghdha, D., Teufel, S.: Unsupervised learning of rhetorical structure with un-topic models. In: Proceedings of COLING 2014, The 25th International Conference on Computational Linguistics: Technical papers, Dublin, Ireland, pp. 2–13 (2014)

OMG: Unified Modeling Language (OMG UML) Superstructure, Version 2.4.1. OMG (2011)

Pang, B., Lee, L.: A sentimental education: sentiment analysis using subjectivity. In: Proceedings of 42th Annual Meeting on Association for Computational Linguistics, pp. 271–278 (2004)

Pang, B., Lee, L.: Seeing stars: exploiting class relationships for sentiment categorization with respect to rating scales. In: Proceedings of the 43rd Annual Meeting on Association for Computational Linguistics, pp. 115–124 (2005)

Pang, B., Lee, L.: Opinion mining and sentiment analysis. Found. Trends Informal Retr. **2**(1–2), 1–135 (2008)

Pang, B., Lee, L., Vaithyanathan, S.: Thumbs up?: sentiment classification using machine learning techniques. In: Proceedings of the ACL 2002 Conference on Empirical Methods in Natural Language Processing, vol. 10, pp. 79–86 (2002)

Pantel, P., Ravichandran, D., Hovy, E.: Towards terascale knowledge acquisition. In: Proceedings of the 20th International Conference on Computational Linguistics, pp. 771–777 (2004)

Pasca, M.: Web-based open-domain information extraction. In: Proceedings of the 20th ACM International Conference on Information and Knowledge Management, pp. 2605–2606 (2011)

Patwardhan, S., Riloff, E.: Effective information extraction with semantic affinity patterns and relevant regions. In: Proceedings of the 2007 Joint Conference on Empirical Methods in Natural Language Processing and Computational Natural Language Learning, pp. 717–727 (2007)

Pauls, A., Klein, D.: k-best A* parsing. In: Proceedings of the Joint Conference of the 47th Annual Meeting of the ACL and the 4th International Joint Conference on Natural Language Processing of the AFNLP, pp. 958–966 (2009)

Petrov, S., Das, D., McDonald, R.: A universal part-of-speech tagset. In: Proceedings of the Eight International Conference on Language Resources and Evaluation, pp. 2089–2096 (2012)

Pitler, E., Nenkova, A.: Revisiting readability: a unified framework for predicting text quality. In: Proceedings of the Conference on Empirical Methods in Natural Language Processing, pp. 186–195 (2008)

Pokkunuri, S., Ramakrishnan, C., Riloff, E., Hovy, E., Burns, G.A.: The role of information extraction in the design of a document triage application for biocuration. In: Proceedings of BioNLP 2011 Workshop, pp. 46–55 (2011)

Poon, H., Domingos, P.: Joint inference in information extraction. In: Proceedings of the 22nd National Conference on Artificial Intelligence, pp. 913–918 (2007)

Popescu, A.-M., Etzioni, O.: Extracting product features and opinions from reviews. In: Proceedings of the conference on Human Language Technology and Empirical Methods in Natural Language Processing, pp. 339–346 (2005)

Prettenhofer, P., Stein, B.: Cross-lingual adaptation using structural correspondence learning. Trans. Intell. Syst. Technol. (ACM TIST) **3**, 13:1–13:22 (2011)

Ramamoorthy, C.V., Li, H.F.: Pipeline architecture. ACM Comput. Surv. **9**(1), 61–102 (1977)

Raman, K., Swaminathan, A., Gehrke, J., Joachims, T.: Beyond myopic inference in big data pipelines. In: Proceedings of the 19th ACM SIGKDD International Conference on Knowledge Discovery and Data Mining, pp. 86–94 (2013)

Ratinov, L., Roth, D.: Design challenges and misconceptions in named entity recognition. In: Proceedings of the 13th Conference on Natural Language Learning, pp. 147–155 (2009)

Reiss, F., Raghavan, S., Krishnamurthy, R., Zhu, H., Vaithyanathan, S.: An algebraic approach to rule-based information extraction. In: Proceedings of the 2008 IEEE 24th International Conference on Data Engineering, pp. 933–942 (2008)

Riabov, A., Liu, Z.: Scalable planning for distributed stream processing systems. In: Proceedings of the Sixteenth International Conference on Automated Planning and Scheduling, pp. 31–41 (2006)

Rose, M.: Entwicklung eines Expertensystems zur automatischen Erstellung effizienter Information-Extraction-Pipelines. Master's thesis, University of Paderborn, Paderborn, Germany (2012)

Rowley, J.: The wisdom hierarchy: representations of the DIKW hierarchy. J. Inf. Sci. **33**(2), 163–180 (2007)

Russell, S.J., Norvig, P.: Artificial Intelligence: A Modern Approach, 3rd edn. Prentice-Hall, Upper Saddle River (2009)

Samuel, A.L.: Some studies in machine learning using the game of checkers. IBM J. Res. Dev. **3**(3), 210–229 (1959)

Sapkota, U., Solorio, T., Montes, M., Bethard, S., Rosso, P.: Cross-topic authorship attribution: will out-of-topic data help? In: Proceedings of the 25th International Conference on Computational Linguistics: Technical papers, pp. 1228–1237 (2014)

Sarawagi, S.: Information extraction. Found. Trends Databases **1**(3), 261–377 (2008)

Schmid, H.: Improvements in part-of-speech tagging with an application to German. In: Proceedings of the ACL SIGDAT-Workshop, pp. 47–50 (1995)

Sebastiani, F.: Machine learning in automated text categorization. ACM Comput. Surv. **34**(1), 1–47 (2002)

Selinger, P.G., Astrahan, M.M., Chamberlin, D.D., Lorie, R.A., Price, T.G.: Access path selection in a relational database management system. In: Proceedings of the 1979 ACM SIGMOD International Conference on Management of Data, pp. 23–34 (1979)

Shen, W., Doan, A., Naughton, J.F., Ramakrishnan, R.: Declarative information extraction using datalog with embedded extraction predicates. In: Proceedings of the 33rd International Conference on Very Large Data Bases, pp. 1033–1044 (2007)

Sinha, R., Swearingen, K.: The role of transparency in recommender systems. In: CHI 2002 Extended Abstracts on Human Factors in Computing Systems, pp. 830–831 (2002)

Solovyev, V., Polyakov, V., Ivanov, V., Anisimov, I., Ponomarev, A.: An approach to semantic natural language processing of Russian texts. Res. Comput. Sci. **65**, 65–73 (2013)

Somasundaran, S., Wiebe, J.: Recognizing stances in ideological on-line debates. In: Proceedings of the NAACL HLT 2010 Workshop on Computational Approaches to Analysis and Generation of Emotion in Text, pp. 116–124 (2010)

Stab, C., Gurevych, I.: Annotating argument components and relations in persuasive essays. In: Proceedings of the 25th International Conference on Computational Linguistics: Technical Papers, pp. 1501–1510 (2014a)

Stab, C., Gurevych, I.: Identifying argumentative discourse structures in persuasive essays. In: Proceedings of the 2014 Conference on Empirical Methods in Natural Language Processing, pp. 46–56 (2014b)

Stamatatos, E.: A survey of modern authorship attribution methods. J. Am. Soc. Inform. Sci. Technol. **60**(3), 538–556 (2009)

Stamatatos, E.: Plagiarism detection based on structural information. In: Proceedings of the 20th ACM International Conference on Information and Knowledge Management, pp. 1221–1230 (2011)

Stein, B., zu Eißen, S.M., Gräfe, G., Wissbrock, F.: Automating market forecast summarization from internet data. In: Proceedings of the Fourth Conference on WWW/Internet, pp. 395–402 (2005)

Stein, B., zu Eißen, S.M., Lipka, N.: Web genre analysis: use cases, retrieval models, and implementation issues. In: Mehler, A., Sharoff, S., Santini, M. (eds.) Genres on the Web. Text, Speech and Language Technology, vol. 42, pp. 167–190. Springer, Berlin (2010)

Stevenson, M.: Fact distribution in information extraction. Lang. Res. Eval. **40**(2), 183–201 (2007)

Stoyanov, V., Eisner, J.: Easy-first coreference resolution. In: Proceedings of the 24th International Conference on Computational Linguistics, pp. 2519–2534 (2012)

Teufel, S., Siddharthan, A., Batchelor, C.: Towards discipline-independent argumentative zoning: evidence from chemistry and computational linguistics. In: Proceedings of the 2009 Conference on Empirical Methods in Natural Language Processing, pp. 1493–1502 (2009)

Tjong, E.F., Sang, K., De Meulder, F.: Introduction to the CoNLL-2003 shared task: language-independent named entity recognition. In: Proceedings of the Seventh Conference on Natural Language Learning at HLT-NAACL 2003, pp. 142–147 (2003)

Toulmin, S.E.: The Uses of Argument. Cambridge University Press, Cambridge (1958)

Trosborg, A.: Text typology: register, genre and text type. In: Trosborg, A. (ed.) Text Typology and Translation, pp. 3–24. John Benjamins Publishing, Amsterdam (1997)

Tsujii, J.: Computational linguistics and natural language processing. In: Proceedings of the 12th International Conference on Computational Linguistics and Intelligent Text Processing, vol. Part I, pp. 52–67 (2011)

Turmo, J., Ageno, A., Català, N.: Adaptive information extraction. ACM Comput. Surv. **38**(2), 1–47 (2006)

van Noord, G.: Learning efficient parsing. In: Proceedings of the 12th Conference of the European Chapter of the Association for Computational Linguistics, pp. 817–825 (2009)

van Rijsbergen, C.J.: Information Retrieval. Butterworth-Heinemann, Newton (1979)

Villalba, M.P.G., Saint-Dizier, P.: Some facets of argument mining for opinion analysis. In: Proceedings of the 2012 Conference on Computational Models of Argument, pp. 23–34 (2012)

Wachsmuth, H., Bujna, K.: Back to the roots of genres: text classification by language function. In: Proceedings of the 5th International Joint Conference on Natural Language Processing, pp. 632–640, (2011)

Wachsmuth, H., Stein, B.: Optimal scheduling of information extraction algorithms. In: Proceedings of the 24th International Conference on Computational Linguistics: Posters, pp. 1281–1290 (2012)

Wachsmuth, H., Prettenhofer, P., Stein, B.: Efficient statement identification for automatic market forecasting. In: Proceedings of the 23rd International Conference on Computational Linguistics, pp. 1128–1136 (2010)

Wachsmuth, H., Stein, B., Engels, G.: Constructing efficient information extraction pipelines. In: Proceedings of the 20th ACM Conference on Information and Knowledge Management, pp. 2237–2240 (2011)

Wachsmuth, H., Rose, M., Engels, G.: Automatic pipeline construction for real-time annotation. In: Gelbukh, A. (ed.) CICLing 2013, Part I. LNCS, vol. 7816, pp. 38–49. Springer, Heidelberg (2013)

Wachsmuth, H., Stein, B., Engels, G.: Learning efficient information extraction on heterogeneous texts. In: Proceedings of the 6th International Joint Conference on Natural Language Processing, pp. 534–542 (2013b)

Wachsmuth, H., Stein, B., Engels, G.: Information extraction as a filtering task. In: Proceedings of the 22nd ACM Conference on Information and Knowledge Management, pp. 2049–2058 (2013c)

Wachsmuth, H., Trenkmann, M., Stein, B., Engels, G.: Modeling review argumentation for robust sentiment analysis. In: Proceedings of the 25th International Conference on Computational Linguistics: Technical Papers, pp. 553–564 (2014a)

Wachsmuth, H., Trenkmann, M., Stein, B., Engels, G., Palakarska, T.: A review corpus for argumentation analysis. In: Gelbukh, A. (ed.) CICLing 2014, Part II. LNCS, vol. 8404, pp. 115–127. Springer, Heidelberg (2014b)

Walton, D., Godden, M.: The impact of argumentation on artificial intelligence. In: Houtlosser, P., van Rees, A. (eds.) Considering Pragma-Dialectics, pp. 287–299. Erlbaum, Mahwah (2006)

Wang, D.Z., Wei, L., Li, Y., Reiss, F.R., Vaithyanathan, S.: Selectivity estimation for extraction operators over text data. In: Proceedings of the 2011 IEEE 27th International Conference on Data Engineering, pp. 685–696 (2011)

Wang, H., Lu, Y., Zhai, C.: Latent aspect rating analysis on review text data: a rating regression approach. In: Proceedings of the 16th ACM SIGKDD International Conference on Knowledge Discovery and Data Mining, pp. 783–792 (2010)

Whitelaw, C., Kehlenbeck, A., Petrovic, N., Ungar, L.: Web-scale named entity recognition. In: Proceedings of the 17th ACM Conference on Information and Knowledge Management, pp. 123–132 (2008)

Wimalasuriya, D.C., Dou, D.: Components for information extraction: ontology-based information extractors and generic platforms. In: Proceedings of the 19th ACM International Conference on Information and Knowledge Management, pp. 9–18 (2010)

Witten, I.H., Frank, E.: Data Mining: Practical Machine Learning Tools and Techniques, 2nd edn. Morgan Kaufmann Publishers, San Francisco (2005)

Wu, Q., Tan, S., Duan, M., Cheng, X.: A two-stage algorithm for domain adaptation with application to sentiment transfer problems. In: Cheng, P.-J., Kan, M.-Y., Lam, W., Nakov, P. (eds.) AIRS 2010. LNCS, vol. 6458, pp. 443–453. Springer, Heidelberg (2010)

Yang, Z., Garduno, E., Fang, Y., Maiberg, A., McCormack, C., Nyberg, E.: Building optimal information systems automatically: configuration space exploration for biomedical information systems. In: Proceedings of the 22nd ACM International Conference on Conference on Information and Knowledge Management, pp. 1421–1430 (2013)

Yi, J., Nasukawa, T., Bunescu, R., Niblack, W.: Sentiment analyzer: extracting sentiments about a given topic using natural language processing techniques. In: Proceedings of the Third IEEE International Conference on Data Mining, pp. 427–434 (2003)

Žáková, M., Křemen, P., Železný, F., Lavrač, N.: Automating knowledge discovery workflow composition through ontology-based planning. IEEE Trans. Autom. Sci. Eng. **8**(2), 253–264 (2011)

Zhang, M., Zhang, J., Su, J., Zhou, G.: A composite kernel to extract relations between entities with both flat and structured features. In: Proceedings of the 21st International Conference on Computational Linguistics and the 44th Annual Meeting of the Association for Computational Linguistics, pp. 825–832 (2006)

Zhang, T.: Solving large scale linear prediction problems using stochastic gradient descent algorithms. In: Proceedings of the Twenty-first International Conference on Machine Learning, pp. 116–123 (2004)

Zhang, Y.: Grid-centric scheduling strategies for workflow applications. Dissertation, Rice University (2010)

Index

The following index covers the major technical terms used in this book. In most cases, a short explanation of the respective term is given at one of its first mentions. The most important terms are explained in more detail in Sect. 2.1.

Printed in the United States
By Bookmasters